W9-ADF-559

ST. MARY'S COLLEGE OF MARYLAND
ST. MARY'S CITY, MARYLAND 20686

TOLD ROUND A BRUSHWOOD FIRE

PRINCETON LIBRARY OF ASIAN TRANSLATIONS

Advisory Committee: Professors Marius B. Jansen, Earl Miner, James Morley, Thomas Rimer

TOLD ROUND
A
BRUSHWOOD FIRE

The Autobiography of Arai Hakuseki

Translated and
with an introduction and notes by
JOYCE ACKROYD

PRINCETON UNIVERSITY PRESS

UNIVERSITY OF TOKYO PRESS

To Professor Furukawa Tesshi

UNESCO COLLECTION OF REPRESENTATIVE WORKS
JAPANESE SERIES
This book has been accepted in the Japanese Series of the Translation Collection of
the United Nations Educational, Scientific and Cultural Organization (UNESCO).

Publication assisted by a grant from The Japan Foundation

Original work: ORITAKU SHIBA NO KI
English translation © Unesco 1979
Translated from the Japanese by Joyce Ackroyd

All rights reserved. No part of this publication may be reproduced or transmitted in
any form or by any means, electronic or mechanical, including photocopy, recording,
or any information storage and retrieval system, without permission in writing from
the publisher.
Printed in Japan

Copublished by
Princeton University Press and University of Tokyo Press

CONTENTS

Acknowledgments vii
Notes on the Translation ix
Introduction 1

Told Round a Brushwood Fire

    Preface 35
    Book I... 37
    Book II 93
    Book III 185

Notes 279
Biographical Notes 309
Appendix 1   Glossary of Titles, Offices, and Names........317
Appendix 2   The Sexagenary System and Era Names 325
Appendix 3   Measures 326
Appendix 4   Pedigrees 327
Appendix 5   Selected Chronology 331
Maps..337
Index 341

ACKNOWLEDGMENTS

This translation was first based on the very faulty unannotated version in the *Arai Hakuseki Zenshū* (ed. Ichijima Kenkichi, Naigai Insatsu K.K., 1906), but later corrected by comparison with a microfilm copy of the *Arai Jippitsu Bon*. In making this comparison I consulted Hani Gorō's Iwanami Bunko transcription (1939), with the additional assistance of the corrections to this transcription supplied by Furukawa Tesshi, now Professor Emeritus, University of Tokyo.

For commentaries and readings I have relied on the annotated editions of Professors Miyazaki Michio (Shibundō, 1963) and Matsumura Akira in the *Nihon Koten Bungaku Taikei* series (Iwanami Shoten, 1964). For aid with some obscure passages I have had recourse to the modernized versions of Professor Furukawa in the *Edo Zuisō Shū* (Chikuma Shobō, 1960), and of Professor Kuwabara Takeo in the *Nihon no Meicho* series (Chūō Kōronsha, 1969). I have also extensively consulted Professor Miyazaki's *Arai Hakuseki no Kenkyū* (Yoshikawa Kōbunkan, 1957), as well as numerous other studies.

For some time I benefited greatly from the personal guidance of the late A. L. Sadler, Professor Emeritus, Sydney University. Discussions with colleagues at the Australian National University and at Queensland University yielded some interesting suggestions. I have occasionally made bold to differ from all my mentors, whether persons or written sources, and take full responsibility for any errors of judgment. Finally, I should like to record my gratitude to my conscientious and painstaking editor, Nina Raj, for her acute scrutiny of my manuscript.

NOTES ON THE TRANSLATION

Transcriptions

For Japanese, the Hepburn romanization system has been employed, long vowels being indicated by a macron. The syllabic "n" is followed by an apostrophe. The reading "bei" has been preferred to "hyōe."

For Chinese names and words, the Wade-Giles system has been used, and for Korean names that of McCune and Reischauer (*The Romanization of the Korean Language*, YWCA Press, Korea, 1939).

Italics

Words, other than titles, bureaux, and geographical names, appearing in the translation in their original Japanese form are given in italics.

Hakuseki's Notes

Hakuseki distinguished short and long notes by writing small in double columns. In the translation, short notes are enclosed in parentheses, long notes appear in indented paragraphs.

Word Form

In word form, convenience rather than consistency has been the aim. Thus *samurai, hatamoto, bugyō*, and *daimyō* (with one exception) are used as plural as well as singular. However, the forms *daimyōs', shōgun's, shōguns, shōguns'*, and Kohō's are tolerated, although it is recognized that, strictly, these are neologisms.

When single Japanese words are quoted in the text, they are placed within quotation marks in the translation.

Names and Titles

The Japanese samurai had (1) a sept or clan name (as Mina-moto); (2) a surname (as Arai); (3) a childhood name (as Hi-no-Ko); (4) a personal or familiar name (as Kageyu); (5) and a given or legal name (as Kimmi). They often adopted a literary pseudonym (as Hakuseki). On retirement, some became lay priests and adopted a Buddhist name (as Jōshin). The *shōgun* was given a posthumous name (as Bunshō-In). Nicknames were often employed, as Yoshū and Kohō.

Unless unnaturalness results, names and titles are given in the order in which they appear in the text: surname, title, sept name or personal name (where given), given name. The Biographical Notes list names of personages appearing (1) several times in one episode under different titles; (2) in two or more episodes, often widely separated; (3) repeatedly throughout the work. In the text, the names of such personages are followed by a number enclosed in square brackets which refers to the corresponding numbers in the Biographical Notes. Those who appear in only one episode, and under only one title, and about whom information additional to that supplied in the text is available, are included in the notes to each book. Scions of the Fujiwara House (so indicated in the Biographical Notes) in the reading of their names used the first character only of Fujiwara (read as "Tō").

The courtesy title "Ason" after names, and "no" between sept and personal names, are regularly suppressed. "Dono" is retained only when it constitutes part of a specific title applied to a (usual-ly) prominent personage, and "kimi" where it is part of a sobri-quet. The reading "Den" is employed for Buddhist priests and lay-priests. Titles are listed in Appendix 1.

In the relatively few cases possible, an English equivalent has been found for official positions, but usually the original Japanese word has been retained. Brief explanations of official positions are given in the notes and summarized in Appendix 1.

Dates

Dates, given in the text by sexagenary cycle and era are con-verted to Western reckoning for convenience of comparison with world events. The sexagenary system is explained in Appendix 2. Japanese era names have been retained only where they refer to a period, their equivalents in European reckoning being given in the notes, and in an alphabetical listing also in Appendix 2. Gregorian calendar dates enclosed in brackets have been inserted by the translator.

It should be noted that (1) Hakuseki makes some mistakes: sometimes, for instance, he gives the right sexagenary cycle symbols but the wrong year of the era; and (2) his method of referring to dates was sometimes vague. Such points are mentioned in the notes, where necessary. The conversion to the Western calendar has necessitated some modifications to the text: e.g., where the Japanese is "the same (lunar) year," the English must occasionally become "the following (solar) year". Where necessary, changes are indicated in the notes. When New Year's Day is mentioned without reference to the Western dates, it signifies the lunar New Year. Ages are left in Japanese reckoning, that is, they are calculated on the basis of a child being one year old at birth. Where actual years are given, calculations of lapses of time have been adjusted to the Western style of reckoning.

Time

Hours of the day, according to the Japanese system, have been converted to the rough Western equivalents. It is recognized that this device is highly inaccurate, as the Japanese system of telling the time marked off the hours of daylight and darkness by sunrise and sunset, and hence the Japanese hour, being a fixed fraction (one-sixth) of the intervals between, varied in length according to the season, each daylight hour being longer and each hour of darkness shorter in summer, and vice versa in winter. The hours of day and night were, of course, equal in length only at the spring and autumn equinoxes, and hence two Western hours long.

It is a convention, however, to take the equinoctial two-hour intervals as the norm. Some authorities equate the Western equivalent to the beginning of the Japanese interval and some to the middle. I have followed Miyazaki in choosing the first alternative.

Measures

Measures have been left in their Japanese form to retain the flavor of the original. Metric and Imperial equivalents are given in Appendix 3.

Departures from the Text

Some liberties have been taken with the text where a literal translation would result in awkwardness. Owing to limitations of space, it has not been possible to include textual notes explaining choice of interpretation in doubtful cases.

INTRODUCTION

Told Round a Brushwood Fire (*Oritaku Shiba no Ki*) is the auto-biography of Arai Hakuseki (1657–1725), the celebrated Confucian scholar. An encyclopedist—he has been compared to Voltaire—and an administrative reformer in advance of his age, sometimes even hailed as the father of modern Japanese scientific thought, he is considered by the Japanese to have been one of their greatest geniuses. The work is a vividly written chronicle, full of often quite ingenuous self-revelation, and ranks as one of the greatest autobiographies of Japanese literature as well as a unique historical adjunct to official records for the first half of the Tokugawa period.

Because of Hakuseki's eminence as a scholar, his position as lecturer to the sixth Tokugawa Shōgun, Ienobu, and his position of influence in the Bakufu administration, he was one of the leading *kangakusha*, or Confucianists, of the day. He was an independent thinker and did not adhere to any school, and the Confucianism he admired was rather the primitive beliefs of the Master himself. He was not interested in devising simplified ethical systems for the purpose of proselytizing among the lower orders, or in elaborating educational programs for the improvement of the position of women or youths. His interests were confined to administration and scholarship.

Hakuseki's view of Confucianism was dominated by his belief in its utility in government. Professor Furukawa Tesshi, formerly of University of Tokyo, points out that the consistent motive of his scholarly works was to seek "information of use in government today." His guiding principle was the dedication of his great learning to the service of the state, and he regarded the eight years when he had so much to say on the subject of good government as

[1]

the most worthwhile part of his life. *Oritaku Shiba no Ki* is thus in large part an inextricable mixture of personal reminiscence and political journal and emphasizes by its arrangement how the pattern of his life was determined by political events and his connection with them.

Hakuseki's Influence on Government

How great was Hakuseki's influence on Japanese government? Practically all the achievements of Ienobu's rule were due to Hakuseki's inspiration and planning. The period when he was able to assist in the government was short, but, despite this, his influence was substantial. He had time only to formulate his plan for the reorganization of the state and to take the first step, the attachment of the title "Koku-Ō" to the *shōgun*. He succeeded in having some economic reforms introduced, but policies concerning the important matters of currency and foreign trade were left incomplete, and many other reforms merely resolved on. After Ienobu's death no unified plan could be carried through.

Hakuseki's times also limited the value of his work. In foreign relations he upheld Japan's prestige, but his adversary was the fairly insignificant country of Korea. The historian Tokutomi Sohō has the interesting comment that had Hakuseki lived in the period between 1854 and 1860, when Japan was forced to deal with the nations of the West, he might have done something notable. He concentrated on removing anomalies in the system of the Bakufu which appeared when it was scrutinized from the point of view of strict logic by adjusting its legal position with respect to the emperor and the *daimyō*. But by this time the materialistic policy of the Bakufu to bring the land under one rule and to suppress the *daimyō* was in process of idealization. It is also unfortunate that Hakuseki's years in the service of the Japanese state were not spent under Yoshimune, the eighth Shōgun, for had he been employ ed by an independent-minded ruler, his talents would have been put to better use.

On economic matters there was much controversy among Confucianists, and in this sphere Hakuseki must definitely be cast among the conservatives and reactionaries. His conservatism limited his achievements too. Though society seemed solidified

[2]

into the feudal pattern in his day, there were already processes of
change at work beginning the transformation toward capitalism.
Hakuseki was not blind to their working, but regarded them as
signs of a decay that must be arrested. He did not criticize the
basic assumptions of the system, like, for instance, Kumazawa
Banzan, a slightly older Confucianist critical of the Bakufu, who
advocated such radical steps as the abolition of the separate class
of soldiers since they had no useful employment in times of peace.
Hakuseki sought to relieve the economic distresses of the *samurai*
but again he did not go so far as Banzan as to urge the relaxation
of the *sankin kōtai* (periodic residence in Edo) system. He saw that
the standard of living was rising, but condemned this trend as
an undesirable taste for luxury, and sought to apply economic
checks. He framed laws for the control of overseas trade, the
expansion of which might have solved many of Japan's economic
difficulties, but would also have strengthened the *daimyō* of the
southwest beyond the capacity of the shogunate to dominate them.

On the practical side, in the sphere of economics he has been
described as "only honest and an economist afterward." As far
as he could see, the *shōgun*'s financial position was fundamentally
sound, but though his statement that the *shōgun* controlled the
wealth of the empire was true in a sense—for despite the *daimyō's* fiscal autonomy the Bakufu did manage to carry on for a long
time to come in one way or another—he underestimated the government's budgetary problems. But as Yuasa Jōzan, an eigh-
teenth-century scholar, observes: "He stood in the first line of
reformers of the unsystematic rule that had existed since the days
of Ieyasu."

The Age and Hakuseki's Administrative Reforms

Hakuseki was born at a critical time in the development of the
Bakufu. This is illustrated by the problems he faced in his own life
and the economic social problems he sought to assist the shogunate
to solve. At this time the warrior classes were being transformed
from fighting men into civilian bureaucrats and reservists. Learning, no longer prowess at arms, was now the road to preferment.
Hakuseki's struggles in childhood and youth to equip himself as
a scholar demonstrate the clash in thinking between the old-style

samurai, such as his father was, and those who recognized that times had changed.

But to be born into a *samurai* house in the Tokugawa period did not guarantee security. Two of the most important social phenomena of the times were the increase in the number of *rōnin*, or unemployed *samurai*, and the deterioration of the *samurai's* financial situation. Due to confiscation of fiefs after the Sekigahara and Ōsaka campaigns, and the Shimabara and Yui Shōsetsu rebellions, and later reductions, transfers, and confiscations because of maladministration or other offenses, the number of *rōnin* by 1650 was in the order of 40,000. Once a *samurai* became a *rōnin* it was very difficult to obtain re-employment. The first volume of *Oritaku Shiba no Ki* throws into relief the tremendous social problems of the *rōnin* through several decades, beginning with the immediate postwar period. Hakuseki's grandfather and father spent part of their lives as *rōnin*, and he himself endured some years in this condition. The indigence to which ex-fighting men were reduced is vividly portrayed in the stories of Takataki and Echizen, and the difficulties of finding re-employment amply illustrated by the experiences of Hakuseki and his immediate forebears.

Economic conditions for the *samurai* were also deteriorating. Perhaps the most important reasons were the change from a subsistence to a cash economy, a rise in their standard of living, and the separation of the military classes from the sources of production. The institution of the *sankin kōtai* system and the growth of castle-towns were factors here. Hakuseki spent much time devising solutions to the economic distress of the *samurai*, but since the fundamental cause was the economic contradictions endemic in the Tokugawa system of centralized feudalism, this problem could not be solved until the system's demise. Hakuseki's regulations for the Nagasaki trade were the only means available of easing the stresses hampering such a commercial activity under the conditions of the Seclusion and they remained in force with only minor changes until the Meiji era.

In his proposals for the refinement of the coinage he clearly grasped that the nation at large handled coins as negotiable goods whose value depended on the intrinsic worth of the metal content. He also apprehended the emergence of a consumer economy and the process of increasing monetization. However, he wished to halt inflation and, to this end, deliberately planned a contraction of the currency. Unfortunately, the recoinage was, as he complained, not carried out as he had recommended: no paper money was issued to facilitate exchange of currencies, and good coins were consequently hoarded. A greater contraction of the coinage thus ensued and at a faster rate than Hakuseki had contemplated, and depression conditions eventually resulted.

Other financial reforms, notably the revival of the Board of Audit, which Hotta Masatoshi, the great reforming prime minister of the early years of Tsunayoshi's rule, had been instrumental in setting up, and the improvements in accounting methods, resulted in increased revenues through the elimination of peculation, and the first adequate budget records in the history of the shogunate.

In the field of justice Hakuseki drew attention to malpractices and inequities which were subsequently corrected in Yoshimune's time. His humanitarian views not only led to later relentment of the penal system but effected the release in Ienobu's time of thousands of unjustly imprisoned sufferers. Finally, his drive against corruption, rife in the Tokugawa bureaucracy, seems peculiarly relevant to modern times.

By this time shogunal relations with the Imperial Court had long entered a phase of rapprochement. The court was impotent and a pensioner of the shogunate, but still the fount of honor and the source of culture. The Tokugawa cult of Confucianism also gave it a peculiar importance, for its very existence raised the philosophical question of "the correct naming of things," and of the proper focus of loyalty of the military classes and the general populace. Many Confucianists addressed themselves to this question, differing on the point of whether the *shōgun's* right to rule were based on force, a delegation of power by the emperor, or inherent.

Hakuseki naturally played a prominent role in this controversy over the *shōgun's* status which continued throughout most of the Tokugawa period. Of the four possible interpretations, about which Confucianists were divided, Hakuseki's became the official Bakufu ideology. His view was that the *shōgun* was the legitimate ruler in his own right. The emperor was above him but had no

[5]

practical connection with the government; he was, however, entitled to the *shōgun's* reverence. Other Confucianists of his day went further; Ogyū Sorai, a contemporary Confucianist of opposing views, viewed the *shōgun* as the actual sovereign and considered his power based on force, and thus amply justified. Some did not go so far, holding that the emperor was the true sovereign but the *shōgun* his rightful deputy. The fourth opinion, according to which the *shōgun* was a usurper, did not appear till much after Hakuseki's time.

Hakuseki's plan for the establishment of a princely house and his own comment on it show him to have had deep reverence for the throne, and his admiration, akin to what Professor Furukawa Tesshi calls a nostalgia, for the primitive age of direct imperial rule is made abundantly clear in his *Tokushi Yoron*. There he condemns the Fujiwara Regents, Minamoto Yoritomo, and Ashikaga Takauji for their behavior to the Imperial Court, though he represents Tokugawa Ieyasu as Japan's savior when the deterioration of imperial rule had gone beyond repair. But as a rationalist, he viewed the then status quo as irreversible and saw a need to have the *shōgun's* nominal title and status accord with his real power and function in the state. Hakuseki's efforts to change the *shōgun's* title in official exchanges with Korea grew out of this position. He does not explain in *Oritaku Shiba no Ki* his proposal for special merit ranks for the military classes but this, too, was an attempt to detach the military classes from the court.

It is important to see Hakuseki's attitude in its proper political perspective: as Tokutomi says, "The situation was that after a hundred years of Tokugawa rule, shogunal authority had come to be regarded as a natural phenomenon, and not only could no one oppose it, but the very idea of opposition was quite extinct." Hakuseki regarded the existing firm basis of the power of the Bakufu as proof that it was a divinely sanctioned institution which he was bound from the point of view of political ethics to support and safeguard. And since his grasp of the processes of historical change enabled him to foresee the possibility of the eventual decline of the Tokugawa shogunate, he recommended to Ienobu that a "master policy" be devised to ensure its survival. On the other hand his policy toward the Imperial Court went no further than the suggestion of certain pious acts, such as ensuring the

[6]

continuance of the Imperial Family and the employment of more respectful terminology in Edo's communications with Kyōto. This attitude toward the Imperial Court, then, was no early presage of the Meiji Restoration. It was merely that he regarded the period of personal imperial rule in the same light as the times of Yao and Shun, a golden age when all men were virtuous, customs liberal, and countries automatically tranquil. At the same time, the measures he contemplated for regularizng the *shōgun's* position, though of little practical impact, might have proved of some constitutional significance had they not been overturned.

The *daimyōs'* state of submission can be judged by the Akō affair of 1701–2, known as the Incident of the 47 Rōnin; not only was a *daimyō* dispossessed and all his clan dispersed because he had wounded an official in the *shōgun's* palace, but his avenging retainers, immediately after accomplishing the killing of that official whose conduct had been responsible for the incident, surrendered to the authorities and obeyed to a man the order to commit suicide. To reduce the *daimyō* to this level of submission, the shogunate had systematically sapped their military strength by financial exactions. By Hakuseki's time economic forces had come into play reducing them to even worse straits and he was concerned to spare them further impoverishment, for the good of the country. He realized their tax exactions bore heavily on the peasantry, and the frequent government moratoria on *daimyō* debts sent merchants bankrupt, despite the improvement in the position of these two classes in other ways. In effect Hakuseki attempted to institute "benevolent government" in the Confucian sense of the term.

Relations with Yoshimune

In view of the high favor Hakuseki enjoyed under Ienobu, and during his successor Ietsugu's tenure of office, something needs to be said about the changed situation under Yoshimune, who became *shōgun* in 1716. It is generally held that on his succession Yoshimune treated Hakuseki harshly, personally slighting him and immediately reversing the policies he had recommended. What seems to have happened, however, was that when he came to power, there was an upsurge of anti-Hakuseki feeling, led by a member of the

Rōjū (or Senior Council), and Hakuseki's rival, the official Bakufu Confucianist Hayashi Nobuatsu. It was probably this faction that was responsible for transferring him to a remote and undesirable house lot without a house on it, when his officially granted residence was requisitioned, and for a close attendant of Yoshimune's burning of the memorials and works Hakuseki had written for Ienobu.

Records exist of Yoshimune actually asking Hakuseki and, later, his eldest son for copies of his writings and also seeking his advice and assistance. He certainly employed men who had been closely associated with Hakuseki. It was rather Hakuseki himself who would have nothing to do with Yoshimune. He took the initiative in severing connection with the government, submitting his resignation two days after being informed of Ietsugu's death.

Not only was Hakuseki obsessed with the idea of its being unethical to serve a second lord—he obviously regarded Ienobu as his one and only true lord—but he and the new Shōgun were in temperament basically incompatible. Hakuseki compared him to the first emperor of the Chin dynasty, famous for "burning the books," because of his despotic style of administration, his dislike for ceremonial, and the destruction of the memorials; and he ridiculed in a discreet indirect way his country-*daimyō* regard for spartan thrift.

However, they actually shared many administrative ideals, notably their admiration for Ieyasu's organization of the state and Hotta Masatoshi's reforms. In fields like justice and finance, the regulation of Nagasaki trade, currency refinement, in the encouragement of agricultural self-sufficiency, and interest in Western science, Yoshimune continued or implemented policies initiated or projected on Hakuseki's advice. It may be noted that it was not till more than ten years after Hakuseki's death that currency debasement was again resorted to, and, while under Hayashi's influence, in the regulations for the military classes and the reception of the Korean Embassy, there was a return to Tsunayoshi's days, even here Yoshimune did not blindly acquiesce and his attitude obliged Hayashi to admit that Hakuseki's innovations were not all undesirable.

It seems that Hakuseki eventually realized he had misjudged Yoshimune, for in a letter to Sakuma Tōgan at the end of his life he acknowledged: "Although I have not given any service what-soever, I have been permitted until now to support my declining years on exactly the same salary as before. Thus the kindness of the present *shōgun* toward me is far greater than that of his pred-ecessor, which is a blessing for which I am truly grateful."

Hakuseki as a Scholar

Hakuseki undoubtedly regarded his years spent in advising the government as the crowning achievement of his life; yet his chief claim to fame is as a scholar; his works cover administration, economics, philosophy, religion, history, antiquities, philology, geography, anthropology, botany, military arts, and poetry. From his contact with Westerners, he gained a rudimentary knowledge of the sciences of physics, astronomy, and medi-cine.

During his lifetime he was renowned as a Chinese poet and was extolled even by his rivals—Ogyū Sorai spoke highly of his Chinese verse, and Professor Miyazaki Michio, a Hakuseki specialist, deduces from the praise of such an uncompromising Sinophile as Sorai, that Hakuseki's reputation must have spread to China. *Hakuseki Shisō*, a collection of Hakuseki's Chinese poems, was widely circulated in Japan and on the Asian continent. Hakuseki refers to his composition of Chinese poetry in *Oritaku Shiba no Ki* but says nothing about his ability in composing *haikai* (17-syllable verse), probably considering such an interest beneath the dignity of a Confucianist. He notes, however, that Uematsu, the man who taught him his first Chinese poem, was adept at *renga* (linked verse), and he himself was apparently an accomplished *haikai* poet by his twenty-first year. He seems to have given it up on his appointment as a Confucianist in the Hotta Clan in 1682 when he was twenty-six; *haikai*, then, were a pastime of his years as a *rōnin*. His *haikai* were included in *Edo Benkei* (1680), edited by Ikenishi Gonsui, and in *Kōyō Gunkan* of about the same time, edited by Tashiro Shōi. Although Hakuseki gave up the practice of *haikai*, according to his diary, complete verses sometimes came to him in dreams; he records five such occasions.

Hakuseki's historical works comprise *Hankampu*, *Tokushi Yoron*, *Koshitsū*, and *Koshitsū Wakumon*, and the lost work called *Shigi,* or

INTRODUCTION

"Historical Doubts." *Hankampu* is the history of the feudal clans from 1600 to 1680, an immense work containing biographies of all the *daimyō* possessing 10,000 *koku* and over, totaling 337 families and branch families in all. *Tokushi Yoron*, Hakuseki's greatest historical work, traces the decline of the Imperial Court and the rise of the military classes, covering the history of Japan from the time of Jimmu to the supremacy of Hideyoshi. *Koshitsū* and *Koshitsū Wakumon* reassess the mythological ages of Japan and illustrate Hakuseki's thesis that the gods were men. The *Shigi* also dealt with the *Nihonshoki*'s account of Japan's prehistory.

Hakuseki's historical writings are all notable for their wealth of documentation and their scrupulous examination of texts and sifting of evidence. *Tokushi Yoron* is outstanding no less for its psychological insight than for its devotion to the task of revealing the pattern of Japanese history. It is not a mere chronicle or continuous narrative but a study of the dynamics of history, distinguishing the various phases by which power passed from the emperor to the Fujiwara, and from the Fujiwara into the hands of the military classes. For his periodization of history he received some help from *Gukanshō* (1220), by a Buddhist priest Jien, and he also quotes extensively from the *Jinnō Shōtōki* (1340), by a court noble Kitabatake Chikafusa. But whereas the former approached Japanese history from a Buddhist, pessimistic viewpoint and the latter from a Shintoist, optimistic viewpoint, Hakuseki interprets history from a Confuciantist, rationalist viewpoint. Historical inevitability plays a large part in all three works, but in Hakuseki it takes the form of a scientific discussion of cause and effect. Though somewhat still trammeled by a scholarly tradition devoted to exposition of the classics, he broke through the current conventions of chronological historical narrative by his grasp of the processes of political change and his perception of the recurring deterioration and rejuvenation of society. *Tokushi Yoron* was adopted as a textbook during the Meiji era and contains suggestions full of value for modern times.

His views on such problems of antiquity as the location of Yamatai and Takama-ga-Hara, propounded in *Koshitsū* and *Koshitsū Wakumon*, are still given serious consideration, and his interpretation of Japanese mythology was completely new and generated valuable lines of inquiry. From the fragments surviving of the *Shigi,* an examination of "doubtful points" in the *Nihonshoki,* it is surmised it would have ranked with Motoori Norinaga's *Kojikiden.*

Hakuseki is also regarded as a "precursor" of the *rangakusha,* as Japanese students of Dutch learning were called. He was not quite the first serious writer on Europe, but nothing like his *Seiyō Kibun* and *Sairan Igen* had previously appeared. These were not his only descriptions of foreign countries, but they are his two major geographical essays. *Sairan Igen* is the first comprehensive and scientifically researched Japanese work on world geography. Christianity is critically examined in *Seiyō Kibun* and though rejected on philosophical grounds, absolved from the charge of territorial aggression if not social and political subversion. *Kishin Ron,* undated but probably belonging to his last years, sets forth his philosophical views, and reveals him not so much as a Neo-Confucianist as an adherent of the original Confucianism, which he saw as providing a workable social and political system.

His *Ezoshi* on Hokkaidō and *Nantōshi* on the Luchus were pioneer ethnographical works, as his main linguistic study *Tōga* was a path-opener in etymology. He was the first to attach the ideographs to the name Okinawa which are used today, and he propounded the view that the Luchuans are of the same race as the Japanese. His *Dōbun Tsūkō* (1711–12), in four volumes, on the origin and history of ideographs presents the conclusion that the so-called Divine Characters, vaunted as Japan's own invention, were merely adaptations of the Korean *onmun* alphabet, and that Japan had, in fact, no writing system of its own.

The discussion of *kokutai* (national essence, or unique nature of the Japanese people) had begun before Hakuseki's time, but he refers to the concept frequently, and he may be viewed as one of one of the forerunners of nationalist feeling in Japan. That this concept, so vital in the thought movements leading up to the Meiji Restoration, was a mainspring of his negotiations with the Korean Envoys is clear from his expressions of sensitivity to foreign attitudes toward Japan in his writings on this subject and others.

Hakuseki the Man

Hakuseki was a typical though superlative product of the system on which he sought to operate, but he was also often a man in advance of his age. Though on many points conservative in approach, some of his administrative reforms reveal him as innovative, and untrammeled by the restrictive bonds of feudal attitudes. He strove to put into practice policies which were later carried to success. Though unwilling to trade his *samurai* status for financial gain, his readiness to employ skilled and knowledgeable men of the merchant classes in the service of the government and his eulogy of Manabe Akifusa, Grand Chamberlain, demonstrated a degree of freedom from class prejudice. It may be thought the incident when as a young man he contemplated the killing of an old couple guarding a gate at variance with this. This was involved in his plan to join his party in an armed clash during a Tsuchiya Clan feud, despite his being under house arrest at the time for a minor misdemeanor. But as far as Hakuseki's resolve was concerned, the incident in question was a classic instance of *giri* versus *ninjō*. The *samurai* code condoned the use of extreme means (even the slaying of the innocent and defenseless) when honor was at stake. And clearly honor was at stake.

Hakuseki was criticized for this scheme by his friend Seki, and some might consider his defense cold-blooded. The main reason for this reaction is the tendency to import modern sensibilities into Seki's speech, so that Hakuseki seems heartless because immune to considerations which deeply moved his friend. Seki says: "It would have been most reprehensible for you, while in disgrace and confined to your house, to leave it by stealth, and worse than that, to have killed those guards and forced your way out of the gate would have been piling crime on crime." What horrified Seki in Hakuseki's projected course was not the slaying of the old couple in itself but the double act of disobedience to his lord which it entailed. Hakuseki's defense was that since Seki had prepared to engage in battle with intent to kill fellow clansmen, he was also contemplating disobedience, but of a more serious degree, because of the difference in rank of the intended victims. In other words, this conversation must not be considered a discussion of homicide, but of acts of feudal disobedience.

The real question under debate was: Should Hakuseki have remained passive in the captivity imposed on him by his lord while his friends imperiled their lives, or should he have flouted his lord's authority in such an extreme degree to stand by his friends? That this is the correct interpretation is suggested by the reaction of Seki's father and his own; they were not outraged but struck with admiration, and even the clan lord Tsuchiya did not withdraw his favor. To most eyes today, the difference between the acts premeditated by Hakuseki and Seki is that the latter contemplated killing in fair combat, while Hakuseki's intended victims were innocent and defenseless bystanders. On this point, we may compare the general admiration for the *samurai*, taken prisoner while fishing, who cut down within a few days three members of the clan on whose land he had trespassed. These victims were innocent, and though warriors, to an extent defenseless because unprepared. Since such was the general attitude of the day, it is unlikely that the young Seki alone would have been so tenderhearted as to grieve over the possible fate of the humble old couple. The importation of rank into the argument may turn the egalitarian stomach, but Hakuseki would scarcely have taken this debating tack if he had discerned any human pity in Seki, so the appeal to the peculiar logic inherent in a hierarchical society reflects as much on Seki as on Hakuseki himself. At this time, clearly, Hakuseki was no worse than his era. It is unlikely that at eighteen he would yet have thought about the philosophical implications of social organization, but it would hardly be a balanced view that would weigh the teen-aged hot-head's words against the consistent, more tolerant attitudes of the mature man. That Hakuseki in his final decade should recall those words without shame may only attest to his amused conceit in his youthful casuistry, just as in *Seiyō Kibun* he exults in the petty-fogging arguments by which he demolished Sidotti's ethical stands, while deeply admiring the man. And reflection suggests that even on a modern humanitarian view, there was, as Hakuseki pointed out, little moral gap between the two young men; killing is killing.

Despite being born into an age when a rigid seclusion policy was in force, he adopted a cosmopolitan approach to foreign nationals. His generous praise of Sidotti's character and learning, his having an ailing son examined by a Dutch doctor, and his exoneration of Christian missionaries from subversive political intent are strong illustrations. His researches, inspired by the primitive Confucian edict on the importance of "the investigation of things," placed him in the forefront of Japanese scientific thought. He clearly grasped the importance of Western learning to Japan's future development.

Phases of Hakuseki's Life

Hakuseki's life may be divided into five phases:
1. his childhood and youth in the Tsuchiya Clan, 1567–1675
2. a) his first period as a *rōnin*, 1675–82
   b) his employment by the Hotta Clan, 1682–91
   c) his second period as a *rōnin*, 1691–93
3. his lectureship in the Kōfu Clan, 1694–1709
4. his assistance in the administration:
   a) of Ienobu, 1709–12
   b) during the shogunate of Ietsugu, 1712–16
5. his last years, 1716–25

Oritaku Shiba no Ki covers the first four phases only, the record of the first phase being preceded by references to his grandfather Kageyu and an account of his father Masanari. For the last ten years of Hakuseki's life we must go to his correspondence, included in his collected works, with a group of important friends: Sakuma Tōgan and Ose Fukuan, two clan physicians, Asaka Tampaku, a historian in the Mito historical bureau, Muro Kyūsō, a fellow disciple under Kinoshita Jun'an, and Doi Motonari, Hakuseki's own lifelong disciple. This correspondence was one of the few solaces of his last years; it throws light on his research, his way of life, his family relationships, and his friendships. A realistic picture of Hakuseki emerges from it, as a man of profound humanity and warmth of feeling.

These last ten years were the period of his perfection as a scholar; he flung himself into research to ease the pain of disappointment. To mention the most important of his later works, in 1716, just before Ietsugu's death, he had completed the revision of *Koshitsū* and *Koshitsū Wakumon*, the first versions of which he had presented to Ienobu when he was still Lord of Kai (Kofu Clan); it was these original drafts that were burned after Yoshimune's succession. In 1717 he completed *Oritaku Shiba no Ki*; in 1719 *Tōga* and, in the same field, *Tōinfu*, and *Nantōshi*; in 1720 *Ezoshi*; in 1721 *Keihō Tenrei* on Japanese ceremonial in 21 volumes of which only a few sections remain; in 1722 *Sombu Heihō Taku*, 13 volumes on Chinese military strategy; and, after two years of feverish application, the 21 volumes of *Shigi*. In this year also he completed a revision of *Tokushi Yoron*, composed in 1712. A few days before his death he finished work on the final revision of *Sairan Igen*.

But his last years were also a time of some distress. It was not till 1721 that he found a permanent residence, and he was saddened by the death of his second son, a grandson, and his friend Ose Fukuan, and the house arrest of Asaka Tampaku. What hurt him most of all about his new obscurity, was, as he explained in a letter to Ose Fukuan, that former intimates ceased to visit him, and another disturbing result was the difficulties it raised in arranging his daughters' marriages, for suitable families were reluctant to ally themselves with a man out of favor. He fell ill on 15th June 1725 and died on the 29th. He was interred in Kōtokuji within Hōonji in Tawara-chō, Asakusa.

Oritaku Shiba no Ki

Hakuseki himself gave no clue in any of his writings as to the derivation of the title of his autobiography, but it is generally considered to have been taken from a poem by the Retired Emperor Go-Toba (1179–1239) in the *Shinkokinshū* (1206):

Omoi(i)zuru	The smoke at evening
oritaku shiba no	of memory's brushwood fire
yū-kemuri	choking me with tears
musebu no ureshi	bitter sweet, never dwindling
wasuregatami ni.	keepsake of those other days.

This suggestion first appeared some time before 1781, but it has been objected that Hakuseki had little interest in *waka* (traditional Japanese five-line verse) outside the *Man'yōshū*. An alternative explanation is that the title is taken from an incident in the autobiography itself where Hakuseki's father and an old ex-warrior friend, Jūrobei, talk through the night of times gone by, while feeding the fire in a rough country cottage. However, neither the experience nor the image of poignant reminiscences around a rustic hearth is unusual in any culture, let alone Japan's, and both must have been familiar to Hakuseki.

[15]

The work consists of a short preface and three volumes or books of varying length. Book I, the most carefully written, deals with Hakuseki's grandfather and father, and his own career to the time of his engagement as lecturer by the Lord of Kai, the future sixth Shōgun Ienobu. Book II chronicles Ienobu's rule and his administrative achievements, and Book III the rule of his infant son, Ietsugu, when attempts were made to carry through those plans of Ienobu left unfinished at his death. It is written in the literary Japanese style of the day, with a number of quotations from the Chinese classics in *kambun*.

The holograph (or *Jippitsu Bon*) of *Oritaku Shiba no Ki* is still preserved by the Arai Family and until the Meiji era was retained as a private document. However, many manuscript copies circulated, 56 in public libraries being recorded in the Iwanami Shoten Kankō's *Kokusho Sōmokuroku*, and more in private collections. There is also another copy (the so-called *Betsubon*) in the Arai Family, mainly in another hand, probably that of Hakuseki's son Akinori, though the last half of the third volume is in Hakuseki's own hand.

The *Jippitsu Bon* is 29 cm × 21.2 cm, in three volumes of 56, 71, and 74 pages, in fine calligraphy entirely in black ink with *furigana* (character readings) and side notes. Each page has 12 columns, with interspersed notes written in double columns in small characters. It is bound Japanese-style in cloth covers with the titles to each volume on attached labels. The *Betsubon* is 27.5 cm. × 19.9 cm. with brown covers and the same format as the *Jippitsu Bon*, though the calligraphy is inferior. Both bear seals used by Hakuseki.

The manuscript copies (*Shahon*) are in six-, five-, four-, two-, and one-volume formats, and contain many errors. The omissions of certain passages included in the *Jippitsu Bon* may well mean these copies were made before the manuscript was completed. The first printed edition was that of Takenaka Kunika in 1881, and others followed in 1890, 1893, 1906, and 1911. Later editions mainly followed the 1906 edition in the *Arai Hakuseki Zenshū*. Hani Gorō's edition in 1939 was the first based on a transcription of the *Jippitsu Bon*, but unfortunately contained many mistakes.

There is a discrepancy between the date at the end of the preface where Hakuseki tells us he began to write after 17th November 1716, and that at the end of Book III where he says he laid down his pen about the middle of July 1716. The fourth anniversary of Ienobu's death fell on 17th November 1716, while the last days of July 1716 saw Hakuseki's retirement after Ietsugu's death. Remembering that Ietsugu's rule had been for Hakuseki an extension of Ienobu's, we can see that these dates had great significance for Hakuseki. It is unclear, however, what relationship they had to actual fact.

The omissions in the *Shahon* of passages in the *Jippitsu Bon* already mentioned suggest that he continued to work on the manuscript even after copies had been made of it. Continual revision was his practice with other works, e.g. *Seiyō Kibun*. The final conclusion is that the book was written after Hakuseki's retirement but that some time elapsed between the commencement and the final revision of the manuscript, during which he made sundry additions. There are passages showing clearly they were written in 1717. The most likely interpretation, then, of "laid down my pen" is "brought my narrative to a close."

Literary Antecedents

Oritaku Shiba no Ki is acknowledged as the first Japanese autobiography proper, and claimed to rank in importance as a pioneer work with Benvenuto Cellini's *Life* (1558–66), the first Western autobiography, and Rousseau's *Confessions* (1764–69), the first of modern times. China, it may be noted, did not produce anything of comparable literary significance till Hu Shih's *Ssŭ Shih Tzŭ Shu* (*Portrait of Myself at Forty*) of 1933. *Oritaku Shiba no Ki* was preceded by Yamaga Sokō's *Haisho Zampitsu* (Last Testimony in Exile) of 1675, of a similar nature but comparatively slender extent, but no notable autobiography followed it till Matsudaira Sadanobu's *Uge no Hitogoto* (an untranslatable title) which traces his life to 1793, and later Fukuzawa Yukichi's *Fukuō Jiden* (Autobiography of the Aged Fukuzawa) of 1898–99.

The sudden appearance in Japan of a work we recognize as an autobiography in the Western sense is intriguing. In the West it was the Renaissance, which liberated the human spirit from ecclesiastical bondage, and the Reformation, which led to the exaltation of the individual's inner life, that bore fruit in such writings as Cellini's and Rousseau's. But in Japan no comparable movements stirred Tokugawa thought currents. On the contrary, in that age in which the theoretic basis was Neo-Confucian ethics, the spiritual and material aspirations of the individual were schooled to subordination to social obligations. Further, there was the example of China, for it was natural that Japanese Confucian scholars, steeped in the traditions of Chinese learning, should turn to China for literary models. Throughout Chinese history owing to the strong collective tradition of the Chinese, scope for individualism was firmly restricted. Neither Buddhism nor organized Taoism, despite their awareness of the individual's intrinsic importance, succeeded in shifting the focus. Not till 1911–12 was there a positive step toward this, when Sun Yat-sen, significantly a "rebel-reformer," published his memoirs. But it was the twenties and thirties ferment which freed the individual from traditional social bonds and the inspiration of Western literature that brought about Western-style biography and autobiography. The great pioneer work of this Westernized movement was Hu Shih's *Ssŭ Shih Tzŭ Shu*.

However, although China did not produce the true autobiographical genre till so late, there was much autobiographical writing of other kinds, though none of it in a sustained form. Examples are the *Ch'ên Ch'ing Piao* (an appeal to the emperor for exemption from conscription to care for his father) by Li Mi of the Chin Dynasty; the *Sung Tung Yang Ma Shêng Hsü* (memo as an encouragement to study) by Sung Lien of the Ming Dynasty, in which he describes his struggles to borrow or copy books; and during the Manchu Dynasty, Chêng Pan-ch'iao's introduction to a poem in praise of the kindness of his wet-nurse. Some *tzŭ-hsü*, or author's prefaces to their works, also focused on the writer's personal circumstances, notably that of Ssŭ-ma Ch'ien, appended to the *Shih Chi*.

There existed also the litterateur's *pi-chi*, or personal jottings, miscellanies preserving informat on about the more private aspects of life. In Japan, the *pi-chi* was represented by the *kikō-nikki-zuihitsu-haibun* (travel record, diary, miscellany, poetic essay) family of genres, spanning the tenth to the nineteenth century. But these were all distinguished by an artistic design, the aim of which was the development of mood, and which required strict selectivity in material and led to fictionalization, a disregard for chronology, and a striving for high literary polish. They were also freely interspersed with poems. They represented a special Japanese point of view, which imposed aesthetic standards not only on the individual's behavior, but on the recording of his experience. They are therefore more forerunners of the modern *shishōsetsu*, or Japanese I-novel, than of autobiography in the sense of a fully rounded portrait of a man as he actually lived. The predeliction of the Japanese for this kind of writing naturally hindered the development of autobiography as is it known in the West. Even when the influence of Western culture was most strongly felt during early and mid-Meiji, it has been remarked, the autobiographical genre attracted little attention. Unless self-revelation was transmuted into an experience of universal validity by art, the prejudice against enlarging on personal affairs was too strong.

But there was another tradition of more relevance. China also had the *lieh-chuan*, or biography, developed to a high point by Ssǔma Ch'ien, a connected account of the achievements of ministers and other public figures, numbers of which were appended to the *shih-chi*, or annalistic records. To the *lieh-chuan* was closely related the *chia-chuan*, or family chronicle, which included information on the subject's association with clan rites, and was transmitted as a private, though not secret, family document, intended to encourage loyalty and public service in family members. Both the *lieh-chuan* and *chia-chuan* set forth the family descent and immediate forebears of the subject, his official career—appointments, promotions, titles, honors, and enfeoffments—rarely dated systematically, anecdotes illustrating the type of man he could be classified as, quotations from his memorials to the throne, actions in his official capacity, and of course posthumous honors and descendants. They were in fact less concerned with the individual himself than with his contribution to society. Hakuseki's *Hankampu* was close to this kind of writing.

Later, in the Sung period in China, the *nien-p'u*, a chronological record of the main events of a man's life, appeared. Some of these *nien-p'u* touched on the subject's personal thoughts and feelings through consideration of his writings. The *nien-p'u* was biographical; the autobiographical equivalent was the *jih-chi*, or diary. As examples of this form may be instanced the *Tsêng Wên Chêng Kung*

Jih Chi of Tsêng Kuo-fan (1813–74); the *Wêng Wên Kung Kung Jih Chi* of Wêng T'ung-ho (1880–1904); and the *Yüeh Man T'ang Jih Chi Ch'ao* of Li Ts'ŭ-ming (fl.ca 1860–1916). These were detailed, covered long periods of time (30 to 40 years), and contained much personal reference as well as social and political comment. They were not autobiographies as such, however, but journals consisting of daily entries. In Japan the *jih-chi* was represented by the *jitsuroku nikki* or *kambun nikki*, factual journals of important events as they happened, kept in Chinese by ministers and others. The earliest examples belong to the ninth century and were travel records of priests who visited China. A large and important group consists of diaries and notebooks of Fujiwara nobles of the tenth to the thirteenth century, of which the *Gyokuyō* of Fujiwara Kanezane, covering the years 1163 to 1200, may be cited as an example. Some diaries and journals of the fourteenth and sixteenth centuries, though preserving the chronological entry form, contain much personal detail and political comment, and can be ranked as close antecedents of autobiography. The *Hanazono Tennō Shinki* may be particularly instanced. There was a notable upsurge in the writing of memoirs in the immediate post-Sengoku (from 1615 on) and Genroku (1688–1703) eras. The impulse in the first case was the desirability of producing a record of meritorious service deserving of material reward, while in the second, it was natural that at a time when the study of history was enjoying great popularity, the warrior class would feel the urge to set down the stories of events of stirring times gone by that they had heard from their grandfathers' lips. There is a strong flavor of these various kinds of writing in *Oritaku Shiba no Ki*, but none of them can themselves be described as autobiographies.

Oritaku Shiba no Ki is very much in the tradition of the Chinese *lieh-chuan* and *chia-chuan*, records of public service, intended to foster loyalty and right conduct in descendants and transmitted as private documents. And these forms seem to have been married in this work with the chronicle organization borrowed from the *jih-chi* or *jitsuroku nikki*, though chronological order is modified by discursiveness and some repetition.

Although Chinese and Japanese models for autobiographical writing existed, in the atmosphere of Tokugawa Japan something more was needed to trigger the writing of such a work as

Oritaku Shiba no Ki, a motive stronger than the edification of one's descendants. This was, it is clear, that Hakuseki felt an overpowering moral obligation to transmit to posterity a true record of the rule of Ienobu and as a postscript that of his successor. He regarded himself as the only man alive who could record the actual facts of two difficult eras and so exonerate the rulers and their advisers from possible criticism for the undoubted maladministration there had been. His loyalty and gratitude to Ienobu were so immense that preserving Ienobu's good name was a sacred trust. And he feared that the actions of the subsequent government might result in its being impugned, for detractions soon began to be uttered. This is the underlying theme of Books II and III of the autobiography.

There was an additional consideration. One of the strongest motives for writing one's own life is the desire for self-justification, especially if exacerbated by a sense of ill-usage and disappointment. This motive is strongly operative, and from the nature of the events related, more prominent in the Books II and III than eulogy of Ienobu, while at the end of the autobiography Hakuseki expressly defends himself against any undue influence on affairs.

Further, Hakuseki had endured a series of disappointments, first in the assassination of Hotta Masatoshi shortly after he took service with him; then in the premature death of his revered lord, Ienobu, within a few years of his succession to the shogunate; and finally in the pathetically early death of Ienobu's infant son, again within a few years of his succession.

Then, Hakuseki's unhappy relations with the next Shōgun, Yoshimune, embittered his last years. One letter to a friend suggests he may have feared exile; his apprehension, he claimed, was not on his own or his descendants' account, but because of the slur it would cast on the memory of the ruler he had taught and advised, and the damage such an event would do to Japan's reputation on the Asian continent. Moreover, the events subsequent to Ietsugu's death, on top of his sense of personal loss in Ienobu's passing, must have produced an irritation of spirits which demanded an outlet.

Significantly the motive of self-justification and sense of ill-usage are obvious in the cases of Sokō and Sadanobu, as of Cellini and Rousseau. Sokō and Sadanobu also found the arena of public life closed against them. In Sokō's case the circumstances were particularly bitter. He had been exiled under the strict Tokugawa thought censorship for his criticism of orthodox Chu Hsi philosophy, and by the tenth year of his punishment had given up hope of pardon. He wrote a kind of will for the benefit of his nephew to defend his good name and his actions, and to accuse those who had condemned him. Sadanobu, aristocrat, administrator, scholar, and author of distinction, after six years of energetic but puritanic reforms, was brought down by a conspiracy of his opponents. He bequeathed his autobiography as a secret document to be read only by those of his descendants who attained the rank of Rōjū. Cellini also frequently invokes the reader's sympathy for the injustices he suffered at the hands of others, and Rousseau too wished to transmit his memory "as he actually was, and not as his unjust enemies unremittingly endeavoured to paint him." It may, of course, be argued that the reference to Cellini and Rousseau, and the observations about Chinese writers, amount to a comparison of *Oritaku Shiba no Ki* as an autobiography with writings of those scholars also as autobiographies. This would indeed be a most interesting avenue of research, but is beyond the scope of this introduction.

The vehemence of Hakuseki's expression bears out the disturbed state of his feelings as he wrote. Clearly, he regarded bequeathing to his descendants a testimony to his own actions and motives as a necessary precaution, his sole means of self-justification, which his own sense of his worth demanded. Hani Gorō in *Arai Hakuseki: Fukuzawa Yukichi* (1936) describes *Oritaku Shiba no Ki* as "an expression of passive resistance to feudal repression," an autobiography of far greater significance than the crude memoirs of the time, which were themselves constricted by feudal bonds; it represents an awakening of individual awareness, and is thus a pioneer work of self-knowledge.

Some may reject Hani Gorō's claim as wide of the mark. However, no one can deny that while Hakuseki was an unequivocal supporter of an ideal Confucian state, he was passionately hostile to the venality, negligence, and stupidity of the Tokugawa bureaucracy. Certainly his whole life illustrated his independence of mind and determined self-assertion and self-realization; during his entire career as Ienobu's adviser, he opposed officialdom, and

Books II and III of his autobiography are replete with strictures on various aspects of the administration. The very writing of *Oritaku Shiba no Ki* after he was excluded from affairs and avoided by society demonstrates a spirit that refused to be quelled. At this time, though under physical restraint—his movement out of his house was restricted—and obliged to be highly circumspect in speech, he yet enjoyed the intellectual freedom to think as he saw fit and to set down his free-ranging thoughts in a private document like *Oritaku Shiba no Ki*. The highly tendentious statements in this autobiography strongly suggest resistance to feudal repression. A similar spirit of defiance, cloaked under an outer mantle of discretion, is clear in Sokō and Sadanobu. And when we note Fukuzawa's impudent flouting of the authorities, we must realize that it is absurd to accept the lip service paid to the force majeure of feudalism as having sprung from the hearts of the strongest intellects.

Sources

Hakuseki himself kept a *jitsuroku nikki* in a mixture of *sōrōbun* (epistolary style) and *kambun kuzushi* (modified *kambun*), composed of 16 volumes, the holograph of which is in the Keiō University library. These are very rough memo-pad type notebooks, made up of sheets of *hanshi* or *mino* paper folded in two or four and fastened together roughly at the top with paper string. Each volume is numbered, dated, and variously titled: Record, or Daily Record, or Particulars, or Daily Particulars after Coming Off Duty. This work is generally referred to as the *Hakuseki Nikki*. It is a journal recording incidents in his public life, with relatively few references to his private affairs, though marriages, births, and deaths in his family are recorded, and he even includes notes on his dreams. It is a repository of factual minutiae, containing records of his lectures, and their topics, memorials and other works, meetings and audiences, regalia worn on ceremonial occasions, official letters, illnesses and absences from duty, salary payments and seasonal presents of clothes to himself and his wife, loans he contracted, public events, and natural calamities. Entries are for the most part laconic in the extreme, and there are notable omissions. For instance, there is no reference to the writing and presentation of

Tokushi Yoron, his great history of Japan, or the dismissal of the Bakufu financial expert, Ogiwara Shigehide, although it was the result of a violent campaign Hakuseki mounted.

The *Nikki* covers a period of over 29 years from Hakuseki's appointment as Confucian lecturer in the Kōfu Clan in January 1694 to 26th September 1723, two years before his death; but subsequent to the death of the infant Shōgun Ietsugu in June 1716 and Yoshimune's succession in August the same year, the entries are sparse and brief: comprising only four for the remainder of 1716, eighteen in 1717, three in 1718, one in 1721, and one in 1723. It therefore principally provides a detailed record of Hakuseki's professional career for just over 21 years. It is of interest also to note that many entries between 1710 and 1716 are written in two other unidentified hands, with occasional interlinear notes in Hakuseki's own.

The *Nikki* was an important source for *Oritaku Shiba no Ki*, and it contains sundry annotations in black and red showing how Hakuseki used it in the composition of his autobiography. For example, he scored the lectures he delivered in order to count them, and also marked in various ways material for inclusion. A study of three important incidents in *Oritaku Shiba no Ki*, each based on comparatively long and detailed entries in the *Nikki*, sheds interesting light on Hakuseki's handling of the facts of his life.

(1) The first incident concerns the discussions among his teacher, the representatives of the Kōfu Clan, and himself preceding his taking service with the clan. Without recounting precise detail, it can be said that in the autobiography he omits information about the actual salary agreed upon, certain private interviews leading up to this agreement, and the contents of a letter sent by his teacher to the clan. He seems to *infer* it contained an acceptance but according to the diary this was not so. Various delicate considerations were involved: the salary at which other lecturers had been hired, concern not to offend the official Confucianist, Hayashi, and through him Tsunayoshi, the then Shōgun, and so on. Nevertheless these suppressions cannot be considered tampering with sources; no fact that could be divulged was misrepresented; what could not be divulged was simply left vague.

(2) The second incident is Hakuseki's refusal to petition for confirmation of his appointment when Ienobu was proclaimed the

Shōgun's heir. In *Oritaku Shiba no Ki*, Hakuseki explains he adamantly declined to join two colleagues in such action, but he omits all mention of his second thoughts and alarm lest standing out might be misinterpreted by the clan authorities, nor does he tell us about the letter he wrote to them explaining his conduct.

(3) The third incident is Hakuseki's request to retire during Ietsugu's shogunate. He reconsidered and was asked to meet members of the Rōjū. His memory of this meeting must have been vivid, for in *Oritaku Shiba no Ki* he considerably expands the entry in the *Nikki* when listing the friendly comments of these officials.

Other sources for *Oritaku Shiba no Ki* were a vast number of memorials and memos he had preserved. One manuscript memo, entitled *Kokusō Jigen*, which, bound together with Muro Kyūsō's *Kokusō Seigi*, is in the University of Tokyo Library (old Nanki Repository), throws interesting light on Hakuseki's method of utilizing these documents. The text is given in full in Furukawa Tesshi's *Arai Hakuseki*, pp. 101–5, and is practically identical with the long passage near the beginning of Book III of *Oritaku Shiba no Ki* which deals with the question of Shōgun Ietsugu's mourning for his father, Ienobu. Differences are that it is written in *katakana*, whereas *Oritaku Shiba no Ki* is written in *hiragana*; it uses many characters where *Oritaku Shiba no Ki* uses *kana*; a number of verbal endings vary, one or two words and some brief phrases have been omitted; and there have been some very slight improvements in grammar. Muro Kyūsō's account is referred to in both *Kokusō Jigen* and *Oritaku Shiba no Ki*, and in the latter Hakuseki also mentions the "document he drafted at that time," obviously *Kokusō Jigen*. When Hakuseki in his autobiography quotes at length from a document no longer extant, we may surmise that a good idea of its contents may be obtained from *Oritaku Shiba no Ki*.

Many documents concerning the Korean Embassy of 1711 survive, setting out revised procedures in detail, containing instructions to the Koreans regarding new procedures, recording discussions with the envoys, letters exchanged with Japanese dignitaries on the subject, etc. Hakuseki, however, gives only a brief outline of the matter, which does little more than list the highlights. But on the change which occasioned most discussion, the title by which the *shōgun* should be addressed, he summarizes a two-part essay on the subject, which occupies twenty pages in the *Zenshū* collection, into one page of equivalent length.

Another interesting transference almost in toto except for a few verbal modifications is the recapitulation of the *Shōtoku Nengō Ben* (December 1712). There is, however, one alteration. In *Oritaku Shiba no Ki* he omits a section listing the era names containing the ideograph *shō* and commenting on the fortunes of the emperors from Ichijō-In to Go-Kōmyō-In, and replaces it by a detailed consideration of the changes of era name which might, but should not, be regarded as precedents in point.

For the regulation of Nagasaki trade, which is dealt with in both Books II and III, Hakuseki has entries under appropriate dates in his diary, but refers the reader to his *Shihaku Gi* (*Regulations for Trading Ships*) and *Shihaku Shinrei* (*New Precedents for Trading Ships*). These are no longer extant, but are contained, probably with little change, in the *Tokugawa Kinrei Ki*. Further, his discussion of the outflow of specie is partly presented in part three of the *Honchō Hōka Tsūyō Jiryaku* and (what is identical in every respect) the sixth proposal of the *Hakuseki Kengi*.

These are but three instances of the voluminous body of works Hakuseki drew on for his autobiography.

The Portraiture of the Oritaku Shiba no Ki

Hakuseki's strongest statement of his attitude to Ienobu is "I tried to make my lord like Yao and Shun." This tells us that Hakuseki viewed himself as a latter-day sage, only more fortunate than his illustrious exemplar in that he found a lord who listened to his advice: "I never hesitated to express my honest opinion, and neither did he disregard my advice," he boasts. Hakuseki even went so far imitated the Master as to remonstrate fearlessly with his lord when he considered him to be deviating from right conduct. But his satisfaction lay not merely in advising a powerful ruler. It was to the state—to the people of the empire—which the ruler symbolized that he dedicated his service; it was the implementation of government for the sake of the people that he took as his life's work. Underlying his self-image as a scholar given the opportunity to fulfill the noblest functions of a Confucian teacher, was his conception of himself as a superior man, benevolent, just, and incorruptible. Prizing scholarship, he prided himself on his learning, but he respected it in others, too; unfortunately, the reverse side of this respect was an inordinate contempt for any defect in another's intellectual attainments, and a proclivity to despise such a person from the heights of his own unassailable erudition.

But he was not only a Confucian scholar; he was a *samurai*. Born into a tradition of self-sacrifice and reckless courage, he was too late by half a century for the proper destiny of a fighting-man. Nevertheless he transposed this spirit in its most uncompromising form to the administrative arena. In exchanging the sword for the pen, he abated not one jot of the *samurai* spirit. He saw himself, in fact, in the old heroic terms: he even went so far as to purchase a suit of armour as an earnest of his determination to fulfill his *samurai* role. He repeatedly stresses that his approach to the tasks with which he was charged was that of the *samurai* resigning himself to death as he prepared for battle. His health, his rest, his reputation, his life itself, he was ever ready to sacrifice for his lord's sake, and this readiness was always in the forefront of his consciousness, informing all his acts and thoughts with an irrefrangible self-righteousness.

Hakuseki recognized in himself a powerful ambition at work: he declared as a child he would rather reign in Hell than serve in Heaven. He saw himself as triumphing over handicaps and misfortunes by superhuman assiduity and willpower. Keenly sensitive to his modest status in the feudal hierachy, he found deep satisfaction in the pressure he succeeded in bringing on the course of events through his unswerving determination. Yet simultaneously he used his essentially unofficial position in the administrative machine as blanket cover against any charge of improper interference; this was adroit, but somewhat specious. Though exulting in the extraordinary fate which had elevated him to a position of such real moment in public affairs, he yet felt himself beset by petty jealousies and bureaucratic frustrations. Specifically, in Ietsugu's rule he cast himself in the role of a prophet crying in the wilderness.

All in all, his self-portrait is essentially honest and clear-sighted. The other portraits presented in *Oritaku Shiba no Ki* of prominent figures in Ienobu's time, though colored by Hakuseki's personal viewpoint, are similarly just. Four examples may be given. His summing-up of Manabe Akifusa seems fair and accurate. Manabe was clearly no upstart adventurer but extremely hardworking and competent, as well as courteous and diplomatic, though also capable of acting with decision. But he had no specialist expertise and no erudition, no abstract theory of administration and no fertility in framing policies.

The portrait of Ienobu that emerges from Hakuseki's autobiography is that of a decisive and conscientious lord, acquainted with every phase of the administration and the source from which the real direction of the state emanated. This view is supported by *Tokugawa Jikki*, which speaks of Ienobu wearing himself out in the service of his people, and other chronicles, which bear witness to his interest in administration and to his determination to improve the quality of government. But there are also references to a degenerate streak in his nature, and Hakuseki himself notes that Ienobu took care not to force on his notice, conduct of which he knew he disapproved. However, though he was a discreet and patient man, he does not seem to have been possessed of any greater intellectual powers than Manabe, and Tokutomi Sohō is probably right when he says neither of them were the sort of men who could use Hakuseki; rather it was Hakuseki who used them. Hakuseki could not be expected to put it quite this way; he could only emphasise his immense utility.

Ogiwara Shigehide was a typical conniving Bakufu bureaucrat, and though it is doubtful if his operations regularly produced the extremes of suffering to the people Hakuseki accused him of, he properly symbolized the lax, ad hoc floundering of the Bakufu administration. Hayashi Nobuatsu was no genius nor a man of great strength of character; his learning was not the equal of his forebears' and though he was hardly the incompetent sycophant pictured by Hakuseki, he drew the criticism of other Confucianists as well, as one who was "given to compromise and avoided vital issues."

Scope and Nature of the Oritaku Shiba no Ki

There is nothing of the confessional about Hakuseki's autobiography, and we should expect a high degree of reticence. Though he regretted that people of his father's generation were so un-communicative that much valuable information was lost, he ad-mired his father's tight-lipped control of his emotions at all times. In design, his autobiography is limited to a record of externals. He makes no attempt to describe himself as a product of or to assess the place he occupied in the particular kind of society of his day. We learn nothing about the social side of his existence, but just the cold bare facts of his achievements as historian and poet. There are no general reflections on the meaning of life and only a little simple intentional introspection. The work is basically a collection of reminiscences of incidents in his career and memoranda on political events of which he had firsthand knowledge, together with summaries of official reports and his own memorials.

Although this sounds objective enough, his manner of dealing with events is highly subjective. In the course of describing the working of the political machine and defining his part in the ad-ministration, he eulogizes or criticizes other prominent figures of the day and delineates his relations with them. And he brings any-thing but a detached approach to the narrative, for he adds as an aid, in elucidating exactly what happened, not only what he thought and felt but also what he imagines others thought and felt on the various occasions with which he deals. As Hani Gorō puts it, "he recalls the past not critically but emotionally."

Hakuseki has some intentionally self-revelatory comments in *Oritaku Shiba no Ki*. He confesses, for example: ". . . as I was born quick-tempered, my anger was harder to control than anything else. However, this also, as I have made my way through life's difficulties, is declining as my years increase, and now per-haps I am not as I used to be." He dwells on his assiduity in study and the persistence by which he overcame the difficulties he en-countered. The whole document is suffused with a strong coloring of self-admiration. His claims concerning his achievements and the nobility of his actions were quite unblushing, and the work is stud-ded with flattering opinions of himself authored by himself and others.

But it must be remembered that Hakuseki addressed himself not to mankind in general but to his own posterity, and he is be-queathing the record of his glories and accomplishments like an heirloom. He explains the motives for sundry actions from his hot-

[29]

headed youthful escapade while in the Tsuchiya Clan to his continuance in administration during Ietsugu's rule. He makes clear
his deep attachment for his father and mother, and his concern
for his sisters; but he rarely mentions his wife and children, except,
for instance, to record gifts from Ienobu, or note when he was
unable to lecture because of their illness. He defends the part he
played in government and pays tribute to the indefatigable
Manabe Akifusa. He makes some solemn comments on his illnesses
and Ienobu's consideration for his rather delicate constitution.
Particularly he dilates on the relationship between Ienobu and
himself, and on the former's qualities as a ruler. He also states
in so many words more than once his utterly selfless dedication
to Ienobu's service.

But there are also many passages of unconscious self-revelation.
His preoccupation with self-justification lends a certain querulous-
ness to some sections. His vehemence in pushing his views, his
scathing attacks on the eminent Confucianist Hayashi Nobuatsu,
contemptuous comments on Amenomori Hōshū, his frenzy of determination in encompassing Ogiwara Shigehide's dismissal, and
in arguing down the objections of the Korean Envoys, his scorn for
the members of the Rōjū, and his attacks on the cruelty and stupidity of the members of the judiciary leave an impression of a harsh
and irascible man. It was simply that his thoroughness as a scholar
and his brilliant intellect made him impatient with lesser minds.

Worse than all, however, comments have come down to us
suggesting that Hakuseki had a brash and uncouth side to his
nature. Muro Kyūsō described his conversation as a continuous
tirade, punctuated by loud bursts of laughter as if there were no
one else in the room. Other records describe how he browbeat
into silence anyone who presumed to question his opinions. So
clearly does this aspect of his personality emerge throughout his
autobiography, that his style sometimes erupts into bitter invec-
tive and sometimes has an overtone of hysteria. Except at these
points, it is dignified and grave as befitted a Confucian scholar
of his eminence writing for his descendants. Often it is charged
with emotion, sometimes tender, sometimes impassioned, but it
is never coarse. His warm and sincere regard for his father, his
obvious family feeling for his mother and sisters, his interest in
his children's futures, his willingness to instruct his friends, his

humanity and energetic defense of the simple common people who fell victim to the rigor of the age, and his ready and boisterous laughter show him a man of quick and deep feelings. His tremendous driving power, which had lifted him to splendid scholastic heights, when focused on any task, had to bring it to what he saw as a successful conclusion over all obstacles, and against all opposition. Under the slow-grinding bureaucratic machine of the Tokugawa Bakufu, the number of times his advice was disregarded or misinterpreted must have built up an overpowering sense of frustration.

He lacked the political temperament and never tried to win people over to his side; he understood only the frontal attack. When victorious in argument he displayed a provocative superciliousness. It was no wonder that he came to be regarded generally as "an arrogant old man." He was also bigoted and narrowminded. Nevertheless he was possessed of great nobility of mind. His disregard of others was usually only the result of his counting the end in view (the welfare of the state as he understood it) as of paramount importance, and when the affairs of individuals were themselves the subject of consideration, he was capable of most sympathetic concern. His ability to appreciate the fine qualities of Sidotti, though at the same time rejecting Christianity as illogical, is one of the most pleasing facets of his character, and his efforts to save that tragic man from imprisonment perhaps the crown of his humane labors in the field of justice. He was no selfish careerist, but sincerely dedicated to the service of the whole state, for he sought the well-being, not only of the Bakufu, but of all social classes.

His importance began to be recognized about the end of the eighteenth century, when Ogyū Sorai's great popularity began to wane. At the same time Confucianists began to appreciate his stature, his work as a pioneer in Western learning gained notice, and from the end of the eighteenth century, *Sairan Igen* became necessary reading for intellectuals. Throughout Meiji his works were published one after the other. With the advance of the twentieth century, his reputation has continued to rise, and in the postwar years there has been a notable upsurge in interest in his life and work.

This introduction has not attempted to do more than to place

[31]

Oritaku Shiba no Ki in its literary context as Japan's first autobiography proper, to provide some background information against which the reader can assess it as an example of its genre, and to present a translation to fill a gap in an important aspect of Japanese literature and historical documentation.

TOLD ROUND A BRUSHWOOD FIRE

PREFACE

In the old days, when people had anything to say, they said it without unnecessary additions, expressing their meaning fully in as few words as possible. My parents were like that.[1]

When my father, in his seventy-fifth year, was on the point of death with typhoid fever, the doctor [1] came and prescribed ginseng. My father had always warned people they must bear in mind that while it may be all right for the young, it is distressing to see an old man die, struggling to breathe with the help of drugs because he refuses to accept that his time has come, and so some said there was nothing to be done. But his sufferings, when in the grip of a spasm, were so pitiful to witness that his family gave him some ginseng in syrup of ginger, and he thereupon revived and finally recovered.

Afterward my mother asked him why, during his illness, he had always turned away in bed from people and said nothing. He replied: "My headache was very severe, but as I had never betrayed suffering to others, I thought it undesirable to depart from my rule. I have seen many cases where people in the grip of a fever have let slip things they should not, so I thought it better to say nothing. Therefore I acted as I did." By this you can judge what he was ordinarily like.

Since he was like this, it was unfortunately difficult to ask him things about which I [2] was curious, and time went by and he died while there was still much I was not clear about. This may be well enough where ordinary matters are concerned, but it is regrettable that circumstances relating to my father and grandfather are not known, and there is now no one I can ask.[2] I know that my children will regret this as much as I.

Now that I have leisure, I have set down past events just as they occurred to me, with no thought-out plan.[3] Since this is not meant for the eyes of outsiders, I have not hesitated to write in a careless style, nor of delicate matters. In particular, with regard to those details that concern His late Highness [3], I am the only man alive who knows the full story, so it would be inexcusable if, unworthy though I am, I did not set it down.

I hope that those who read this record, even unto the descendants of my sons and grandsons, will not swerve from the path of loyalty and filial piety when they remember the laborious rise of their father and grandfather, and the extraordinary kindness of His late Highness to their father. I, an old man of sixty, of the sept name Minamoto, and holding Honorary Rank, took up my pen on the 17th November 1716.[4]

BOOK I

M y father said that as he lost his mother at the age of four and his father at the age of nine, he knew little about his parents. Grandfather's name was Kageyu, and grandmother was the daughter of someone called Someya. Both ended their days in Shimozuma-no-Shō in Hitachi Province.[1]

The Arai sprang from the Minamoto clan of Kōzuke Province.[2] The Someya were descended from the Fujiwara of Sagami Province, but for some reason they moved to Hitachi Province. There is a traditional explanation, but as it was not positively stated by my father, I cannot accept it.

My father told me: "Your grandfather said he lost his fief for some reason and went into hiding on the estate he used to possess. I remember that his eyes were large, his beard thick, and his expression stern. When he died, his hair had not yet turned white."

Whenever grandfather ate, he always took his chopsticks from a black lacquered box, decorated in gold with irises, and when he had finished eating, he put them back in the box and placed it by his side. When father asked his old nurse about it, she told him that once, after grandfather had taken a good head in a battle, the general said to him when he presented himself: "You must be weary with fighting.[3] Eat this." He pushed forward his dinner-tray and gave it to grandfather with the chopsticks. This became a famous incident at the time, and so grandfather would never let them leave his side. My father added: "Since I was a child when I heard the story, I am not certain when she said it happened, where the battle took place, or who the general was."

My father once said: "One other thing I remember. When I was playing with a companion of the same age, your grandfather heard me say to him: 'You're the fellow who called me a fool.'

Your grandfather said to me: 'It is a great insult for a man to be called a fool. Though just now you were only speaking in jest, it was as bad as if you insulted yourself. You should not say such things.' "

Father told me: "After your grandfather's death, by an arrangement made by my elder brothers, I was brought up in the house of a certain man.[4] He was not like your grandfather, but was very rich and had many servants and a great collection of bows, muskets, long spears, etc. He was very fond of me, but when I was thirteen, a friend I had had a quarrel with said: 'What can a fellow understand who does not know that he has become the son of his own retainer?' I could not understand, and since there was no one else to ask, I went to the house of my old nurse and asked her about it; she told me not to bother myself about such things. More and more perplexed, I persisted. Then she wept and said: 'Since those you now regard as your parents were mindful of past kindnesses, your father died peacefully. Now, this man is rich. He could adopt anyone's son, but he has adopted you and loves you better than his own son because he bears in mind that you are the son of his lord. You must devote yourself to serving him dutifully.'

"When I heard this, I felt a deep resentment against my elder brothers, and so I went to the priest who taught me calligraphy and borrowed 100 copper coins. Fastening up some clothes in wrapping paper, I hung them on my sword hilt, did up the coins in my belt, and set off. Having gone two or three *ri*, I fell in with two couriers on their way from Mito to Edo. I inquired about the road to Edo, and they said: 'If a young fellow travels alone, he will be in danger of robbery. Come along with us.' Thinking this was so, I went with them. When they asked where I was from, whose son I was, and whose house I was going to in Edo, I did not reply immediately, but as they were kind, and let me ride when I was tired, I thought there was no reason to be so fearful and told them how things were. They were sorry for me, took me to Edo, and looked after me. With their help, I found a master.

"Twenty-five years after your grandfather's death, desirous of visiting his grave, I returned to my native village.[5] My three elder brothers were dead, and my elder sister alone survived. My sister told me that my second eldest brother, grieved at not knowing my whereabouts, had gone to Edo every year inquiring for me everywhere, again and again, but now he was dead. Later I heard that she too had died shortly afterward. After that, there was no one to visit in my native village."

My father's mother died on the 2nd April 1604, and his father died on the 25th September 1609.[6] My father was born in 1601. He left his native province in 1613.

A man called Ryōya [4], a former abbot of Kōtokuji, told me that when he was still a child, in the time of the abbot who preceded him, someone called Arai Kansai visited this temple.[7] Ryōya took word to my father, who came to meet the visitor, and the two stayed together all day. The visitor sometimes came every year, and sometimes after an interval of several years. Ryōya heard he was a cousin but was not sure, nor did he know where he came from. I do not know whether my mother knew about this, much less did she dare tell me. Why were people in olden times so reticent? Even Ryōya did not tell me of this until thirty years or so after my father's death.

Not long after the civil wars, when my father was still young, men were chivalrous and were accustomed to setting a high value on nobility of spirit, in contrast to the situation today.[8] My father spent some years wandering no one knows where. At the age of thirty-one, when he first entered the service of Mimbu-no-Shō Minamoto Toshinao (Tsuchiya) [5], three foot-soldiers (at that time called *kachizamurai*) were accused of night burglary. They were arrested and confined above the firing gallery in the gate-tower and placed in the sole charge of my father. On being informed of this, father said: "If these men are committed to my custody, I hope their long and short swords will not be taken away from them." My father's request was granted, and their weapons were handed over to him. Giving them to a servant to carry, he climbed up to the floor above the gallery and returned them to the three men, saying: "If you intend to escape, cut off my head and go. I alone am no match for the three of you, so my own weapons are useless." Then he wrapped his two swords in a piece of toweling and laid them aside, and so he slept and ate with the men. After about ten days, the charge against them was proved baseless. Nevertheless they were dismissed from the Kohō's [5] House on the grounds that he did not want such men in his service.[9] When that time came, they said to my father: "We felt that the lord committed us to the charge of only one man because he considered us contemptible. We intended to prove otherwise, but if we had killed you, unarmed as you were, he would have concluded that we were as despicable as he had thought, which would have been unbearable. There was nothing for us but to wait for death, but still we planned, if by some lucky chance our lives were spared, to take our revenge. Owing to your kindness, our weapons were not confiscated, and now we can take our place in the company of warriors again. We do not wish to be unmindful of your kindness, and we feel that our resentment has been done away with." With this they parted. This is the story as my father told it to me.

Shortly afterward, he was selected for special duties, and at last became a permanent retainer in the Kohō's House. Later he was appointed a surveillance officer (at that time called a *metsuke*).[10]

The events which I now relate are my own recollections dating from the time when I first began to understand things.

My father's daily routine was always the same and never varied. He always rose early at about four o'clock, bathed in cold water, and dressed his own hair. When the nights were cold, my mother wanted him to use warm water, but he would not countenance putting the servants to this trouble and forbade it. When he was past seventy, my mother said that she too was getting on in years and could no longer endure the cold nights, so hot coals were placed on the ashes in the hearth, and they lay down with their feet toward it. A kettle of water was placed by the side of the fire, and when my father got up, he bathed with the hot water.

Both my parents were devout Buddhists. My father never neglected to make obeisance to Buddha each morning, after he had done up his hair and put on his clothes. On the anniversaries of his parents' deaths, he prepared rice and placed it on the altar with his own hands, without troubling the servants. While the night was still dark, he sat up waiting for the dawn, and as soon as it was light, he went on duty.

My father's house lay to the south of the Kohō's, but when he went on duty, he had to enter by the north gate. In the morning, he approached from the east and in the evenings, set off toward the west.[11] He wore footgear which had leather soles and walked with loud footsteps so that everyone knew it was my father coming and little children hushed their crying.

In the eighth lunar month every year, the Kohō went to his fief in the district of Mōta, in Kazusa Province, and returned in the middle of the twelfth.[12] On his return he would always send for my father and, taking him aside, ask him what had happened while he had been away.[13] Every year my father would reply that there was nothing to report. After some years had passed, the Kohō said: "Although we are a small clan, there is quite a large number of retainers on duty here while I am away. During my long absences, how can nothing have happened? I do not understand why, notwithstanding this, you always say there is nothing to report." Whereupon my father replied: "We notify you of important matters at once; those in charge during your absence discuss and decide on small matters. That is why there has never been anything else to tell you." Thereafter, when the Kohō returned from Kazusa Province, he would always summon my father and tell him what had happened there, and they would be together a long time before my father would take his leave. Father told me that the Kohō never again asked him about what had happened in the Edo mansion while he was away.

In the autumn of 1645, when the Kohō was put in command of Sumpu Castle, my father went to Kazusa Province to take charge of affairs there and did not accompany his lord.[14] The following spring, he was sent for urgently and went from Kazusa to Suruga. At that time, the military encampment at the castle was surrounded by only a bamboo fence. My father was told that he had been sent for because many of the younger *samurai* went out for their amusement over the fence every night; the older retainers did not seem to be able to stop them. My father wished to avoid the scandal which would have been caused by punishing even one of the young men for such an offense. He surveyed the surroundings of the camp at once and posted sentries at suitable places. In addition, he had four or five guardhouses built and set two foot-soldiers in each to keep watch, and every night from dusk to dawn, he personally visited the sentries, encouraging those who were diligent and rebuking those who were lazy. Until the Kohō was relieved, my father did not take a single night's rest, and the surreptitious night excursions of the young *samurai* stopped of themselves.

In 1647 and 1649, the Kohō was put in charge of the Fire Guard at the Nikkō Tōshōgū.[15] His guard duties there lasted for a hundred days on each occasion. In 1649, he was also made castle commandant at Ōsaka (called the Ōsaka Auxiliary Guard).[16] My father accompanied him to both places, and during those journeys, father never lay down to sleep but only dozed on horseback on the way. Even after they arrived at Ōsaka, he did not go to bed night or day but only napped sitting up, when the occasion offered, during daytime duty, so that for a long time afterward, he suffered from night blindness. He told me laughingly that on the way back from Ōsaka, having arrived at Mishima post-station after sunset, he could not distinguish the lamps that shone from every house.[17]

Afterward, when I asked why he had done this, he said there had been a very good reason. A certain young hereditary retainer had committed a serious crime. Thinking he could not escape punishment if the crime were discovered, to give it the appearance of an honorable vendetta, he killed a child and fled. The Kohō was thoroughly disgusted by this, but though a search was made for the wanted man, he could not be found. It was thought that if the criminal's old mother were seized, he would give himself up. His mother was accordingly arrested, but the man did not appear. After many months, his mother died in prison. My father received secret information that the fugitive had sworn to avenge this and, disguised as an itinerant priest, was lying in wait for the Kohō. Father thought that if there was any truth to the rumor, the criminal would take advantage of such a journey, so without any fuss, he posted guards at intervals and went the rounds himself, as in Suruga. People thought that he was only following his former practice.

After my father's resignation, when he was talking to me on one occasion, he said: "A man called Ashizawa lost his father at an early age and was given his father's estates and honorably employed, but when he was about twenty, I was summoned, and when I went, the Kohō was seated with his combat sword stuck horizontally in his belt. I thought his expression was different from usual, and when he bade me approach, I went to lay aside my short sword, but since I was told to come as I was, I approached. The Kohō told me he had just then summoned Ashizawa and that he was going to kill him with his own hand, and that I must be present. When I did not answer, the Kohō said: 'You don't answer. Is there anything on your mind?' I said: 'There is. Ashizawa has always said that one who lost his father at an early age and had grown up thus far, owing to the immense favor of his lord, should feel more than ordinary gratitude for this kindness. He is a naturally audacious fellow, and, moreover, is still young. He has committed many follies. I do not know what offense he has committed, but men who are not like this when they are young are often good for nothing in later years. Because I was turning all these things over in my mind, I was slow to answer, for which I beg pardon.' The Kohō said nothing more, and I too was silent. After a while the Kohō said: 'The mosquitoes have gathered on your face. Brush them away.' I moved my head, and six or seven mosquitoes that had grown as big as silverberries gorged with blood fluttered to the ground. Taking some paper from my bosom, I wrapped them up and put them in my sleeve. A little later, I was told to go home and rest, and I withdrew.

"This Ashizawa was always fond of *sake* and used to get drunk. I talked this over with a man called Seki, who was friendly with him, and the two of us constantly urged him to give up drinking. After some years, he was finally appointed to his father's office. Although the Kohō is now dead, I hope that he will carry out his duties so that what I said in the beginning does not prove wrong." Father added this because, after a long time, Ashizawa had taken to drink again.

In the Kohō's house, there was a man called Katō. When I was twenty, he seemed already over sixty. His grandfather was said to have held a castle in a place called Sanuki, in Kazusa Province, as a *samurai-taishō* of the Satomi of Awa Province.[18] (He is said to have been called Katō Iga-no-Kami; I never heard his given name.) In his house, there were two precious swords called "Snake-Sword" and "Monkey-Leader." I definitely saw "Snake-Sword." It had a narrow blade three *shaku* long. The reason "Monkey-Leader" was so called was because he had begged it from a monkey-leader who had it, so it is said.[19] I must have seen it.

When he was sixteen, Katō had killed with his own hand a young *samurai*. The accepted version was that he had cut him down while the man was chopping up the makings of a fish salad and struck the celadon dish at the same time, cutting it slant-wise. Once, after my father had retired, when the story of the sword was mentioned, he said: "The story is told this way only because there was no one present at the time. One should not necessarily believe what everyone says. The sword which cut that dish in two was, in fact, the one I gave you when you were a child. At that time, the barracks where Katō was quartered were next to my house, and Katō, who was upstairs, was quarreling with his retainer in a loud voice, which I considered unseemly. When I heard Katō rushing downstairs, I thought: 'Something must be up!' and took my sword and hurried to the scene. Katō had already struck at the man, but his blow was weak, and the fellow seemed to be unwounded. When he turned on Katō with a kitchen knife, I drew my sword and cut him through slant-wise, from the upper part of the shoulder. My blow struck the dish, which was before him, and cut it in two. I said: 'Give him the coup de grâce quickly,' and wiped the blood off my sword blade. Returning it to the scabbard, I hurried away. Afterward, people came thronging around him, and in the end, the monkey-leader's sword was credited with the glory."

My father continued: "My own sword originally belonged to a man called Gotō, a native of Kōzuke Province. His elder brother had cut an enemy's head clean in two with a horizontal blow of this sword. Gotō said he used that skull for a plaything when he was a child. After I heard the story, I begged the sword from him for many years, until finally he gave it to me. You must never let it leave your side and must hand it on." That sword is the narrow decorated one called "Lion."

"The short sword with a blade by Kunikiyo belonged to the grandson of a man called Okabe Tamba-no-Kami, in the House of Takeda of Kai.[20] (He was called Okabe Motome. His direct descendants are still serving in the Mutsu branch of the Sōma House.)[21] He was the cousin of Tadanao, the Kohō's father.[22]

[44]

When Tadanao was in Echizen, he was requested to take Okabe into his House as a retainer, and when Okabe was still a child, he was sent for. Tadanao died soon afterward, and Okabe ended his life in the Kohō's House. In the autumn of his thirteenth year, Okabe went out on to the moors with a sixteen-year-old companion to catch butcher-birds. A wounded wild boar suddenly charged them. The retainer immediately abandoned his lord and climbed a nearby tree. The young Okabe waited with his back to the tree. When the boar tried to rush him, he drew his short sword and cut at it. It took the sword-guard in its mouth, with the blade foremost, and tried to throw him down, but because he was backed up against a large tree, he was not easily thrown. While he kept up a steady pressure, the boar chewed about a *sun*'s length of the silver sword-guard it had in its mouth, split itself on the blade from the tip of its nose to the middle of its head, and fell dead. Okabe was the grandson of no common man, and he performed many such deeds from his boyhood on. My father asked for and obtained the sword, and it came down to me."

My father also said to me: "You should not boast to people of the qualities of your sword. When I was young, I heard a certain man talk of the sharpness of his sword. I said: 'How shamelessly you talk! Who would wear a sword that cannot cut things? Now then, let's see whether it will cut or not.' I drew my sword, but those standing round restrained me, and the matter was eventually smoothed over." My father added: "People were like that in the old days."

A certain old man called Asahina constantly swore by the gods and buddhas. My father said: "Ordinarily, people who tell a lot of lies swear by the gods and buddhas to make their words sound true. Although this man was not normally a liar, he was headstrong and uncircumspect in his conversation. Swearing by the gods and buddhas had become a habit. So you must take care," he warned.

My father had a friend called Seki [6], who was five or six years younger than he. When Seki was past seventy, he became senile in speech and act. Father, noting the many signs of this, said: "It is in the nature of man that his powers decline with age. When the time comes, however much care we take, we cannot help growing old, but if you train yourself from your boyhood years on, you will not, even when you are old, be thought silly by those you meet. What makes people think of you as old is when you say and do foolish things. In short, you strike people as old simply because you forget what you are doing. There is a routine for both young and old. It is generally better to confine your activities. If people attempt to do too many things, they may do them or they may not, but inevitably they will be guilty of inconsistencies. From my youth, I have attempted only a few things, but what I have attempted I have done with all my might, and I have done them myself without relegating them to servants. I have a place for articles of daily use and never move them from it, so that even at night, I can find them in the dark without groping. It must be because I have become so thoroughly accustomed to every part of my routine that when I do things it is just like the various parts of my body performing their functions involuntarily, in response to my wishes.

"There is something to be gained from asking old men about bygone days. Just as it is difficult to forget what we learned when we were children, so the experiences of childhood remain in one's memory even in old age, and when people inquire, it is well to answer. Though we hear about new and strange things, we should not talk about them. We forget people's names that we have heard only once. Everyone sometimes forgets where and when a thing happened, even a short while afterward. When a young person forgets, people think that it is only on that one occasion, but when an old man is uncertain of something, they say he is senile. As a man grows older, he should, in every respect, be more careful than he was in his youth. Seki was honest by nature, and he was also resourceful above the average, but from his youth, he was self-indulgent and showed little circumspection in speech and action, and in the end he has become as he is now."

I shall now set down what I have seen myself since I reached years of discretion.

In my earliest recollections, father had few black hairs. His face was square, his forehead high, his eyes large, and his beard heavy. Although he was short in stature, he was thickset and powerful-looking. He was not a man who showed his feelings, and I never remember him laughing loudly, much less did I ever hear him scolding people roughly. When he spoke, he used as few words as possible; his manners were imposing, and I never saw him surprised, perturbed, or lacking in self-control. For instance, when he had the moxa applied, he said it was useless to put on a few small applications, and he would order many large applications, in five or more places, without betraying the least sign of pain.

When he had leisure, he swept clean the room he regularly used, hung an old painting on the wall, placed a few seasonal flowers in a vase and spent the day in silent contemplation before them. He also painted but did not like the use of colors. Except when he was ill, he did not have servants to wait on him but did everything for himself.

In the morning and evening, he ate no more than two bowls of rice. Holding a bowl in his hand, he would judge by its weight the amount of rice and would take more or less of other dishes, in accordance with the weight of the rice, so that the amount of food he ate should not be excessive. He said: "If you eat a great deal of one kind of food, even though you are fond of it, it inevitably leads to illness. When you eat a little of everything that is put before you, one food balances the other. Then I think it would be rare if one became ill from eating." Usually, he ate whatever was brought and did not order anything in particular, though he insisted on having the foods of the four seasons, as soon as they were readily available, and ate them with his retainers. He was easily affected by wine, so he joined in festivities by merely taking the cup in his hand. He liked tea.

When at home, he always wore freshly washed clothing and never anything soiled, even in bed, but when he went out, he always wore fine, new clothes. He never wore what was not suitable to his rank. He said: "In the old days, people tried to avoid doing what would lead to their being criticized after death. People drop and lose intimate personal things, like fans, when in company; from such things, you can discover the character of the owner." My father used a fan about a *shaku* in length that was painted in an old-fashioned style, with unlacquered ribs and paper speckled in gold and silver. He would not use any fan that was not executed by masters of the first rank, and he was even more particular about weapons, like his two swords.

When he was past seventy, his left elbow troubled him, and though he offered his resignation on this pretext, the Kohō would not accept it. Thereafter, when on duty, he wore only a short sword without a guard, one *sun* six or seven *bu* in width and over one *shaku* long. When he went out, his long sword was carried by a retainer. Although I can see now that this was strange, no one censured him, and much less did the Kohō make any comment. It seems my father thought that if a man encounters trouble while wearing a sword he should use it, but if you are ill and unable to wield a sword, it is better not to have the useless thing with you.

Until the day of his death, he never let this sword leave his side, and I sent it to his adopted son [7] in Mutsu, as he had directed in his will.[23] Its ornaments were of steel, carved in a wave design. It had a scabbard of black lacquer, and the rattan binding on the hilt was lacquered gold. On taking the tonsure, he put the scabbard into an ornamental leather cover.

Many years after my father's death, Ryōya [4], the former abbot of Kōtokuji, told me of an incident which he had witnessed as a boy and of which he had never seen the like. It happened when father was past eighty, and Ryōya had seen it with his own eyes. A drunkard came into the temple brandishing a sword and put everyone to flight so that no one would face him. Father came out from his cell, leaning on his stick, quite unaware of what was going on. Ryōya, who was peeping through a chink in the door, thought he was in danger but was at a loss what to do. It appeared that father went up to the man and suddenly, with all his might, grabbed the man's sword-arm. He then kicked the fellow down, and, taking the sword from him, flung it into a ditch, and went back to his room. The man did not rise but fell into a drunken slumber where he lay, while the young priests came out from their various hiding places and kept guard over him. "When he awoke from his sodden sleep, they sent him on his way, or so I heard," Ryōya said. There are sure to be some who say it was most inappropriate for an old man to do such things, and care should be taken not to repeat such behavior to people. However, he was not the kind to be unaware of such considerations, and one should reflect on why he acted as he did.

When I was seventeen or eighteen, I accidentally dropped,

in my father's presence, a *torinawa*, a finely wound green cord with a hook at the end used for tying people up, which I was carrying in my bosom. Saying: "What is this?" he picked it up and looked at it. After a short pause he said: "Long ago, when I was in office, I used to keep this by me in my flint bag. I thought that if I ordered men to seize and bind some disorderly fellow, they might not have it in readiness. When I retired, I had no further use for it, and I kept it for tying up the cat. It is proper that a warrior should know every part of his duties. However, there are things which a man should or should not do, according to his station. This cord is not something you should keep about your person, and you are old enough to know better."

My father said that when he was young, there was a certain man named Takataki who served in the House of the Lord of Shisawa, in Harima.[24] (He was commonly called Kichibei; I do not know his given name.) This man suddenly disappeared. After some days had passed, the story went about that, being fond of fishing, he had gone out with what is called a casting net, and, taking off his clothes by the riverside, had told his servant to guard his two swords carefully while he himself, carrying the net, went into the water. As he walked along catching trout, he crossed the border of the territory of Hayashida.[25] The lord of that region had forbidden fishing in that place, and Kichibei was seized by two guards. When they went to tie him up with a rope, he pleaded piteously with them; they grudgingly let him go free, and off he went.

He then disappeared, perhaps because he thought that the affair would eventually become known. It was being said that he had suffered this misadventure because of his fondness for so frivolous a pastime when that year drew to a close. On the day of the lunar New Year of the following year, he cut down one of the chief *samurai* among the large number on duty in front of the great gate of the Hayashida mansion. He left a card describing in detail the circumstances of what he had done, stating that it was in order to wipe out his shame, and fled. Thinking that he had not fled far, they sent out parties to search for him, but they were unable to find him. The next day he cut down another man and left his card as before. Although no time was lost in making a search, once more he could not be found. Five days later he cut down yet another man, left a card, and fled as before. Despite a thorough search, they were never able to discover where he had gone. People said that to do such a deed once was easy, but to do it twice and three times proved his courage beyond a doubt.

My father said: "After I went to serve in the Kohō's House, I used to relate this incident. Later, when I went to take charge of affairs in Kazusa, my companions and I came to a place called Takataki where we stopped in at the house of the headman.[26]

"When night fell, a crowd of villagers came in and one of them, a man close to sixty, who was seated at the other side of the fire that was burning in a long hearth, caught my eye and then averted his face. His glance seemed peculiar, so I stared in his direction, and he also looked back at me and then away, two or three times. I was puzzled and got up from my seat, went across to him and asked him who he was. At first he turned away saying only that he was a native of that place. Afterward he said: 'How can I conceal myself in this way? I am the ruin of that Takataki whom you once knew.' I was astonished, and exclaimed: 'How do you come to be living here?'

"Thereupon he said: 'I am descended from the Kazusa branch of the Takataki who were retainers of the Kamakura Bakufu. I am a grandson of the Takataki who bore the title of Sakyō-no-Jō at the time of the Satomi of Awa who annexed this province.[27] When the House of Satomi was destroyed, I entered the House of the Lord of Shisawa. After that incident occurred, I fled here. My ancestors had held this place for generations, and the people here sheltered me for the sake of the past. When I heard that a man called Arai had come here, I wondered if it was the man I had met. I came to see, but you were surprised and spoke in an embarrassed way, and so I was ashamed.'

"When my companions asked me if I knew the man, I said: 'He is the Takataki who, it is said, cut down three men in Harima Province in the space of seven days, and each time set up a card.' They were all astounded. How hard it is to foresee the vicissitudes of a man's life."

My father also told me the following story: "When I was young," he said, "there was a fellow by the name of Echizen." (He was called Kurobei. Echizen is an unusual name, but my father said that in those days people often called themselves after

their native province; perhaps his native province was Echizen.)
"This man also disappeared. Several years later, when I was
setting out from Mutsu for the San'yōdō, I came to Kashinokinosaka and passed a fellow with a load of firewood on his
back.[28] I had gone a little way past him when I heard a voice
call my name from behind. I looked round, and the fellow with
the firewood put down his load and, taking off the scarf about his
face, came toward me. Puzzled, I went back, and he said: 'Since
it is such a long time ago, you do not recognize me, I see. I am so-
and-so. Why are you traveling along this road alone? I feel as
if I am dreaming.' I looked at him, and although he was much
changed from the way I remembered him in the days of his
prosperity and youth long ago, I had not forgotten his features.
Looking at him as in a dream, I said: 'How did you fall to this
condition?' When I told him about myself, he said: 'So you too
are now a masterless man. I would like to talk with you about
what has happened since we parted and also about our friends.
Please spend tonight at my house. I live not far from here.' When
he had led me some distance, he added: 'I had no means of
supporting my old father, so I asked for help from some people
I knew in a place called Higai in this neighborhood, and I
now live by doing this work.[29] It was disgraceful to call out the
way I did, but I revealed myself to you because I was overcome
by memories of the past. My father is a strict man, holding to
the old ways, and will be put out if a stranger comes. I must first
tell him about you. Wait here a little while.' He made me wait
outside a rough-looking house which he entered.

"After a time he came out and led me in. An old man of some
eighty years was tending the fire. He said: 'Although we have
asked you to stay here as our guest, there seems to be nothing I
can offer you. But as I hear you are a friend of my son's, I must
not be ashamed. Please partake of our poor fare and spend the
night here.' With these words he added some mixture to a bowl
of gruel and gave me a portion of it. When night fell, the old man
said: 'You will not be able to speak freely while I am here,' and
retired to another room and lay down. The two of us sat facing
each other, feeding the fire, and talking of the past and the
present. When the night was far advanced, Kurobei went into
the room where his father was sleeping and brought out two

[51]

bamboo tubes that looked like carrying poles. Opening the ends, which were fashioned like a lid, he drew forth a long sword, about three *shaku*, and a short sword, more than two *shaku*. He also took from his bosom two sword-guards. With his back to the fire-light, he drew the two swords from their scabbards and laid them before me. Both the blades shone like ice. The scabbards were covered with 'shark-skin,' and decorated with steel ornaments. 'When I was a *samurai*, I lacked the ability to qualify for a salary sufficient to support my father. As there was no one but myself to care for him, I forsook the world and have become as I am now. I do not regret any part of the equipment I possessed in the past, but, while my strength lasts, I intend to keep my set of swords with me. Happily I have not yet parted with them. As you see, my father will not live long. If I am fortunate enough to support him to the end, I may meet you again.' As he said these words, he wept.

"In the morning, he prepared breakfast for his father and me. Later he accompanied me about a *ri* on my way, and so we parted. I had no way of making inquiries afterward. I wonder what happened to him. Nobody saw him again."

My father was still unmarried when he entered the Kohō's service. He had adopted the third son of a great friend and given him the name Masanobu [7]. (His name as a boy was Ichiya.) I believe he was a descendant of a certain Gunji who served in the House of Daijō, in Hitachi.[30] When the Kohō's second son succeeded to the Mutsu branch of the Sōma House, he took the sixteen-year-old Masanobu with him and employed him there.[31] (When he grew up, he was called Yaichiemon.) After my father left the Tsuchiya House, Masanobu sent an allowance to support his old age. Later on, he transferred his estate to his eldest son, who, with his younger brother, reverted to the name Gunji. (Masanobu took the tonsure and assumed the name Chihō.) After I began to receive a salary, we refused the allowance Masanobu sent. He died shortly afterward and so did his eldest son. His second son succeeded to the estate, but he also died young. The son of his second son is still a child, but he has succeeded his father. (Masanobu's eldest son was called Gunji Ichirobei; his younger brother was called Gunji Yaichiemon. The latter's son

[52]

was called Ichiya. For some reason the spelling of the name Gunji was changed.)[32]

The Kohō's grandfather was a *samurai-taishō* in the service of Takeda Shirō Katsuyori, of Kai, and was called Tsuchiya Uemon-no-Jō Masatsune.[33] After his elder brother, Uemon-no-Jō Masatsugu, was slain in battle, he succeeded him. When his lord's House was overthrown, all the hereditary retainers turned traitor. Masatsune alone did not abandon his lord's side and finally perished with him. Two warriors in the company he commanded, Shimizu and Kambe, taking Masatsune's wife and child with them, sought refuge in Suruga Province. As the Abbot of Seikenji was known to Kambe, they offered Masatsune's son to him as a disciple.[34] When the boy was six years old, the Ōgosho [8] saw him, and on hearing that he was Tsuchiya's child, said: "He is the son of a hero. Will you give him to me?" Ieyasu [8] took him and entered him in the service of Takechiyo [9]. The lad gradually won advancement, and after his coming of age, was given court rank and called Mimbu-no-Shō Tadanao.[35] He was the father of the future Kohō.

I wonder what happened to Shimizu's descendants. Kambe's descendants became outstanding hereditary retainers in the House of Tsuchiya. Kambe had three grandsons. The eldest grandson succeeded to his father's inheritance. The second served in the House of Matsushita who was castellan of Miharu in Mutsu.[36] (He was an elder of the House and was called Kambe Saburōemon.) The third also served in the Kohō's House. (He was at first called Jūbei.) Saburōemon's wife was my mother's elder sister. As my mother was the younger sister of the wife of Jūbei's elder brother, Jūbei arranged the marriage between her and my father.

The priest Sorin, the former Abbot of Tenneiji in Ōme in Musashi Province, was Saburōemon's son, and so was my cousin on my mother's side.[37] Jūbei, in spite of his reputable descent, for many years suffered a succession of misfortunes. At the beginning of the winter of his sixtieth year, he discussed the question of the care of his children with my father, saying that he thought of becoming a priest. Before thirty days had elapsed, the Kohō's younger brother, Tajima-no-Kami Kazunao, who had been appointed a member of the Rōjū, asked that one of the descendants of the Kambe Family be enrolled in his service and immediately made Jūbei an elder of his House.[38] Such good fortune in old age I have seen with my own eyes. However, I consider it due to the merit accumulated by his ancestors. (He was thereafter called Kambe Shin'emon.) His eldest son served in the House of Kazunao with his father. The second son remained in the Kohō's service but died young. The descendants of the eldest son are prospering today.

My father must have been well past forty when he married my mother. Their first children were two daughters, but both died before they were three years old. (The first daughter was called O-Matsu, and she died on the 26th April 1653; the second was called O-Yone, and she died on the 31st December 1654.) The next child, also a daughter, died at nineteen. (O-Tei died on the 26th February 1671.) I also had one younger sister who died at the age of eighteen. (She was called O-Made. She died on the 8th June 1677.) I was born when my father was fifty-seven and my mother forty-two (March 1657).

I do not know what sort of people my mother's parents were. She had an elder and a younger sister, but although, from the time I could reason, I took every opportunity of asking her about my maternal ancestors, weeping bitterly she would reply: "Should one conceal one's parentage from one's children? It is not a thing I should tell you, therefore I do not talk of it. There are many examples, in both modern and ancient times, of distinguished persons being born of humble women. Even if you do not know about your mother's parents, why need you be ashamed? But when you grow up, you may think about these things, so take my word for what it is worth, that my father and grandfather were not unknown. They have left a name which is not without honor in the *Shinchō Ki*.[39] Moreover, someone has left an account of my maternal grandfather's attack on a castle in Korea.[40]

When the daughter of Niwa Saishō was married, my mother became her lady-in-waiting and went with her to the House of Asano.[41] Afterward, my mother came back from the Asano House and went to serve at Nihommatsu, in Mutsu, where the nun Chōshō-In lived.[42] There she married my father. This nun was the younger sister of the Saishō and was the widow of Furuta Daizen-

Daibu.[43] I remember from childhood that she continued to write until her death.

In letters written by my mother's elder brother and returned to her after his death, letters which she carefully kept, he signed himself as Bansan.[44] He wrote a fine hand, such as is rarely seen nowadays. It closely resembled my mother's handwriting. As my uncle's letters were always kept with the greatest care, they are even now preserved, just like my mother's correspondence.

My mother not only wrote a fine hand, but also studied traditional poetry, and often read, with my sisters, the anthologies of different ages and the classical romances. She was skilled at go and shōgi, and she also taught me these games. I once saw her put some koto finger-picks in a bag in an incense-burner box, so perhaps she was fond of music too. From my own observation, she held that weaving and sewing were a woman's chief work, and every year she herself wove pretty striped cloth and silks of various patterns. She had her servants weave also, and even now I have a few of the things she gave my father and me also to wear.

In the words of a vulgar proverb, "like marries like," and both in speech and action, she differed in no way from my father. When my father retired, she also took the tonsure and earnestly practiced the way of the Buddha until she died. She had said that she was sixty-three that year. (She died on the 28th June 1678.)

My father was seventy-five when the Kohō died (on the 17th June 1675). Near the time of the Kohō's death, my father was very ill. Miraculously he recovered, but he remained in seclusion, for some reason or other, and earnestly petitioned to be allowed to retire.[45] The Kohō's heir, Yoshū [10] (called Yorinao), gave him an allowance to support his old age, saying it was to requite his years of faithful service, and also granted his request. So with mother, father took the tonsure and built a retreat in Hōonji in Asakusa and lived there.

In the winter of the following year, 1676, Yoshū's second cousin, an elder of his house and friendly with my father, complained that Yoshū's conduct was disgraceful. He therefore decided to set up Yoshū's son as lord. My father, hearing this and realizing that the time was unripe, used every argument in his power to dissuade him. But when the scheme, whose momentum could not be checked, was carried out, my father threw in his lot with the chief members of the House. The plot failed, as he had expected, and its instigator was turned out by Yoshū. As father had also been one of the party, employment was closed to me, and I left Yoshū's House. (This happened on the 25th March 1677.)

On the 8th June that year, my younger sister died prematurely, and mother was cast down thinking of our continued misfortunes. On the 25th June of the following year, she was mournfully rehearsing the events that had taken place in the previous year, when she suddenly took ill, dying on the 27th of that month.[46] After that, father lived alone.

In April [1679] of the following year, Yoshū was finally expelled from his fief, and his son was granted only a part of the domain.[47] Word was immediately sent from the son's house to me that I was to go to see him. I said that I was reluctant to do so, since I had incurred his father's displeasure, but he said I must not hold back, and so I went and met him. He told me: "I have as yet no adult name. I wish to consult you officially. You must choose the characters for my name." I then gave him the name Tatsunao.[48] (Until then he had been called Chikara.)

With this, my career as a *samurai* was automatically reopened, and on a certain person's recommendation, I entered the service of the clan of Shōshō Masatoshi of Koga [11].

I thought I would now be able to take care of my father as I wished. On the 12th July that year [1682], he visited me, and we spent the whole night in talk and mutual consolation. The following day, he returned to his lodgings. I received word that he had been taken ill that same morning and hurried to him. He was on the point of death. He heard that I had come and opened his eyes and looked at me, and, stretching out his hand, took mine. He died as if he had gone to sleep. Barely a hundred days had passed since I had found employment, and although I was stricken with grief at his loss, it was at least a blessing that he had died without anxiety for his posterity. He was eighty-two that year.

Until my father was past eighty, he did not change in any respect from what I remember in my childhood, and although this must have been due to his natural gifts being above average, I also think that it was because the regularity of his way of life allowed him to preserve his strength of mind.

From the time that I was old enough to understand, what I

remember best, among the many things he taught me, is his saying: "A boy must learn to endure. It is necessary to learn this in everything. If you begin by enduring what you think is most difficult to endure, after some time, you will not think it so difficult." From this oft-repeated lesson, by the time I was eight or nine, I had gained self-confidence in many things, but I was born quick-tempered, so my anger was harder to control than anything else. However, this also, as I have made my way through life's difficulties, is declining as my years increase, and now, perhaps, I am not as I used to be. I most earnestly desire that those who come after me should regard this as an ancestral precept, and take it to heart above everything.

Among the things he taught me, he also said: "I left my native province at the age of thirteen and have grown up among strangers. The reason I have been able to mix successfully with all those I have been close friends with, even to the end, is that I have been careful about two things only. These two are what we call greed and lust. Over the years, I have seen many men, and all have differed in endowments and character, but only those without these two desires have in every case avoided men's hatred." Later on, my teacher [12] also told me: "Men of old said, both greed and lust breed a hatred nothing can remove. You must understand this." This is something I want to warn both young and old against.

Touching my birth: The Kohō's mansion burned down in the fire of March 1657.[49] Consequently, his maternal grandson, Naitō Ukon-Daibu Masachika, who was then a child, was removed to Yanagihara.[50] (He afterward became Tamba-no-Kami. His name as a boy was Kin'ichirō. He was the son of the Kohō's eldest daughter, Sōkō-In.) A temporary residence was hastily erected, and his retainers were also sent there. It was here that I was born at eight o'clock on the morning of the 24th March, that year, and that is why the Kohō gave me the name Hi-no-Ko, or "Child of Fire."

The Kohō's mother (called Shōgaku-In, daughter of a certain Morikawa Kin'emon) saying: "He is the first-born son of his father," always sent for me from the time when I was a baby, and when I was three [1659], the Kohō came and was much taken with me. From that time on, he sent for me daily and always kept me by his side. I heard that this behavior aroused suspicion among the people of his house, who said: "He does not even treat his own son like that. This child may perhaps be the son of a concubine!"

When I was about six [1662], Nambu Shinano-no-Kami Toshinao of Mutsu came and saw me in attendance at the Kohō's side.[51] He expressed a wish to adopt me, as he had no son of his own, but the Kohō replied: "He is the child of a retainer. My mother is fond of him, so I always keep him by my side. I cannot give him to you." Toshinao persisted, saying: "Well then, let me take him without adoption. I will bring him up in my House, and when he comes of age, I will give him a fief of 1,000 koku." The Kohō replied: "Although he would benefit materially if I gave him to you, neither my mother nor myself would have anything to solace our tedious hours with." A man called Makino said: "How unlucky this child is! If they were to accept this proposal, his future would be secure; whatever the Kohō intends, he cannot give him a stipend of 1,000 koku." (He was commonly called Rokurozaemon. I do not know his given name. He later served the Kohō's third son.)

On New Year's Day the year I turned seven [1663], I fell ill with smallpox. When I was in great danger, the Kohō's mother sent a constant stream of messengers to inquire about me, called in priests with a reputation for healing, and had prayers recited by my bedside. Although my father did not favor such procedures, it was by order of his lord's mother, so he could not prevent them. The Kohō also sent two of his personal servants (called Seki and Yamamoto), and when he heard that medical skill had failed, he sent various kinds of foreign medicines, saying they might help. After I was given some Unicornis, the infection was immediately allayed and I broke out in a rash, and from that time was out of danger.[52] Jun'an's [12] physician, Gensaku, the one who gave me the medicine at that time, told me this when I was past twenty, saying that my cure was not due to medical skill. (He was called Ishikawa and later received an official appointment.) The ceremony of wearing a sash and putting on a hakama was performed before the proper time, and the Kohō himself tied my sash and provided and arranged the hakama.[53] His mother died when I was nine years old, on the 1st January. (This was in 1666.)

When I was a child, there used to be a picture-book called *Ueno Monogatari*.[54] This book illustrated such things as crowds of people flower-viewing at Kan'eiji.[55] It may have been about the spring of my third year [1659] when, lying on my belly with my feet stretched out in the foot-warmer, I was looking at that storybook and asked for brush and paper and made a tracing. One or two of the ten characters were properly drawn, and when my mother saw it, she showed it to my father. When father's friends came and saw it, people got to hear about it, and the tracing was handed round. When I was sixteen or seventeen, I was able to see that tracing when I went to Kazusa Province.

Also, about that time, I wrote my name on a screen. Two of the characters were well written, and the screen was kept afterward. Later it was burnt in a fire. None of the things from that time remain with me. Henceforth, in my daily play, I would always be, brush in hand, practicing characters. Gradually, without any special effort, I came to be able to recognize them, but as I had no one to teach me properly, I only learned to read elementary primers.[56]

In the Kohō's House was a man called Tomita. (He was first called Koemon, and afterward Kakushin.) He was said to have been born in Kaga Province. He had a commentary on the *Taiheiki*, which had been handed down to him, and he used to lecture on this.[57] Every night, father and others would gather to hear his lecture. From the time I was four or five, I was always present and listened to him, and however late it grew, I never left until the end. When the lecture was over I would ask questions about difficult points. People said I was exceptional.

About the summer of my sixth year [1662], a man called Uematsu, who was something of a scholar, taught me a seven-syllable Chinese poem and explained its meaning. (He was called Chūbei. He was a descendant of the Uematsu who was a retainer in the Suruga branch of the Imagawa House and was very fond of verse-capping, at which he excelled.)[58] I memorized it straight off, so he taught me three more poems, which I expounded to people. (The poems were, first, the one containing the line, "Even foolish rumors, if oft repeated, will win general credence"; second, one made in the Taikō's [13] presence by a seven-year-old Korean child; and third, one made by a priest called Jikyū Zōsu, at Enoshima.)[59]

Uematsu said: "This child has literary talent. You should certainly find him a teacher and set him to study." But other stiff-necked old-fashioned people argued: "There is a saying that has been handed down by word of mouth since ancient times: 'No one can become a scholar without intelligence, diligence, and affluence.' This child was born with intelligence, but he is still young. It is impossible to tell whether he has diligence. Since his family does not appear to be rich, we do not know about affluence." Father also said: "The Kohō is so fond of him that he could never bear to let him leave his side. I cannot send him to school or put him under a master. However, the Kohō takes pride in telling people he could write from the time he was a baby, so at least I want him taught to write." In the autumn of my eighth year [1664], after the Kohō went to Kazusa Province, father arranged for me to be taught calligraphy. When the Kohō returned home that winter, about the end of January [1665], he continued to keep me by his side, as before. In the autumn of the following year, when he again went to his province, he allotted me a daily task, directing me to copy out 3,000 semi-cursive and cursive characters during the day and 1,000 at night.

When winter began, the days were short, and sometimes the sun set before I had finished my task. I then took my desk out on to a bamboo verandah, facing west, and so finished my writing. Also, when practicing calligraphy at night, I would be overcome with sleepiness, so I secretly arranged with the man who waited on me to have him draw and set ready two buckets of water on the verandah. When I grew very drowsy, I would take off my clothes and pour first one bucket of water over me, dress again, and study. Although at first I felt awakened by the cold, after a while I became warm and sleepy again, so, once more, I would pour water over myself, as before. With the help of the second lot of water, I would get through the greater part of my task. This happened during the autumn and winter of my ninth year [1665].

From about the time I was thus engaged, I wrote, in the prescribed form, the letters my father sent to people. In the autumn of my tenth year [1666], the Kohō set me another task, namely

[60]

to study the *Teikin Ōrai*, and in December he told me to make a fair copy in ten days.[60] Having finished it as he had ordered, I had it bound and presented it to him, and he praised me warmly. From my thirteenth year [1669], on the Kohō's instructions, I also wrote the greater part of his day-to-day correspondence.

The son of a friend of my father, called Seki [6], excelled in the art of fencing, and as he took pupils, I asked him to instruct me in this art. I was only eleven at the time. He said: "You are still a child. You will have time to learn this art later." I said: "I may be a child, but if I do not understand at least something of how to use a sword, is it not indeed pointless for me to wear two swords?" "You are right," he answered and taught me one stroke.

After this, a sixteen-year-old lad (the second son of a man called Kambe) said he would try a test of skill with me. We had three contests with wooden swords, and I beat him every time. The spectators also enjoyed the match, laughing heartily. From then on, I acquired a firm partiality for martial pursuits. Although I did not care for calligraphy, I took delight in reading. There was nothing by way of Japanese literature or popular tales I did not read.

In my seventeenth year [1673], when I visited the house of a young *samurai* (called Hasegawa) engaged in the same service as myself, I saw on his desk a book entitled *Okina Mondō*.[61] Wishing to know what sort of book it was, I asked to borrow it and took it home with me to read. For the first time, I learned of the existence of what is called the Way of the Sages, but though I resolved henceforth to apply myself to the Way, there was no one to teach me.[62]

A certain Kyōto physician [1], who had a little learning, came daily to the Kohō's house. Turning to this man, I told him of my desire, and he taught me to read the Introduction to the *Hsiao Hsüeh*.[63] (This was the man who, as I explained above, gave my father the ginseng when he was ill. He was called Ema Ekian. His given name was Gemboku.) After that, he also taught me how to read the *Ssŭ Chên* of the sage Ch'êng Tzŭ, and henceforth I studied the *Hsiao Hsüeh* day and night.[64] When I had completed this task, I wanted to study the *Four Books*, and after that the *Five Classics* also, but there was no teacher who could instruct me in the construing.[65] I therefore studied them by myself with the aid of the *Yün Hui* and *Tzŭ Hui*, but I made many mistakes, as I later discovered.[66]

Having no literary training in Chinese, I found it terribly hard to understand the meanings of the characters, but when I occasionally had leisure to study, I studied prose composition, poetry, and metrical prose. About December of that year, I composed a seven-syllable Chinese poem, "Extempore Piece on a Winter Scene." This was the beginning of my composition of poetry. When someone criticized this poem, I immediately wrote an essay rebutting his attack, and that was my first attempt at prose.

However, I kept my studies carefully concealed from my father because of what he and his friends had said when I was a child. As I could not obtain books, I confided my ambitions to my mother. By the time I left Yoshū's [10] House, at the age of twenty-one [1677], I had become acquainted with men of similar interests and was able to pursue my studies, though for reasons of my own, I did not try to find a teacher.

At this juncture, I became friendly with a man called Abiru [14], a Confucian scholar in the province of Tsushima. In the spring of my twenty-sixth year [1682], I re-entered the service of a military house.[67] In the autumn of that year, an embassy arrived from Korea. Through the kind offices of my friend Abiru, I requested the three leaders of the embassy, who were fine scholars, to write an appreciation of a collection of a hundred verses of occasional poetry I had composed. They agreed to write a foreword but said they would first like to meet the author. I went to their lodgings on the 1st October. There, I met the interpreter Sung Wan, the secretary Ri Tam Re, and the military attaché Hŭng Se Tae. We spent some time together composing poetry, and that evening, Sung Wan sent me the foreword he had written for my collection of poetry.

This year, the learned Kyōsei Boku (Kinoshita Heinojō) [12] was appointed lecturer to the Shōgun [15], and my friend Abiru entered his school to study. Later, when I went to Yamagata, in Dewa Province, I wrote a volume describing my travels.[68] (This happened in the autumn of 1686, when I was thirty years old.) Abiru showed this volume to his teacher, Kinoshita, and told him about the foreword composed by the

Korean ambassador. As a result, he said he would like to meet me, and Abiru introduced me to him. Some time afterward, when Abiru fell ill and was on the point of death, he expressed to me his wish that his teacher should compose his epitaph, and he asked me to do the calligraphy. (Abiru was afterward called Nishiyama Juntai. He died on the 26th September 1688.)

Some years after I also had entered Kinoshita's school in consequence of all this, I became his intimate disciple, although I had never observed the proper entrance formalities.[69] Although there were many senior disciples who had spent a long time in his school, he always placed me above them, and in the end, when Bunshō-byō [3] was still residing in his clan mansion, Kinoshita recommended me to his service.[70]

When I think back over all this now, it seems to me that if, long ago when I first learned how to write at the age of three, I had had a qualified teacher, I should not have been so deficient in calligraphy; further, if, when I studied the recitation of poetry at the age of six, there had been someone under whose guidance I could have worked, I should perhaps have made a little progress in literature also. More important, if, at the age of seventeen, when I first became interested in Confucianism, I had had someone to instruct me, I should not have been as I am now. After I entered the service of the Lord of Kai, I bought some books and was also given many; however, as I was then pressed by duties, I had little time to read. Before this, I had always been poor and had had to borrow books from others. Anything I needed copied out, I had to do with my own hand, with the result that I read very few books. There have been few less fortunate than I in the path of learning. I have made such progress as I have because, as I explained earlier, I have always forced myself to endure that which was most difficult to endure, and because what ordinary people do once, I have done ten times, and what they do ten times, I have done a hundred.[71]

The incident I now relate happened the year before the Kohō's death. In the autumn of my eighteenth year [1674], he visited his fief as usual, and I accompanied him. About the middle of December that year I unexpectedly fell into disgrace and was placed under house arrest. (I had secretly been watching a hunt during the time I was to have been on night watch.)

[63]

Toward the end of that month, a dissension arose among the young *samurai*, and their relatives and supporters divided into two parties. There were few of the Kohō's retainers who were not involved, and finally, by the beginning of the following January, both sides were on the point of coming to blows. The supporters of one party, who were all long-standing friends of my father's, assembled at Seki's [6] house, and it was decided to set out to engage the adversary at about two o'clock that afternoon.

When someone informed me of this, I sent a sharp-witted fellow to Seki's house telling him to bring me back word with all speed when he saw them set out and start fighting. I impressed upon him that even though they should set out, he was not to come back until the fighting had actually begun. I instructed the rest of my servants that, if anyone should come, they were to say I had felt a cold coming on since morning and was lying down. I put chain armor on next to my skin, dressed in fresh clothes, and lay down to wait, pulling the bed quilt over my head.

By sundown my messenger had still not returned. I wondered what had happened, but at about nine o'clock, he returned and reported that our side had been on the point of setting out at about six o'clock, but certain intermediaries had negotiated with both sides and effected a compromise and the quarrel had just then been settled. He also said that Uematsu had caught sight of him and questioned him, with the result that he had told him he was there on my orders.[72]

Toward evening the following day, one of Seki's sons [16] came and said: "Yesterday I was told that you too had intended to come and help us." When I replied: "Such was my intention," he said: "How did you, when you were then in disgrace and confined to your house, intend to get through the gate of our lord's mansion?" I explained that I had intended to get out by the small wicket gate on the west. "That gate is open during the day, but it is closed at night," he pointed out. "How could you have got through?" I told him: "The other gates are all strongly guarded and it is impossible to pass through them. The small wicket gate on the west is guarded only by an old couple who live in a hut beside it, and the key is in that hut. I thought, if I went to them and explained the situation, telling them that as I was going out to die, there would be no need for it to be known that

I had escaped that way, and therefore they would incur no guilt, they would not refuse to let me out. However, I thought, if I could not prevail, there was no other way than to kill the old couple, steal the key, open the gate and go." (The Kohō's mansion was within the earthwork surrounding Kururi Castle, where the lay-priest Satomi Yoshitaka lived in former times.[73] Behind the castle was a high mountain.)

Seki [16] replied: "Your father and mine have been close friends for many years, and so I cannot find words to thank you for wanting to come and help us. However, it would have been most reprehensible for you, while in disgrace and confined to your house, to leave it by stealth, and worse than that, to have killed those guards and forced your way out of the gate would have been piling crime upon crime."

At this I burst out laughing and said: "If so, I think it is surely a crime for people to go thither with the intention of joining battle. Those whom you planned to kill were all prominent members of this clan, whereas my intended victims were an old couple guarding a small gate. On the score of planning to kill our lord's retainers, we were equally guilty, but comparing the rank of those involved, my crime would have been much lighter than yours. Suppose I had not been in disgrace at the time, and although aware of your plans, I had not gone to help. The Kohō might have said nothing, but in his heart he would have thought my conduct despicable. Therefore, despite the fact that I was in disgrace, I was not bound hand and foot, so if I had stayed shut up in my house alone, once I had heard from some other source that you were going to start a fight, people would have thought I had taken advantage of my plight to save my life. I may have behaved in a lawless way, but why should I fear my lord's displeasure? Were I of sober years, there may have been a more fitting way for me to act, but I am not yet twenty and so my only concern was to avoid dishonor. I do not expect thanks." He had nothing to say in reply but, it seems, went home and told his father [6], who exclaimed with tears of joy, "Ah! He is a true son of his father."

At this time, I thought that even if the Kohō forgave me, my father would never see me again, and I was very upset at the notion. Afterward, when the Kohō sent for me as before, my father was also highly gratified. Because he never spoke about my

[65]

having fallen into disgrace, I thought he did not know about it. Afterward, I heard that old Seki [6] had written him, giving him a detailed account of how I had intended to go and help, of what I had said to his son, and also that father had showed the letter to mother, telling her to read it. My mother said it was due to this that he had relented. When I reflect upon it now, it is tragic to realize that this disturbance was probably the first omen of the downfall of the Kohō's House.

On the Kohō's death [1675], his heir, Yoshū [10], succeeded. This fellow had such a wicked disposition that he finally brought his House to ruin, so it is not surprising that he had been out of favor with his father. When I was little, the father and son were still on speaking terms, but later, they never met except at the formal audience on New Year's Day. The Kohō's relatives knew nothing of Yoshū's evil conduct and suspected that, out of fondness for a concubine's son, the Kohō wanted to make him his heir. After Yoshū divorced his wife, she bore him a son whom the Kohō sent to Kazusa Province to be brought up. When the boy was twelve or thirteen, the Kohō wished to bring him to his fief and present him to the retainers. Yoshū suspected that his father intended to make this grandchild his heir and thereupon trumped up excuses, so the boy was never sent for. When the Kohō was on the point of death, he sent for his grandson for the first time, and died, fearing that his House would end with him.

Thus, Yoshū looked with disfavor on those whom the Kohō had trusted and was even more displeased when my father resigned, without having served him for a single day. Since he had only just succeeded, however, and stood in fear of what his retainers would think, he accepted father's resignation, giving him a stipend sufficient to support his old age. He did not, however, transfer my father's salary to me, nor would he take me into his service because he could not bear the thought that the Kohō had brought me up at his knee from childhood. After a year [1677], he brought false charges against us, deprived my father of his pension and expelled me from his clan, thus closing to me the career of *samurai*. Hence, my hopes of obtaining employment in any other clan were destroyed.

My father and mother were supported by their adopted son in Mutsu, and without any idea of what my future would be, I took

[66]

myself off to Edo with one servant. Old friends had suggested I make a living by teaching their children calligraphy, but I did not care for the idea. Morning and evening, I attended the houses of those who gave lectures and, during the day, visited my parents. Soon after this, in a dream I saw my elder sister, who had died when she was nineteen, and, in some distress, hurried to my parents' house at dawn. I learned that my younger sister was in labor, and I went to see her.[74] The child was delivered safely, but my sister died shortly afterward of complications. Thereafter, I stayed with my parents. The following year, about the middle of summer, I again saw my sister in a dream. I hurried to my parents' room but both were well. An hour later, my mother suddenly took ill and died some time later. There were only the two of us left, my father and I, and our many sorrows were beyond description.

Long ago, there was an old man who used to visit the Kohō's House. (He was called Suminokura Ryōnin and was over eighty years old at that time.) He had been in the service of the lay-priest, Oda Naifu Jōshin, and was now retired.[75] This man came to my father's house and said: "Since Yoshū nurses a deep resentment against those whom the Kohō trusted, it is impossible that there will ever be an opportunity for your son to re-enter his service. I have watched him from a child, and even I am grieved at this, so I understand how you feel. A rich merchant, who is an old friend of mine, has only one daughter but no son. He wishes to marry her to the son of a worthy *samurai* and make him his heir; he has discussed his plans with me. Now, if your son will only agree to my friend's proposals, he will be able to look after you comfortably. The purpose of my visit was to put this proposal to you."[76] On hearing this, my father replied: "I can never forget your kindness, but my son is not a child and I cannot make decisions for him. You must talk to him yourself." When I came the following day, my father told me of Suminokura's proposals. I said: "Very well," and went to the old man's house. After expressing my gratitude for his overwhelming kindness, I said, that for reasons of my own, I could not fall in with his request. On returning home, I said to my father: "I am not insensible of your distress that I should be in this situation, and I am deeply grieved when I see you reduced to such desolate circumstances, but I was born your son and have no intention of becoming the son of any other man. In spite of our sad circumstances and despite the fact that I am debarred from serving in a military house, as far as I am concerned, I shall never abandon the life of a warrior, which my father and grandfather followed, to become a merchant's heir. This was the answer I gave him." With a joyful countenance father said: "In matters of this kind men feel differently, and even between father and son it is difficult to say for certain whether they will take the same view. You have answered well. It is filial piety to sacrifice oneself to care for an aged father, but this falls short of true filial piety like yours. When I first renounced the world, I resolved to endure just such a position as I am now in. You must never grieve over me."

After that, another man taking thought on my behalf said: "When one considers the men who practice medicine as a profession today, one discovers that most of them cannot even read books on their own art. With your talents, and just a little application, you would far outstrip those charlatans. In these times, it is not an ignoble profession. I wish you would decide to take up this profession to support your father." I replied: "Whatever the situation may have been in ancient times, in succeeding ages medicine has been known as the benevolent art. Therefore, if a man who could not achieve his ambitions buried himself in this profession, it might not be a bad thing. However, as I have always been negligent, I am not versed in that profession; if I were to make a mistake in prescribing, I would not be fulfilling the aim of the benevolent art. Medicine is not a profession I could do well at. I have heard the saying, 'In ancient times, doctors did not kill a single innocent man.' "[77]

Also at this time, the son of a merchant, said to be the richest in Japan, became a student friend of mine, and he said: "My father has seen you and thinks that you will become the greatest Confucian scholar in Japan.[78] He wishes to marry you to the daughter of my elder brother, who is now dead. With landed property bought for 3,000 gold pieces to support your studies, devote yourself to learning. He told me to tell you this." When I heard this, I said: "Your kindness is quite unforgettable. Someone once told me the following story: 'Several people went to Ling Shan in the summer, and one of them put his feet into a pond and a little serpent came and licked his big toe, suddenly disappeared, and then suddenly reappeared and licked his toe again.[79] While doing this, the serpent got much bigger and eventually seemed likely to swallow his toe, so he drew his dagger, laid it on his toe with the edge up, and waited. When the serpent came again to bite off his toe he cut upward at it, and it fell backward and disappeared. The man ran home and shut the sliding doors. Before his companions could ask him what it was all about, stones began to fly, trees fell, and the earth quaked for more than an hour. When he opened the doors a little and looked out, there was a great serpent more than one *jō* high, fallen dead, with a wound a *shaku* or more long from its mouth to the top of its head.' Whether this was so or not I do not know, but it is very like what you said just now. When the serpent was quite small it could be cut with only a dagger, but when it got big, the wound was more than a *shaku* in length. I am now poor, in difficulties, and unknown. If I carry on the line of your late elder brother, and remain as I am at the moment, the flaw would be only a small one, but if, as you say, I become a well-known Confucian scholar, the flaw will appear very serious. To throw away 3,000 gold pieces for me to become a Confucian scholar with a big flaw is not a good policy for you. However small the flaw may be, I myself do not wish to suffer such a wound. So pray take this as my answer." As I later heard, a distinguished Confucian scholar married the girl. (The name of the wealthy man was Kawamura. His grand-daughter's husband was called Kurokawa.[80] His father and forebears were distinguished Confucian scholars.) When I told this story to my father, he laughed and said: "It is not a new story, but it was an apt illustration."

Yoshū's House was dispossessed about the summer of my twenty-third year [1679], and as I noted above, my career as a *samurai* reopened automatically. Someone recommended me to Chikuzen-no-Kami Ki Masatoshi [11] in the third month of my twenty-sixth year [1682], and I entered the service of this lord.

After a year, in the autumn of my twenty-eighth year [1684], the Hotta incident occurred, and although Masatoshi's son, Shimōsa-no-Kami Masanaka [17], was permitted to succeed him, nothing but ill fortune continued.[81] Later, the support he could give his retainers was not to their liking; when all had their salaries reduced, many of them resigned. Although I had never been on confidential terms with the father or son since I first entered the service of his clan, seeing that he had become my lord and I had become his retainer, I thought I ought not to leave at such a time.

Although I was attached to an unsatisfactory service and had barely enough to support a wife and family, I had plenty of leisure, and at this time I read deeply in the Chinese classics and histories.[82] However much I stinted in my personal wants—for the saying goes that poverty is the usual lot of the *samurai*—one engaged in service has many commitments connected with it, so my funds at length gave out and my strength was exhausted. In the spring of my thirty-fifth year [1691], I explained the situation in a letter and asked for my dismissal.

When I had previously confided my feelings to my friends, they had said: "Since you receive a rice stipend, you are not in danger of death from starvation, but if you give that up, you will not be able to supply even your daily needs, for you have exhausted the money you had. If you have indeed made up your mind, you must do it, but how are you going to care for your young wife and helpless babe?" But I said: "If the lord to whom I looked for support, had not been unfortunate, I would not have continued to serve this clan until now. It was just because I bore in mind that he had become my lord, and I his retainer, that I have patiently endured all manner of hardships until this year. If I give up my stipend and immediately depart with my wife and child, my true feelings will be clear. If there is an omniscient Heaven, things will not be so bad as you suggest."

Sōshū [17], for some reason of his own, gave no reply, but when spring had passed and summer was far advanced, he sent a message saying that I must definitely postpone the idea of leaving his House.[83] (The messenger was an elder of the House called Ōtagaki.) However, after I had made a second request, at the beginning of autumn my son Akinori [18] was born, and at length I was given leave to resign.

At this time, when I came to reckon up the capital I had at home, it amounted to 300 copper pieces and 3 *to* of polished rice. I thought I should not be in danger of immediate starvation, so I took my family and went to Kōtokuji, where I had had a parishioner's connection for many years, and moved soon after to a house I rented near Asakusa.[84] Still, I did not have the means to support the one man-servant and one maid we kept, but when I told them they must do whatever they thought best, they said that they would work at anything, even if not used to it, and so keep themselves, for they did not want to part from us.

Unexpectedly, word was sent by messenger, from Sōshū's younger brother (the present Bingo-no-Kami Toshihiro), that while we were in this plight, he would provide for my whole family.[85] (This messenger was an elder of the House called Tsuboi.) This must have been because he felt grateful for the assistance I had given him with his studies for several years. In consequence of this unlooked-for good fortune, at the end of that autumn, I moved my residence east of the castle and my pupils increased daily.[86] Quite a few outstanding men came to study under me.

The following year [1692], a certain man (called Tani) said to me: "You come from the clan of a lord who is out of favor at this time.[87] On top of that, you are studying under a master who has no special standing.[88] Therefore, however brilliant your scholarship, your advancement is bound to be difficult. Do change your school and look forward to future prosperity."[89]

The first time I only burst out laughing, but when he persisted in his advice two or three times, I said: "You speak for my good, I know, but actually what you urge would not be to my benefit. You have probably heard about the followers of Confucius long ago. If it were permissible for them to change their master just because he suffered misfortune, why were they obliged to follow him despite all kinds of hardships while he was in Ch'ên and Ts'ai?[90] A man should do three things with all his might in gratitude for being born. He should serve his father, his teacher, and his lord unto death. My father is now dead, and I have no lord to serve. I have only my teacher to follow unto death." After that he said no more.

My teacher [12] intended to recommend me to the Lord of Kaga, in whose service he had formerly been employed, and had given me an outline of the matter, but a man of Kaga, called Okajima (known as Chūshirō), came to me with the plea that he had an old mother in his home province and begged me to ask our teacher to recommend him.[91] I explained the matter to the teacher in detail, stating positively: "I will serve in any province without expressing any preference, but as the position in question is in a province where Okajima's old mother is living, I support his request that you recommend him in my place. I firmly and finally decline your recommendation of me to that province." He listened attentively and, with tears in his eyes, said: "There are not many today who would speak like that. It is indeed like meeting, in these latter days, a sage of old." He never wearied of telling people this story. As a result of my request, he immediately recommended Okajima to that province.

On the 7th November in the winter of my thirty-seventh year [1693], Kōriki Yoshū [19] came to my teacher's house and said: "Who is the best among your disciples? Toda Chōshū [20] said to make informal inquiries." (Toda was at that time an elder in the Kōfu clan.)[92] So Kinoshita [12] replied that I was, as he well knew. On the evening of the 12th, Kinoshita said to me: "It is some days since Yoshū was here," and he directed me to go to his house. I went, and he questioned me, and I answered him. On the 31st December, Yoshū again visited my teacher, bringing a message from Chōshū that he intended to recommend me as clan lecturer in the House of Kai.

However, there was one aspect of the matter with which my teacher was not satisfied. He told Yoshū he would first speak to me and then give him an answer. That evening, he sent for me and we talked it over. On the 1st January [1694], Yoshū added something further and, as a result of what I said to Kinoshita that evening, a letter was dispatched to Yoshū on the morning of the 2nd.

Kinoshita had at first been dissatisfied with the stipend offered, namely rations for 30 men.[93] He said: "Of course, the standard of a man's scholarship cannot be judged by the size of his income. However, it is the way of the world to think that if a man's salary is high, his learning is great, and that if his salary is low, his learning is poor. No one from my school has accepted such a low salary, although none of them is equal to him. Furthermore, he has not always been a professional scholar. You must take into account the stipend he received as a *samurai*. You will not get him to come under the terms you offer."

After that, Yoshū again came to Kinoshita and said that

his objections were not unreasonable, but as to our demand for 40 men's rations, he himself could say nothing. However, if I came according to the present offer, it might well be that the terms could be adjusted at a later date. That night, Kinoshita sent for me and told me what Yoshū had said, but he insisted he was still of the same mind and could not consent.

I then said: "The House of Kai is not to be compared with any other. If I do not accept this offer because of the salary, even if later on I receive offers from other Houses, I shall be unable to accept them unless they promise a very large salary. It is impossible to know what my destiny will be. I think it best to agree with Yoshū's conditions." He said there was plenty of time to reply, and that I must give the matter due thought, but I continued to press my view, and at length he agreed and sent a letter to Yoshū.

I heard later that, at first, a request had gone from the clan mansion asking Daigaku-no-Kami Tō Nobuatsu [21] to send a disciple, but Nobuatsu, for reasons of his own, replied that he had no disciples that he could send.[94] After my name was mentioned, Chōshū arranged to have a man he recommended become a disciple of Nobuatsu in the spring of this year. After that, it was suggested that I should be invited.

The man Chōshū recommended is now called Funabashi Han'emon [22]. He was then called Yoshida Tōhachirō. At the time he was invited to Edo, he was a disciple of Jinsai of Kyōto.[95] He was thereupon enrolled as a pupil of Daigakuno-Kami, and as soon as the Lord of Kai [3] was appointed Heir, he was made one of the personal attendants.

On the evening of the 10th of that month [January 1694], a letter came to Kinoshita from Chōshū, bidding me come to the clan mansion on the following day, so at about ten o'clock on the morning of the 11th, I went there. Toda, Tsuda, Koide [23], and others introduced me, and Koide conveyed to me a message that I was to be made a clan retainer.[96] On the 13th of the month, I was received in audience for the first time, and on the 21st began to lecture on the *Ta Hsüeh*.[97]

At the end of January, my lord said that henceforth there should be three lectures on the *Four Books* and one each on the *Hsiao Hsüeh* and *Chin Ssŭ Lu*, and since the Way of the Sages was not yet clear to him, I must arrange his future study program.[98] The gist of my answer was: The Way of the Sages, as regards the control of self and the government of men, is contained in the *Four Books*, and if this is followed in principle and action, nothing more is needed. In order to understand the fundamental principles and teachings of the Sages in detail, you should perhaps also study the *Five Classics*. Since you are still young, and your future is full of hope, if you are diligent, you will accomplish that task. He said to begin with the *Shih Ching* and the *Li Chi*.[99] Hence two of us were directed to give daily lectures, and I was ordered to lecture on the *Shih Ching*. (Yoshida was appointed to lecture on the *Li Chi*.)

At that time my eldest daughter caught smallpox and died on the 24th February. Akinori [18] also caught it. On account of these events, I did not begin lectures on the *Shih Ching* until the 8th March. I lectured for 162 days until the 5th January the following year [1695], and so ended my work.[100] (I had had pictures of flowers, trees, birds, and animals drawn by the painting teacher, and as they had been prepared previously, they were of great assistance in giving these lectures.[101] These pictures are still preserved in my house.)[102]

Afterward he told me to lecture on the *Shu Ching*.[103] Though he heard daily lectures this year, he said there was still time to spare, and he would also like to learn about the successive vicissitudes and upheavals since the Three Dynasties.[104] I answered that this was very auspicious for Confucian learning and asked him if would he like to study, between whiles, Ssŭ-ma Kuang's *Tzŭ Chih T'ung Chien* or Chu Hsi's *T'ung Chien Kang Mu*.[105] He said he would read the *T'ung Chien Kang Mu* and asked me to lecture on it.

On the 8th March of the same year, 1695, I began lectures on the *Shu Ching*, and on the 12th, I began lectures on the *T'ung Chien Kang Mu*.[106] This year I lectured 71 days and finished on the following 25th January.[107] After this, he said I was to lecture on the *Ch'un Ch'iu*, and this year also, when lectures on the *Li Chi* finished, I heard I was to lecture on the *Chou I*.[108]

On the 28th February 1696, I began lectures on the *Ch'un Ch'iu*, and gave additional lectures on the four commentaries, *Tso Chuan, Kung Yang, Ku Liang, Hu Chuan*.[109] Lectures on the

T'ung Chien Kang Mu continued, simultaneously, as before. The lectures on the *Ch'un Ch'iu* went on for almost six years, up to the 16th January 1702, in all some 157 days.[110] After that, my lord diligently attended lectures on the *T'ung Chien Kang Mu*, year by year, and had finished the *Hsü Pien* by the time he died.[111]

After the lecture was over, he always asked me to stay and would ask questions about Japanese and Chinese history. He was particularly interested in the Divine Ancestor's [8] unification of Japan, and when the lectures on the *Shu Ching* came to an end on the 19th January 1701, he asked me if I would undertake to write an account, in the intervals of my lectures, of all the feudal clans with an income of 10,000 *koku* and over from the earliest days.

Then, on the 18th February the same year, 1701, the order was issued, and on the 21st, I submitted a draft plan of the work.[112] The lord approved it, so next I collected information about all the clans and began to write on 14th August. By the beginning of November, I had finished the manuscript.

I began from the year 1600 and went down to 1680, 80 years in all, and dealt with 337 clans, their first grants, the successive generations, confiscation of income, and so on. The main work was in ten volumes, with an appendix of two volumes, and an introduction and table of contents comprising one volume, thirteen volumes in all. These were divided into twenty books.

Having made a fair copy of the work, I presented it the following year, on the 17th March 1702. He had previously chosen the name for the work himself, calling it the *Hankampu*.[113] (Besides this, in accordance with his orders, I composed and presented many other works, of two or three volumes each. There is no space to deal with them all.)

From the time I was first required to lecture on the *Shih Ching*, I lectured simultaneously, every year, on the *Four Books*, the *Hsiao Ching*, the *Chou Li*, the *I Li*, and so on, except when I was absent as envoy in Kyōto, and attending to arrangements for the reception of the Korean Embassy after my lord became Shōgun, so that I gave lectures for about 1,299 days over a period of 19 years.[114]

Besides myself, there were three others who gave lectures, some daily, and they too must each have given as many as I. His Highness thus became very well versed in almost all the classics and histories, and writings of the Hundred Schools. In fact, I have never heard of anyone who was more devoted to both Japanese and Chinese literature, both ancient and modern. (After the daily lectures on the *Chou I* were completed, I was asked to lecture on the *Ta Hsüeh Yen I,* and by the time that His Highness died, we had finished both the main section and supplement of this as well.)[115]

At the end of the autumn of 1695, he gave orders that a list should be made of the Japanese and Chinese works which he should always keep by his side and read constantly.[116] I replied that I must consult with my teacher, and after I had done so, I presented a list, and he gave instructions to purchase the books. After a diligent search, I presented over one hundred volumes of Japanese and Chinese books.

On the 25th January [1696], he set the other lecturer [22] and myself to cataloguing 200 Chinese and Japanese books and told us to mark those each of us desired.[117] These were books which he had hitherto kept by his side. After the two of us had deferred to each other, those bearing my colleague's mark included two out of every three. I marked only eleven of the remainder, for some I had myself, and, of the others, I said it would be more useful if he distributed them to his close attendants. He ordered that each should be given what he desired. He detained me for a time and said: "I have been fond of these for many years. You must hand them on to your son," and he gave me the *Six Classics.*[118]

The man who transmitted his orders at this time was the present Echizen-no-Kami Tō Akifusa [24], when he was still called Kunai. The *Six Classics* which my lord gave me are a good edition from the Chikuko.[119] The bindings and cases and the cabinet with its keys were finely wrought and beautiful, and they are still in my house. It is regrettable that what he gave to the other lecturer was soon afterward all destroyed by fire.

At the beginning of February the same year, 1696, I gave a feast and showed my teacher these books that were a special gift, and consequently he kindly wrote an inscription. Two years later (on hearing that my house had burned down on the 9th October 1698), my lord presented me with 50 gold pieces on the 12th of the same month. (He said this money was to build a temporary dwelling.) I was the only one among my lord's retainers, many of whom had had their houses destroyed, who received this special kindness.

I reflected that even without this, I was not without the resources to build and furnish a house, and moreover, at this time, fires were frequent, so if I were to apply this gift to such a purpose, I might lose it in another fire, and, if that were to happen, his kindness would be in vain. I turned over in my mind what I had best do, and finally, I bought a new set of armor with the money he had given me.

This is the armor I have now, the one with navy blue lacing and a helmet with lacing of the same color, surmounted by metal ornaments. It was to be worn when the time came to requite the kindness of my lord by my own death, and my descendants must bear this well in mind. This armor, and the sword which he gave me afterward, must be transmitted to my heirs. Five years later, in January 1704, fire broke out again, as I expected. My house and other things were again lost, but, as I always kept this armor by my side, I have it yet.

My teacher [12] had died on the night of the 23rd January 1699, a few months after I suffered the first fire. In accordance with his will, I arranged his obsequies. (This happened in the eleventh year of the Genroku era. According to his will, Sakakibara Gensuke of the Kii House and I had charge of his obsequies.)[120]

At the beginning of every year, there was a ceremony of beginning lectures. Previous to this, my lord asked me to submit a lecture schedule. When that day's lectures were finished he would give me two sets of seasonal clothes. It was a custom which he never altered. (This ceremony was the yearly inauguration, and it became the custom to commence lectures by selecting an auspicious ode from the *Ta Ya* or *Hsiao Ya*.)[121]

From the time His Highness was lord of the Kai clan, and after he became Shōgun, a lecture was given at the New Year celebration, and then, after the fifteenth day of the lunar month, the daily lectures began and continued until the end of the lunar year, except at times of serious trouble, and of course, on the first and fifteenth days of the month. Otherwise they were never interrupted, even on days of seasonal celebrations.[122]

[77]

After my lord perceived that I was liable to illness and found mid-summer and mid-winter difficult to bear, he told me to attend after sunset in the hot weather, so the lectures were evening ones. During winter, they were in the morning. A large brazier was put between his seat and mine, and when the cold was intense, he would have another big brazier put behind my back. If it rained or snowed on the day of the lecture, he would send a messenger to tell me not to come.

As to the way in which he attended the lectures, in spring, autumn, and winter, he wore lined formal dress, in summer, light semiformal attire. He came down from the seat he usually occupied and sat in a seat placed about nine *shaku* away from me. However hot it was in summer, he never used a fan, and in the evening, when there were a lot of mosquitoes, he did not brush them away. On one occasion, when he had a cold and his nose troubled him, he would stealthily turn aside, take out some paper from his bosom, and wipe it from time to time. And so you can understand that he was perfectly quiet throughout the lecture, though it was apt to last more than two hours.

When he went to his villa every year in the spring and autumn, he ordered me to accompany him. He always assigned me a room and sent wine and cakes by messenger. Often, he asked people to write verses. My lord also presented clothing to everyone at the four seasons, and, at the end of the year, he gave everyone presents of money. That which he gave to recompense their labor did not vary from year to year. Even after he became Shōgun, to the last, these customs did not change.

In the spring of [1705] the year following that in which he was appointed Heir, he gave me, in particular, various beautiful silks and told me to give them to my wife and children. In the summer of that year, he gave me summer clothes similar to what he had given me before, and he also presented me with boxes of cakes, telling me to give these to my wife and children. This henceforth became a yearly custom and, even after the predecessor [25] of the present Shōgun [26] succeeded, everything was done in the same way, as when he was alive. People said that these things were done for no one but me.

During the early part of my residence at Yushima, there was a violent earthquake, sometime after midnight on the 30th De-

[78]

cember 1703.[123] No sooner had I opened my eyes than I snatched my sword, sprang up, and rushed out, and just then, all the doors and windows throughout the house crashed in. I ran to where my wife and children were sleeping and found that all had risen and fled. The rear part of my house was close to the foot of a high ridge, so taking everyone with me I went out into the large garden on the east. I had some of the shutters that had collapsed fetched and laid out and made everyone sit on them in case the ground split open.

I changed into fresh clothes, putting a loose traveling cloak on over lined formal dress. Telling two or three of my men-servants that I was going to inquire about my lord's safety and that they were to come with me and the rest to stay at home, I set out at a run.

I had thought I might get breathless on the way, and on entering the house, which was tossing like a small boat in a heavy sea, got out a medicine chest, and put it on one side. But when I changed my clothes, to my shame, I clean forgot about the medicine in my haste.

Running on in this way, I was just passing the east gate of Kanda Myōjin when there was another severe shock.[124] The houses of the shop people in this quarter stood wide open and crowds had gathered in the alley. The lights in the houses were still burning, so, as I hurried by, I shouted to them to put them right out in case of fire should the houses fall.

Nearing Shōhei Bridge, I met Kagehira (then called Asakura Yosan) hurrying toward me. I told him to go to my house and take charge, and rushed on.[125] Crossing the bridge, I continued in a southerly direction, turned west, and just as I was about to turn south again, I came upon a man who had pulled up his horse. By the light of the moon, I recognized Fujieda Wakasa-no-Kami.[126] A chasm had opened and water was rushing through. It was difficult to judge how deep or wide it was, and this is what had seemingly held him up. "Follow me, men!" I cried, and jumped over the water which was running more than one *jō* wide, and my men did likewise. I got my feet wet jumping across, my straw sandals grew heavy and walking became difficult, so I changed them and hastened on.

As I drew near Kanda Bridge, another violent tremor occurred. There was a noise like a lot of chopsticks snapping, together with the hum of a swarm of mosquitoes. This must have been the sound of buildings falling and the shouts of men. Stones rolled from the walls, the earth crumbled, and clouds of dust hung across the sky. I thought the entire bridge had collapsed, but only three or four *shaku* between the bridge and the abutment had fallen in, so we sprang across and passed through the gate.

The siding had peeled off the houses and fell across the roadway like strips of silk curling in the breeze. When I reached Tatsu-no-Kuchi, I saw in the distance that fire had broken out in the clan mansion, and as the glow was close to the ground, I was very anxious lest my lord's apartments had collapsed and fire had broken out.[127] Though my heart rushed ahead, my feet seemed to stand still.

I had gone on for about four or five *chō*, when I heard a horse's hooves behind me, and looking back, I saw Fujieda gallop up. I had got so far, but it was difficult to calculate what lay ahead, so I said: "You are surely Wakasa-no-Kami. I am worried about the state of that fire." He answered: "So am I! Come on! Pray excuse me for going on horseback," and hurried on.

I soon arrived at the Hibiya Gate.[128] The guardhouse had fallen, and the cries of the crushed and dying were pitiful to hear. There I saw someone dismounted from his horse; it was Fujieda. This time he was stopped trying to get over the heaps of tiles that had fallen off the eaves on the north and south sides of the gateway. I told him to come with me, and together we climbed over the tiles and passed through the wicket gate. We saw that the barracks north of the clan mansion had fallen down and were in flames, but my lord's apartments were a long way off. We felt our hearts expand.

The great gate on the west of the clan mansion stood open, and it seemed the guards' barracks had collapsed.[129] Fujieda made to enter here. I said that as I was accustomed to enter from the small wicket-gate on the west, I would go in that way, and left him. When I passed through the wicket-gate, I saw that the buildings had all tumbled down. The road was blocked by the people who had rushed out, and I could not go on.

[80]

I skirted that point, and when I arrived at the place where I usually entered, I found the buildings there had also collapsed, and I was unable to get in. I again found Fujieda standing nearby, and together we entered by the Onando-no-Kuchi.[130] We passed through a part where the ceiling had fallen in here and there, and when I entered the room where I was usually received, I met the present Echizen-no-Kami Akifusa [24] coming toward me.

I heard from him that my lord was safe, and observing that I had ventured to come without leave at such a time, I passed on to my lord's day apartments. A building on the east had collapsed onto the verandah. His personal attendants were standing in the southern court, and they said that my lord was in the garden beyond. The elders, Toda [20], Koide [23], Inoue [27], and the rest, were standing in the court when I came in. I consulted with a certain Igarashi (Ichijūrō was at that time a young man; he was a member of the *okonandoshū*), and laid about ten mats, which had been spread on the verandah, in the garden, and had everyone sit down on them.

The tremors continued, and the bank of the pond behind where we were sitting crumbled making the leveled earth narrower. At this point, Sakai Saemon-no-Jō Tadazane came, saying that he was acting under orders and fought the fire. If the fire got a hold, it was said, my lord would have to move, so he just put a loose traveling cloak over his trousers and came out to the south side of his day apartments. Seeing that I was present he called me, and when I came up to the verandah, he asked me all sorts of questions about earthquakes, after which he went in.

When dawn began to break, I heard that he was going to inquire about the Shōgun's [15] safety, so I said into Nagato-no-Kami's [20] ear: "The tremors are continuing. It is very unwise that he should go."[131] "I think so too," he replied, "but there is nothing I can say to stop him." Meanwhile, my lord had gone out.

And so I went to where the fire was blazing and saw that they had dragged out the injured and dying from the wreckage. The numerous wells and springs had all gone dry and, without water, there was no way of putting out the fire. (When it was suggested that at such a time they should draw from the garden

pond, the present Magaribuchi Shimotsuke-no-Kami [28] replied that it would be needed later on and would not permit it.
I wondered why, but I have been unable to find out.)

At this point, the present Oki-no-Kami Tō Akiyuki, [29]
led me into the garden of his elder brother Akifusa's house and
offered me a meal. During the night, the clan physician, Sakamoto
(who was called Yōkei), on coming into the garden, had drawn
me aside and given me some food which he took out of his sleeve.
It was a bowl of rice soaked in hot water. It was some time since
I had eaten that, so I ate and drank heartily and left. As I was
passing before the house of the present Ichi-no-Kami Tō Masanao [30], I was invited in and offered tea.

When I had partaken of it, I heard that my lord was returning, and stationed myself where he would enter. I welcomed
him, and from there three elders and myself escorted him down a
narrow corridor, somewhere or other, continued on in the direction of his day apartments, and arrived at a place where they
had just repaired one section. Although all had straw sandals in
their sleeves, it appeared that Toda had come unprepared, and I,
feeling that decorum should be preserved, took out the sandals I
had put in both sleeves and gave them to him when I first entered
the garden.

My lord came out again where he had before and called me over
and said: "It reminds me of the crowds flocking to the flower-
viewing at Ueno when I was a child," and smiled. After some
time, they put out the fire, and it must have been about one
o'clock when my lord came out again and called me. When I
came, he said: "Have you heard how your wife and children are
since you came?" I replied that since I had come last night I
had been here all the time and had heard nothing about them.
He said: "When I was on my way to my villa at Yanaka,
someone pointed out your house to me, at the foot of a high
ridge."[132] "That is so," I replied. "A very alarming thing," he
said. "The tremors will probably continue for many days. If they
are as violent as in the beginning, do not dream of coming again.
Go home at once!"

I went off and sought out my servants. When I asked them if
they had been here all night, they said that as those whom I had
left at home had hurried there early this morning and relieved

them, they had gone home and eaten and returned. Owing to this, I knew that my wife and children were safe, and returned home with my mind at ease when it was some time after two o'clock in the afternoon.

On the following day when I went to the clan mansion, my lord's residence was all aslant, so that he had moved to a temporary shelter in the horse-exercise ground on the east.

As the tremors continued, I thought that fire would certainly break out, and though my storeroom had not yet collapsed, there were many places in the walls where the plaster had crumbled and fallen down. I had the crumbled plaster moistened with water and the rents patched up. As I had expected, at dusk, on the 6th January [1704], fire broke out.

I wondered whether I should leave all my possessions in the storeroom. I could not guess whether the room would fall with the repeated shocks. The plaster, where I had patched it up, was not yet dry, and it was difficult to tell whether, if the fire became fierce and a space opened between the new and the old plaster, the fire might get in. So I quickly had a hole dug nearby, and taking out from the room the books that I had been given and also extracts that I had copied out by hand, put them into the hole, laid six or seven mats over them, piled earth thickly on top, and fled.

Our way was stopped here and there by the fire, but when it had died down somewhat, we returned home through the burned-out streets. We saw that a house on top of the bank near the hole where we had buried the books had burned down, and the fire had not yet gone out. We doused it liberally with water and put out the fire. When we dragged away a pillar of the burned-out house, we found that, when the house collapsed, it had scattered the earth away from the place we had covered up and had burned through the mats we had piled on top. The fire had already reached the bottom-most mat by the time we returned home. The storeroom, contrary to my expectations, had not fallen, nor had it burned. We laughed at our wasted effort in digging the hole and putting the books into it in the first place.

On the 31st December 1704, hearing that my lord had been proclaimed the Shōgun's Heir, I hastened to congratulate him. I had got as far as the neighborhood of Tatsu-no-Kuchi when I found that, as he was just about to enter the Western Palace, pedestrians had been stopped (by the *okachishū*).[133] I gave my name, saying that I had come on official business, and they allowed me to pass.

When I reached the clan mansion, I found a number of people who had come to escort him (Mino-no-Kami Yoshiyasu [31] and others of the Shōgun's suite). When I inquired for Akifusa, they told me he was eating, so I went in and conveyed my congratulations.

After he had finished eating, I detained him as he was leaving his seat and said: "I have, I need not say, told the Heir many things about the empire in these recent years, and I come today to say that if he does not forget them, it will be very fortunate for the empire. My only purpose in hastening hither has been to say this. So please let him know this, if you will," and took my leave.

Afterward, I heard from someone that on some occasion, apropos of what I do not exactly know, His Highness turned to Akifusa and said: "Shall I forget what Kimmi [2] came immediately to tell me when I first entered the Western Palace? I certainly have never forgotten it for a single day."

After this, I just remained at home. When about 20 days had passed, a certain man came and said: "Those who have served for many years have, each according to his rank, been taken into his service. We alone have not been sent for, and it appears that others have sent petitions in. As I too intend to send in my petition, I have come to let you know."

The man who told me this was Shibazaki Jūroemon [32]. It was Murata Jūroemon [33] who had sent in his petition through Akifusa's younger brother [29]. Shibazaki was anxious because he had heard that when the Heir was still the Lord of Kai, Murata had visited the houses of those in charge of us and made representations.

I thought to myself, what felicity can exceed this, to see the man whom I have served for years past in such a position? What else can I desire? Although I am a humble fellow, nevertheless I have been for many years the tutor of a man who has become the Heir. In accordance with the dictates of right conduct, my promotion, or otherwise, has nothing to do with my own personal importance. I do not feel that I can put forward my claims like other men. So I replied: "I have no words to thank you for your kind thoughts, but as I have views of my own on the matter, I cannot make such a petition."

Scarcely one day later, on the evening of the 21st January, a message came saying that the officials had received orders to make arrangements for me and others.

This information was conveyed by a man called Sakabe, who had been one of the *metsuke* when the Heir was the Lord of Kai. The message was to the effect that seven of us, Arai Kageyu [2], Murata Jūroemon, Shibazaki Jūroemon, Yoshida Tōhachirō [22], Hattori Tōkurō [34], Hattori Seisuke [35], and Doi Genshirō [36], were to be under the control of the *osobashū* of the Western Palace.

At about four o'clock on the 22nd, an order came through Akifusa that I was to go to the Western Palace; I went at once. Those who had received orders and were to conduct me, came out to meet me and led me where I had to go.

Servants posted outside the Great Gate conducted me to the Naka-no-Kuchi.[134] Yamamoto Den'a was waiting there, and when he reported that I had arrived, Yamamoto Gen-chō, who was the clan physician, came out to greet me and led me to the Tokei-no-Ma.[135] This was because the Heir knew that Genchō was a friend of mine.

Toda Nagato-no-Kami Tadatoshi [20], Koide Tosa-no-Kami Ariyuki [23], and Inoue Tōtōmi-no-Kami Masakata [27] met me. (It had been ordered that these men were to take charge of us.) After Murata and the others arrived, Akifusa came out with Koide, and when the Heir's instructions had been transmitted to us, everyone withdrew. (At this time, Shibazaki and Hattori Seisuke did not appear; perhaps they had not been sent for. I do not know.) I alone was told to wait here a while.

These were instructions concerning those in charge and where we would be received hereafter. When everyone had gone, Koide came up to where I was sitting and said: "Henceforth, matters concerning the Heir touch the welfare of the empire. We, as you know from previous experience, are wanting in ability and wisdom. We depend entirely on you. Although I do not need to mention it, I say it because it is my inmost thought." As this was after Akifusa had gone into the lord's presence, he said it to me alone. This man shortly afterward departed this life, overwhelmed by misfortune. It was indeed regrettable.

After this, I was informed, through Akifusa, of the events of the past weeks, and told that lectures would commence after the New Year. I returned home at about eight in the evening. (I was told that thereafter I was to come in from the Naka-no-Kuchi, go past the kitchens, and enter the private apartments.)

On the 24th [January 1705], I was told that I was to attend the lunar New Year's ceremony of congratulation in the Main Palace.[136] (Word came about this matter from Toda. In the letter, it said that I was to be seated next to the *yoriaishū* of the Main Palace.) On the 25th January 1705, I attended at the Main Palace to offer congratulations.[137]

On the 4th February, I commenced my lectures in the Western Palace. After that, my presence at daily lectures was no different from the time when the Heir was the Lord of Kai.

On the 3rd May, this year, two men, Murata Jūroemon and Yoshida Tōhachirō, were promoted to the *konandoshū*. Murata was originally a retainer of the House of Yagiū.[138] His master, Yagiū, had served the Heir when the latter had studied swordsmanship in his youth. After I was summoned, orders were given for the Yagiū House to send a disciple, and Murata was sent. The appointment of Yoshida was, as I have explained earlier, because Toda had recommended him and made him a pupil of Daigaku-no-Kami [21]. Since Daigaku-no-Kami was the tutor of the then Shōgun [15], many of his pupils entered the ranks of the Shōgun's personal attendants, thus Toda, in order to recommend Yoshida, also recommended Murata.

Whatever the present custom may be, the duties given to these men were those performed by the eunuchs in ancient China, and although this was disdained by *samurai* and superior men, some of the younger people, who were unaware that the Heir accorded me respectful treatment even though I had not risen in rank, and had so far been friendly, now became somewhat reserved toward me. Then, after barely ten days, when I had finished my lecture, on the 14th of this month [May], the Heir said: "The garden here has some beautiful views," and told Ichi-no-Kami Masanao [30] to take me around it. After I had seen the various parts and come back again, he presented me with five rolls of several kinds of silk, saying that they were for my wife and children. This was the first time he sent presents to my family. It was then that even those who had been distant toward me came and congratulated me.

On the 23rd October of this year, Shibazaki Jūroemon retired. He had taught the Heir horse-riding from his youth. He must have been over seventy. He was the most famous horseman of his time.

When the Lord of Kai became the Heir, Toda had wished to recommend a riding-master he knew called Nagasaki, so he slandered Shibazaki, but the Heir took no notice. This Shibazaki was an excellent horseman but of a headstrong disposition. He said exactly what he thought, and because he criticized people's riding openly, he was much disliked. When the keeper of the Shōgun's stables, whose name was Suwabe, I think, complained, Hōki-no-Kami, Masatake, who was attached to the staff of the Heir at that time and had always been on friendly terms with Suwabe, plotted with Toda and slandered Shibazaki.[139] Shibazaki, unable to contain his anger, on the 16th October this year requested permission to resign. His request was immediately granted, but not many days had passed before he died of indignation.

He and Murata and I had been colleagues for many years. Whatever he thought, he spoke kindly of me, and though he brought it on himself, it was sad that he should die in such circumstances.

It happened about this time that there was an argument between Koide and Inoue. Koide was immediately relieved of office, and shortly afterward was deprived of the additional grants he had received. This too was because Toda had plotted with Masatake. Although, in the beginning, when the Lord of Kai was appointed the Heir, Toda was taken into employment at the same time as Koide, Toda had for some years been dissatisfied with Koide. Inoue's elder brother, Kawachi-no-Kami Masamine [37], was then a member of the Rōjū. Also, Ukyō-Daibu Terusada [38] was his cousin on the maternal side, so that Inoue had some connection with Shōshō Yoshiyasu [31]. This invited someone to comment that from the start slanders were easily manufactured. Although I do not know the truth or falsehood of the matter, as I wrote before, since Tadatoshi [20] had had charge of my appointment, I could not forget this.

Although I had no special connection with Koide, I heard it said that, being an honest fellow, he said what he thought without reserve, and so the story may be true. I remember what he said to me when the Heir was first appointed. Toda appeared to be very skillful in worldly affairs, and a man of deep cunning. When the Lord of Kai was appointed the Heir, he used to come, very early in the morning, and privately make representations through Akifusa. Also, when anyone presented petitions through Toda, he would hear what they had to say and tell them: "I understand. Explain it to my colleagues." People thought that the success of their recommendations was due to Toda, and that when they failed, it was his colleagues who had objected. These things I witnessed myself. Although shortly afterward Toda attained a salary of 10,000 *koku* and the Fourth Rank, scarcely a year had passed before he was deprived of office on the 19th November 1706.[140] Whatever the reason was, I did not hear. After the Heir became Shōgun, I said to him: "Although when the previous Shōgun [15] was alive, Toda was relieved of office, he was very fortunate in salary and rank. I hope something will be done to reward Koide's services to you when you were the Heir." His Highness answered: "These two men enjoyed considerable favor under the previous Shōgun, but when I was still the Lord of Kai, they both always spoke disparagingly of his government. That they were visited by this misfortune was their own fault. By this one thing alone, one can judge what kind of men they were."

Although these are not matters I should record, as I think my posterity should understand the conditions of society, I have set down one or two of them here.

On the 10th September this year [1706], orders were given newly appointing the officials to whom I and others were responsible. (In a letter dated this day Inoue said that orders were given that the four of us, Hattori [34] and his son [35], Doi [36], and I were to be controlled by the Wakadoshiyori.)

Next year, on the 18th June 1707, a house lot, timber, and 200 gold pieces to build a house were given to me.

The two men, Nagai Izu-no-Kami Naohira [39] and Ōkubo Nagato-no-Kami Norishige [40], informed me that I was to be given 355 *tsubo* of land outside the Kiji Bridge. When the matter was completed, I was ordered to present myself at the Heir's private apartments, so I went and expressed my thanks for the gift of the house lot. This was because when the houses of those who served in the clan mansion in Hama were destroyed, the house of Hachiya Gempachirō was left, and the Heir thought that he would give it to me.[141] He now gave me that house. However, shifting it to the ground he had given me was beyond my means, so he gave orders, through Akifusa, that I was to be given 100 gold pieces for removal expenses. On the 29th June, when he heard that his gift was insufficient, he gave me another 100 gold pieces.

On the 23rd August, he heard that I had shifted to my new house and, on the 27th, gave instructions about the gates I should use when I came on duty. (This was that when on duty I should enter and leave by the Momijiyamashita and Ura gates because he thought they were nearer to my new residence.)

On the 25th September, there was a performance of *sarugaku*, at the Main Palace.[142] This was to celebrate the birth of the lord Iechiyo.[143] Orders were received that the baby's maternal uncle, Ōta Naiki, and I were to attend.[144]

The baby had been born early in the morning of the 7th August. Instructions about the performance to be held on this day were conveyed over the joint signatures of Nagai and Ōkubo. Also, in accordance with orders Ōkubo had received previously, we were introduced by his relative Ōkubo Sakyō. It was because it was the first occasion on which the two of us had been present at such a ceremony. After this, in circular instructions concerning all matters, Ōta and I were addressed jointly.

I was told to come on the afternoon of the 16th December. The night before, there had been an earthquake, and at noon on this day, there were rumblings. When I left my house, white ash was falling like snow, a black cloud hung in the sky to the southwest, and there were continuous flashes of lightning. When I arrived at the Western Palace, the ground was covered with white ash, and the trees and grass had also become white. On this day, the Heir attended at the Main Palace and returned at three o'clock. (His visit was occasioned by the fact that, on this day, the two sons of Yoshiyasu [31] were raised to court rank.) I was shown into his presence at once. By this time, the sky was very dark, so I lectured by candlelight. The ash ceased falling by eight o'clock, but the rumblings and tremors continued.

On the 18th, the heavens again darkened, and there were rumblings. When evening came, there was a heavy fall of ash, and it was said that this was because Mount Fuji had erupted. After that, black ash fell constantly until the end of December. On the evening of the 1st January, it snowed, and by this time, there was no one who was not suffering from a cough.

Early in the new year, there was an unusually heavy downpour on the 23rd January 1708. On the 28th February, a tax to pay for the removal of the ash and sand caused by the eruption of Mount Fuji, which had buried the provinces near Edo the previous year, was laid on all provinces. (It was for the sake of the three provinces of Musashi, Suruga, and Mikawa. The tax was 2 gold pieces for every 100 *koku*).

On the 20th March, orders were given for the minting of the Great Cash, called "Ten Mon Pieces."[145] In April, there was a report that patches of grass like white hair had been discovered on the ground, and soon afterward, this wonder was also observed on my ground.[146] This year drew to a close with no end to the heavenly portents and natural calamities besides this. However, I have not set down anything here I have not seen with my own eyes.

At the end of July, the district near my house was relocated. (This neighborhood was called Iidamachi.) It was reported that many people's houses must also be moved to one place or another. They said it was because a palace was being built to the north of the castle.[147] Toward the end of September, I heard that the cutting of horses' hair was forbidden.[148] After this, the horses people led and rode all came to look like wild horses. Toward the middle of November, orders were given concerning the circulation of the Great Cash.[149] In December, three decrees were issued for the protection of animals, and thereafter people whose rank entitled them to ride on horseback did not ride but only led their horses.[150]

It was also reported that the merchants objected to using the Great Cash. With daily exhortations that without a single exception rich and poor alike, old and young, men and women, must send in their promise that they would circulate the Great Cash, the year drew to an end.

On the 10th February 1709, owing to the Shōgun's [15] illness since the previous year, he requested the Heir to deputize for him at the reception at the lunar New Year. On the 16th, I was ill and did not go on duty, but remained at home. Some time past noon on the 19th, I noticed people hurrying back and forth and, at sunset, the Shōgun's death was announced.[151] I was deeply shocked.

BOOK II

On the 19th February, in the spring of 1709, the Shōgun's [15] death was announced, and orders were sent out for all the officials to attend at the Western Palace on the following day. I also went on that day, the 20th.

At that time, I put a document in my sleeve, intending to present it through Akifusa [24], but I was unable to see him, and so presented it through his younger brother, Nakatsukasa-no-Shō Akihira [41]. (He is the present Awaji-no-Kami.) In this document, I set forth the three matters most urgently requiring attention at this time.[1]

That day it rained toward nightfall. It was the first time it had rained since the 1st December of the previous year. On the 21st, I again went and presented a document. That evening it rained again and continued until dawn.

Although I went daily, I did not see Akifusa. On the 24th, I saw him for the first time and heard about the petition I had presented earlier. On the 26th, orders were published abolishing the Great Cash.[2] That evening, it rained again and continued until dawn. It must have been about this time that the relocation of residential districts was stopped.[3]

As I have explained earlier, since the winter of the previous year, the merchants had had to send in pledges that they would circulate the Great Cash, and exhortations about this had continued until the day of the Shōgun's death.

In consequence of the orders that residential districts must be relocated, houses had already been demolished, buildings erected, and materials and tools transported by the lunar New Year. In accordance with precedent, on the Shōgun's death, artisans and merchants suspended their activities for

[93]

seven days, but when this time had elapsed, both trade and construction recommenced. Consequently, these orders were issued on that day because without them the people's minds could not have been set at rest, and it was impossible to leave things as they were.

When I went on the 28th, I received a message from His Highness about the Genna Regulations, so I returned home, and that evening I composed a volume, "In Explanation of the Laws of the Divine Ancestor [8]," with the intention of presenting it the next day.⁴ I was summoned at dawn, so I went and presented the work. I returned home toward two o'clock but was again summoned and went. On this day, I heard that the Kindness to Animals Statutes, which had been issued in the previous reign, had been repealed.

On the 3rd March, the funeral took place. It was said that it was postponed until this day because it had rained continuously from the 26th February to the 1st March.

Someone said that the postponement of the funeral until this day was not really because of the continuous rain, but that the true reason was as follows:

One day when His Highness [3], who was then Heir, had visited the former Shōgun [15], the latter had sent for Shōshō Yoshiyasu [31], Ukyō-Daibu Terusada [38], Iga-no-Kami Tadayoshi [42], Buzen-no-Kami Naoshige, and others from among his personal attendants and had said: "However unreasonable my protection of animals for some years past may have been, if you do no more than retain these orders when I am dead, as when I was alive, you will be acting in accordance with filial piety. I want all those present to pay heed."⁵

However, owing to these statutes protecting animals, for many years past myriads of people had been punished, and the corpses of nine, who died in prison before judgment on their cases had been given, had been pickled in brine, and there were also many who lay under sentence of death.⁶ Unless these statutes were abolished, it would be impossible to bring the sufferings of Japan to an end.

However, it would have been improper to abolish, as soon as His Highness came into power, statutes which had been in effect until that time. As His Highness wished somehow to obey the injunctions of the dying Shōgun, he first summoned Yoshiyasu and explained his intentions. Yoshiyasu also thought that these decrees were evil, and although the former Shōgun had showed him special favor, the future was difficult to foresee, so he agreed that what His Highness said must be called the extreme of filial piety. His Highness therefore directed Yoshiyasu to convey his wishes to the officials who had been thus far in charge of this matter, of whom Terusada was the chief. When Yoshiyasu informed them of His Highness's intentions, none of them raised any objections.

Yoshiyasu informed His Highness of this. So on the 1st March, His Highness stood before the former Shōgun's coffin and said: "As far as I am personally concerned, I will never depart from the orders you have given. However, I have some anxiety touching the people of the empire, and so I must crave your permission." Then he summoned those who had heard what the former Shōgun had said about this matter long ago and told them what he had done. After that, he gave orders that the prohibitions be removed. As the funeral had not yet taken place, these were generally regarded as the final injunctions of the former Shōgun.

Also, among the personal attendants who had been obliged to be present with His Highness on this occasion, were many who wished to take the tonsure. However, with regard to these old customs, there was a regulation limiting the number of such people, so His Highness told Yoshiyasu and other officials to choose those who should do so.[7]

At this time, Yoshiyasu himself expressed a desire to take the tonsure, as an expression of loyalty to the former Shōgun. His Highness said that since Yoshiyasu had received unparalleled favor from the former Shōgun, his desire was understandable. His Highness therefore could not stop him. However, on considering the precedents of generations, there had never been a case of such high-ranking officials taking the tonsure as an expression of loyalty. The practice of following one's lord in death had been discontinued long ago in the time of Gen'yū-In [43], and it would be very unsuitable to

[95]

inaugurate a practice of this kind at the beginning of his own rule.[8] But if Yoshiyasu, after resigning from office at the conclusion of the funeral ceremonies and handing over his estates to his son, took the tonsure as he wished, he would not be departing from long established precedents, and he would also be accomplishing what he himself desired. So Yoshiyasu accordingly retired.

As His Highness did not personally inform me of these two matters, I do not know whether they are true or not, but the man who told me was not one to spread idle rumors, so I have set down what he said here.

This day [1st March 1709], I heard that His Highness had given orders to Daigaku-no-Kami Nobuatsu [21] about the inscription for the late Shōgun's sarcophagus.

I had been summoned on the 27th previous [February], and when I had come, His Highness had asked me what the form of the inscription on the late Shōgun's sarcophagus should be, so I had told him that there were Chinese and Japanese precedents for it. As he directed me to compose one, I presented a draft on the 28th together with a separate commentary on the ancient Chinese and Japanese precedents.

On this day, I heard that at first Nobuatsu had said that as the epitaphs of the *shōguns* had been written by his House for generations, he had composed the epitaph at the time of the death of Shōgun Ietsuna [43]. When Nobuatsu presented his draft, His Highness thought that what he had written about the former Shōgun was not in order and also that the form of the composition was unsuitable, and therefore asked me about it and requested me to submit a draft as well.

After that, he summoned Sado-no-Kami Nagashige [44] and told him to go to the Nikkō Jugō [45] and ask him which of the two forms was correct.[9] The Jugō said that the second form could not be bettered. Accordingly, His Highness directed that my draft should be handed to Nobuatsu and that he should be instructed to write the epitaph in this form.

When I went on the 8th March, I again presented a document. The gist of it was: "The Divine Ancestor [8] was endowed by Heaven with wisdom and courage and so unified the country.

[96]

Through his prosperous protection of the empire and the accumulated virtues of his ancestors, he was able to establish the control of his heirs permanently. He had many sons and daughters, and although some of them died early, four became lords of great provinces, and their descendants continue to flourish.[10]

"Of the sons of the second Shōgun [46] who were granted provinces in fief, after the suicide of Suruga Dono [47], only the descendants of Aizu Dono are left.[11]

"The third Shōgun [9] had two sons who were granted fiefs.[12]

"The fourth Shōgun [43] had no son to succeed him, but at his death, as his only blood relative was your uncle [15], who has just died, he was adopted as Ietsuna's [43] son and succeeded to the shogunate.[13]

"When that former Shōgun first succeeded, he had a son, but this child soon died, and since he had no children after that, he adopted Your Highness, who are now Shōgun, as his son.[14]

"And so, since the third Shōgun, the ruling line has failed twice, and it cannot be without reason that before a hundred years have been accomplished through the virtues of the Divine Ancestor, the ruling line has come to this pass. I was even more grieved at heart when the former Shōgun adopted Your Highness as his son.

"The continuance of the fine government carried out by the Divine Ancestor is the best way to ensure that Heaven will take pity on the calamity that has befallen the Tokugawa House at this time of crisis and bring about some change in its destiny. But since I have lectured about these matters for the past 20 years, there is no need to speak about them now.

"However, there is one thing I wish to discuss: During the Genkō and Kemmu eras, the imperial line divided into the Northern and Southern Courts, and the Southern Court soon came to an end.[15] As the Northern Court had the support of the military classes, its fortunes rose and fell along with theirs. And when they were overthrown during the long-continued disturbances after the Ōnin era, one can imagine the plight of the Imperial Court.

"When the Divine Ancestor gained control of the empire, he revived the former glory and restored the dignity of the Imperial House, but no change from the days of its eclipse was made in the custom whereby all the imperial princes and princesses, with the exception of the Crown Prince, took Buddhist vows.[16]

"The humblest man and woman, if they have children, always want to get them married. This is the natural feeling of all people of all ages. Also, now, even farmers, artisans, and the merchant class divide their property among their sons and seek marriages for their daughters. Much less are these arrangements ever neglected among those of the rank of *samurai* and above.

"Because a long time has elapsed since this custom has arisen, now of course there is no complaint from the Imperial House.[17] We cannot, however, argue that they therefore desire this state of affairs. And even though they say nothing, unless Your Highness's government takes steps to put this matter right, those responsible cannot claim to have done their duty to the Imperial Court.

"As at this time the Imperial Court is possessed of considerable estates, even if the Emperor's sons are proclaimed Shinnō, it will not be necessary to give them much land.[18] Even if marriages are arranged for imperial princesses, it will not be necessary to expend much of the national resources. If the descendants of the Divine Ancestress in Japan are in their present condition, how unreasonable it would be for the descendants of the Divine Ancestor of your House to expect to flourish unshakable forever.[19]

"But if my proposals are put into effect, some may be anxious lest, in the future when the generations of imperial princes and princesses increase in number, they may become a financial embarrassment to the empire. Although since ancient times, there have been many ages when there were scores of imperial princes and princesses, those who have survived to this day are not numerous. Sages of old said their number was divinely ordained. These things cannot be calculated by human intelligence. One can only discuss whether or not a certain line of action is right or wrong.

"Again, it may be argued that it will be unprofitable for the military classes if the descendants of imperial princes become numerous. Although the Minamoto Family throughout Japan arose in response to the edict of Takakura-no-Miya, this was because it was the time when the House of Hei Shōkoku Nyūdō was

[98]

destined to be destroyed because of the master's many ill deeds.[20] If we consider this a warning, was it not the former prince, the Abbot of Nashimoto, who issued a call to arms when the lay-priest Takatoki [48] was destroyed?[21] So, even though imperial princes become recluses, we cannot say that disasters of this kind will not happen. It all depends on the efficiency or otherwise of the military government. Your Highness must give your serious attention to these matters."

After His Highness had perused this memorial and made two or three comments, he said: "What you say is very reasonable, and as it is of great importance to this country, I must consider it carefully."

Soon after, he gave orders that Hide-no-Miya, the son of the Retired Emperor, should be proclaimed Shinnō, and later it was arranged that a princess should be given in marriage to the previous Shōgun [25].[22]

Thus I, born in this land, was able in some way to repay gratitude to the Imperial House.

However, as I had secretly feared, the previous Shōgun died, and the extinction of the line could not be prevented by human agency. Nevertheless, it must be considered a great blessing for the empire that, owing to my words, the present Shōgun [26] has succeeded, just as Heaven had wisely planned for years to come.[23]

Touching the matter of Hide-no-Miya, I heard that although some highly born person had argued that it has always been difficult to establish a princely house, this view was not followed, and the question was referred to the court nobility.[24] It was indeed a blessing. However, as I did not hear this directly, I have not set it down in the main text.

In this document I had cited ancient and modern Japanese and Chinese precedents, and as it was exceptionally long, it was not easily understood by the unlearned, hence I have just set down an outline of it here. (I presented this document at this time since it had a bearing on His Highness's [3] proclamation as Shōgun.)

In response to a summons, I presented myself on the 13th March [1709]. His Highness informed me through Akifusa [24] of the following: "Since the death of the former Shōgun [15], the mem-

[99]

bers of the Rōjū have been taking turns on duty in the Main Palace, but they have said it is most unfitting at such a time for me not to be in residence in the Main Palace for a single day, and that I must move at once. According to precedent, the former Shōgun reconstructed the official residence and moved there. At this time, it is necessary to construct a palace for the Ōmidaidokoro [49] to move to permanently, but when the Rōjū came to discuss it, they found that the treasury was already exhausted and that there were no funds for future requirements.

"Under the former Shōgun, Kaga-no-Kami Tadatomo (Ōkubo) [50] had been in charge of state finances, but they had actually been entrusted to Ōmi-no-Kami Shigehide (Ogiwara) [51] alone, and Shigehide had consulted with Mino-no-Kami Yoshiyasu [31] and Tsushima-no-Kami Shigetomi (Inagaki) [52]. And so even Kaga-no-Kami did not know the details, much less did the rest of the Rōjū have any say in the matter.

"Now Shigehide reports: 'The shogunal estates yield 4,000,000 *koku* and the annual income is more than 760,000 or 770,000 *ryō*.[25] (Ōmi-no-Kami said that this included 60,000 *ryō* he collected in customs at Nagasaki and 6,000 *ryō* in transport tax on *sake*.)[26] After subtracting from this, 300,000 *ryō* for biannual salaries, some 460,000 or 470,000 *ryō* remain.[27] But the expenditure for the previous year reached about 1,400,000 *ryō*, and besides this, about 700,000 or 800,000 *ryō* were required to pay for the construction of the Imperial Palace.[28] And so the present deficit exceeds 1,700,000 or 1,800,000 *ryō*.

" 'Even if there had been no funeral, there would have been no funds for future requirements. The situation is very much aggravated with the present urgent expenses for the memorial services for the former Shōgun, the construction of his mausoleum, the ceremony of His Highness's proclamation as Shōgun, his move to the Main Palace, and on top of these, the construction of the Imperial Palace.[29] Yet there now remains in the treasury only 370,000 *ryō*.

" 'Of this 370,000 *ryō*, 240,000 *ryō* came about as follows: In the spring of the preceding year, a tax of 2 *ryō* for every 100 *koku* of territory had been imposed on all the provinces to be used for the removal of ash from the three provinces of Musashi, Sagami, and Suruga, and 400,000 *ryō* had been collected, of which 160,000 had been used for that work.[30] The remainder, namely 240,000 ryō, had been set aside for the construction of the palace to the north of the castle precincts.[31]

" 'Besides this total of 370,000 ryō, there are no funds to meet state expenses. Even if we apply this to defray the expenses of the present time, it will not even cover one-tenth of what is needed.'

"Everyone, including Kaga-no-Kami [53], was appalled. When the members of the Rōjū consulted with Ōmi-no-Kami a second time, he said: 'In the time of the former Shōgun, yearly expenditure was always double the income, and when the treasury was bare the gold and silver coinage was debased in October 1695, and thereafter.[32] From that time on, the profit from yearly recoinage had totalled 5 million ryō, and the constant deficit had been made up with this. Owing to the great earthquake in the winter of 1703, however, even the profit this brought in yearly was immediately exhausted in repairing damages and destruction. Thereafter, the original deficit in the state finances reappeared, and in August 1706, the silver coinage was debased a second time. Still this was insufficient for the year's expenditure, and in the spring of the previous year [1708], in accordance with the advice of Tsushima-no-Kami Shigetomi, the Great Cash known as "Ten Mon Pieces" was minted. (Even Ōmi-no-Kami said that the idea of the Great Cash was not a good one.) There is no way of tiding over the present emergency except by debasing the gold and silver coinage.'

"Even though Kaga-no-Kami has been in charge of these matters for some years, he says he still does not know the details, but that the rest of the Rōjū, who were hearing about these matters for the first time, were even more at a loss what to suggest. His only advice was that it would be best to be guided by Ōmi-no-Kami. I said that although I too thought that for some time the state finances were not balanced, I had no idea that the situation was so bad. However, I did not approve of the plan of debasing the gold and silver coinage, and I told Ōmi-no-Kami he must think of some other plan.

"Ōmi-no-Kami then said: 'Ever since the gold and silver coinage was first debased, the people have privately criticized this policy, but if we had not resorted to this, how could we have supplied the expenses of government for the past 13 years? Or in particular, if we had not resorted to this, how could we have dealt with a sudden emergency like that which arose in the winter of 1703? So it will be very easy if we first of all supply the needs of the time by these means, and later, in years of good harvest and ample funds, we can restore the gold and silver coinage to its former value.'

"Everyone agreed with this and said: 'It is impossible to foresee natural disasters, and if the present situation is handled in this way, when something unexpected occurs hereafter, we can deal with that emergency by some means or other. We must do just as he [51] says.'

"I replied to this: 'Although what Ōmi-no-Kami says sounds reasonable, we cannot know whether calamities would not have come if the coinage had not first been debased. If, in the future, unexpected disasters occur and we have no means of dealing with the emergency, the line of the Divine Ancestor [8] will come to an end with me. Why must I too bring suffering to the people of the empire? You must think of some other way.' "

On hearing this, Ogasawara Sado-no-Kami Nagashige [44] wept bitterly and could say nothing. After a while, Akimoto Tajima-no-Kami Takatomo [54] said: "We thank you for your words." Whereupon they all retired.

"This is a matter of great importance to the empire. Consider it well." And with this, Akifusa concluded his narration of the Shōgun's message.

When I heard this, I said: "At this time, we have here only the remainder of the tax collected from the various provinces in the spring of last year, but how about the money in the Shōgun's storerooms in Ōsaka?"[33] Akifusa replied: "When His Highness also asked about that, it was reported that it was already used up." I then said: "I have heard that in the time of the Divine Ancestor, large gold ingots had been cast of 1,000 gold coins each and these had been inscribed: 'Not to be used except for the prosecution of war or the defense of the castle.'[34] What has happened to those?" When I made this inquiry, I was told that His Highness had also inquired about them, but it had been explained that only one or two remained, the rest having been used to defray minting expenses.

I said: "It appears in the *Chou I* that when things are at their worst, a solution appears.[35] The situation at the present time is not as bad as that, for though the treasury is bare, His Highness possesses the wealth of the empire. There is bound to be a solution. Let him not distress himself about these matters. Tell him I will think of a plan," and retired.

On the 14th [March], there was another matter I wished to speak about, and when I heard about this question of finances also, during that night I wrote out what I advised in connection with this question and at dawn, putting the two documents in my sleeve, I waited on Akifusa. The gist of my advice on this matter was:

"The first principle set down in Confucius' discussion of government in the first book of the *Analects* is: 'Respect things and believe. Spend economically and cherish men. Employ people at the right time.'[36] In the *Ta Hsüeh*, it is written: 'If producers are many and consumers are few, if workers work fast and users use slowly, there will always be enough.'[37] As I have lectured on these matters for years past, there is no need to go into them now. If, henceforth, we follow this path, it will not take many years before the treasury is full. And so Your Highness's rejection of the advice to debase the coinage again must be called a great blessing for the empire.

"As has been urged, the funeral ceremonies, the construction of the mausoleum, and Your Highness's proclamation as Shōgun cannot be delayed even if there is no money. But even if there were ample funds, the sympathy between lord and subject would not countenance the immediate demolition of the former Shōgun's residence and the construction and occupation of a new one. Because it is now the custom to conduct important ceremonies in the Ōhiroma and the Goshoin, no matter what ceremony is concerned, Your Highness should go there as before and conduct them, and when the time comes that the national finances are balanced, you should reconstruct the official residence and move.[38]

"Furthermore, I cannot understand what Ōmi-no-Kami says touching the critical condition of the national finances at the present time. The reason for my doubts is that according to what he says, the funds to meet this year's expenditure are only a bare 370,000 *ryō*. I do not agree. The funds which he says were expended last year [1708] were the proceeds of the taxes from the year before that. And so to meet this year's expenditures, even if things are as he says, there must be more than 1,100,000 *ryō* all told, if we add together the 760,000 or 770,000 *ryō* gathered in last year and the 370,000 *ryō* here at present.

"Moreover, if we do not pay for ordinary needs, we will be able to pay for the urgent needs of the moment. If we apportion the 1,100,000 or so *ryō* according to the urgency of the matter, either paying the whole or paying the half, and if we pay the whole next year, we will be able to pay for all necessities. And what will it matter if it takes us six or seven or even more than ten years from now to pay off the whole of the outstanding debts which are a result of the deficit from the time of the former Shōgun? And so, Your Highness should not distress yourself about these matters. In ancient times, Fêng I of the Later Han Dynasty prayed: 'May your Majesty never forget the sufferings north of the Yellow River.'[39] I also pray that you will never forget today, and if you use the national funds sparingly for the sake of the empire, it will be a great blessing for the people."

On reading this document, His Highness was overjoyed, and when I came on the 16th of the same month [March], I was told that he said it would be unseemly to demolish the official residence of the former Shōgun immediately, and that the debasement of the coinage was not to be suggested again.

This was the first time I was consulted about affairs of state.

Could Ōmi-no-Kami not have known that this year's expenses are met out of last year's taxes? His failure to explain this and his statement that the funds for this year's expenditure did not exceed 370,000 *ryō* were in order to gain his own ends by intimidating His Highness. His secret designs are dealt with below.

Later, Ōmi-no-Kami said that last year's income had amounted to more than anticipated, and since its collection had been completed without impediment, he again recommended that His Highness should build the official residence in the main castle enclosure. It was constructed at once, and on the 2nd December this year [1709] the lord moved there.

However, this matter was not carried out as I had planned, and the cost of construction consumed 700,000 *ryō* or more. Also, I heard that the construction of the mausoleum cost 200,000 *ryō*. The high cost was because the abuses rife in the time of the former Shōgun had not been reformed; therefore, when any construction work was carried out, those in charge, whether high or low, only applied themselves to the enrichment each of his own House, and the various artisans and merchants conspired together and divided up the public funds.

From that time on, these undertakings yearly became increasingly difficult to carry out, but I wonder if, under the present Shōgun [26], things are as bad as they used to be.

Earlier, on the 12th March, I had presented a document touching the General Amnesty.[40] The gist of it was: "In ancient times amnesties granted pardon to those who had committed offenses when these had arisen through mistakes or through misfortunes, and did not, as in later times, pardon all crimes great and small, already detected and not yet detected, of those already sentenced and those not yet sentenced.

"If we look at recent precedents, we find that when a general amnesty was carried out, the petitions of the criminals' relatives were written in the register at the places of release. This register was called the Amnesty Register. It was handed to the Bugyōsho, and the *bugyō* were requested to decide who should be pardoned and who should not, and those to be pardoned were assembled at the place of release to receive their pardon.[41]

"Therefore, even though a man might be due for release when an amnesty was granted, unless he had relatives to petition for him, he could never, as long as he lived, receive the benefit of this mercy. Furthermore, this pardon was limited to those who had been sentenced by the Bugyōsho. Others, whose cases had fallen within the jurisdiction of *daimyō* and *hatamoto* in the empire, did not qualify for it. And though nominally a general amnesty is said to have been carried out, it is nothing more than the observance of ancient precedents, and there has been nothing like an actual extension of mercy to the empire at large. How can this be equated to what was called benevolence in ancient times?

"When we consider what has happened recently in the previous reign, we find that those who administered the law exerted themselves to investigate even mild offenses, and for the sake of a single bird or beast, men suffered the extreme penalty, and even their relatives were put to death, while others were deported and exiled. People could not live in security. Their fathers and mothers, sisters and brothers, wives and children were turned adrift in untold thousands. Unless a general amnesty is proclaimed in the empire now, how can we bring ease to the people's sufferings?

"Also, when you consider ancient Japanese and Chinese precedents, an amnesty was always carried out at times of reform or rejoicing. It was not something which took place at the death of a ruler, as in modern times. If we adhere to existing precedent, will not criminals in the state secretly hope for the death of the ruler?

"The ancient proverb says: 'One man's prayer cannot prevail against many curses.' And this is a very unhappy state of affairs. Nevertheless, this precedent cannot be changed suddenly. Therefore, first an ordinary amnesty should be carried out according to precedent at the time of the late Shōgun's memorial service, and when the ceremony of His Highness's proclamation as Shōgun is held, there should be a general amnesty in the empire.[42] This will be the first step toward the reform of long-standing abuses.

"Kuan Chung said: 'There is small gain and great loss in an amnesty.'[43] Also K'ung-ming said: 'Govern society by great virtue and not by small favors.'[44] I have paid great attention to these sayings. Hsün Yüeh also said: 'Amnesties should be granted at times of crisis, not at ordinary times.[45] When the empire is disturbed and the people cannot live in comfort, at times like these should they be granted.' What I proposed was at bottom based on these sayings."

On the 14th of the same month [March], I presented another document which discussed the question of a general amnesty. This was because His Highness had asked for details.

On the 17th of that month, my eldest daughter fell ill with smallpox, thus confining me to my house. The Ōmidaidokoro [49] died on the 20th, and news of this was brought to me by the personal attendants. They also informed me that on the 30th His Highness had given orders that a general amnesty should be carried out.

Since the winter of the preceding year, an epidemic of smallpox had been raging in Edo, and the former Shōgun [15] had died from this disease. Of those who contracted it, few, either young or old, let alone children, escaped death. On the appropriate day, I climbed to a high place and counted the flags flying for the Boys' Festival over the houses, and over an area of two or three blocks, they were displayed in only one or two places.

Then my eldest son and younger daughter caught the disease, and critical symptoms appeared in each, but we could do nothing for them. After some time, the disease subsided without casualty in either case. Our doctor said their recovery seemed like divine intervention. The announcement of the General Amnesty coincided with my eldest daughter's falling ill. Was this not according to the rule that after travail comes ease?[46] It must have been owing to the blessings of the grateful nation.

At this time, His Highness sent for the records of trials during the previous reign and studied them himself every night until dawn. Nine hundred and fifty-six persons were pardoned. Soon after, His Highness granted another amnesty, on the death of the Ōmidaidokoro, and himself pardoned 92. In the houses of *daimyō* and those of lower rank throughout the empire, 3,737 were released.

On the 8th June, the ceremony of His Highness's proclamation as Shōgun was performed, and on the 30th of the same month he gave orders for a general amnesty throughout the empire. At this time also, as before, he himself pardoned 2,901, and 1,862 were pardoned in the houses of *daimyō* and those of lower rank throughout the empire. The grand total of those pardoned this year was 8,831. Among them, those pardoned in the houses of *daimyō* and those of lower rank totaled 5,599. There has never been an example of such mercy since the Tokugawa House gained control of the empire.

At first, orders were given to *daimyō* and those of lower rank throughout the empire, but as this had no precedent, there were no signs of compliance. So His Highness gave orders again that detailed reports must be submitted, and this time everyone obeyed and wrote out a detailed report. His Highness directed me through Akifusa to make out a detailed report on all these matters. This must have been because it was I who had spoken of them previously.

Later, he sent for the reports on criminal cases judged at the Bugyōsho, read them himself, and afterward sent them to me, telling me to write my opinion under each case. As my opinion sometimes differed from what he had previously resolved, he questioned me in detail about my opinion and afterward pronounced sentence. I have not heard of such benevolence since ancient times.

Also, in connection with the ceremony of the proclamation of the Shōgun, after the General Amnesty was granted, an edict was issued prohibiting gamblers, fire-hook coolies and such-like ruffians, and women of ill fame, such as dancers and prostitutes who loiter in the streets.[47] I was ordered through Akifusa to draft the Shōgun's decree about these matters, also because of what I had said.

On the 31st March, orders had been given about the personal attendants of the former Shōgun. (They were either attached to the *yoriaishū* or the *gobanshū*.) On the 16th April, orders were given that henceforth all those with incomes above 10,000 *koku* should be elevated to court rank. (Orders were given because they were to attend on the day of the proclamation of the Shōgun.) On this day, those who had been domiciled in the houses of Mino-no-Kami Yoshiyasu [31] and Ukyō-Daibu Terusada [38] in the previous reign were dismissed, and each was given a house lot.

On the 11th May, congratulations had been offered on the inauguration of His Highness's rule. On the 15th of the month, the sons of the *hatamoto* in the Shōgun's service, 731 in number, were received in audience. They presented a congratulatory message through Akifusa.

This ceremony was called Goban-iri but had been discontinued for a long time.[48] By former precedent, those above sixteen or seventeen years of age took part in the ceremony. Although at this time the orders stated that the ceremony was for sixteen- and seventeen-year-olds, it was said that many were barely thirteen or fourteen. His Highness was pleased when he heard this. He smiled, saying that their parents would have been terribly disappointed if their sons had not enjoyed this honor because they were not of full age.

Prior to this, on the 27th April, when my son Akinori applied for his first audience, I was informed through Akifusa that His Highness directed that he should not only request an audience but should apply to be taken into his service. When I heard this, I said that according to ancient precedent, retainers' sons who were taken into the Shōgun's service were the eldest sons of those who held office or belonged to the *gobanshū*. There had never yet been an instance of the employment of a son of a member of the *yoriaishū*. Now I, unworthy as I am, had been promoted to the *yoriaishū*. Although I had received this favor through his special grace, I did not wish mine to be the first case in which he violated precedents. After that, all our sons were summoned, and on the 27th April Akinori was received in audience for the first time.[49]

Concerning the ceremony of the Shōgun's proclamation on the 8th June, when I presented myself on the 6th June, orders were conveyed to me through Akifusa that His Highness wished me to view the ceremony on this occasion, and that accordingly, on the previous day, the Rōjū had been informed that I was to attend on that day, together with the Shōgun's personal attendants. His Highness gave orders concerning my ceremonial robes to Akihira [41] and Masanao [30].

On that day, I first attended at the Western Palace. I was lent a *hoi* costume.[50] I went to the Main Palace in the company of the personal attendants. I was permitted to stand inside the curtains of the Shōgun's dais. On the 10th and 11th days of the month, I viewed the ceremonies as before.

On the 9th January 1710, at the memorial service for the late Shōgun, Inaba-no-Kami Masakuni [55] had the office of sandal-bearer, and I was attached to him.[51] (Masakuni is the present Murakami Noto-no-Kami. On this occasion, I was again lent a *hoi* costume.)

As on the occasion of the Shōgun's proclamation, I was permitted to view the lunar New Year celebrations from the 30th January to the 1st February this year, and, of these occasions, on the evening of the 1st February, Akifusa was behind His Highness and I was on the right of his seat (north of the screen around his dais).[52] There was no one in close attendance on him except the two of us. This was so that if discussion of those ceremonies should arise, His Highness could ask me about them.

When I came in obedience to a summons on the 29th July [1709], I presented a document. This said:

"In the time of the former Shōgun, people spoke only of the

empire at peace in congratulatory terms, and to refer, in the slightest way, to war was considered taboo. During the earthquake
of 1703, the military storehouse collapsed and all the weapons
were destroyed, but there has been no intimation that these have
been replaced. When the contents of the Shōgun's storehouses are
aired in the summer, the Shōgun should, after inspecting them,
give instructions to that effect."

I do not know whether His Highness privately made inquiries
about the matter, but my suggestions were not carried out this
summer. It was said that, as it was most important for the national polity that gossip concerning the neglect of the empire's
military preparations should not be bandied about among the
common people, His Highness should issue decrees about the
matter on some fitting occasion. And first of all, in anticipation
of his moving into his new residence, he gave orders concerning
the banners.[53] After that, these matters were dealt with in decrees
touching the forthcoming visit of the Korean Embassy.[54]

When His Highness was about to visit the Tōshōgū at Nikkō
on the one hundredth anniversary of the death of the Divine
Ancestor, it was reported that he would issue these decrees, but
he died soon after, before he could attend to the matter.[55] It
is one thing which must be regretted.

Since the demolition of the Shōgun's ship, the *Atake-Maru*,
at the beginning of the rule of the former Shōgun, the ships
here in Edo had fallen to pieces as the years went by, and
those at Ōsaka were in like condition.[56] It was formerly the
custom for the Shōgun's ships at Ōsaka to escort the Nagasaki Bugyō on their way here and back, but from the time
of the former Shōgun, the duty of escorting them was imposed
on the *daimyō* of the Western Provinces, so that the Ōsaka
sailors had no practical training in navigation.[57] After
returning from my tour of Kyōto and Ōsaka as Shōgunal
Envoy, I made proposals about these matters, so that the
ships here and at Ōsaka were repaired in preparation for the
Korean Embassy.

Also, orders were given to make ready a tiger-skin spear
for the ceremonial escort at the time of the Korean Embassy.
Under the previous lord, the use of birds' plumage and
animals' skins had been forbidden, so that now there is no

one who even knows how to make it. The officials discussed whether an imitation one should be made of yellow woolen cloth, but I said that this was a ceremonial spear which had been used for generations, and that it would not have been thrown away, so they sent for any tiger skins in the Shōgun's storehouse. Two or three skins were sent from the *onando* with a message that these were the only ones they had. There had been a fox-bewitching in the time of the former Shōgun, and these skins had been issued nightly for officials to wear, with orders for their return each morning. However they were now not fit to be used as half the fur had been pulled out.[58] A maker of artificial skins was therefore summoned to make one. From this sort of thing you can infer the rest.

The previous Shōgun [25] was born on the 8th August [1709]. He was given the name of Serata.[59] It had been necessary to change his name owing to a taboo. (Under this taboo, those born in the year of the ox were called by another family name.)

The Abbot of Chōrakuji at Serata in the Nitta District of Kōzuke Province, Kōkai Sōjō [56], had been an intimate friend of mine for some years.[60] In the storehouse of that temple, there were documents of many eras of the Kamakura and Ashikaga shogunates as well as one volume containing an old pedigree of the Nitta Family.[61] It differed from the popularly accepted pedigree, and as matters concerning my family name appeared in it, Kōkai had it copied for me upon my request.

Since I thought that on comparison with that account there were points that were not clear in the popularly accepted pedigree of the Tokugawa Family, when the question of His Highness's pedigree arose after his proclamation as Heir, I wrote out ten queries concerning the popularly accepted account and presented them.

Later, when the present Taikō [57] showed His Highness a letter Konoe Ryōzan [58] had sent to his son, Sammyaku-In Den [59], I found information in it about the pedigree of the Tokugawa Family which agreed with what I had said, causing His Highness to express his admiration.

Since the child was given the name of Serata at birth, the Sōjō [56] offered, through the Nikkō Jugō [45], to present the Nitta pedigree. On the 3rd September, the Jugō conveyed this message to His Highness and the Sōjō presented it (on the 5th September).

The one-volume Nitta Pedigree in my house is the traced copy the Sōjō had had made by a man called Saitō who served in the Sōjō's temple. Also, when His Highness asked me to copy out the letter purporting to have been from Ryōzan, which was written on small-size, thick, white paper, cut in two and joined together, and which he had had the Taikō show His Highness, I asked if I might also make one copy, and he said: "Do as you wish," so I copied it.

Prior to this, when I came in response to a summons on the 24th July [1709], I was informed that the Midaidokoro [60] had been promoted to the Lower Third Rank on the 18th previous, and on the 25th congratulatory visits had been made.

On the 5th August, Yamato-no-Kami Shigeyuki [61] conveyed a message summoning me the next day, but being ill, I did not go. When I attended on the 11th August, His Highness conferred on me a new grant, bestowing 500 *koku* of territory in the two districts of Saitama (Yagiū village) and Hiki (Naranashi and Otsuhata villages) in Musashi Province.[62] In view of His Highness's moving into the Main Palace on the 1st December, he gave orders that I should be given the use of a room at the Naka-no-Kuchi entrance, and that I should enter and leave by the Hasuike Gate.[63] (On the 3rd of the same month, the *kobushin bugyō*, Takeda Tamba-no-Kami, handed the room over to me.

On the 9th of the month, I received orders to question the Roman about his reasons for coming.[64] As a detailed account of this affair is given in other documents, I have not dealt with it here.[65] On the 8th May of this year, I had received orders about Nagasaki harbor.[66] This matter too I have dealt with in a separate document.[67] Since it is also dealt with below, I shall not discuss it here. And so the year drew to a close.

I have already described the ceremonies which took place from the 30th January to the 1st February 1710. On the 9th, I was shown the armor which was displayed on this day.[68] After that, I was also invited to the Verse-Capping Party.[69]

On the 13th, I heard that orders had been given on this day for the construction of the Nishi-Kuruwa Gate (now called

the Shibaguchi Gate). This was also because when I was summoned on the 29th July the previous year [1709], I had been told
that if there was anything I wished to say touching the visit
of the Korean Embassy, I should write it out and present it. On
the 11th November, I had presented a volume containing proposals about this affair. In it, there was one section dealing with
the fact that the Nishi-Kuruwa as yet had no castle gate. As a
result, when His Highness mentioned the matter that day, he also
told me about the gate.

On the 20th of this month [February 1710], I again presented
supplementary proposals concerning the Korean Embassy.[70]
On the 28th February, I presented another two volumes of
proposals concerning the reception of the Korean Embassy.[71]
As all these matters are dealt with in another document, I have
not dealt with them here, except for one or two special points.

As it was at first reported that Hayashi Daigaku-no-Kami
[21] said that there was a precedent for the reception of the
Korean Embassy to be entrusted to his House, His Highness
questioned him about it and he presented two volumes.
When His Highness questioned him further about certain
points which were not clear to him, his replies were unsatisfactory. Therefore the Shōgun turned to me and directed
that I be invited to make any recommendations I wished.

On the 13th May [1710], the New Regulations were promulgated.[72] As I have recorded earlier, after the death of the Sho-
gun the previous year, His Highness consulted with me on the 28th
February about the Genna Regulations.[73] Later, as everyone
proposed that the regulations should be promulgated in accordance with established precedent, Sagami-no-Kami Masanao
[62] placed that resolution before His Highness. Furthermore,
since it was the custom of the preceding rule, Daigaku-no-Kami
Nobuatsu was charged with this matter.

On the 17th March of this year, I was asked to present a draft,
and on the 23rd of the month I was questioned about it. In obedience to another order, I presented a Commentary on the New
Regulations on the 25th.[74] On the 13th May, the New Regulations
which I had drafted were promulgated, presents were made to
Masanao and Nobuatsu, and my Commentary on the New Regu-

[113]

lations was given to Daigaku-no-Kami with instructions that if anyone found the New Regulations difficult to understand, he should copy it out and give it to him.

When the Genna Regulations were promulgated, a draft was written by Den Chōrō [63] of Konji-In. Those regulations were modeled on the *Shikimoku* of the Jōei and Kemmu eras.[75] Those were postwar days, people were learning nothing but military matters, and there were not many who could read and write. Nevertheless, the Genna Regulations were composed in Chinese. The reason for this was that from this time on an attempt was made to administer the government on literary principles, but the regulations issued in succeeding ages were all written in *kana*, and this is one sign of the gradual decline of learning in Japan.[76]

His Highness told me, however, that if the New Regulations followed the style of the Genna Regulations, people would be dissatisfied. The New Regulations should use Chinese characters, as in the Genna Regulations, but *kana* should be used to write particles and verbal terminations. Later on, when people had learned Chinese characters, the *kana* could be done away with, and they would still understand how to construe the text. I was ordered to write the draft in the above style.

His Highness showed this to Masanao, but he replied that if it were written thus, it could not be put forward at this time. His Highness said if it were accompanied by a commentary, it could be done, hence he now asked me to draft one, and so I drafted the commentary also.

When these New Regulations were set forth, a certain Yoshida, a physician who was in the employ of Masanao, came to me and asked: "What is the meaning of the word 'Jōsai' which appears in the New Regulations, and in which authoritative sources does it appear?"[77] I laughed at this and replied: "The characters in the New Regulations do not constitute an attempt to imitate the style of the codes and regulations of Japan.[78] They simply come out of the *Shikimoku* and *Teikin Ōrai*.[79] As to the word 'Jōsai,' I have known it ever since I was a boy. It appears in a letter of the seventh month in the *Teikin Ōrai*."

When I asked why he inquired about this, he said: "I
have heard that Daigaku-no-Kami told my lord that he
could not understand the use of 'Jōsai' in the New Regulations because the character 'Jō' referred to the emperor,
and that he did not understand anything else in the New
Regulations either." I said: "The character 'Jō' is of course
used for the emperor. However, we use the expression
'Uesama' for the military ruler, and this has been so ever
since the Kamakura period.[80] It is said that the use of the
expression 'Kubō' for the *shōgun* began with the lord Rokuon-
In in Kyōto.[81] And we find the expressions 'Jōchō,' 'Jōbun,'
etc., also in the statements of your own lord and others,"
and I laughed at him.[82]

When I came in response to a summons on the morning of the
16th May, it was because of the ceremony for the Konoe Daishōkoku's [57] audience on this day. I was summoned on the 23rd
of the month, and the lord said: "I have spoken to the Daishōkoku,
and you must meet him." (I met him for the first time on the 31st
May.)

On this day, I heard that Ogiwara Ōmi-no-Kami [51] had
incurred His Highness's displeasure. This was because of the
following incident: There was a precedent whereby the biannual
salaries paid to shogunal retainers could be paid in money
according to the current price of rice.[83] When a table of the
amounts to be paid in cash was sent to His Highness from the
Kanjōsho, the secretaries were ordered to make a record of it,
and it was posted in the entrance used by those going on duty.
On this occasion, when His Highness inquired about the price
of high-, medium-, and low-grade rice selling in the market, he
was informed that high-grade rice was 37 *ryō* per 100 bales (a bale
is 3 *to* 5 *shō*), and so His Highness ordered that the retainers be
given 38 *ryō* each, but Ōmi-no-Kami wrote down 28. When His
Highness heard of this, he was annoyed, but when he questioned
him about it, Ōmi-no-Kami apologized, stating that he had made
a clerical error.

He made an error in writing what was called the Salary
Rice Bulletin, which was pasted on the wall of the Naka-no-
Kuchi.[84] Before this, money paid in salaries was usually not
at a rate equal to the price of rice in the market. Since His

[115]

Highness was aware of this, he said that his orders at this time were for the convenience of the low-salaried retainers, so that with the money they received at the price of high-grade rice, they could buy medium- and low-grade rice for food.

Earlier, on the 16th April, His Highness had Ichi-no-Kami Masanao [30] show me a section of a tree which someone from Kyōto had presented and which was probably more than a *shaku* in circumference. On the face of that section, the characters "Tenka" were naturally formed.[85] When I asked: "Was this not a persimmon tree?" Masanao was surprised and said: "How did you know it was a persimmon tree? A persimmon tree growing in a temple was cut down and when it was split for firewood, these characters were discovered. Since it is an auspicious omen, someone from Kyōto presented it." I said: "The appearance of such things in persimmon trees is recorded in ancient documents. I think that when the tree was young, the characters were written on it with something like bamboo, and as the tree grew they were absorbed into the wood, and this has come about. It is not worth regarding such a thing as an auspicious omen."

On the 5th June, His Highness had Masanao bring out a piece of thin mulberry-paper on which the four characters "Tenka Taihei" were inscribed, saying that I must look at it.[86] I looked at it carefully and said: "I have been told that many examples exist in China of characters said to have been written by supernatural beings, but the paper on which these characters are written is of Japanese manufacture, so this writing does not appear to be of Chinese origin.[87] However, it does not look like the writing of an ordinary human being." Masanao asked: "If so, have you ever seen anything written by a supernatural being?" I replied that I never had. He asked: "Well then, why do you think this does not look like the writing of a human being?" I said: "I thought this since it bears the same relation to human writing as the clouds in the sky to material objects when they accidentally appear to resemble their shapes." He said: "Tell me, then, what manner of being wrote it?" I replied: "Perhaps it is the writing of a god or demon such as was heard of in ancient times. However, since people say neither gods nor demons exist in a peaceful era, I do not consider it an auspicious omen."

Masanao returned to His Highness and came back a short time later, saying: "His Highness was amazed by what you said and remarked: 'It could indeed be described as written by a god. This was written by a maiden possessed by a fox and presented to me.'"[88] (A fox recently possessed the daughter of someone connected with a servant employed in the quarters of the Midai-dokoro [60], and it seems that this writing was the result.)

I heard about it later, but it may have been about this time that it was said that grass had grown on a stone near the pond in the palace gardens. They did not inform me of that. (It happened in the Fukiage Garden.)[89]

There is another incident which comes to mind because of this. It was when His Highness was Heir. On the 24th April 1706, when I had completed my lecture on the chronicle of Chuang Tsung of the Later T'ang Dynasty in the *T'ung Chien Kang Mu*, I presented a paper through Akifusa in which I stated that the popular operas of China were the forerunners of the *sarugaku* of today.[90] As His Highness was particularly fond of *sarugaku*, I said that if he went no further than he had up till now, it would be all right, but he must regard what happened to Chuang Tsung of Later T'ang as an example for a ruler.[91]

When later he asked how the present *sarugaku* resembled the popular Chinese operas, I presented a document about them on the 28th of the same month. Later, he again asked if there was anything written about Chinese drama. I said that these dramas had been brought to Japan, and in accordance with His Highness's orders, I presented 56 volumes of the *Yüan Ch'ü Hsüan* through Masanao on the 12th October.[92]

Although I heard that he witnessed *sarugaku* after becoming Shōgun, he never invited me.

He was fond of *sarugaku*. However, after I had spoken thus, a certain person said that in former times, both the Divine Ancestor [8] and Tokubyō [46] had performed *sarugaku*, and that even if His Highness himself took part in performances, there would be nothing wrong with it. He showed His Highness the record, in the account of the Divine Ancestor written by Daigaku-no-Kami Nobuatsu [21] and others, that the Divine Ancestor had performed in the time of the Taikō Hideyoshi [13], and that Tokubyō had also performed before the Divine Ancestor.[93]

When Masanao showed me this, claiming that it was his own idea to bring this book and get me to look at these statements, I said: "I do not need to look at such a claim. In ancient times, Confucius in writing the *Ch'un Ch'iu* drew his examples from the history of the state of Lu.[94] What do you think of that?[95] Also, what the ruler does is transmitted as ancient tradition, and so those who record history should have understanding. What honor will it bring to Japan if we transmit this incident to future generations? As the Taikō humiliated the Divine Ancestor to boast before the world, we do not need to talk about such insults.[96] If Tokubyō's performing was like the performances given today before His Highness, we could probably excuse them by comparing them to the action of Lao Lai in donning a brightly colored costume.[97] Is there any record of performances being given in the time of the Divine Ancestor and Tokubyō continuously as they are now, or after the establishment of the Tokugawa shogunate? You should carefully seek out the answers to these questions."

Perhaps it was on account of these things that after His Highness became Shōgun he never obliged me to witness these performances.

The following incident also happened when His Highness was the Heir. His Highness said that in the time of the former Shōgun, orders had been given to Daigaku-no-Kami Nobuatsu to select materials and write an account of the Divine Ancestor, so I lent it to His Highness and he read it.

On one occasion, when I had finished my lecture, His Highness said to me through Akifusa, in reference to a place in Nobuatsu's history where it was recorded that a personal attendant had drawn his sword, stabbed the father of the Divine Ancestor, and run off, and people had cut him down: "This incident is dealt with in the biography of Uemura in the *Hankampu* which you composed some time ago.[98] There it is stated that Hirotada was pierced through the thigh. In Nobuatsu's history, this fact was not mentioned. If Hirotada was stabbed but was not so deeply wounded as to be killed on the spot, and if he did not himself pursue the assailant, future generations would form a poor opinion of him. It ought to be recorded that the sword pierced him in the thigh. This account was written by a historian who did not understand the code of the warrior.[99] What do you think of what I have said?"

Later, when His Highness first became Shōgun, he said he was considering having an account of the Divine Ancestor written, and I heard that he was going to give orders about it in the year he died. Shortly afterward, he died owing to illness before he could attend to this matter.

As it is apropos, I attach the following here: After His Highness succeeded, Daigaku-no-Kami Nobuatsu asked to be permitted to resign. When His Highness spoke of this to me, I said: "He has been the instructor of the former Shōgun and is therefore respected by the people. He is not yet seventy years old, and if his request is granted, people will probably misunderstand you." His Highness replied: "But when the province of Kai was granted by the former Shōgun to Mino-no-Kami [31], I understand that Daigaku-no-Kami drafted the deed of enfeoffment. I asked Daigaku-no-Kami: 'How was it that you came to do such an unprecedented thing?' To this he replied: 'At that time, Mino-no-Kami could get whatever he wanted.' By such acts as these we can judge Daigaku-no-Kami's cunning. Such a man is completely unfit to teach and lead people. However, I agree that there is no doubt that the people today would think as you say." His Highness did not permit him to retire.

On the 16th July [1710], after the lecture, His Highness told me through Akifusa about what had happened in the days of the former Shōgun [15] in connection with the dispute between the two abbots of Kōfukuji in Nara (Ichijō-In Den [64] and Daijō-In Den [65]). A decision had been given and was about to be ratified when the Shōgun died. Therefore envoys from Ichijō-In, with the heads of the branch temples of Kezō-In and Hosshin-In, were sent to speak about it.[100]

But Konoe Shōkoku [57] said he knew all about the circumstances and related them as follows: "The lay-priest Tōgu-In, the former Kampaku Sakihisa (that is, Ryōzan) [58], had two sons, the elder of whom was known as Daiō-In Takataka [66], Abbot of Ichijō-In. The second was the former Kampaku, Sammyaku-In Nobutada [59]. Tōgu-In was on very friendly terms with the Divine Ancestor [8] for some years, so that when the latter went to Kyōto from his mansion at Fushimi, he would go and stay at the Konoe mansion, and the two of them would set their pillows side by side and lie there and chat with each other.[101] Takataka was then known as Tarō Gimi and Nobutada as Jirō Gimi. When Tarō Gimi was eleven years old, the Divine Ancestor said: "I am always coming here, but so far I have not given you anything much, so tell me what you would like and whatever it may be, you shall have it." "I do not want anything in particular," was the answer, "but since Kōfukuji is my ancestral temple, I should like to have the management of it, so that I could restore it to its former state." The Divine Ancestor thought this quite an extraordinary request, and after Takataka entered Ichijō-In, he was eventually made its administrator, and restored it and revived its prosperity.

"When the Divine Ancestor became ruler of the empire, he did not forget his former promise. He presented Takataka with the donations for the encouragement of priestly learning and issued a decree with his personal seal which stated that the descendants of Takataka, even though they did not hold the office of administrator, should in the future control the scholar monks at Ichijō-In. In the days of Gen'yū-In Kubō [43], the former Imperial Abbot Mibota-In Den [67] (Shingyō Hōshinnō) was again granted a shogunal decree, and again in the days of the former Shōgun [15], an imperial decree was issued, stating that the Abbot of Ichijō-In would be appointed administrator on the sixth day of the Yuima Service, and that after the lecture at the Yuima Service was concluded, the Abbot of Daijō-In would be appointed to office.[102] But the present Abbot of Daijō-In [65] was the brother of the Midaidokoro [49], so that as a result of confidential representations, the arrangement was altered, and eventually it was decided that the grants donated by the Divine Ancestor for the encouragement of learning at Ichijō-In, which Daijō-In coveted, should be confirmed to it as requested.[103] However, before the decree could be ratified, His Highness, the present

Shōgun [3], succeeded. There was a feeling that the decree of the Divine Ancestor should not be set at nought, but should be continued as it had been previously."

Representations to this effect were made in detail from the Bugyōsho with the request that a decision should be given.[104] Therefore His Highness ordered that a judgment about it should be submitted to him, so in accordance with this order, I received a copy of the shogunate's decision on the subject with the documents submitted from the Bugyōsho. I went home and examined them, and on the morning of the following day (the 17th), I submitted a memorandum. The gist of this was: "Leaving aside for the moment the question of rights in the case between the two temples of Nara, the allegations of the Shōkoku [57] are quite unreliable. As to the Divine Ancestor going from his Fushimi mansion to the Konoe mansion in the capital, and making a promise to Tarō Gimi when he was eleven years old that when he entered the monastery he should receive the donations for the scholar monks' support, the Divine Ancestor resided at the Fushimi mansion while Japan was enjoying peace, that is after he had visited Kyōto in November 1586.[105] According to the *Kugyō Bunin*, the former Kampaku, Sammyaku-In, died at the age of fifty on the 25th December 1614, so that he would have been twenty-two in 1586.[106] Daiō-In was his elder brother, it is said, so it is possible to estimate his age, and he could not have been eleven years old when the Divine Ancestor was at his Fushimi mansion.

"If the Divine Ancestor visited Kyōto when Daiō-In was eleven, since the latter must have been a year or two older than his younger brother, he would have been eleven in about 1573 or 1574, but there is no record of the Divine Ancestor being in Kyōto at that time. Furthermore, at that time, he was fighting the Takeda of Kai for Tōtōmi Province and continuously engaged in battle.[107] How then could he abandon his campaign in his own province and make his way through many others to the capital?[108] He certainly did nothing of the sort. So, on careful consideration, it is, as can be seen, difficult to agree with what the Shōkoku says.

"Also, on examining the material sent from the Bugyōsho, the

[121]

decision of the former Shōgun appears to have been entirely reasonable. If His Highness decides according to this evidence, not only will the suit between the two temples of Nara go on unendingly, but a continuous quarrel will certainly arise, like that between the temples of Hieizan and Miidera.[109]

"And according to what the Shōkoku says, the former decision was influenced by the Takatsukasa Family. So if the former decision is again altered, I should not wonder if the people say that this is due to the influence of the Konoe Family.[110] If His Highness permits, I will argue the matter to the utmost of my capacity. Therefore, I shall not return the material sent to me yesterday, but, with His Highness's permission, I will submit the document as he has ordered."

After His Highness had read it, I was summoned on the 20th, and when I went, I was told that His Highness had considered my proposals and that I was to submit a formal recommendation. I was further told: "In the days of the former Shōgun, the Nikkō Jugō [45] had requested that the common people be forbidden to trespass near Hieizan. The villagers of Yase complained that they had lost their livelihood.[111] The case has not been settled yet and is still pending. These people have unfortunately been kept waiting a long time and consequently have suffered great distress. You must submit a recommendation about this matter."

On the morning of the 21st, I first heard that I would be consulted about the Yase affair. Then I was summoned and allowed to see the documents which had been presented by the Bugyōsho. On the morning of the 22nd [July 1710], I presented my recommendations.

When I went on the 24th, His Highness said that the complaint of the Yase villagers was not without reason, but the prohibition of trespassing at Hieizan could not be abolished now. Instead of the ground at Hieizan, to which the villagers were now forbidden access, it would be better to give them other land and rice fields so that they could have the wherewithal to make their living. I was told to draw up a judgment to that effect and presented it on the 25th. His Highness also gave further orders on the matter, and on the 30th July, he handed down a decision which he himself had written out.

Touching this matter, the Nikkō Jugō had told the for-

mer Shōgun that the prohibition of trespassing at Hieizan
had been established long ago, but subsequently the villagers of Yase had trespassed on the hills to cut timber,
and as a result the holy confines of this national tutelary fane
were polluted by women, oxen, and horses, which was a
highly unfitting state of affairs.[112] Therefore, in January
1709, the Kyōto Bugyō went there and erected a palisade. At
this, the villagers presented many ancient documents as
proof, alleging that they had lost their rights to cut firewood
and make a living by it, and continued to urge that the prohibition be abolished. And this they have continued to do
right up to the present time. Therefore, the private land and
temple land in their village were exchanged for other land
elsewhere, that land was given to the Yase people, and their
taxes and all their forced labor were remitted.

I first presented this decision written out in Chinese characters, but His Highness revised it himself and wrote it
out in characters mixed with *kana*. It was a very gracious act
to write out the document by his own hand.

In the winter of this year, I went to Kyōto as Shogunal
Envoy, and on my way back from visiting Hieizan, I passed
through Yase and went into a house situated by the road-
side, while the servants took their mid-day meal, and sat
down on the verandah. The mistress was an old woman whose
son had gone to Kyōto. When I inquired about the circumstances they had complained of, she said that after the palisade had been constructed, the people here had lost their
means of livelihood, but now, owing to His Highness's kindness, they felt as though restored to life and prayed for the
long continuance of his House. But all the same, since they
had not yet learned how to cultivate gardens and rice fields,
they wondered how they would fare, but no doubt they
would be all right in the end.

On the 4th August [1710] the two abbots of Kōfukuji in Nara
presented two volumes in support of their law suit. In connection
with it, the chiefs of the Ichijō-In party were called in to state
their case (from Kezō-In and Hosshin-In). Similarly, those of the
Daijō-In party were also summoned and interrogated (from
Shōrin-In and Fumon-In). Then the Ichijō-In representatives

replied but got the worst of the argument. Afterward, His Highness ordered that both parties were to be reconciled so that all might be well in the monastery, whereupon the two chiefs of Ichijō-In became ill and died, and the abbots' envoys (Naishihara Gyōbu and Kitabō Suruga) requested permission to take their leave and return home. On the 15th November, I presented a draft of His Highness's orders to them and the two messengers received these and retired to their respective temples. As this affair is recorded in detail elsewhere, I have only given a summary of it here.

This law suit began in October 1600, when the Divine Ancestor [8] entered Ōsaka Castle after the Battle of Sekigahara, as there was a dispute among the monks of Kōfukuji concerning its domains. On the 21st December, the Divine Ancestor gave a decision and a sealed order to the Five Controllers, and it was also given to the administrator of that time, the Abbot of Ichijō-In, in the form of a written document.[113] This was when Daiō-In Takataka Sōjō was the administrator.

Later, in the days of Gen'yū-In [43], the Abbot of Ichijō-In, Mibota-In Den, was Shingyō Hōshinnō [67], son of the Retired Emperor Go-Mizu-no-O. When he was the Abbot of Ichijō-In, he made the following request: "The special sealed document, granted in former days by the Divine Ancestor to the Abbot of Ichijō-In, had been kept in the library of the Retired Emperor because it was a great treasure of the abbot. After some time, the Palace burned down and this document was destroyed with it. Since it was a document granted by the Divine Ancestor, we should like to obtain a document from the present Shōgun [43] to replace it," and he brought a copy of the previous one, issued to Daiō-In in December 1600. And on the 9th December 1665, this was duly sealed as they desired.

At the beginning of the rule of the preceding Shōgun [15], the Imperial Court alleged that since Kōfukuji was the tutelary temple of the Fujiwara House and thus of the maternal relatives of many generations of emperors, its affairs should be decided by them, and so it was settled. Then in the

Jōkyō era, on the sixth day of the Yuima Service, an imperial decree was issued promising that the Abbot of Ichijō-In would be appointed administrator and that after the lecture was concluded the Abbot of Daijō-In would be appointed to office.

After this, the members of Kōfukuji were permitted to wear yellow robes, for the first time.[114] The Shōgun [15] directed that as the donations for the scholar monks' support had been granted by the Divine Ancestor to Ichijō-In, even if the Abbot of Ichijō-In was not the administrator, he should have the income and should also have the control of the monks. Therefore, Daijō-In naturally placed a complaint, and their envoy, one Matsui Hyōbu, a monk official of great ability, proceeded to state his case.[115] Mibota-In was greatly perturbed by this and died. Matsui pressed for a decision, but the years went by and at last he became ill and also died.

Now, since they say that the special sealed document, alleged by Ichijō-In to have been granted by the Divine Ancestor, had been destroyed in a fire, and only a copy of it was produced, there must be some doubt about it. This copy had no official seal, only a handwritten signature. Moreover, though the day of the appointment of the administrator was defined in the suit, since from olden times, both abbots have been appointed to this office alternately, there was no distinction between them. Also, it does not seem that the donations for the support of the monks were given to Ichijō-In in perpetuity by the Divine Ancestor's order, nor does it appear that, even if the Abbot of Ichijō-In was not the administrator at the time, he should have these and the control of the scholar monks. It was only because Daiō-In was the administrator at that time that Ichijō-In received these.

For instance, when an order is made for Miidera, it is given to the present administrator Shōkō-In Den. And supposing this had the effect that Ichijō-In would suggest, it would mean that the control of Miidera would go to the head of Shōgo-In whether he was the administrator or not. And if the order were made as Ichijō-In wished it, the heads of Emman-In and Jissō-In would begin law suits about Miidera against Shōgo-In Den, if he made such a claim.[116]

When His Highness interrogated them in accordance with the arguments I put forward about all these matters, the chiefs of Ichijō-In were entirely refuted and gave way. They gradually altered their story and confessed that what they had first declared to be the sealed order of the Divine Ancestor was merely a letter from the Divine Ancestor. Also, their assertions did not seem to be in agreement with what is said in ancient documents. All this made them feel very upset, no doubt, and they both immediately became ill and died, one after the other, and the envoys returned home before the judgment was pronounced.

In the winter of the following year [1711], I went to Nara, and the *bugyō* there, Miyoshi Bizen-no-Kami [68], told me that the decision was naturally very pleasing to Daijō-In, and even the monks of Ichijō-In approved of it. I stayed there a while to quietly enjoy the views of the famous historic sites, when an old monk of Ichijō-In called Jōshin-In brought a message from Konoe Sesshō [69].[117] He suggested that I should have an interview with Taki-no-Miya [64], but I thought that if I had an interview with Taki-no-Miya it would not be correct if I did not also see Daijō-In Den. I thought that I would be criticized if I were to see these men, and so saying that I must get back quickly and could not see him this time, I stayed there only three days and then went back to Kyōto.

I later heard that Mibota-In [67] had been very friendly with Konoe [57] and his son [69], and that the old monk was related to Jijū-Den, the mother of Konoe Taikō's [57] daughter [60], and he too had been friendly with Mibota-In. Since he had such influence, Jōshin-In spoke to the Taikō about it, and before Konoe left Kyōto, he sent the envoys of Ichijō-In and the chiefs of the branch temple to Edo, thinking that they would in this way win their case. But the affair turned out differently. I was able to see the letter that they brought to the Taikō, so the latter thought it was I who had encompassed this decision and therefore spoke badly of me to His Highness on various occasions, but His Highness passed it off by pretending to know nothing about it.

When I presented myself at the palace on the 19th August [1710], His Highness asked me about the correct procedures to be followed for his visit to Taiseiden on the 28th.[118] When I was summoned on the 23rd, he gave orders for me to write out the procedure for his visit to Taiseiden in detail and present it, and on the following day, the 24th, I wrote it out. Previously, he had also given me other orders, and on the 25th August I instructed him in the traditional national ceremonies of worship. On the 28th of the same month His Highness's visit to the temple took place.

As regards this, in the first place Daigaku-no-Kami Nobuatsu [21] had written out the procedure for the Shōgun's [15] visit during the previous regime. It appeared that he formulated the ceremony by adopting only the procedures of that time, and these did not accord with ancient etiquette. So, His Highness directed that it would be most unfitting if, when he visited Taiseiden, the ceremony were not in accordance with ancient custom, and that the procedure must be modeled on the ceremony of worshiping Confucius as observed in China.[119]

Private discussions were held as to whether or not His Highness should use court costume. His Highness said: "The present flat court cap is styled after the headdress of later ages, but the pointed court cap of Japan is styled after the court cap which was introduced from the Chou Dynasty. Also, the ceremonial robes of the ancient kings were all long robes with loose square collars.[120] The circular collar appeared in the dress of the northern Chinese barbarians." Therefore His Highness wore a pointed court cap and a loose-collared robe.

Also, as regards the *chêntungpai*, one of the ancient forms of the "nine obeisances," giving as his reason that it was stated in the writings of Chêng Ta-fu that that custom had survived in Japan, he ordered that I must instruct him in the procedure, which I did.[121]

On the 16th September, there were orders that I was to be sent to Kyōto as Shogunal Envoy. First I was given 100 gold *ryō* for my traveling expenses. As regards my itinerary, I received private instructions that I should leave Edo after the arrival of the Luchu Envoys in November and return in January.[122] (I was privately informed that this was in order that I might witness the Emperor's [70] coronation ceremony on the 30th December.)

This day, also, I was given instructions through Nakatsukasa-no-Shō Akihira that I might enter and leave the Shōgun's Palace at night.[123]

When His Highness discussed this matter with the Rōjū, they said that there was no precedent for this, and that it was not permissible. Whereupon His Highness said: "It is not necessary to follow the precedents applicable to other men."

Accordingly, His Highness gave orders that I could enter or leave without restriction, day or night, by any of eight places, the Ōte, the Uchisakurada, the Hyakuningumi, the Naka, the Gogenkan, the Hasuike, the Sakashita, or the Momijiyamashita gates.

On the 8th October, His Highness gave orders about the disciplining of Zenkōji in Shinano Province.[124] I had presented a draft of a decision discussing that matter.

On the 4th November, His Highness attended the Buddhist memorial services for Seiyō-In Den, and I accompanied him.[125] (My attendance at this ceremony was like my accompanying him previously to Kan'eiji at Ueno).[126]

On the 18th of the same month, he proceeded to the Shiroshoin, and gave orders about sending me as Shogunal Envoy to Kyōto.[127] Afterward, Kaga-no-Kami Tadatomo [53] conveyed His Highness's orders to me and gave me five pieces of gold. I was also summoned to His Highness's official residence a second time, and was given seasonal clothes and a loose traveling coat (two sets of seasonal clothes and one coat). This day I was given a shogunal seal for requisitioning bearers and horses along the route.[128] (Before this, orders had been given about the number of servants and packhorses to accompany me.) On the 25th November, I was given various kinds of silks and pongee made in Hachijō Island for my wife and children (three rolls of dyed outer material for short-sleeved *kimono*, and two rolls of striped weave). On the 1st December, I paid a formal visit to His Highness before setting out for Kyōto on the following day. After I was summoned into his presence and he had given me my instructions, he himself gave me presents (a medicine case and a money bag). And so I set out on the 2nd December.

I had intended to set out after the Luchu ambassadors arrived in Edo, but owing to contrary winds, they failed to arrive by the expected time. I left without waiting for them and entered Kyōto on the 14th of the same month. On this day, the Luchu ambassadors reached the post-station of Ōtsu.[129] On the 30th December, I was privileged to witness the coronation ceremony.

On the 3rd January 1711, His Highness told Akifusa [24] that as a result of a request from the Sesshō [69], I was to remain for the Emperor's coming-of-age ceremony in February, and as my stay had been extended, he gave me 100 gold ryō, saying they were for my expenses.[130]

I was immediately informed of this in Kyōto, and I went to Ōsaka on the 13th January. From there, on the 20th January, I went to Nara, intending to return to Kyōto on the 23rd of the month, but when I arrived at Uji, I spent the night there and returned to Kyōto on the following day, the 24th.[131]

As I have recorded all these events in another document I shall not deal with them in detail here.

On the 17th February 1711, I witnessed the Emperor's coming-of-age ceremony.[132] On this day, I had the good fortune to observe the imperial countenance at close hand.

Later, I heard that the Luchu ambassadors, having completed their mission and being homeward bound, were stopping at Fushimi. On the 24th of the same month, I went to the residence of Satsuma-no-Kami [71], which was in Fushimi, and was able to meet the two princes Misato and Toyomigusuku. This was because His Highness had previously given instructions that I should do so.

On the 9th March, I left Kyōto and returned to Edo on the 21st of the same month. On the 2nd April, when His Highness proceeded to the Shiroshoin, I was summoned, and His Highness thanked me for my services. On the 18th April, orders were given that I could enter and leave during the day by the Tayasu, Shimizu, or Takehashi gates.[133] On the 10th May, I accompanied His Highness when he inspected the shogunal ships which had just been repaired.[134] On the 26th July, I was promoted to *hoi samurai*.[135]

On the 7th August, I tendered details of the reception, entertainment, and farewell ceremonies for the Korean Envoys, as I had been bidden to do after my return to Edo. On the 7th October, I was privately ordered to go and meet the envoys on their way and was presented with 100 gold *ryō* as traveling expenses. On the 3rd November, I was told by Sagami-no-Kami Masanao [62] that His Highness's orders were that I was to go and meet the Korean Envoys when they arrived at Kawasaki post-station. I was presented with two pieces of gold and also with the shogunal seal for requisitioning bearers and horses during the journey.

On the 20th November, I was promoted to court rank and appointed Chikugo-no-Kami.[136] I was summoned to audience with His Highness, and he presented me with clothes for the season (three sets). As I retired, Akifusa [24] was bidden to give me a sword (corded and gold-mounted) by Suetsugu and a court costume suitable for those of the fifth rank, and all the accessories. I understand that these had all been ordered to be prepared the day before so that my rank might be raised today.

I set out on the 26th November and arrived at the Kawasaki post-station about noon. That same evening, I met the Korean Envoys, and on the 27th at dawn we left Kawasaki and arrived at the lodgings in Asakusa at about three o'clock.[137] After giving the officials the necessary instructions, I reported to His Highness that I had returned. On the 28th, I attended at the palace to offer thanks for my promotion.

On the 10th December, the envoys' audience with His Highness took place. On the 12th there was a banquet for them. On the 13th, there was an exhibition of Korean horsemanship. On the 20th, the envoys took leave of His Highness, and on the 28th December they departed westward.[138]

On the 31st of the same month, as a reward for my efforts in connection with the visit of the envoys, I was granted an additional 500 *koku* of land in the Kamakura District of Sagami Province (the villages of Ueki and Shiromeguri) and in Kōza District of the same province (Kami-Ōtani village).

I returned the estates I had previously been given in the

Hiki District of Musashi Province and requested that I might receive another instead at Yagiū village in Saitama District. This was permitted, and I therefore obtained the whole village of Yagiū as my estate. So my whole fief in the provinces of Musashi and Sagami amounted to 1,000 *koku*.

As I have recorded everything which happened at the time of the Korean Embassy in separate documents, I shall not deal with it in detail here.[139] However, as public criticism about me dates from this matter, I also set down an outline of the events here.

In the beginning, after the Taikō Hideyoshi [13] invaded Korea, the Divine Ancestor [8], at the outset of his rule, gave orders that friendly relations were to be established with neighboring countries, as during the Ashikaga shogunate long ago. But the prince and people of Korea professed deep hatred of Japan, and it was more than ten years before envoys were sent for the first time.[140] At that time, the foundations of the shogunate were being laid down, and so it was impossible to arrange ceremonies for receiving ambassadors.

This year the envoys arrived after the Ōgosho [8] had moved his seat to Sumpu in Suruga Province. He informed them that he had handed over the administrative affairs to his son in Edo, and that they must go there. So the envoys went to Edo and carried out their mission. When they passed by Sumpu on their return, they were sent for by the Ōgosho, but they had brought no presents, and as only a minimum of ceremony was observed, one can imagine how matters were carried out. These matters are dealt with in the *Sōgyōki* and other works.[141]

The Korean Embassy in the Tenna era appears to have followed the precedents of Kan'ei.[142] There is no evidence that reference was made to information handed down concerning ancient precedents when ambassadors from foreign countries visited Japan or when our ambassadors went to their countries. In the Tenna era, those in charge of the envoys' reception merely followed the customs of the time, and there were many things not suitable to the national polity.

It is said that ceremony arises within a hundred years.[143] It was therefore time to settle these matters, and accordingly, His High-

[131]

ness made inquiries about them, but the answers were not clear, so he turned to me and finally gave orders that I should make proposals concerning the ceremonies.[144]

Among these, the most difficult was the restoration of the *shōgun*'s title. The problem was as follows: From the commencement of friendly relations between the two countries, the Koreans had used the title of "Nippon Koku-Ō" in their letters. This was in accordance with the precedent dating from the Kamakura and Ashikaga periods whereby foreigners had addressed the Japanese emperor as "Nippon Tennō" and the military ruler as "Nippon Koku-Ō."[145] But after orders were given in the Kan'ei era that he should be addressed as "Nippon Koku Taikun," this became the custom in later times. (This was owing to some trouble between the *daimyō* of Tsushima Province and his retainers.)[146]

However, "Taikun" is an official title granted to a subject in Korea, and so to give orders that the *shōgun* should be addressed by this title is like receiving an official title from that country.[147] It also appears in Chinese books as another name for the emperor; since this is so, there would be confusion with the emperor in Japan.[148] Therefore, His Highness gave orders to Tsushima-no-Kami [72] that he should be addressed as "Nippon Koku-Ō" as originally.

When I informed Taira Naokata [73] (an elder in Tsushima Province called Hirata Naoemon), a retainer of Tsushima-no-Kami Taira Yoshikata [72], of this at the beginning of the affair, he said there was no difficulty. To think of the emperor as "Heaven" and call him "Nippon Tennō," and to think of the *shōgun* as "Controller of the Country" and call him "Nippon Koku-Ō," is as natural as the unchangeable positions of Heaven and Earth. To call both by the title "Nippon" was like bestowing the title "Chou" on the King of Chou and the Duke of Chou, prince and subject alike. But the rustic scholars who were in Tsushima Province did not know this and expressed various opinions, and I heard that the retainers refused to use the title "Koku-Ō."[149] When I again sent a letter to Naokata setting the matter forth, as Naokata had said in the first place, the Koreans brought documents with the title altered to "Nippon Koku-Ō," without any objections having been raised in Korea.[150]

Also in the Tenna era, in accordance with the precedents

of Kan'ei, tribute was presented to the Heir Apparent also.[151] However, as the Heir Apparent was still a child, Shōshō Masatoshi [11] acted as his representative. When it came time for the envoys' audience with him, they went home without paying their respects, pleading that on the day they received their official orders, they had been told they must pay their respects to the Heir Apparent, but nothing had been said about paying their respects to an administrator. At the present time also, the Heir Apparent was still a child. His Highness, deciding that it would be troublesome to have disputes about these matters, also, sent a message to Tsushima stating that it was not necessary for the envoys to pay their respects to the Heir Apparent as he had not yet left the nursery.

Also, recently, a custom had arisen of the Korean masters-of-ceremonies sending communications to our administrators. Although formerly under the Ashikaga shogunate, communications from the Korean government were still sent to the Tandai of Kyūshū, Korea probably no longer wished that custom to be followed, and Japan also did not require it.[152] His Highness informed Tsushima that this too should be discontinued.

Although a Korean official called the Togunegi-Fūsu, or some such, sent a communication making representations concerning these two matters to Tsushima-no-Kami, this also was carried out in accordance with His Highness's instructions.[153]

Also, recent custom was that at all places through which the envoys passed, they were entertained at morning and evening meals of three courses consisting of seven, five, and three dishes, respectively, and one at midday consisting of three courses of five, five, and three dishes respectively.[154] This is not done even when we entertain imperial envoys, and, in particular, it entails incalculable waste for the provinces that lie along their route. They were informed at Tsushima that henceforth, as was done for our envoys in Korea, except at four places along the road where feasts would be given, they would be given money instead.[155] To this their envoys had no objection, as they had always found the banquets tedious and the presentation of money was more convenient.

Also, according to recent custom, the envoys entered their lodgings riding in their palanquins. Even when our messengers visited their lodgings, there was no welcome or farewell ceremony.

These arrangements were not at all in conformity with ancient customs, and they also differed from the custom when our envoys went to Korea in former times. They were informed at Tsushima that henceforth, the envoys would alight from their palanquins before entering their lodgings, and when our messengers arrived at their lodgings, the ceremony of welcome and farewell at the foot of the steps would be the same as was formerly observed by our envoys when they went to Korea.

With regard to these two pronouncements, the envoys disputed the etiquette by referring to recent custom, and though they had already arrived at Ōsaka, they would not attend the banquet on this account, it was said, and all the people criticized it, but eventually this matter too proceeded as His Highness ordered.

Also, according to recent custom, on the day the envoys arrived here in Edo, the administrators, as the Shōgun's Envoys, went to the Korean Envoys' lodgings and thanked them for coming.[156] What are called administrators in Japan correspond to councilors in the Korean government, but when our envoys went to Korea, the custom of their councilors coming as envoys to our envoys' lodgings was not observed.[157] Why should our administrators give thanks to their ambassadors? Therefore, on this occasion, the *kōke* were employed as envoys. However, the reason the Korean Envoys said nothing about this was because, as none of the Japanese Envoys conveying thanks at Ōsaka, Kyōto, and at country places had been an administrator, now they could not object to it.

As soon as the Korean Envoys arrived in Edo, orders had been given to Tsushima-no-Kami to present them with a document containing six articles describing the amended procedures. In this it was said that, according to recent custom, when the Korean Envoys were received by the Shōgun, the letters from their king had previously been presented by one of the *changchangkwan*, but this was incorrect and now it was to be done by the Chief Envoy himself.[158]

Also, they had previously been given seats in the same place as the Lords of the Three Houses, but this too was not correct, and more suitable seats would be allotted to them.[159] Also, at the banquet, they had previously been placed with the Three Lords. This was not done even in the case of the envoy from the

[134]

Imperial Court. Nor was it in accord with ancient custom. The entertainment our envoy had received in their country was not so either. Therefore, the procedure had been amended.

But on the point of their being placed with the Three Lords, up to the day of the banquet, and after the envoys were installed in their seats in the palace, they disputed about it for a long time with me, though they eventually gave way, and the ceremonial was carried out as ordered by His Highness.

When the ceremony of taking leave was completed, I was spoken to about their statement that, in our reply to their letters, we had violated the taboo of an ancestor of their king, seven generations removed, and that we must change it.[160]

I replied: "The ancient rule is that no taboo lasts beyond five generations. The son avoids it in the case of the father, and the vassal in that of his lord. This is because of the feelings of delicacy in these relations. But why should the princes of neighboring countries avoid each other's taboo as if they were sons and vassals? And if the lords of both countries did avoid each other's taboo, there is no case in ancient lore of avoiding one in the seventh generation. There is also the principle of not doing to others what you do not like done to yourself. And when we examine the credentials brought by Korea, we see that there is a definite violation of the taboo of an ancestor of the present Shōgun.[161] In spite of the fact that it is said we must respect a taboo in the seventh generation of that country, why do they bring something which violates ours? All their statements were impolite. There is nothing I can say about such claims."

They did not desist but approached Tsushima-no-Kami about the point. Before His Highness had given directions about it, a great commotion arose with everyone saying that if the envoys could not order matters as they wished, it looked as if they were determined not to return to Korea alive, and that war might result between the two countries.[162] At this juncture, high-ranking people remonstrated with me. However, this statement of the envoys and the first part of our dispute were all unimportant points of etiquette and not worthy of discussion, but since I thought that the avoidance of the Korean taboo and matters connected with it were of the utmost importance, and, moreover, as I had borne certain matters in mind from the beginning, I too swore on my death that I would not change my first words.

And so His Highness said: "If in the letters from Korea, they first avoid the taboo of our country, my answer will also avoid the taboo of their country," and finally, also as His Highness ordered, after they altered the letters from their king, he sent our official letters altered.

In all the matters concerning this event, I have been more abused by my own compatriots than by the Koreans. Naturally, they would not say anything against His Highness, and so they directed all their criticism against me. That Confucius performed valuable services at the meeting at Chia Ku was natural, seeing that he was, as we know, a sage.[163] Why should the present discussions be criticized since they are not unlike the cases of Ts'ao Mo of Lu and Mao Sui of Chao?[164] Why has this state of society come about, in which people are ignorant of the shame put on our country? It is said that of old, there were men who forsook society and lived retired. It has also been stated that the superior man loses no time.[165] Reflecting on all this, I composed a letter to the effect that I intended to resign from office as from today and sent it to Akifusa toward two o'clock on the day the mission left Edo.

Akifusa did not give any answer but told me to come at once, as His Highness wished to say something to me urgently. I was anxious to know what he would say, so I went immediately and was told: "I am surprised at your proposal. This is because of the various criticisms people have made. I heard these sorts of things were being said from the beginning, and I know from where these views originated.[166] Relations between the two countries depend on their respective strength and prestige, and as the matter was very important, discussions were held about it from the beginning, and as your views were exactly in agreement with my wishes, you were placed in charge. Although the Korean Envoys had much to say about it, everything was done as we had decided. But when the affair was almost concluded, a problem unexpectedly arose, and when there was talk about it, I told Echizen-no-Kami [24]: 'As this was the first occasion, I had entrusted this matter to Chikugo-no-Kami [2], and he would make no mistake. It cannot be called a complete success if even one point out of a hundred is not settled. Would it not be regrettable if all he had accomplished so far were to be rendered in vain because of this one thing? Buddha speaks of "two bodies but one mind" and that describes myself and Chikugo-no-Kami.[167] If he has made a mistake, it is of course mine, and if I have made a mistake, he must have made a mistake. And so now I have nothing to say. You must take care not to be misled by the populace in what you say. Just carry out matters as he arranged,' and, in the end, it was all carried out as I wished. But if you now do as you propose, people will probably say that I have dismissed you because now I, too, disapprove of what you did. If that were to happen, your previous distinguished services would be thrown away, exactly as I said before. You must not think that all these things are your responsibility alone. They are all mine as well. However you regard it, you must think only that it was done for my sake and refrain."

And when His Highness spoke thus of our being "two bodies but one mind," I was overcome with emotion and wept despite myself, and could say nothing except that I would do as he said.

On the 30th of the same month [December 1711], an order was conveyed through Yamato-no-Kami Shigeyuki [61] that His Highness had something he wished to tell me on the following day. When I went on the 31st, I was first told by Akifusa that today His Highness had given orders through the Rōjū about rewarding me, and that as he had said the other day, whatever I felt, I must raise no objections. He then presented me with an increase in fief as a reward for my services on this occasion, sending Kaga-no-Kami Tadatomo [53] to inform me of this. Thereafter, he also said through Akifusa that, as he knew that if he rewarded me in a fashion suitable to the occasion, I would refuse it, he barely repaid my services. I said: "Everything on this occasion depended on His Highness's divine intention. What services did I perform? However, I would not presume to disobey his orders," and retired.

When the Divine Ancestor [8] first became Shōgun, letters were sent from foreign countries on many occasions. At that time, a man called the San'yō Chōrō had charge of these matters.[168] This had come about because, when the Divine Ancestor had moved to the Eastern Provinces in Hideyoshi's [13] time, San'yō was head of a school in Ashikaga-no-Shō in Kōzuke Province and had been charged with looking after these matters.[169] It was afterward called Enkōji. After this Chōrō died, Sūden Chōrō [63] had charge of it. He later became Sōroku of Konji-In, and after this Sōroku died, Hayashi Dōshun Hōin [74] took charge of these affairs.[170]

When the present Shōgun succeeded, since nothing was as it had formerly been, Daigaku-no-Kami Nobuatsu [21], wishing he could reinstate himself in favor as before, claimed that since ancient times Korean affairs had always been entrusted to his family.[171] As Masanao [62], who heard this, had always been on good terms with Nobuatsu, he transmitted it to His Highness, who accordingly gave directions that Nobuatsu should write out a program for it. So Nobuatsu prepared and presented two volumes. When His Highness asked him about some matters contained therein, as he was not really an expert on these matters, his answers were not clear, so His Highness turned to me and eventually entrusted it to me.

When Masanao was first entrusted with these matters, he inquired about the precedents from Nobuatsu. He also summoned and questioned those among Tsushima-no-Kami's [72] retainers who happened to be here, but when, later, different counsels emerged on these matters, Masanao, who was no scholar, did not understand where the significance of such lay. It was only natural that he should feel like a rudderless boat in a swift current.

In particular, I heard that it was Nobuatsu's grandfather [74] who had proposed the title "Taikun" when the use of the title "Nippon Koku-Ō" was discontinued in the Kan'ei era. Also, it could not have been unknown in Tsushima Province that this title was an official designation in Korea. When I put forward the opinion that the use of this title could by no means be continued, unexpectedly everyone agreed with me. However, it was thought that it would probably be impossible to overturn this one detail only, and that therefore none of His Highness's commands could be carried out, whereupon even Masanao was perplexed by these conflicting views. When Masanao put forward these various opinions, His Highness agreed with me completely

[138]

and gave orders, and eventually everything was carried out as he ordered.

The fact that His Highness mentioned that he knew where these views originated shows that he must have been well aware of all the slanders against me. I have heard that even now there is some argument about this matter of the title "Taikun." I think that people who disregard our national disgrace and suggest that it was a mistake do not understand human righteousness.

About that time, one of the most far-fetched slanders against me was that I had accepted large bribes from Tsushima Province. Among Yoshikata's [72] retainers, a man called Taki Rokurōemon came and said: "When Hirata Naoemon [73] returned to his province, he said something to me. It was that I must ask if, in regard to the responsibilities you have undertaken at this time, there is anything you find difficult to do. Now when the envoys return, I have heard that they will pass by your dwelling place. In spite of the fact that your fame has spread even to Korea, your residence appears to be small, and moreover this does not redound to the credit of Japan. As there still remains some timber that was used for building the residence of my lord some time ago, I will rebuild your house for you."

I replied: "His Highness has said there is no need to rebuild the houses which the envoys will pass on this occasion, but unsightly defects should by all means be repaired. Although my house is small, there is nothing shabby about it. If I were to rebuild it, it would be most embarrassing if it came to light that, despite the fact that His Highness has said not to, those in charge of the ceremony said that it would actually be better to rebuild it. I will not forget your kindness."

After that, also, when I received orders that I must go to meet the envoys on their arrival at the Kawasaki poststation, the fellow came again and said: "It is for the sake of Japan. It will be unfitting if you do not change your traveling apparel on the journey. I have hastened hither in order to receive your orders about this." I said: "Last year when I went to Kyōto as Shogunal Envoy, I had plenty of traveling clothes made. From Edo to Kawasaki is but a single day's journey, so the traveling expenses will not be heavy. But if I do lack anything, I will come to you." However, although he talked till late at night, he knew that my mind would never change, and saying: "If you have any requests, we shall do anything at all," he went back. If I had not been charged with carrying out His Highness's orders at this time, I would not have had these approaches made to me.

All these propositions concerned public affairs. I thought I must not regard them as private matters, and since I explained this point of view in detail, there could be no doubt about my intentions in the opinion of the world at large. But those who did not understand public morality probably thought in their hearts that I was just taking care of my own welfare, not knowing that I had dedicated myself to my country.

There is no need to seek for distant examples in Chinese and Japanese history. In recent times, a man called Yamamoto Dōki was a military adviser in the House of Takeda of Kai.[172] When Takeda fought against Uesugi of Echigo, at a place called Kawanakajima in Shinano Province, this Yamamoto, realizing that his own side was defeated, flung himself into the forefront to die.[173] That was the conduct of a man of honor. And I too thought that if anything I advised on this occasion was not in accordance with His Highness's commands, even though he himself did not criticize me, I should have no countenance left to appear before him again. Therefore, from the time that I received these orders, I regarded myself as non-existent. I took this resolution because I thought that if I made a mistake, whatever happened to me at home, abroad dishonor would fall on Japan.

The letter I sent, when I heard that the people of Tsushima Province refused in the matter of the restitution of the *shō-gun*'s title, was the beginning of my argument about this matter. The draft of this letter is still in existence. Later, when I presented the draft of the letter I was going to send Tsushima-no-Kami, on hearing that the envoys were disputing the ceremony in Ōsaka, His Highness approved it, but when it was reported that the ceremony had already taken place, it became unnecessary to send it. However, as he had read this draft, I shall transmit it to my posterity.

The present Yamato-no-Kami Shigeyuki [61] witnessed the incident when the envoys later disputed with me about ceremony within the Shōgun's palace. Other witnesses besides him must still be alive. Seeing that His Highness had already taken his place, everyone was disturbed, but I was unmoved and finally overcame the three of them with my arguments. You can infer how resolute my heart was at these times. After that, when the question of the national taboo arose again, there was not a single person who was not upset. That I alone was unmoved was because I had steeled my resolution from the beginning. As these facts were also known to His Highness, he said: "Your suggestions are right and proper," and as he said nothing more, everything I proposed was eventually carried out.

All this was due to the Divine Spirit of Japan. It could not have been achieved by human power. It is not fitting to say that it was because of my services. It would be much more unfitting if I boasted of my services. If even one single point in my proposals had not been carried out, where would my merit have been?

We should let nothing pass by that we see or hear. We should seek the origin of everything carefully. This is in fact what was called natural philosophy itself in ancient times.[174] Although they are trifles, there were not a few matters which I had seen and heard long ago which proved to be useful in connection with the Korean Embassy, which I have described above. I shall set down one or two here.

For instance, when I was studying the *Teikin Ōrai* as a child, among methods of house building discussed, if I remember correctly, in a section of a letter dated the third month, there were some, not heard about or seen now, which were difficult to follow.[175] However, as soon as I was capable, I began to read ancient stories and old diaries, and, in the course of time, came upon information that threw some light on them. I also heard that in Kamakura there was a plan of the palace of the Kamakura *shōgun,* and it occurred to me that it might refer to what I had read about in the *Ōrai.*[176] I searched for many years and finally was able to obtain a copy of it, but, upon examination, it did not appear to belong to the Kamakura period. Nor did it appear to belong to the period of the Kamakura Kanryō during the Ashikaga shogunate.[177] It seemed rather to be the plan of a mansion of someone of a later period, which had been handed down in the family of some master carpenter living in Kamakura. I also happened to hear that in the Kujō Palace there was a sketch of the "Congratulatory Banquet" for the Ashikaga *shōgun.*[178] When I visited Kyōto, I requested to be allowed to see it and was permitted to borrow it. I was also able to see a plan of the gate in the Konoe Palace called the "Kaimon" and was able to get an insight into the construction of houses as described in ancient documents.[179]

Later, I was ordered to design a new "middle gate" for the visit of the Korean Embassy. The theory was then advanced that it was an ancient custom dating from the time of the Udaishō [75], the Kamakura *shōgun,* not to use roof-coverings on gates in the houses of the military classes. It is said that in proof of that statement, a plan dating from the time of the Udaishō was presented.

When His Highness asked me about this, I replied: "I have for many years made a practice of noting down items of interest I have come across. I have a copy of this plan myself. However, it does not belong to Yoritomo's [75] age, and this can be proved without trouble. The first appearance of what is now called a 'long-spear' occurs in the *Taiheiki,* and the fact that a room called the 'long-spear room' is shown in this plan is proof of the period the plan belongs to.[180] Nor is it necessary to cite examples in China or in ancient times. The stone foundations of gates, dating from about the era of Kan'ei, in the Nijō Palace are still in existence."[181] (The hip-roofed gate and the Chinese gabled gate constructed at this time were removed to the Retired Emperor's Palace afterward.[182] Now only the stones remain.) "Also the palace gate of Konji-In in Nanzenji is one which the Divine Ancestor had transported from the Juraku-Dai long ago.[183] Therefore it is clear that for many generations, the Tokugawa Family has used hip-roofed gates and Chinese gabled gates, and it is only that these gates have not yet been constructed in Edo Castle. Such assertions as that under discussion are completely unfounded, and His Highness should not follow such advice," I replied. I heard that after I wrote out these comments, those who had advised about this matter ceased their arguments.

I heard that Daigaku-no-Kami Nobuatsu [21] himself said that the fact that there was a place called the long-spear room was proof that it was not a plan belonging to the age of the Kamakura shogunate but of more recent times. I said: "It is claimed that the ancient custom of not using covered gates in warriors' houses was because of taking banners in and out. But, as regards the problem they have brought up of taking banners in and out, it is not necessary that they should be taken in and out of this gate only. If, among all the other gates, there were none without roofs, there might be some reason for their objections." His Highness thereupon said: "It is not necessary to discuss the question fundamentally." I heard that the reason Nobuatsu put forward all these conflicting opinions was because, as I recorded before, he was determined to oppose every change His Highness intended to make on this occasion.

Also, it was the custom for the box containing the letters sent from Japan to be made of silver and for gold rings and scarlet cords to be attached. (This had been the custom from the age of Tokubyō [46], as can be seen in the *Kokushi Nikki*).[184] When His Highness asked me about this, I recommended a style of box and stand for the presentation of the official letters which I had seen in Kyōto, so that on this occasion we adopted that style. Also, since on this occasion the envoys had to alight from their palanquins outside their lodgings, I spoke to Tsushima-no-Kami [72] about an enclosure outside the gate, so that at Ōsaka, it was said, they provided wooden shaft-rests (wrapped in carpet) within the enclosure, and when they heard about that in Kyōto they provided Chinese chairs within a striped curtain. Since this was done to meet a sudden demand, it could not be helped, but I said that such preparations were unsuitable, and had a variegated curtain and stools brought posthaste from Kyōto, and at Edo we provided these stools within the variegated curtain. I heard that when the former Sesshō [57] heard about this he praised it.

[143]

When I was ordered to go to the post-station of Kawasaki to meet the envoys, I considered the costume I should wear on that occasion. This was what in ancient times was called an informal meeting, and so what was worn at Edo Castle was not suitable. It was the ancient custom of the military to wear a tunic with rosettes on all military occasions, and I intended to wear this; while I made inquiry unofficially, the envoys had sent a messenger to Tsushima-no-Kami to ask what sort of headgear and robe I as guest would wear on that evening, so that they would know how to appear. Tsushima-no-Kami communicated this to me. I replied that the occasion was a meeting at an inn, that I intended to wear the ordinary military dress, and that they should also wear their ordinary dress. At the ceremony that evening, I wore a lacquered court cap with a brim, a tunic of yellowish red with rosettes belted into the trousers, and a silver-mounted slung sword. I thought that some of their officials would probably come out to meet me, so I put a pair of sandals into my palanquin. Just as I thought, when I got to the gate, some high officials appeared to be coming out, so I at once brought out the sandals, put them on, and went in. All these matters, both pertaining to the national polity and the ancient customs of the military, are things that do not admit of discussion with those who know nothing about them.

There are one or two other things I remember in connection with my account of the visit of the Korean Envoys. First, when I passed through Ōgaki in Mino Province on my way to Kyōto, I noticed that in all the houses in this town, measurements had been marked off and notices stuck up stating that one *jō* was to be cut off here and one *shaku* off there.[185] They said that when the officials in charge of the Korean Embassy had come this way (the *ōmetsuke, kanjō bugyō*, etc.), Tsushima-no-Kami's retainers, who accompanied them, had said that the road here was narrow and they would have trouble when the large banners were carried along, and so they ordered these adjustments to be made. When I asked if it was the first time the envoys had passed this place, they replied that every time the envoys came, they had always passed along this route. In my letter reporting my arrival in Kyōto, I mentioned this matter and said that this kind of thing must be a burden in all the provinces along the whole route. There had never been any difficulty since the envoys first came, therefore, it was most unfitting that there should be such orders now. I afterward heard that these schemes were all put a stop to.

Also, the duty of supplying saddle horses for the party on the envoys' journey from Kyōto to Edo and back was imposed on the *daimyō*. This was the custom. It seems that in the document presented, which described the precedents for assigning that duty, the duty on the road east of Tōtōmi Province was imposed on the *daimyō* of the Western Provinces, and the duty on the road west of Mikawa Province on the *daimyō* of the Eastern Provinces. The performance of that duty was limited to one day, one day coming and one day returning, and in no case did it exceed two days.

When I saw this document, I said: "I do not consider this arrangement a suitable one. We should assign the duty on the road west of Mikawa Province to the western *daimyō* and the duty on the road east of Tōtōmi Province to the eastern *daimyō*. After the retainers of the *daimyō* of the Western Provinces have seen the envoys off on their way to Edo, they should return to the residences of their respective *daimyō* in Ōsaka, and, on the envoys' return, they should set out sufficiently ahead of time to greet them. Also, the retainers of the *daimyō* of the Eastern Provinces should assemble in Edo after they have greeted the envoys and should see them off on their return. If this is done, it will be convenient for everyone and travel expenses will be automatically reduced by half. Furthermore, it is not sensible to limit the performance of this duty to just one day. It makes little difference to the *daimyō* of the various provinces whether they perform this duty for one or two days. If it is limited to two days going and coming, and those who are too distant or of insufficient income are exempted from this service, the number of *daimyō* charged with this duty will be reduced, and, moreover, the matter will be accomplished with half the number of saddle horses."

His Highness said: "Your advice is perfectly reasonable, but if I give a new set of orders about these arrangements, those who misunderstand their intention will be unable to carry them out effectively. Therefore you must write out your recommendations." I presented them the following morning. "How did you do it so quickly?" he asked. I replied: "I arranged it so that the *daimyō* of the various provinces do not go more than 100 *ri* from their own castles in carrying out this duty, so the details were simple to work out." (According to the first plan, as arranged by Ogiwara Ōmi-no-Kami Shigehide [51], merchants supplied pack and saddle horses and the *daimyō* paid for these services. I did away with this arrangement on the grounds that it was most unfitting to the national polity.)

Also, it was said that His Highness would give orders to the members of the guard companies that on the day of the banquet for the envoys on their way through Sumpu in Suruga, they should serve as stewards for the high officials and above, and to Naitō Buzen-no-Kami Kazuo that he should provide the stewards for those of lower rank.[186] (It was because he was Commander of Tanaka Castle in Suruga Province.)[187] I said: "This is a foolish arrangement also. We cannot impose double duty on the *daimyō* in our preparations on this occasion. All the *daimyō* whose fiefs border on the Tōkaidō have the duty of meeting the envoys. If in addition to that, His Highness imposes this burden, he will be imposing a double duty on these men only. When I passed by Sumpu in Suruga on my mission as Shogunal Envoy, I noticed the fine appearance of the local inhabitants as a result of the long residence there of the Divine Ancestor. If merchants' sons are chosen and charged with this duty, they will do far better than rough country *samurai*." His Highness gave orders in accordance with my recommendations on this matter also.

When I was summoned on the 17th August of this year, I heard about the extraordinary happening in which 4,116 farmers from 85 villages on the fief of Murakami in Echigo Province made a disorderly protest.[188] It appears that upon this, orders were given to the feudal lord that he must punish them severely. His Highness gave me the letter from the Bugyōsho (*kanjō bugyō*) and told me to consider it. The letter from the Bugyōsho said: "Last year when Matsudaira Ukyō-Daibu Terusada [38] received Murakami Castle in fief, the farmers in Mishima, Kambara, and other districts, territory producing 40,000 *koku* of rice, petitioned for that territory to be taken under the direct control of the *shōgun*. When it was explained that their request could not be granted, they returned home, but the villagers concerned would not obey the orders of the *daikan* and also would not pay last year's tax. At this time, we summoned 50-odd leaders to the Hyōjōsho and questioned them about the reasons for their dissatisfaction, and they said that they wished to become farmers under the direct control of the *shōgun*. Although they were told many times that their request could not be granted, they would not obey. Shall we now send other messengers to question them, or imprison the 50-odd ringleaders and send two or three messengers to the fief of Murakami to deliver the remainder at once to the feudal lord? (The *daikan* should be employed as messenger.) As for those who had defied orders, should they, on the authority of the feudal lord, be put to death or banished or imprisoned, and their lands and houses forfeited to the feudal lord, according to the gravity of their offense?" A letter from the Daikansho in that province, dated the 6th July, was attached. (The residence of the *daikan* was in Kurokawa, and his name was Kawara Seibei.)[189]

Furthermore, the *daikan*'s letter asserted that rumor had it that the remainder of the group had been deeply aroused by the arrest of the 58 ringleaders at this time. They had written many pledges, swearing a firm oath to one another, and more than 100 farmers who had gone to the prison with the arrested men had decided that if the 58 were sentenced, they themselves would bring forward a complaint, and if they were also punished, the other 4,000-odd farmers would also come and they too would make a complaint. It was stated that all regarded the *daikan* as their enemy, and so they had willfully seized last year's tax-rice for sale and loaded it on boats. Although the village headman had forbade them, they had defied him. (According to rumor, they had made a priest of the Ikkō sect their commander and had made preparations for war, but this was not stated in the letter.)[190]

On the following day I presented a memorial. The gist of it was: "I have finished reading the letters which you handed to me yesterday. Now, who is there to whom the poor unprotected people of the empire can complain at such a time? It has been considered a crime that they disregarded the orders given by the *bugyō* in the first place and protested. In addition, a conclusion, based merely on rumors which appeared in the report from the office of the *daikan*, has been reached, and now they are judged guilty of rebellion. Those who should be the father and mother of the people should not have taken up this kind of attitude.[191] If it were actually a case of rebellion, as these rumors suggest, they would not sell tax-rice and thus deprive themselves of their military provisions. On the other hand, if it is a case of rebellion and they do not know that they ought to make such preparations, there is not much to fear. Moreover, it is unreasonable to assert that men who petition to become farmers under the direct control of the *shōgun* intend to rebel. They have just come complaining because there are things that they cannot bear. I will be their surety that they have no rebellious intent. Now, even if the officers of the Bugyōsho are given orders to question them again, if those who make complaint and those who hear them are mutually indignant and resentful, it will be impossible to get at the truth and induce them to obey. I suggest that the *bugyō* send different messengers to question them. In particular, they must direct the messengers to find out the reason for their complaints. They must choose very mild and sympathetic men for this mission."

In due course, three men, Yokota Bitchū-no-Kami [76], Suzuki Hida-no-Kami [77], and Hotta Gen'emon [78] received special orders, and when they questioned those summoned to the Bugyōsho on this occasion, as I expected, the complaint was not without reason. (This interrogation began on the 24th August.) Furthermore it was not because this land had been given to Matsudaira Ukyō-Daibu that this complaint had arisen. Sixty years ago, when Matsudaira Yamato-no-Kami Tadamoto was given Murakami Castle in fief, he received additional territory of 40,000 *koku* in the districts of Mishima and Kambara.[192] After this, the local inhabitants called this land "the fief of 40,000 *koku*." The year before last [1709], when Honda Nakatsukasa-Tayū Tadayoshi [79] was given that castle (at that time his fief was 50,000 *koku*), "the fief of 40,000 *koku*" was divided into two parcels. A fief of 20,000 *koku* was made a shogunal estate and the remainder was made the fief of Murakami. But the Honda fief was 20 or 30 *ri* distant from Murakami Castle, and it was separated by three great rivers, chief of which was the Shinano.[193] There also was an embankment of 15 or 16 *ri* or more, and every year, on account of the spring and autumn floods, the embankment was destroyed, and the cost of repair of this destruction and also of labor were incalculable. Moreover, in "the fief of 40,000 *koku*" there had formerly been ten *ōjōya*, and great suffering had been caused by these men for many years. Eight of these ten were at this time attached to the fief of Murakami. Because of these circumstances, a petition had been presented to the *daikan* in Kurokawa requesting that this territory be exchanged for lands in the neighborhood of Murakami Castle, but there was no reply.

All these appeals from the farmers of the 85 villages have good grounds. Ever since the time of the former Shōgun [15], whenever *daimyō* and *hatamoto* have been transferred, fertile farmland and profitable forests and river flats have been made shogunal territory and the remainder annexed to private fiefs. Thus not only have the farmers complained, but the feudal lords have also suffered distress on account of it and this is the general state of affairs.

In February the previous year [1710], three farmers had been chosen and sent to the magistrates' office to make a complaint. (The three men were called Sangobei, Shingoemon, and Ichibei. They had made their complaint to the *kanjō bugyō*, Nakayama Izumo-no-Kami [80] and Ōkubo Ōsumi-no-Kami [81]).

In May, before a decision was given about this also, they intercepted Kawachi-no-Kami Masamine [37] when he was en route to take up duty and had made a complaint. The *bugyō* had refused to consider this complaint as it had not been made to the proper authorities, and had arrested the three men. At the end of June, the three men were summoned to the Bugyōsho and told that, at this time, Matsudaira Ukyō-Daibu [38] had been given Murakami Castle, that their petition could not be granted, and that they must return home at once. But they had returned to their home province mistakenly believing that their petition had been granted.

The people of the villages had rejoiced greatly. However, when the three men, unable to understand why the 20,000 *koku* of territory remained annexed to the fief of Murakami as before, had again petitioned toward the end of October, they had immediately been cast into prison. Their fathers and brothers had also been summoned and imprisoned. Two had died in prison (Sangobei's father and younger brother). The Murakami farmers had become more and more perplexed, and their complaints still did not receive government notice, and so, not knowing whether to send this year's tax to the *daikan* or to the feudal lord of Murakami, they had not obeyed the demand for payment. In March this year, the *bugyō* had said they would summon and interrogate the farmers in their territory, and had sent for the 58 who were said to be the ringleaders.

At this time, those who had received special orders from His Highness heard the Murakami farmers' complaint, but said: "Although their demands seem reasonable, it will be very unwise to grant their petition now and have these happenings set a precedent for the future. In spite of everything, they must submit to the orders of the Bugyōsho." When they heard this, they said, "Henceforth, we will certainly not resist the government's orders. However, if things proceed as they have until now, our parents will die of starvation and brothers, wives, and children will be scattered because of what the *ōjōya* and *kojōya* say, so what will the men in their home province decide to do now? Now, if 20 or 30 of those who are here are granted leave and return and convey this order, we can reply after hearing what the Murakami farmers have to say."

As there were many who considered that it was very unwise to permit them to return, His Highness consulted me about the matter again. I said: "The saying about setting loose a tiger in the wilds depends on the circumstances. In this case, you will have no problem if you let them return to their home province. If they do not return and convey your decision, who else will inform the people in their home province of its purport? Also, it is imperative to interrogate the *ōjōya* against whom they made their complaint." So His Highness granted their request, and 32 men were sent back to their home province. The *ōjōya* and *kojōya* were summoned, and about the beginning of October an investigation was held by Yokota [76], Suzuki [77], and Hotta [78].

About the middle of October, the *bugyō* again sent a report from the Daikansho. In that report, he had said: "Since the government had sent back those they first summoned, they had heard that the farmers of the villages had gathered together and discussed matters," and it appeared that they had also secretly gathered in the whole of this year's harvest. Shortly afterward, twelve farmers from those eight divisions came and gave thanks for the Shōgun's gracious decision.[194]

The eight divisions were attached to the eight *ōjōya* on "the fief of 40,000 *koku*." They were formerly called "the ten divisions," but, as stated earlier, two of the *ōjōya* had become *shōya* on the shogunal lands. The districts which belonged to the remaining eight were called "the eight divisions."

After that, they summoned all these men and the three men who had first been imprisoned at the Bugyōsho and questioned them about the *shōya*. When they again had the *shōya* interrogated, the *shōya* had nothing to say.

For instance, from the end of November the year before last until the middle of February last year [1709–10], when two *daikan* came to Kurokawa during a span of 80 days, the *ōjōya* had forced the farmers of the villages to disgorge 950 *ryō* as living expenses for the *daikan*. There were any number of these cases, but the *shōya* had nothing to say in excuse.

On the 21st November last year [1711], a decision was given on this matter, and it was announced that henceforth illegal acts by the *shōya* were forbidden, and that the 4,116 farmers from the 85 villages of that territory of 20,000 *koku* would be transferred to the territory of Murakami. (This was the message which was sent down to the feudal lord at this time.)

On the 2nd February 1712, it was said that the tax for the two years 1710 and 1711 was paid in full to the feudal lord.

And so the first rumors that they had sold two years' tax-rice were unfounded. Later, there was a report that farmers, in a place called Sakaimura, one of those 85 villages, and the Abbot of Fukujōji of the Ikkō sect had revolted.[195] When they were summoned and questioned at the end of February this year, it was found that all these reports were mistaken, and the farmers were dismissed to their homes.

As I have recorded all these matters in another document, I have only set down an outline of them here.

On the 29th January this year [1712], fire broke out in the vicinity of Shinobazu Pond.[196] A violent northwest wind was blowing and many tens of thousands of houses were engulfed in the spreading flames. Ever since the great fire of 1657, such disasters had been frequent, and some city blocks had suffered in these holocausts ten or more times. People therefore felt unsafe in their homes, and in addition to this anxiety, after every disaster the prices of commodities rose.

As the area afflicted was extensive, His Highness said: "You must consider how we can avoid these disasters." It was natural that he should ask others about this too. But seeing that he asked me first, I wrote out 15 articles in all concerning the causes of these disasters. Four dealt with natural causes, two with those due to topographical conditions, four with those due to human agency, and five with ineffective means of fire prevention. (As this draft is still in existence it may be consulted.)[197] His Highness consulted the *machi bugyō* and and those charged with extinguishing fires, but none of their replies seemed to pay proper attention to fundamentals. They merely agreed that the moat at Shirogane-chō should be enlarged.[198] Although there was something similar to this among my proposals, my suggestions differed from theirs. However, in accordance with their suggestions, His Highness ordered this moat to be enlarged. He died before my proposals could be carried out.

This year, 1712, as deeds of enfeoffment had to be distributed to the *daimyō*, His Highness directed me to draft them. After obtaining His Highness's instructions, I wrote the drafts between the 29th and 31st March. After that, His Highness directed that I write documents to be sent to shrines and others. (These were title deeds for nobles of the Imperial Court, temples, and shrines.) His Highness died before this was finished, too.

Also, I received orders that I was to meet the Dutchmen who were to come this spring and question them about the foreign countries of the southwest.[199] From the 31st March to the 14th April, I went to their lodgings and questioned them.[200] These matters are recorded separately, so I shall not deal with them here.[201]

At that time, I offered recommendations concerning another matter. The gist of these was: Since the time of the former Shōgun [15], the services exacted from the *daimyō* have been heavy, and in addition the *daimyō* have given many voluntary presents.[202] All the privations and distress of the military classes and commoners are due to this.

The performance by the *daimyō* and *hatamoto* of services to their suzerain should be based on military service.[203] Since this military service was first fixed in the Genna era, there have been the divisions of "full duty," "half duty," and "one-third duty" in carrying it out.[204] In the Kan'ei era, military service was revised, and thereafter it was light as compared with the Genna era.[205] But in view of the long continued peace, it was useless expenditure which mounted yearly, and seeing that there were hardships in carrying out that service, the government considered what was suitable to the time.

It is much more unfitting, now, when we are still further removed from the Kan'ei era, that when military service has been lightened, ordinary duties should be unreasonably heavy. It is not necessary to discuss far-off examples in China. If we consider periods of disturbance in Japan, the causes from which those disturbances have arisen were none other than the waste of the substance and the exhaustion of the strength of the people of the empire. It is written: "First make the people prosperous, then teach them," and also: "When their storehouses are filled, they will understand."[206] But now since there are these heavy duties, there will be adverse criticism however good the government. Whatever other urgent needs there may be at this time, there is nothing more important than to lighten the burdens of the people. Give orders to reduce the number of bearers and horses the *daimyō* bring with them when they come to Edo, and to reduce the number of guards on duty at every gate from the castle gates to the outside gates. In carrying out special services, work on the principle of requiring either "half duty" or "one-third duty" in each case according to its circumstances.

Before this, on the 14th May 1710, the number of places where the *daimyō* had been ordered to do fire-guard duty under the former Shōgun was limited to 15, but the large number of men called out in times of emergency such as fighting sudden and spreading conflagrations was because no firm regulations had been established.

Turning to the question of gifts, if the tendency to increase the frequency of presentation and the number of articles is curbed, and if, in cases where these bad tendencies have become firmly established, orders are given that gifts to all ranks from members of the Rōjū down are to be reduced in number and frequency, I am confident the habit of flattery will be reformed and bribery will also cease. "Careful consideration should be given to these matters," I said.

Owing to this, His Highness had inquiries made about the number of guards on gate duty and fixed their number. There was also a decree that the number of bearers and horses the *daimyō* brought with them during their obligatory period of residence in Edo should be kept to a minimum. But I heard that people raised objections over present-giving, and my proposals were not put into effect.

    Certain people criticized my proposals by saying that the giving of presents was an expression of respect for superiors. Since ancient times, the frequent giving of presents had been a matter of pride in their houses, and it would be most unfitting if regulations about this were issued. Did they honestly feel this, I wonder?

In April this year [1712], regulations were issued about the highways. This was because in March last year, after I returned from Kyōto, I had spoken about the Tōkaidō.[207] As a result, His Highness had given orders in April of that year to the *bugyō* in charge of the highways (Matsudaira Iwami-no-Kami [82] and Ōkubo Ōsumi-no-Kami [81]) in connection with the visit of the Korean Embassy.[208]

Among the many proposals the officials made in response, the most important was the following:

"The inns along the highways have grown poor over the years and are experiencing difficulties. There are many reasons for this, but, in particular, for some time now the attendants on court nobles and military men have increased in number, and there are not enough bearers and horses at the inns for their use. Even those places charged with the duty of providing auxiliaries are having difficulties.[209] Furthermore, since the removal of the Arai Ferry, most travelers of all ranks go by the Nakasendō.[210] The inns along the Tōkaidō have lost business while the inns along the Nakasendō cannot continue to supply enough bearers and horses.

[154]

"Therefore, the burden should be imposed on all the provinces, and contributions should be collected to defray the expense of increasing the number of bearers and horses at the inns on the various roads. When the number of bearers and horses has been increased, those who live close to the roads should be relieved from the duty of supplying auxiliaries. If this is done, not only the inn-keepers as a matter of course, but those who supply auxiliaries will also be relieved of hardship. Next, if in the future, travel on the Nakasendō is restricted, the inns on both the Tōkaidō and Nakasendō will have a fair share of business.

"These are the most important matters, but in all questions touching the distress of the people who live along the roads, unless the officials actually visit these places themselves, they will not be able to understand properly. We request that officials should be attached to the *bugyō* to be responsible for sending frequent inspectors to make inquiries."

Their petitions included several tens of articles in all. After receiving these, His Highness consulted me, so I wrote out proposals and presented them. Among the many matters I discussed, I mentioned that when I went to Kyōto as shogunal messenger, I traveled along the Tōkaidō and saw the actual state of affairs with my own eyes.

The large number of attendants on travelers places no strain on the innkeepers. It is only a worry to those who live close to the roads and have the task of supplying auxiliaries. The reason for this is that in the time of the former Shōgun, inn inspectors were appointed for the first time, and in the inns on shogunal lands officials, called clerks of the Daikansho, had charge of the control of the inns.[211] When travelers on official duty passed through, the innkeepers conspired with the inn inspectors and doubled and tripled the number of bearers and horses which were actually needed, and demanded them from the places which were required to supply auxiliaries. The number of bearers and horses supplied by the latter sufficed to cover the number requisitioned for official purposes, while the bearers and horses actually belonging to the inns were used for the transport of ordinary travelers, and the conspirators pocketed the hire. If the number of bearers and horses sent by the places charged with the duty of providing auxiliaries fell even slightly short, the inn inspectors held those con-

[155]

cerned to be guilty of negligence and pocketed the fines imposed as a forfeit. Unless the attendants on travelers are numerous, the innkeepers make little profit; therefore, they worry only when the retinues are small. Those charged with supplying auxiliaries not only wear out their bearers and horses, but have already exhausted their resources in paying fines for their offenses. The result is that those who hold fiefs as far as five or ten *ri* from the post-stations are at the end of their resources because of the yearly reduction of their tax receipts. Also, when the attendants of travelers on official business see large numbers of bearers and horses assembled to meet and see them off, why should they worry? Why should they tramp long distances carrying heavy loads themselves? It is the natural desire of the lower orders to use these bearers and horses instead of their own labor. The best way of removing all these abuses is, first, to dismiss the inn inspectors.

Next, it has been stated that as travelers in recent years avoided the Arai route because of its difficulties, innkeepers along both the Tōkaidō and Nakasendō have been suffering hardship. That assertion arises from knowing only one side of the question and not the full story. In the time of the former Shōgun [15], permission was given to increase the transportation charges as requested by the innkeepers along the Tōkaidō. Ever since then, large numbers of travelers of all ranks have gone by the Nakasendō in order to economize on their traveling expenses. When I passed up and down the Tōkaidō as Shogunal Envoy, I was advised to take the Honzaka Road.[212] But I did not follow that advice, and when I went via Arai, I encountered no hardships. If the *bugyō* wish to increase the number of travelers on the Tōkaidō, the best thing is for them to decide to return to the old rate of charges for bearers and horses at the post-stations. It is a foolish plan to restrict travel on the Nakasendō.

Again, with regard to the imposition of a permanent tax on all the provinces to defray the cost of bearers and horses at the post-stations along the roads, in the time of the former Shōgun, a tax was imposed on all provinces in order to build the Daibutsuden in Tōdaiji and to remove the ash resulting from the eruption of Mount Fuji.[213] Although these were only temporary taxes, people complained about them. Complaints would be much more bitter if a yearly tax were demanded from all provinces so as to provide bearers and horses for the post-stations along the roads.

Also, at the post-stations along the Tōkaidō, the number of bearers required is fixed at 100, and the number of pack horses at 100, and at the post-stations along the Nakasendō the number of bearers required is fixed at 50, and the number of pack horses at the same figure. These numbers have been unaltered since olden times. If His Highness gives orders that the retinues of travelers must be regulated according to the number of bearers and horses and also that the inns must not accede to requests for even a single bearer or horse in excess of the fixed number, the demands on those charged with the duty of supplying auxiliaries will automatically be reduced. But at this time, there are not many post-stations which maintain the full complement of bearers and horses as laid down. As this arrangement was originally set up to make provision for needs in times of war, it has very important implications. The best thing to do is for His Highness to issue orders at once that these numbers are to be brought up to full strength, and to lend the money to those places actually lacking the means to do so.

I presented seven articles setting forth these recommendations. (This memorandum is still in existence.)[214]

In March 1712, for a start, the inn inspectors were dismissed, and, later, a decree was issued concerning various matters in connection with the roads, but, in compliance with a request from the *bugyō*, *yoriki* and *dōshin* were appointed. According to a report which was lent to me, sent in by the *bugyō* in September, at the 53 post-stations along the Tōkaidō, the number of bearers and horses requisitioned the previous year by travelers bearing the shogunal seal totalled 230,550 and 41,234 respectively. This year, after orders were given about the matters connected with the roads, these numbers were reduced by 122,589 and 4,823 respectively to 107,961 bearers and 36,411 horses.

In the seven articles in the memorandum I presented were included several scores of items. Among them I discussed the *bugyō*'s initial statement that they were quite unable to control the lawlessness of the casual bearers along the road. That is to say, both in Edo and in Kyōto and Ōsaka, there are so-called casual bearers who are hired as temporary attendants by travelers passing from one capital to the other. One example of the lawlessness of these bearers is that they say they are tired and demand horses and palanquins and then ride themselves while they make the regular bearers carry what they themselves should carry. Telling the regular bearers that if they want to return home quickly they will let them go, they exact money and then let them go. Also, if they have a grudge against anyone at the post-stations, they tell their fellows, and in the end, they take revenge on him in some way, so that innkeepers at the post-stations will give no information. As the *bugyō* were unable to discover who are actually responsible for these acts, it was difficult to take action against them.

When I heard this, I said: "It is very easy to stop these practices. There are places which control this kind of person in Edo, Kyōto, and Ōsaka also. These are called agencies for day-laborers and casual bearers. If those who wish to hire them send orders to these agencies, they will send them immediately. If they disobey the orders of the agencies they will lose their jobs on the spot and will be unable to support their wives and children. They respect the agency managers like masters. If they behave lawlessly, the agency managers must be punished, and if this regulation is strictly enforced, this abuse will be reformed." As this regulation was established, these happenings ceased as I expected.

I also wrote out three items arguing against the request of the *bugyō* for *yoriki* and *dōshin* to be appointed, but as certain officials supported this request, His Highness [3] finally acceded to it. After he died, at the time of the Buddhist ceremonies at Nikkō Temple, those new officials, like their predecessors, requisitioned excessive numbers of bearers and horses to be sent as auxiliaries to the post-stations.[215] Also, there was some dissatisfaction among *daimyō* with orders issued by the Bugyōsho for innkeepers on the Nakasendō, and what happened was what I had warned against. I made other suggestions which were not carried out at that time, but as His Highness died soon afterward, many abuses still remain as bad as ever. It was a case which might be compared to building a house too close to the road.[216]

As I have recorded the incidents of this time in another document, I have just set down one or two items here.[217]

On the 25th April [1712], I became seriously ill and was forced to remain at home. In May, Akihira [41] and Masanao [30] came as messengers from the Shōgun to inquire how I was and whether I would be able to attend at the palace should His Highness send for me soon, for he had something to discuss with me. I replied that I was still unable to attend, and on the 9th, His Highness sent Ichi-no-Kami [30] as his messenger to inquire about my health. I later heard that when His Highness inquired about me, Masanao undertook the mission and reported to him that he had asked my physician, who had given his opinion that my spleen was seriously affected and my strength failing. He had added that although innumerable applications of moxa had been made to the lower back, no results were yet noticeable. His Highness, on hearing this, said: "His concern for the welfare of the country is all-consuming. Perhaps that is why he has fallen ill. His spirit is broader than Japan and extends over the four seas. I wonder how he can bear so many applications of the moxa." (I shall never forget his words.) He sent Akihira, Masanao, and others to inquire five times after that. On the 31st May, having recovered my health, I went on duty and expressed my thanks for His Highness's solicitude through Akifusa.

At this time I said: "While I was confined to my bed, I heard reports that His Highness had sent for large numbers of dancing girls. Since he had prohibited such people when he first became Shōgun, I do not think there can be any truth in this report.[218] However, maybe these girls were summoned by His Highness's consort [60] to entertain the Taikō [57] during his visit. Although it is ridiculous to believe the rumors one hears nowadays, I am reporting this because it came to my ears." I then withdrew.

When I again attended a few days later (I think it was on the 7th June but I do not remember the date exactly), His Highness sent the following message through Akifusa: "During the time of my predecessor [15], when my consort visited the Shōgun's mother, dancing girls were provided to entertain her, and she said there was no harm in having dancing girls to beguile an idle hour.[219] Therefore later when the Shōgun's mother or his consort visited the Shōgun's apartments, it was the custom to have such entertainment.[220] Even after I succeeded, when my children's mothers entertained my consort, and also when my consort entertained them, these diversions were held, and, as you said, these entertainments were also held to entertain the Taikō.[221] In view of the fact that I prohibited them when I first succeeded, I ought to have stopped it; it is a serious error on my part that I have followed former custom and not done so. After hearing what you said to Akifusa, I have already given orders to dismiss these people immediately."

It was about spring that I heard this. It may be that the Taikō spoke about these matters to his daughter, His Highness's consort [60]. I knew that if I were to speak of this matter, it would certainly be very embarrassing to His Highness, but I finally spoke as I did because I had heard that even after the Taikō had returned to Kyōto on the 16th May, these entertainments continued.

Some things come to mind in recording this matter. Some time ago, the Confucianist of Tsushima Province, Amenomori Tōgōrō Toshiyoshi, came to visit me and said: "Although after the present Shōgun [26] succeeded, people criticized you in respect to the two previous ages, there was not a single thing on which you could be found wanting.[222] But I am in some doubt as to whether there may have been just one thing that might seem to agree with the general opinion." When I asked him to tell me about it, he said: "When the Shōgun before last [3] was alive, he asked whether it was true that in China there was such a thing called the 'Battle of the Flowers,' and you replied 'In the age of Hsüan Tsung of the T'ang Dynasty, there was something called *fêngliuchên*.[223] It is generally so referred to.' And when you presented pictures which you had commissioned from an artist, he thought them interesting and afterward played that game himself." I said with a stern expression: "I lectured to His Highness on the words of Yao and Shun, and I tried to make my lord like the lords Yao and Shun.[224] That I did not make him like them was my fault alone. I had nothing to do with what you are talking about. We have known each other for thirty years, ever since I first studied

[160]

under Kinri [12], when you were seventeen or eighteen and I was over thirty. For you to doubt me now in such matters is like saying that friends of long standing have just met.[225] It is difficult for anyone to find another who understands him. Things said by people who have not always known me do not surprise me." Whereupon he said with a heightened color: "If I had thought you would do such a thing, how could I say it to your face? But the fact that you say such things shows that you do not know me either." I then understood that this man was speaking with tongue in cheek to test me and without replying burst out laughing. When I retold this story to a friend who had attended the same school, he said: "You understood him I think, but you must not blame him too seriously." I afterward heard that the Hōin Yōboku copied a painting of the ancient game *fêngliuchên* and presented it to His Highness, and that His Highness at once gave it to someone.[226] It appears that people had said that it had been my idea to have this copied. It was completely incomprehensible.

I attended the Buddhist memorial service on the 11th June as before.[227]

When I was summoned on the 22nd June, His Highness informed me through Torii Iga-no-Kami Tadahide that, as he had heard that the house lot I had had until now was too small, he had given me another one in exchange outside Hitotsubashi.[228] On the 25th June, I moved to my new house and returned my former house lot on the 2nd July. On the 22nd July, he heard that the house he had given me at this time was damaged in several places. He told me through Akifusa that he would give me 100 gold *ryō* for the cost of repairs.

Although the grant made to me at this time was 800 *tsubo*, the land I then received was only 600 *tsubo*. His Highness said that later, after he had moved the Government Rice Mill, he would give me additional land. After he died, I received that addition of land and now have 800 *tsubo*.

On the 26th July, it was reported that a group of 16 members of the Matsudaira Family, chief of whom was Matsudaira Izumi-no-Kami Norisato [83], had broken off relations with their relative, Matsudaira Samon [84], because he would not heed their advice.[229] The facts of the case were as follows: Hearing that Samon's hereditary retainers were angry at his employing a man who was disloyal, Izumi-no-Kami warned him about this matter in May of this year. Samon paid no attention to Izumi-no-Kami's admonitions, and on the 8th of this month all his relatives broke off relations with him. Eleven of his hereditary retainers who heard of this left him on the same day, and on the following day, one took the tonsure and retired into a monastery, whereupon the man whom he had employed asked for his dismissal and resigned, and two of his family did the same.

When I was told of this incident, I said that if Samon's conduct was as had been described, I did not think he had acted properly. However, whatever his hereditary retainers said, we could not necessarily conclude that the man he had employed was not a suitable person.[230] In any event, the matter could only be decided after interrogating both lord and retainers. First, Samon was placed in the custody of Mizoguchi Hōki-no-Kami Shigemoto [85], and afterward lord and retainers were summoned to the Hyōjōsho, and the matter was investigated. Also, there were matters which were ordered to be investigated among his relatives (Matsudaira Iwami-no-Kami [82] and Matsudaira Iki-no-Kami).[231] When the retainers of the House were summoned, and the contesting parties confronted with each other, the testimony now elicited differed from what Samon's hereditary retainers had said in the first place, and no one had anything to say against the man called Maeda (Sadaemon) whom Samon had employed at that time. Also, Samon's relatives had accepted without question the unsupported assertions of one man, called Takagi (Hachibei), chief of the retainers, and had uncompromisingly demanded Maeda's expulsion, but Samon had refused. After these matters had been carefully investigated, some of the hereditary retainers were banished and some were expelled. Maeda was reinstated, Samon was confirmed in possession of his fief, and the family was censured for their carelessness. As there is a contemporary record of the details of this affair, I set down a summary here.

I had certain ideas I wished to express, so I put forward a proposal, in which I stated: What is now called the Kanjōsho is what Ta Yü and Pê I administered in ancient times in China.[232]

These were the duties of the Ta-szŭ-k'ung in the time of the Three Dynasties, and in the ages of Han, T'ang, Sung, and Ming all boards of accounting had charge of other important duties besides.[233] If we compare the official system of the Imperial Court of Japan, it had charge of four offices, including the three ministries of internal affairs, finance, and justice, and the provincial inspectors, and of the six or seven offices under them. As the production of wealth, and the disbursements and receipts of the empire were all the concern of this board, the weal and woe of the people of the whole country depended on whether or not it was possible to find suitable persons to take charge of that office. One man cannot be expected to discharge these burdensome duties, and a board of audit should be established as in former times.[234]

When His Highness asked me what that office should have charge of, I replied, first, the taxes of the shogunal domains, and the efficiency of the shogunal stewards; second, transportation of the tax-rice; third, all construction works including embankments; fourth, highway post-stations; fifth, gold, silver, and copper mines throughout the country. On the 2nd August, orders were given to revive this office and carry out my proposals.

Sugioka Yatarō [86] and Hagiwara Genzaemon [87] were appointed to this office. These two men were chosen from the chiefs of the Kanjōsho.

By the time of the former Shōgun [15] the tax-rice from the shogunal domains had decreased yearly till it had fallen to 28.9 percent of the original yield. It seems that the quantity of rice sent in by the farmers on the shogunal domains was exactly the same as in former times, so it must have been because the clerks of the Daikansho appropriated it to their private use. Also, the expense of repairing the embankments increased yearly. It appears that this, too, was because the clerks each worked for his own advantage.

The year after the Board of Audit was established, the tax-rice from the shogunal domains increased by 433,400 bales, and the farmers were very pleased. The expenses for repairing the embankments also decreased by 38,000 ryō, and there was no anxiety about flood or drought. As regards sea transportation also, until this time, every year several tens of thousands of bales of rice had been sunk in the sea, but henceforth we did not hear of loss in wrecks. The other things I spoke of all produced good results.

I presented another proposal containing matters spoken of by my teacher [12]. I said it is the Hyōjōsho upon which the weal and woe of the empire depends, so that matters connected with it are of the greatest importance. Recently the officials of this body have been negligent in their work and have handed over their duties to lower officials. This is most reprehensible. Furthermore, cases involving loans to *daimyō* and those of lesser rank have come under the attention of the Hyōjōsho, and this is most injurious to the dignity of the State. As a result of my representations on these matters, on the 6th August, His Highness issued directions to the members of the Hyōjōsho, and furthermore directed that, in judgments concerning money borrowed by those of high rank, the recommendations of the officials of the Hyōjōsho must be submitted to him.[235] He requested me to present proposals, but he died before he could deal with it. As my drafts about these matters are still in existence, I have only set down an outline here.

On the 11th October [1712], Ogiwara Ōmi-no-Kami Shigehide [51] was deprived of office and confined to his house. People were overjoyed although they did not know the reason. Actually, it was because, since April in the spring of this year until the previous day (the 10th), I had sent in fully three petitions. They were lengthy, but I will set down one or two points contained in them.

As is known far and wide, ever since Shigehide was given control of the finances of the State in the time of the former Shōgun [15], the fine laws of our Divine Ancestor [8] have been destroyed and the military classes and the common people have been caused continual suffering.[236] There is no need to speak of it now. I have referred above to the fact that at the beginning of the present reign, Shigehide wanted to remint the silver coinage, but owing to the admirable determination of His Highness, this was not carried out.

As mentioned previously, he later recommended that His Highness should reconstruct his official residence. As a result, people said that the work of construction at this time had beggared the State. For example, it was even rumored that one pavilion was entirely constructed of sandalwood, and that from this one fact you could infer the rest.[237] When I heard this, I said through Aki-fusa [24]: "At the present time, people are saying many things which I cannot accept. However, according to report, a sandal-wood pavilion was constructed during the T'ang Dynasty, and the rebellion in the T'ien Pao era arose because of this.[238] Therefore, I do not consider that the installation of His Highness in his new residence is a cause for rejoicing at this time." Shortly after this, His Highness sent a message through Ichi-no-Kami Masa-nao [30] that he would have me shown what had been built at this time, and that he would have Masanao conduct me. Ichi-no-Kami showed me everything without reserve, even where ordinary people do not enter. We came to the pavilion, said to have been constructed of sandalwood, which I had heard about. This was near a hill beyond a pond in the south garden. It appeared to be one *jō* high by two *jō* wide. Pointing to a circular tree about one *shaku* in circumference around which vines were entwined here and there and which was serving as the alcove pillar, Ichi-no-Kami said: "This is the sandalwood you heard about." When I examined what Masanao indicated, I found that it was not Japa-nese material. "In the summer of this year," he explained, "when His Highness took inventory of the dried rice in the granaries in the northern part of the castle, a tree one *jō* long, which tradition had it was of sandalwood, was taken out and presented to him. Although it appeared to be sandalwood, perhaps because it had been there so many years, when it was burned for incense, it had no characteristic fragrance. As this happened just about the time they were building this pavilion, His Highness told them to use it as timber for it."

Looking down from this place, I could see everything that had been rebuilt at this time, and everything I saw contradicted the rumors being circulated. Furthermore, it could not be maintained that it had exhausted the national finances to the extent that peo-ple had claimed. I could not understand it. However, when Shige-hide first gave orders about the construction, he said that the timber in the shogunal warehouse was not usable, so he obtained timber from the merchants' warehouses. It was the custom at this time to calculate the price of one length of timber as 100 gold *ryō*, but Shigehide said it was a waste of time to argue about the price in a case like this and agreed to buy the timber at whatever price was quoted. With the addition of the cost of construction, he spent more than 700,000 *ryō* of gold in all, it is said.

Much building was undertaken under the former Shōgun [15], and ever since then the rise in the price of timber has been unprecedented, both in ancient and modern times. Since ancient times, the price of sandalwood and aloeswood has been calculated as so many times their weight in silver. Nowadays, they say, the price of a square *sun* of cedar is double its weight in gold. And so merchants who deal in timber enrich themselves in no time, and it is impossible to count those who have amassed hundreds of thousands or even millions. Rumor had it that it was not only they who benefited. Those who grew rich by dividing the spoils with them were also without number.

From the spring of the following year, 1710, on, there were discussions on the advisability of reminting the gold coinage. This was because His Highness had heard that many of the gold coins paid as salary that spring had broken and bent, and those on small salaries had been particularly distressed. When he inquired about this, Shigehide had replied: "Though the weight of a gold *ryō* reminted in the previous regime was the same as the old standard, owing to the increase in the quantity of silver contained in it, the proportion of silver to gold had been increased and its quality had deteriorated, so that when it knocked against anything, it either bent or broke.[239] If it was desired to prevent the breaking and bending, it would be best to restore the proportion of gold and silver to the old standard. However, if the coinage were to be restored to the old standard, the amount of gold in circulation at the present time would necessarily be reduced by half. So the simplest thing would be, first remove the amount of silver which had previously been increased, and restore the quality to the old standard, even though one *ryō* of gold would not weigh as much as formerly, and later on, by using the gold produced from the mines throughout the country, restore the weight to what it was before."

The ladies in attendance on His Highness's consort [60], the pages who waited on the chamberlains, the under-servants, and the like complained that many of the coins

[166]

paid in salary this spring broke and bent, and this had reached the ears of His Highness. I cannot understand this. Among the gold and silver handed over to the government, in each case, the coins in both the Gold and Silver Mints which were not in the least broken or bent were chosen. When the government paid them out, there should not have been any like that. But there must certainly have been some reason why such a thing happened.

When I heard that everyone had agreed with Shigehide's advice, I presented my opinion. This was that ever since the re-minting had been carried out in the Genroku era by increasing the amount of silver in the gold, and the amount of copper in the silver, people had complained about the deterioration in the quality, and eventually the prices of commodities fluctuated.[240] If the coins are now reminted again, even though they are restored to the old standard in quality, people will be sure to be suspicious if their weight is half what it was formerly, and they will not circulate. Therefore His Highness should appoint officials with the duty of calling Ōmi-no-Kami [51] to account if the quality of the gold he had orders to remint at this time varied in the slightest from the standard. In accordance with my advice, His Highness gave orders for the silver and gold to be reminted, and appointed one ōmetsuke and two metsuke to take charge of this affair.

This order was issued on the 13th May [1712]. Yokota Bitchū-no-Kami [76] was appointed ōmetsuke and Nagasaki Hanzaemon and Nagai Saburōemon metsuke.[241] Nagasaki is now Iyo-no-Kami.

At this time, Shigehide had the mint present a sample of gold to His Highness. The gold coins, equivalent to those of former times, were thinner in quality and smaller when compared with those of the preceding ages. But those in which the silver content was greater than in former times were not so thin and small, even though they were not as poor as the gold coins of Genroku. I was summoned and shown a sample by Akifusa [24].

When I looked at them, I said: "Some years ago, someone sent two barrels of *sake* to the house of a friend of mine, and after the lapse of some time, all that *sake* had changed to vinegar. This was because it was mixed with water. The recipient was very disappointed and said he preferred *sake* unmixed with water, even if it were only one small bottle. Although this is a vulgar illustration, it applies to this case. The best thing to do will be to reduce the quantity of silver in order to prevent the bending and breaking and to make them of the highest quality, however thin and small the coins may become." His Highness said: "My ideas are exactly in agreement with the opinion you have expressed," and he gave orders that the quality was to be restored to the ancient standard, however thin and small they became.

When a second sample of the coins was presented, His Highness showed them to me saying: "By making them this way, they seem to be trying to trick people." I had a look at them and found they were the same as the old coins in quality, and a little bigger and thicker than those we saw before, but when examined closely, the central part was as thin as paper while the outer edge was thicker.

At this time I also said: "It appears that the expense of recoinage is heavy, but there is one thing I do not understand. What has been done with the silver previously removed from the gold? If it is used, the expense will be greatly reduced." Doubtless, His Highness inquired into this matter, but I did not hear what Shigehide [51] replied. I afterward heard that at this time he had already secretly reminted the silver too and had used the silver recovered from the gold for the new silver coinage.[242] The gold recoined under Shigehide's supervision at this time was commonly called "Kenjikin."[243] I heard that officials at the Gold Mint said that the gold was still not equivalent in quality to that of former times.

While all this was happening, I heard that a great deal of debased silver had been coined and circulated.[244] I did not understand this, and presented the following message: "Since permission to mint debased silver was refused even when we faced a national emergency like that of last spring, it is hardly likely that this could be true.[245] However, as the rumor is widely circulated, I wish to inform you of the fact."

One day later, His Highness said: "You must read these documents," and had Akifusa [24] bring them out. On reading them, I found it was a sworn declaration by certain members of the Kanjōsho. When those who had superintended the reminting of the silver, which Ōmi-no-Kami had been ordered to carry out, were questioned, in their replies they had declared that the silver reminted at this time did not contravene the law which was revised in August 1706. I replied: "Those who have superintended the work, and those who have carried it out have said the same. I can no longer dispute this," and retired.

This happened in June or July [1710]. However, I forget the date. The letter which Shigehide presented at this time was signed by two men called Hogi Yaemon [88] and Komiyama Tomoemon [89], heads of the *kanjōshū*, who were the Shōgun's clerks at the mint. As I later heard, on the 18th April this year the three men, Shigehide, Hogi, and Komiyama, had secretly given orders to coin debased silver. This was commonly called the "Futatsuhōjigin." Shortly afterward, on the 13th May, an even more debased coinage was again minted. This was commonly called the "Mitsuhōjigin."

When I was in Kyōto in the winter of this year, I visited the Sesshō [69], and he said: "What do you think about the reports that Ōmi-no-Kami [51] has received fresh rewards?" I replied: "I have heard that these are rewards for Ōmi-no-Kami's unremitting labor. If a man's rank and salary exceed his merit, it cannot be called a blessing, but if Shigehide reforms his old behavior in gratitude for these rewards, that will not only benefit him alone but will also be fortunate for our own times."

Shigehide's new rewards came about because at the beginning of His Highness's reign, the ceremony of his inauguration as Shōgun could not be performed, owing to the exhaustion of finances, but through Shigehide's contrivances, not only was this ceremony carried out, but His Highness's official residence was fortunately reconstructed. Even though the cost amounted to a vast sum, again by Shigehide's contrivances, the matter was finished without difficulties.[246] Many praised him saying that these things could not have been so easily accomplished if he had not been there at the time, and therefore His Highness rewarded him.

However, he accomplished all these things by perpetrating his evil designs, and by employing fraudulent shifts, skillfully adapted to changing circumstances. For example, when the palace to the north of the castle was to be built at the end of the previous regime, the *bugyō* searched for material but they could not obtain any, so orders were given to Shigehide, whereupon, in no time at all, he managed to get hold of a vast quantity of fine materials, much to the amazement of everyone.[247]

This was because Shigehide had for years held the financial power of Japan in his hands, and none of the rich merchants throughout the country dared oppose his wishes. Moreover, the price of materials difficult to obtain at that time was high, and the profit to the merchants was great, and there were not a few cases where Shigehide obtained his share.

On the pretext that the treasury was already exhausted at this time, he alarmed both His Highness and the officials, then twice announced to the world that he had succeeded in carrying through undertakings by his own special plan. However, he had no other plan than secretly recoining the gold and silver. He took a share of the profits for himself and also used them to eke out the national finances. I wonder how big his share from the recoinage of the gold was at this time. When he refined the silver, Shigehide took more than 260,000 *ryō* as his share while his retainer, Nagai Hanroku [90], received 60,000 as his share. And it is impossible to list all the famous paintings and curios that came Shigehide's way in addition.

When the members of the Silver Mint, those whose hereditary work was minting silver, were accused of treason, a ledger kept by one Fukae Shōzaemon [91] was seized, and in it we can see Shigehide's operations in detail.[248] This was just during the short time that he minted the "Futatsuhōji," "Mitsuhōji," and "Yotsuhōji."[249] But for the space of 30-odd years, from the beginning of the Genroku era to the present era of Hōei, the facts were obscure.[250]

Shigehide was also directed by His Highness to take charge of the reception of the Korean Embassy. I do not think what he did was for the good of the State. The one item concerning the saddle horses used for receiving and seeing off the ambassadors was, on

[170]

account of my advice, imposed by His Highness as a service on all the *daimyō* in accordance with former precedent.

In recent times, when any work has been undertaken, it has been carried out by calling tenders from the merchants and giving the contract to the lowest bid. For example, when the repair of the lodging houses for the visit of the Korean Envoys was undertaken, the *bugyō* in charge published a list of the repairs needed and invited merchants to submit estimates. Each merchant prepared his estimate, wrote it down on a slip of paper, and sealed and sent it in. This is called submitting a tender. The *bugyō* summoned the merchants who had participated, opened the tenders, and gave the job to the man who put in the lowest tender. This is called accepting the lowest tender. After the work was finished, the price was paid publicly from government funds. This is the normal procedure.

Although this seems fair, actually it is not. Nowadays, the merchants first of all give the magistrates sometimes 100 *ryō*, sometimes 1,000 *ryō*, according to the size of the contract, and call it a "gift in anticipation," saying: "If you give me this contract, when I get paid by the government, I will give you a percentage in addition to this." This they call a "thank-offering." Those who give small "anticipatory gifts" and "thank-offerings" are not permitted to submit tenders; much less chance, it is unnecessary to say, have those who do not give any such presents. And so every time a tender is called, the *bugyō* in charge of the work always makes 1,000 gold *ryō*. Things which do not cost 100 *ryō* when built by ordinary people, cannot be done for less than 10,000 *ryō* when the government does it. The exhaustion of the treasury in the previous regime was chiefly due to this. And so, for the reception of the Korean Embassy at this time, it is easy to see why the merchants did nothing except by contract, no matter what the job was.

Thereafter, as time passed, people grumbled about the debased silver, and all commodity prices became unstable. It was said this was because of the construction work during the previous regime and the visit by the Korean Embassy. I have heard that in ancient times the achievements and shortcomings of the government were assessed every three years, but three years have already passed since the present rule began, and the condition of the empire does not appear to have changed from what it was at the beginning.[251]

In April this year [1712], I presented a document discussing these matters. His Highness replied: "Those who have talent have no virtue, and those who have virtue have no talent. It is very difficult to get conscientious men. We have no one who can handle the finances of the empire. For years, there has been nothing about Shigehide's character that we did not know." I argued: "Since ancient times, it has been difficult to obtain conscientious men, so it is unnecessary to speak of it, but Shigehide has neither talent nor virtue. You think that though Shigehide has no virtue, yet he has talent. That is quite incorrect." As I have already mentioned before, I had sent in a petition suggesting the establishment of a board of audit in the Kanjōsho.

About this time, there was a dispute between the peasants in shogunal and private domains, and they were summoned by the Hyōjōsho. On Shigehide's word alone that it was all the fault of those on the private domains, the officials dared not discuss the case or give a decision. Also, Shigehide even told the members of the Rōjū at this time that His Highness's own orders were mistaken, and that he would discuss the matter with them. In consequence, I wrote out ten articles on His Highness's mistake in employing such a wicked fellow and presented a petition on the 10th October [1712]. His Highness was surprised at the vehemence of my words, and on the morning of the following day, the 11th, Akifusa was directed by His Highness to inform me that Shigehide had been deprived of office.

Before this, there was a boundary dispute between the farmers of the villages of Ukawa and Uchishita and those of the village of Kita-Komatsu in Shiga District, Ōmi Province.[252] When that dispute was decided at the office of the *machi bugyō* of Kyōto, the people of Ukawa made a complaint. His Highness appointed a *daikan* as investigator, and he examined the matter again, but the people of Ukawa still complained, so they were put into gaol but they still did not cease their complaints. They said that their complaint must now be decided by the Hyōjōsho.

In the spring of this year, His Highness told me about this.

I replied: "This case is by no means as simple as it appears. On the contrary, it is very complicated." When His Highness asked why, I said: "The people of Kita-Komatsu have unearthed trees and stones, and argue that they are boundary marks. It appears that on these grounds, they have annexed this land to Kita-Komatsu. But it is rumored that they carefully planned this action years ago. Hence I spoke as I did before." When in due course a decision was given by the Hyōjōsho, Ōmi-no-Kami [51] said that the proofs which Kita-Komatsu had were clear.

Again, merchant ships from Funatsu in Kii Province, driven off course by storms, reached the shore of Shinohara in Tōtōmi Province, whereupon the farmers on the shogunal domains mobbed together, broke up the ships, and stole the cargoes.[253] Ōmi-no-Kami argued that what the people on the shogunal domains had done was no crime, and wanted to punish the sailors.

Again, the farmers on the shogunal domains in the neighborhood of Nihommatsu in Mutsu Province were wounded by the *samurai* of Niwa Sakyō-Daibu Tadashige because they insulted them.[254] Ōmi-no-Kami said it was a crime that the farmers had been injured by the *samurai*, and tried to punish Niwa's *samurai*.

At about this time, cases before the Hyōjōsho were decided by two men, Shigehide and Honda Danjō-Shōhitsu Tadaharu [92], in consultation. The officials did not dare take part in their discussions. Shigehide also bragged that he did not think that the orders His Highness had given the Hyōjōsho in the past were correct, but that once he had discussed the matter with him, they would do as he said.

About 40 days before Shigehide was relieved of office, on the 2nd September he had again had the silver recoined.[255] This time, he gave out that it was at His Highness's secret orders. I thought it was strange, but according to what I heard afterward, His Highness had said to Shigehide at the end of the previous month, August: "About the summer of the year before last [1710], I heard that new silver was circulating, and when I asked about this, you presented a written statement that this was by no means so. I thought it was as you said. But then even after that, rumors did not cease, and finally I heard that the people's distress was due to this. You must explain matters immediately," whereupon Shigehide replied he had good reasons for what he had done.

On the following day, he presented a document in which he said: "Owing to the fact that the treasury was already exhausted at the beginning of your rule, I urged that the silver must be recoined. But I was told that this matter could not be discussed again. However, as there was no other way than this to provide for government expenses, ever since the year before last [1709], I have secretly had the silver recoined, with the result that matters have proceeded without mishap until today. I knew all along that this was a crime, nevertheless I admit it."

His Highness was greatly surprised when he heard this. While he wondered what to do now, Shigehide, on the other hand, thinking: "I have already said what I had to say. There is nothing to be afraid of now," again issued an order for the reminting of the silver about mid-September [1711], stating in it that these were the secret orders from His Highness.

Without the entries in Fukae's [91] ledger, as mentioned before, and judging only by this document of Shigehide's, it would appear that although he defrauded the people, Shigehide's aim was to sacrifice his life for the sake of his country. Even this assertion of his reveals the extent of his cunning. I said: "This statement, being written in Shigehide's own hand, is proof that His Highness was ignorant of the whole matter from beginning to end. Do not lose it." It must be in Akifusa's house now.

Although Shigehide was dismissed and died soon afterward, I do not think the persistent poison he injected into the empire will ever be removed. In particular, preparations were deficient in respect to armaments, and there is no way of repairing the public and private harm resulting from the economic deterioration. Never since the dawn of time has there ever been such an evil, worthless fellow. For 30-odd years, there was no one throughout the length and breadth of Japan who was not aware of it. Although there were many hereditary retainers of the Tokugawa House of high standing during the rule of these two Shōguns [15, 3], there was not one who sacrificed himself for his lord's sake and spoke of this matter. I, by the exertion of my little strength, took up my brush and did not cease to petition. When I had petitioned as many as three times, His Highness reached a firm decision. There will never be another ruler like him. As he died the following month [1712], if he had delayed his decision, he would probably have been blamed in later times. It was a critical matter. People in ancient times boasted of accomplishing one-twentieth of what Shun did, so it will not be a bad thing if the documents of Akifusa belonging to that time and the drafts of the three petitions which I wrote are transmitted to my posterity.[256] Also, my posterity will understand the relations between His Highness and myself at that time.

This year [1712], just about the time spring was over and summer had come, His Highness's health gradually declined, and even when the heat abated and the weather became somewhat cooler, medicine was without effect. From this time on, his recovery was despaired of, and on the 25th October he sent for me and presented me with the *Twenty-one Histories* which he had planned to give me as a last keepsake.[257] After a day's interval, he sent for me on the 27th and inquired of me privately through Akifusa as follows: "That which hath no beginning may be confident of no end."[258] Therefore it is always necessary to take thought about matters after one's death. And this is much more necessary when one is ill. If, because we are afraid of death like women and children, we take no thought about such matters until we are on the brink of the grave, it is impossible to avoid making mistakes. During my illness, I have thought about what is to be done after my death, and I can see only two alternatives. I have sent for you because I will make up my mind in accordance with your decision. Unexpectedly, the succession of the line of the Divine Ancestor [8] passed to me, and although I do not lack a son to inherit after me, no one should regard the empire as his private property. Since ancient times, whenever there was a child ruler, disturbances have been frequent. The Divine Ancestor established the Three Houses for just such an emergency as this.[259] Perhaps I should make Owari Dono my heir, and if my child, by good luck, grows to manhood, entrust the question of his succession to the right feeling of him who inherited from me.[260] Or perhaps, since among my several sons, only one survives to inherit from me, until he grows up—if he is so fortunate—I should establish Owari Dono in the Western Palace, place the control of affairs in his hands and if by some misfortune my heir should die, let Owari Dono succeed.[261] Consider these two alternatives."

When I heard what His Highness said, I replied: "The lowliest parents pray for the good fortune of their own children. And it is indeed a blessing that His Highness has given thought to this problem. But I do not think that either of his suggestions will ensure the well-being of the country or of society. It is not necessary to go far afield to find examples. In the time of the Divine Ancestor, before Yūki Dono's [93] premature death, people were uneasy in their minds. During the rule of the second Shōgun [46], while Suruga Dono [47] was still alive, again the people knew no freedom from anxiety. Even where relations between fathers and sons and brothers are sound, as the vulgar proverb has it: 'Misfortune comes from below,' and since people commonly work each for his own advantage, they fabricate stories and make enemies of those who were good friends, until it comes to a point where a man will slay his own brother.[262] This sort of thing happened even in ancient times. Hereafter, as society deteriorates with the passage of time, it will happen more and more. If His Highness does as he has suggested, society is bound to split into two factions and disturbances will ensue like those that broke out during the Ōnin era.[263] During the history of your ancestors, there were many examples of children succeeding their fathers. Among these, how can we criticize what was done in the case of the Divine Ancestor?[264] While your family—and in particular the Three Houses—and the hereditary retainers are there to support him, what can go wrong if your young son succeeds?"

Then he sent a second message to me saying: "I understand the point you wish to make. But a child ruler is, to use the common phrase, like 'foam upon the waters.' Unless I made provision for the possibility of his death occurring a short time after mine, I would not be looking very far ahead. Please consider what I should do in case that happens."

I replied: "As His Highness said in the first place, it was for just such an emergency that the Three Houses were established." When His Highness heard what I said, he replied: "I have made up my mind what to do about affairs after my death. When

[176]

I shortly rise from my sick bed, we will laugh about how we worried needlessly about these matters today." At this I only wept.

Shortly afterward, I said to Akifusa [24]: "I did not expect that today would be the end of my labors and anxieties for years past. Please convey these sentiments to His Highness." I spoke thus because there was something on my mind, but at such a time he did not ask me about it again, nor did I speak of it again.

I heard that immediately after this His Highness made thorough and far-sighted plans about affairs after his death, and just mentioned them vaguely to his consort [60]. When his death drew near, he summoned the Rōjū and told them that he had spoken about what was to be done after his death to Echizen-no-Kami [24], and that they must ask him if there was anything they wanted to know.[265] Again, when I said that my service would end that day, he must have wondered what I meant, and so I thought I should explain my meaning, but as he did not refer to it, I too did not mention it again. Afterward, I spoke about this matter to Akifusa. However, that too was before His Highness's line came to an end.[266] It is all like a fleeting dream.

After Shigehide retired, the recoinage of the silver was stopped, and His Highness asked me to draft orders stating that the question of the gold and silver coinage was to be discussed with the general public.[267] On the 7th [November 1712], he gave orders to the Rōjū that they were to issue this order on the 9th.

That evening, officials hurried about saying His Highness's illness had taken a critical turn. When I also hastened to the palace, Aoyama Bizen-no-Kami Akiyuki received me, and when he said: "I am worried about what will happen after His Highness's death, but since you have come, my mind is at ease," I replied: "That question is already settled."[268] "If that is so, that is very fortunate," he said. In this emergency, there was no one who spoke of such matters. I was impressed, thinking: "He is indeed the descendant of illustrious men."

From this time forth, His Highness spoke of nothing but affairs after his death. About noon on the 12th, the day he died, he summoned his consort first, and then the mother [94] of his young sons, and said: "Today I feel better. If I go on like this, I'll soon be up and with you again." Then he summoned all those of high rank, and after he had given them orders about affairs after his death, he summoned all those who had served near his person and thanked them for their services until that day. After that, he summoned me through Akihira [41]. Akifusa was in attendance by his pillow and Masanao [30] behind. His Highness said nothing, but just opened his eyes and looked fixedly at me. This was the end of our daily meetings that had continued for more than 20 years.

After that, His Highness said to Akifusa: "I think there is nothing more that we ought to discuss now, but if there is anything you still wish to say, I will listen." As Akifusa replied: "Nothing remains," he then said: "Raise me up." Those in attendance said: "Why should you speak so?" His Highness said: "I have said what I wanted to say. There is nothing on my mind now. I only wish to be out of pain." Even now, those who were in attendance weep when they speak of what happened at that time.

It is said that at this time a man called Mizuno, who had been his personal attendant for some time, was summoned. As he was involuntarily choking back sobs. His Highness said: "You are an unexpectedly foolish fellow.[269] A man's death is nothing to fuss about." It was a case of showing one's humanity by the mistakes one makes.[270] Mizuno's behavior moved one to pity. Also, for His Highness to have spoken thus at the hour of his death proves what a fine lord he was.

From the beginning of His Highness's rule, copper currency for carrying on foreign trade at Nagasaki harbor had been insufficient, and commerce being difficult to carry on, the populace lost their employment. As a result there were reports from the Bugyōsho, and His Highness questioned me about them. I replied: "I think this is a very difficult matter to discuss. I will give you my opinion after I have carefully looked into the causes."

As the drafts I presented since that time have been made into many separate pamphlets, I shall not set down the details of them here.[271] The gist of them was, since the time foreign trade began during the shogunate of the present rulers, for the space of a hundred years, the treasure of Japan has flowed abroad and we have already lost the greater part.

We have lost one quarter of the gold and three quarters of the silver.[272] This is an estimate based on official statements.[273] The total amount is probably higher, but there are no figures to go on.

It does not take any special knowledge to foresee that within a hundred years from now the treasure of our country will be completely exhausted. Our country yearly produces a variety of goods. Taking a comparison from the human body, we can liken the Five Cereals to the never-ceasing production of hair.[274] The Five Metals are like the bones which are not produced a second time.[275] Even in the case of the Five Cereals, there is good and bad soil, and there are good and bad years. But the situation is even more difficult in the case of the Five Metals, for there are few places which produce these and the yield is not constant. Spending the useful wealth of Japan in exchange for useless foreign goods is not a far-sighted policy. Since ancient times Japan has never needed the assistance of foreign countries, and even today, except for medicines, we want nothing. Even if no foreign ships visited our shores, as was the case in ancient times, it would not be impossible for us to obtain everything we need. In the regulations of the ancient kings, it is said: "Estimate the income, and plan the expenditure."[276] Therefore, if we continue unavoidable trade, by comparing the amount of treasure circulating in Japan at this time, and the amount produced every year in the various provinces, we can estimate and fix the yearly amount to be sent to China, the countries of the south and west, Korea, and the Luchus.[277] Even if the price of articles bought and sold in Japan is double, the anxiety is still less than exhausting the treasure of our country and pouring it into foreign countries. I discussed such things in detail. His Highness said: "Well then, you must first draft regulations concerning foreign trade for me," and he many times gave orders to the Nagasaki Bugyōsho based on these regulations.

I argued as follows: "In such matters as these, though clever people make plans, if the material necessary to put them into effect is lacking, nothing can be done in practice. Even though there may be sufficient material, if knowledge is lacking, it is impossible to make plans. The situation is much worse when there is neither material nor knowledge, for then nothing can be done. And so it will be difficult to carry out this plan." But the government has received nothing but complaints last year and this year about the amount of copper being insufficient for trade and the townspeople of Nagasaki being thrown out of employment with the threat of starvation daily growing more serious as a consequence. In addition to this, on account of private trade (commonly called undercover buying and selling), much silver coin has flowed out of the country. When His Highness heard about this, he said: "Such a state of affairs is bad for the present and future. If we look back to ancient times, we see that there was no small quantity of goods like medicine produced in Japan. Cotton, tobacco, and the like were not heard of in ancient times, but at present they are produced everywhere.[278] Even as far as commodities never before produced in Japan are concerned, if we obtain the seeds and test the quality of the soil, we can introduce them. I have heard that in ancient times in China, there was something called Japanese brocade, and there was also a great amount of cloth woven in our country. These still do not require foreign materials. First have such things woven as a trial."

The Kyōto Bugyō received those orders, but the cloth which they had woven and presented to His Highness reached the palace when his illness was already critical (perhaps about the 10th October [1712]—I do not remember for certain). He was pleased to hear about it and gave orders to Akifusa to have them shown to me. I was reminded of the search for the mandarin of everlasting life.[279] How sad it was!

In the spring of this year, Ichijō-In-no-Miya was granted permission to wear a scarlet robe on the occasion of his visit to Edo.[280] As a consequence, it was reported that the head of Daijō-In had said that there was no example of a priest of Kōfukuji being granted a scarlet robe before completion of his studies.[281] He feared that owing to such a mark of favor, a distinction would also be made between the two branch temples in the future, and that quarrels would arise. When this statement was communicated to the Court, the reply was made that the Imperial Decree granting Ichijō-In-no-Miya permission to wear a scarlet robe at this time was because he was an imperial prince, and they said much besides.

His Highness replied: "There must be no confusion between the fact that respect must be paid to the Imperial Family and the fact that there should be no difference in rank between the tem-

[180]

ples. And so henceforth, in the ceremonies and regulations of temples, should we issue decrees in accordance with the ancient rules? Also, if there were any difference in rank between these two branch temples, we could not expect the whole of Kōfukuji to maintain peace. And so henceforth, shall we prevent imperial princes from entering Ichijō-In, or shall we require imperial princes to enter Daijō-In also? There must be an imperial decision concerning these three points." (This letter was sent on the 29th October, I think.)

After His Highness's death, a letter dated the 11th November and signed by Dainagon Kin'akira (Tokudaiji) [95] and the former Dainagon Shige'eda (Niwata) [96] arrived saying that the necessity for respecting the Imperial House and the fact that there was no difference between temples should not be confused. So when he took part in Buddhist ceremonies, Ichijō-In-no-Miya should wear a white robe while his studies were still incomplete. Furthermore, if the Shōgun were dissatisfied, the entry of imperial princes into the Ichijō-In would henceforth be discontinued. His Highness had asked my opinion about these things. So I drafted his official letter to the Court, but everything became like a transient dream.

His Highness died on the 12th November, a little after dusk, it seems. When the officials assembled on the following day, and his will was read, the eyes of all present were moist.[282] On the 18th, the body was conveyed to Zōjōji.[283] I too followed in the cortege. About this time, snow fell every day, and when you caught the flakes in a vessel, they were gleaming yellow like thistles. They fell, borne by the wind. After some time, they crumbled into powder.

On the evening of the 30th November, the interment took place. As there was no precedent for mourning clothes, those who escorted the body wore ceremonial dress, with the tail-piece of their headgear folded, and black-lacquered scabbards for their swords. It was sad to be included in the number also.

About that time, everyone said that a great star appeared and circled the moon, but I did not see it. While the body was passing from the temple to the burial ground, I remember that hail pelted down. It fell in particularly large quantities on top of the funeral pavilion, and it was gathered and presented. It was all like gleaming white jewels. For two or three days, the streets were blocked with crowds of people gathering hailstones in various places. Such things do happen. If I had heard about such things, I would not have believed them. During the mourning period for His Highness, the voices of young children could not be heard.[284] I have read of the populace grieving as for their own parents, but it was indeed a grateful thing to witness such grief with my own eyes.[285]

On the 21st November, the results of the deliberations of the officials concerning the gold and silver, about which His Highness had given orders to the Rōjū on the 7th previous, were put into effect. I heard that there were some who said that I had fabricated this order after His Highness's death. But as they had received orders on the 7th that it was to be put into effect on the 9th, the Rōjū knew that it had not proceeded from me.

Among those who received orders at that time, three men, Sagami-no-Kami Masanao [62], Kawachi-no-Kami Masamine [37], and Bungo-no-Kami Masataka [97] are still alive now. There was a rumor that people had seen a placard stuck up on the gate of my house saying: "The place where shogunal decrees about gold and silver are made."

There is another incident which comes to mind in connection with this. At the beginning of His Highness's rule, there were many critical scribblings.[286] Although this had happened during the Empō era, it was not as bad then as now.[287] The members of the Rōjū said: "It is most unfitting that this outbreak should grow worse day by day. We must absolutely stop it." His Highness said: "In this way, the people can say what they think without fear. As I consider that it may provide valuable warnings for myself, or may be useful for the administration, I have told the young *samurai* who wait on me personally, to copy whatever is written and show it to me. You should also seek out such scribblings and read them. It will be most unfitting to stop the people's means of criticism by forbidding these activities."

Also after that, His Highness gave orders to the Hyōjōsho about the decision in the case of the shipwreck of a boat from Funatsu village in Kii Province on the coast of Shinohara in Tōtōmi Province. (I forget now the date of this affair.)[288] It arose when this boat, driven off course by the wind, was stranded on Shinohara coast, and villagers in the neighborhood came out and broke up the boat and stole the cargo. When they did so, the sailors drew their swords, and a villager was wounded. The decision of the officials of the Hyōjōsho was that, although there was no doubt that the people of this neighborhood had mobbed together and stolen goods from the boat, as there were so many of them, it was impossible to punish them all; furthermore, although the sailors had said that boxes of money had been stolen, actually such articles had not been stolen, and in view of these lies, these men should be put to death.

When His Highness asked me about this, I said: "If it is certain that goods from the ship have been stolen, it is not difficult to punish those who stole them, no matter how many of them there are. In a regulation dated the 1st September 1636, it is written that if sailors conspire with those on the shore to steal the cargo, the sailors, it goes without saying, and those who conspire with them will all be put to death, and each house on the coast will be fined 100 *mon*. When an earlier Shōgun [9] laid down these laws, they must have been intended to deal with such cases as this. It is even more unfitting not to put the laws of the land into effect when those who have broken the law are numerous. According to the regulations of the Kan'ei era, if the crime of the ringleaders is clear and we make every house on the coast that participated in the attack pay 100 *mon* and give the money to the sailors, it will make up to a small extent for what they have lost. Also the reason that the sailors at first said that their money-chests had been stolen was because they were very angry, and they wished to magnify the enormity of the crime against them. Even if this did not happen, the goods on the ship have been stolen by people all along the coast, and no trace of them can be found. Perhaps the sailors thought that if they did not say that the money-chests had been stolen, they would not have been able to get a judgment. We must not blame the lower classes severely for harboring such ideas. In addition, which is the lighter and which the more serious crime, to steal things or tell lies? It would be very wrong for those who have committed the serious crime to escape, and those who have committed the trifling crime to be punished." So His Highness said that I must present a draft of the judgment in accordance with what I had said. I presented the draft, and after he died, I heard that it was put into effect.

BOOK III

During those years past, the service I rendered His late Highness [3] and the treatment he accorded me were quite exceptional. I never hesitated to express my honest opinion, and neither did he disregard my advice. But now that he was dead, even though I were to advance an opinion, there was no one who would pay any attention to it. It was for this reason that I had stated earlier that my service to my country would come to an end with His Highness's death.[1] However, I felt that I should like to try to carry out those far-reaching plans for the country and the people, which he had told me of but had not been able to put into effect up to the time of his death.[2] In matters other than these, there were many to assist the present Shōgun [25], and therefore they were no concern of mine.

I spoke to Akifusa [24] about the official diary, for which I had received instructions from His late Highness in the spring of this year [1712].

At that time, His Highness had considered the compilation of a history of the Divine Ancestor [8] and had placed the project in my hands, but when I examined the diaries of the time, I found they were unsatisfactory.[3] His Highness therefore directed me to prepare a model plan and to obtain information from the Wakadoshiyori about events of primary importance, and from the *metsuke* about those of secondary importance. He gave instructions about this to the present Yamato-no-Kami Shigeyuki [61] and Katō Ukon (a member of the *metsuke*). I told Akifusa that as there was no way of carrying out His late Highness's intentions now, affairs were sure to relapse to their former condition.

Meanwhile, in December it was announced that as the present

[185]

Shōgun was still a child and was not required to wear mourning for his father, the messengers bearing the divine offerings would be sent to Nikkō and Ise immediately.[4] I was amazed to hear of such a decision. I approached Akifusa on the subject, and he said that Daigaku-no-Kami Nobuatsu [21] had so advised on the grounds that a child under seven years does not wear mourning for its parents.

As I have previously observed, I no longer had anything to do with affairs of state, so I ought not to have interfered, but on this one point alone I could not remain silent.

I explained that though it is stated in the *I Li* that there is no mourning *for* children under seven years, this does not mean that there is no mourning *by* children under seven years for their parents.[5] Much less could such an inference be drawn in the case of the present Shōgun, who has inherited the control of the empire and is the overlord of all the people. He is not to be compared with an ordinary child.

Accordingly, Akifusa questioned Nobuatsu on this point, and his reply was: "In the *Bukukiryō* of the Genroku era, which I had the honor of framing, the immutable regulations of Japan are laid down and these admit no exception.[6] Whoever put forward such a preposterous suggestion?"

Akifusa then told me that the Rōjū had already agreed to Nobuatsu's proposals, and in view of Nobuatsu's uncompromising stand, it was impossible to induce them to change their minds now.

I immediately presented Akifusa with a document setting forth my views. In this I stated: "This question has profound implications. It would, however, be out of place for me to enter into controversy with the officials on this point, and I realize it will have no bearing on the welfare of the state whether my opinion is followed or not, but I beg you to make it known to those in authority."

My opinion was as follows: "When the sages of old laid down the regulations for mourning, their aim was to strengthen moral ties, particularly those between father and son and between lord and retainer.[7] As time went by, even in China some generations departed from the ancient rules, while the regulations of Japan differed to a greater extent still from those of ancient times.[8] Nevertheless, all these later regulations are based on those of the

[186]

sages of old, yet they are not wanting in provisions which take into account the convenience of their own times. When the *Bukukiryō* were revised during the Genroku era, there should have been no deviation from the intention of the ancient sages. However, at the beginning of his rule, probably because he had some special purpose in mind, His late Highness inquired of me in detail about the mourning regulations of ancient and modern times in China and Japan. I presented a document containing explanations with illustrations attached. But up to the present time, no decrees have ever been issued about these matters.

"If I may be permitted to make the observation, in the Genroku Regulations it was stated that there is no mourning *for* or *by* children under seven years.[9] It might appear that this regulation is in accordance with the regulations of Japan, but although these state that there is no mourning *for* children under seven years, they contain nothing to the effect that children under seven years do not mourn for their parents. In view of the fact that it is stated in the ancient Chinese rules for mourning that children observe a period of mourning for their parents, how can it be asserted that neither parents *nor children* wear mourning for each other? If this ruling is accepted, it seems there is to be no mourning on this occasion on the grounds that a young child is involved. Furthermore, it is also stated in the regulations of Japan that a retainer shall observe one year's mourning for his lord, but since rules regarding the mourning of a retainer for his lord have also been omitted from the Genroku Regulations, it does not seem that on this occasion the Shōgun's retainers will observe mourning either.[10] If the Genroku regulations are taken as the model in all these matters, no revised decrees will be issued even now.

"But consider: Although His late Highness had many children, only our present lord has by great good fortune survived and succeeded to the shogunate.[11] Yet because he is a young child, he is not to observe mourning. And although His late Highness ruled the empire and had many retainers in his service, they are not to wear mourning either. Therefore, what is there to mark this as a period of national mourning?

"In Japan, we have what is called 'heart mourning,' which means that though we do not wear mourning clothes, we observe a period of mourning in our hearts.[12] Therefore, even though in accordance with the Genroku Regulations neither the Shōgun nor his retainers wear mourning, if at least for the duration of the mourning period, no auspicious observances are carried out, there will certainly be no conflict with the Genroku regulations. The sentiments of His late Highness's retainers and of his son will then be a little deepened, and in this way correct relations between father and son, and lord and retainer will be upheld throughout Japan.

"However, it may be objected that if the question of 'heart mourning' by the Shōgun is raised at this juncture, the populace will suspect there are points open to question in the Genroku regulations. But even if the whole nation were assailed by doubt, it would only be concerning that one point of children under seven wearing mourning for their parents and nothing else would be affected.

"Furthermore, the government and laws of Japan are in every particular aimed at enforcing codes of moral conduct, and since we consider the foundation of morality to be service to father and lord, is it more important to avoid arousing doubts in the people concerning the one point of children under seven wearing mourning for their parents, than to sacrifice the foundations of the empire and destroy the bases of its morality?

"In ancient China, there were similar incidents during the reigns of Ying Tsung and Shih Tsung of the Sung and Ming dynasties, and when these emperors came of age, they punished those who had been their ministers at the times in question.[13] Our lord is still a child and does not understand anything about this, but bear in mind that when he grows up, he will reconsider the matter."

Akifusa took my petition and first consulted the officials, but they were entirely prepossessed by what had been proposed in the beginning, and it seemed unlikely that my proposals would be put into effect. So he presented my petition to the Ōmidaidokoro [60] and told her what my sentiments were. She read it together with the present Shōgun's mother [94], and they said: "Divine retribution would be terrible if, in common with ordinary people, the Shōgun [25], simply because he is a child, did not wear mourning for his father [3], who was lord of the empire.[14] Moreover, when he grows up and learns what happened, he will regret it. It is our wish that he observe 'heart mourning.' " Since this order was transmitted to the officials, it was impossible for them to argue further. It was therefore decided to defer all Shintō and other ceremonies until thirteen months had elapsed.

Nobuatsu was greatly angered by the rejection of his opinion. He enumerated every example, comparing Chinese and Japanese mourning regulations, to prove that wearing mourning is stated to be mutual in the *I Li* of the Duke of Chou, the *Chia Li* of Chu Tzŭ, and the regulations of the Ming Court.[15] He also presented a document to the Rōjū on the 27th December stating: "Regarding the question of whether children under seven do not wear mourning, I state positively that they do not wear mourning for any relative, including father and mother. The *Shintō Bukukiryō*, *Yoshida-Ke Bukukiryō*, and *Kinri Bukukiryō* all support this statement."[16]

Akifusa showed this document to me also. I said to him: "As this question has already been settled by Shogunal Decree in accordance with my advice, there is no need for me to discuss it again. However, my reason for throwing all my heart and soul into this matter as I have done was because it was my desire to formulate the moral code for father and son, and lord and vassal in Japan in accordance with the pronouncements of the sages of old. The assertion that my arguments are not in agreement with the rules laid down by the Duke of Chou and Confucius will not only delude the people of today but misrepresent the sages of old. This fellow had the good fortune to win some slight favor, and thus attained the position of instructor to the people of the empire. But if his views were put into effect, he would only use the sages to lead them into disloyalty and unfilial conduct. This would indeed be a calamity with far-reaching consequences. In support of my contentions, I presented a document in which I stated that reference to the words of the *I Li* and the *Li Chi* could not fail to demolish his false views."

I wrote out seven articles excerpted from several works ranging from the *I Li* and *Li Chi*, to the *Hui Tien* and *Chi Li* of the Ming Dynasty, and stated: "Consultation of these authoritative works shows that every single one of them prescribes mourning for fathers and mothers by children under seven years."[17] But I observed that he must have found certain material which he considered clear and sufficient proof that no mourning is prescribed in this case in the *I Li, Chia Li,* and regulations laid down during the Ming Dynasty, and that he should set this down under each article." I also wrote out two articles taken from the *Sōsōryō.*[18]

When Akifusa questioned Nobuatsu about my assertions, he replied: "Among the five kinds of mourning clothes enumerated in the *I Li* and *Chia Li,* etc., mourning for fathers by young children for whom mourning is not worn is not explicitly prescribed, I therefore wrote as I did at first. Other than that, there is no clear proof that children under seven years do not wear mourning for their parents. If we accept the words of the classics on rites as conclusive, it is difficult to assert there is no mourning, so there is nothing I can say in reply." In his reply to the two articles I had written out separately, he cited the commentary on the *Genji Monogatari* called *Kachōyojō,* or some such thing, and stated: "It is the custom of Japan for children under seven years not to wear mourning for their parents.[19] If mourning is prescribed on the authority of the classics on rites, then also on the authority of these classics, should not mourning for parents continue for three years?'

When I saw this, I said: "It was because he said that my opinion was not in accordance with the rules of the Duke of Chou and Confucius that I quoted the words of the classics on rites to refute him. In view of the fact that this fellow has hereby sent an apology stating that what he said before is not found in the classics on rites, this admission alone is sufficient to demonstrate to future generations in Japan the truth of what I say. In discussing such important ceremonies of Japan as this, if a man holding the position of Daigaku-no-Kami quotes from a commentary on the *Genji Monogatari,* and goes so far as to say we ought not to observe the rules of the ancient Chinese sages in Japan, future generations of our countrymen will surely publicly condemn him. Consequently there is no need for me to comment further." I asked for the documents which I had presented, was given them, and returned home. Since these documents not only formulated correct relations between parent and child, and lord and vassal in Japan in my time, but also preserved the principles of the Duke of Chou and Confucius forever in our country, it would not be inappropriate if they were handed down to my descendants. The details of this incident will be found in the documents I drafted at that time and in Kyū-sō's [98] *Kokusō Seigi,* and reference should be made to these.[20]

I later heard that someone, who said he had heard it from a disciple of Nobuatsu, had stated that when Nobuatsu was questioned by Akifusa on this occasion, he was completely at a loss and unable to think up anything to say in reply. The disciple, perceiving this, had inquired the reason for his dismay, and had said he remembered there might be something in a commentary on the *Genji Monogatari* about when the emperor, father of the young prince, died. Nobuatsu, on hearing this, had said: "Look it up," with the result that he concocted an argument based on the *Kachōyojō*. Thus he revealed his own teacher's shame to an outsider. One can only say that such teachers produce such disciples. This was the sort of relation existing between Daigaku-no-Kami and his disciples. Alas, it shows the decline of Japanese learning that things have come to this pass.

About this time, too, Nobuatsu presented a document to the Rōjū in which he asserted that the use of the character for "shō" in era names was inauspicious, and that the present era name "Shōtoku" should be changed at once, citing in support of his contention the three works *Shu Tu Tsa Ch'ao, Pi Chi,* and *Ch'ien Pai Nien Yen.*[21] Akifusa asked my opinion about this and, having been asked, I could hardly refuse to reply. Although my advice was unlikely to be heeded, I wrote out a document and presented it. The gist of it was: "In recent times, a Chinese scholar wrote an essay discussing era names, in which he asserted that calamities had occurred during those periods when the ideograph 'shō' ['chêng' in Chinese] had been employed in the era name and that the ideograph should be avoided in literary usage. Now, this sort of argument occurs in many books besides those cited by Nobuatsu, but none of these is the work of men of superior intelligence. Social disturbances and untimely deaths are sometimes due to heavenly decree and sometimes to human agency. How could good or bad fortune depend on the ideographs in an era name?

"The fate of men like Ch'i-wang Fang and Kao-kuei-hsiang-kung, of Wei, Prince Wu Ling of Liang, King Yang of Chin, and the Emperor Shun of Yüan was in every instance due to their lack of virtue.[22] Even if the ideograph 'chêng' had not been employed in the era names of their reigns, these princes would surely have lost their kingdoms and their lives. The events of eras of Chêng-t'ung and Chêng-tê during the Ming Dynasty were entirely due to lack of virtue and to weakness in the administration, not to the fault of the ideograph in the era name.[23] It is well to bear in mind Mencius's dictum: 'Do not blame the times.'[24]

"To demonstrate how social disturbances and untimely deaths do not depend on the ideograph in the era name would involve a very lengthy exposition and waste a great number of words indeed, so I shall just set forth a simple illustration which anyone who hears will understand. A man is described as a child, a youth, an adult, a man in his prime, a man past his prime, an elderly man, an old man, and a senile man.[25] The names may be different, but this only signifies the passing of years, and he is still the same man. Similarly, just as in the third month of his life, he is given a hereditary name, at twenty takes his adult name, and at fifty is addressed by a title of respect, although his name alters, the course of his life is in no way affected.[26]

"Although years, months, days, and hours all have different names, the hours pile up to make a day, the days pile up to make a month, the months pile up to make a year. Just as childhood, youth, adulthood, maturity, decline, advanced age, old age, and senility are different, yet a man himself is still the same, so also a year has a name, and a month has a name. This is also like a man having one name at three months, another at twenty, and a third at fifty.

"If it is unlucky to use the ideograph 'chêng' in the name of a year, it must be unlucky to use it in the name of a month also. Yet since the time of the ancient sages until now, the first month of every year has been called 'chêngyüeh' ['shōgatsu' in Japanese]. Even in the regulations in the *Ch'un Ch'iu* of Confucius, when the 'Four Beginnings' are spoken of, the first month of every year is referred to as 'chêngyüeh.'[27] If indeed the ideograph 'chêng' is unlucky, then every year since ancient times has begun with an inauspicious month, so it cannot be said that in all that time there has ever been a year which has been wholly auspicious. This is such an obvious example that it might be described as being unable to see the nose in front of one's own face. If the ideograph 'chêng' is unfortunate in the name of a year, I should very much like to hear if there is any reason why the same ideograph is fortunate in the name of a month.

"We are told that the superior man, by his actions, provides a model for the morality of the empire, by his behavior in society a model for the laws of the empire, and by his words, a model for the regulations of the empire; also, that the superior man is one who understands his own fate.[28] Therefore, I do not think that a superior man would express such a worthless opinion as that under discussion.

"Furthermore, in Japanese era names the ideograph 'shō' has been used sixteen times, but it does not seem that there have always been unfortunate happenings. It will be argued that after the military classes gained control, the Kamakura shogunate was overthrown in the era of Shōkei, and the Ashikaga shogunate in the era of Tenshō. The overthrow of the lay-priest Taira Takatoki [48] did actually occur in July 1333, during the Shōkei era. However, since the time of Takatoki's ancestor, Sagami-no-Kami Tokimasa, for a period of nine generations, the ideograph 'shō' had been used seven times in the era names of Shōji, Shōka, Shōgen, Shōō, Shōan, Shōwa, and Shōchū, yet the Hōjō Family was not destroyed during these eras.[29] That it was destroyed on the occasion in question does not appear to have been due to the ideograph in the era name. The downfall of the family was a misfortune that the Hōjō brought upon themselves. The overthrow of the Ashikaga shogunate actually took place on the 31st July 1573, during the Genki era, and was due to the flight of Yoshiaki.[30] It was because of these happenings that the era name was changed on the 25th August and the name of Tenshō then adopted.

"Since the time of Tōji-In Den, for a period covering thirteen generations, on as many as five occasions the era names were Shōchō, Kōshō, Kanshō, Bunshō, and Eishō.[31] Yet during all that time, there was no case of a *shōgun* being overthrown. If we were to make a detailed investigation of the events of the successive eras since we began to use era names in Japan and designate this or that as having been inauspicious, every ideograph would prove to have been inauspicious. The reason is that in both China and Japan, the change of an era name has practically always been owing to natural disasters of celestial or terrestrial origin, floods, droughts, plagues, and the like. Thus in the course of time every single ideograph that has been used in era names has become associated with misfortune.

"If we worry lest misfortune is bound to proceed from an era name, it would be far better if we had none at all, as was the case in ancient times. Yet in both China and Japan, even in ancient times, when there were no era names, there was no period when social disturbances and untimely deaths were unknown. When I met the Italian and the Dutch I made detailed inquiry about current affairs in foreign countries.[32] I discovered that no more than two or three countries employed era names. All the rest, instead of employing era names, counted so many thousands, hundreds, and tens of years since the creation of the world. Nevertheless, about twenty years ago, upon the death of one of their paramount rulers, many of the countries of western Europe have been plunged into turmoil over the question of his successor.[33] I was told that large numbers had died in battle in the winter of the previous year and that spring. What inauspicious influence was responsible for these misfortunes? Thus, even though they had no era names, because Heaven ceased to favor them and their own conduct was lacking in virtue, it seems they could not escape destruction.

"Among the generations of Chinese emperors also, of those who have used the same era name, there have been quite a few cases where one grew strong and another was overthrown. Take for example the era name Yung-lo. At the beginning of the Five Dynasties, a barbarian by the name of Chang Yü-hsien took the title of Chung-t'ien-ta-kuo-wang and chose Yung-lo as the era name of his inauguration, but he was shortly afterward put to sword.[34] Later, during the Sung Dynasty, a man called Fang La proclaimed himself emperor and used the era name Yung-lo, and within eight months he was executed.[35] Later again, T'ai Tsung of the Ming Dynasty used the era name Yung-lo upon his succession, and he accomplished a prosperous reign of 26 years.[36] There are innumerable examples of this kind.

"Also, many era names in Japan are the same as those in China. For example, it was in the era named Chien-wu that Emperor Kuang-Wu of the Later Han Dynasty restored the Family of Han and himself endured for 31 years.[37] Although Emperor Go-Daigo used this era name [Kemmu], before he had reigned for two

[194]

years the empire was again thrown into confusion.[38] Tenryaku was the era name of Emperor Murakami, and although it has been handed down in Japan as an example of a prosperous reign, Wên Tsung of Yüan used this era name [T'ien-li], but in five short years he was dead.[39] These examples are also innumerable. Thus if we consider events, ancient and modern, in China and Japan, there is an absence of connection between social disturbances and untimely deaths, and the characters used in era names.

"Also, coming to recent times in Japan, the only matter on which the emperor's edict runs throughout the whole country is the era name. Discussions of this question are also found in Chinese books. Ever since ancient times, it has been customary to change the era name in Japan because of the inauguration of a new reign, 'revolution,' 'reformation,' or 'triple-conjunction' years, natural calamities of celestial or terrestrial origin, floods, droughts, plagues, military uprisings, or famines.[40] And never, since the military classes came into power, has there been an example when the era name was changed because of the death of the *shōgun*. Because there are perhaps one or two instances open to doubt among these examples, some will again assert that this has actually happened. So I must discuss this question in more detail.

"On 9th February 1199, during the Kenkyū era, the former Udaishō Yoritomo [75] died. On the 7th May of that year, the era name was changed to Shōji.[41] This was occasioned by the inauguration of the reign of Emperor Tsuchimikado. On the 23rd February 1218, during the Kempō era, the Udaijin Sanetomo was assassinated, and on the 10th May of that year the era name was changed to Jōkyū.[42] This was on account of a 'triple conjunction' year and natural calamities. On the 28th December 1367, during the Jōji era, Hōkyō-In Yoshikatsu died, and on the 16th March of the following year the era name was changed to Ōan.[43] On the 26th April 1489, during the Chōkyō era, Jōtoku-In Yoshihisa died, and on the 15th September of that year the era name was changed to Entoku.[44] These changes were due to military uprisings and natural calamities. Besides these, on the 27th January 1428, during the Ōei era, Shōjō-In Yoshimochi died.[45] On the 20th February of that year, the era name was changed to Shōchō.[46] This was to mark the inauguration of the reign of Emperor Shōkō.[47] Before this, on the 3rd February 1408, during the Ōei era, Rokuon-In Yoshimitsu [99] died, and on the 7th March 1425, during the same era, Chōtoku-In Yoshikazu died, but there was no change in era name.[48] Also, on the 16th August 1443, during the Kakitsu era, Kyōun-In Yoshikatsu died, and on the 23rd February 1444, the era name was changed to Bun'an but this was because it was a 'revolution' year.[49] Although Fukō-In Yoshinori was assassinated on the 12th July 1441, during the Kakitsu era, there was no change of era name.[50]

"Although these doubtful instances exist, as I have amply illustrated, they had no connection with the *shōgun*'s death. But if the Shōgun now requests the Emperor [70] to change the era name of Shōtoku on account of His late Highness, what will happen if the officials of the Imperial Court object, basing their arguments on these examples? Even if no objections are raised and the Emperor changes the era name in accordance with the Shōgun's request, when men of later generations in our country who are versed in ceremonial discuss this, those advising the Shōgun at this time will not escape censure. Therefore, you had best give these questions your earnest consideration." As a result of my words and whatever steps Akifusa took, this proposal was not put into effect.

Nobuatsu's acceptance of the theories of the Ming Confucianists and his notion that the era name of Shōtoku was objectionable were the result of a devious plot, so the whole affair was quite contemptible. For why did he not mention this in the time of His late Highness? Instead, he brought the matter up now, probably because he calculated that the officials would conclude it was the fault of those on whose advice His Highness had relied that no one had mentioned this in the previous age. However, it was when his father and grandfather [74] were alive that the era name had been changed to Shōhō.[51] So if the fact that no one raised objections to the era name of Shōtoku was the fault of those whom His late Highness trusted, then the fact that no one raised objections to the era name of Shōhō was the fault of his father and grandfather. When this is taken into account, we see how first of all he had said that in the case of a child *shōgun* it is unnecessary to wear mourning, and then he said that even in ancient times three years' mourning was considered too long, imagining that high-placed persons, such as the Ōmidaidokoro [60] and the present Shōgun's mother [94], would take notice of what he said.[52] Now, on top of that, he imagines that when he says the era name of Shōtoku is inauspicious, high-ranking persons, including these ladies, will believe him. In such ways as these, with the perverted talents of literary sycophants of his kidney, he has hatched a wicked plot in a desperate bid to regain his former popularity.

An incident comes to mind in connection with the matter recorded above. In the time of His late Highness, after lectures had finished on the 29th September 1711, His Highness showed me a report of a complicated case.

According to this, a man of Matsushiro-no-Shō in Shinano Province came to stay in Edo to trade.[53] His wife was the daughter of a farmer of Komabayashi village in Kawagoe-no-Shō in this province.[54] On the previous 29th August, his wife's elder brother had come and invited him to Kawagoe. On the 2nd September, this man again came and told his sister that her husband had returned to his native village to trade and that he would soon return, and that while he was away she was to come to their father's house to wait for her husband's return. On the 3rd of the same month, her brother took her to their father's house. Although many days went by, her husband did not return, so she asked her father when he would come back. Her father told her that her husband would certainly return about the 10th, but three days passed and still he had not returned.[55]

Fearful of what might have happened, and hearing that a man had been found drowned in a nearby river, she rushed there in great agitation to look, but the man was lying face down in the water and she could not positively identify him. Although she told her father and brother she was very anxious to examine the dead man, they would not listen to her and said it was impossible for anything like that to have happened to her husband. Unable to endure her suspense, next day she informed the headman of the place, and when he had the body taken up, she recognized it as her husband.

This spot was within the fief of Tajima-no-Kami Takatomo (Akimoto) [54], and the officials in charge during his absence summoned the wife's father and brother and also the servants of the house and questioned them. Suspicious of the replies given, they searched the house and found the clothing and effects of the son-in-law. When they questioned them about their possession of these articles, they were unable to offer any explanation, and the father and brother confessed that, on the evening of the 31st August, they had together strangled the son-in-law and thrown him into the water. The crime of the two men, in killing the son-in-law, was clear, but as there was some doubt in connection with the woman's crime in informing against her father, Takatomo had sent a report to His Highness.

I replied: "This case is one involving the three basic moral obligations and cannot be decided by ordinary arguments. What worries me personally has to do not only with relations between father and child, and husband and wife, but also with the question revolving around the all-important principle of relations between lord and retainer." As a result, orders were given for members of the Hyōjōsho to investigate if there were any precedents bearing on this case.

After I returned home, I consulted privately with my friend Kyūsō [98] about this matter, and in a letter which he sent me on the morning of the following day, he quoted an article on the wearing of mourning in the chapter on mourning in the *I Li*, with the comment: "If the case is decided according to this article, it admits of no doubt."[56] In our first discussion, the opinions he expressed agreed with my interpretation, and now I was overjoyed that we could find adequate support in this book.

After the lecture on the 4th October, His Highness showed me a copy of the precedent presented by the members of the Hyōjōsho saying: "This does not seem to be applicable. What is your opinion?" On examining the report concerning this precedent, I found that in May 1687, a woman had given information concerning the adultery of her husband and her adoptive mother. The two adulterers had been beheaded and their heads exposed. Since the woman had informed against her mother and her husband, she was given one year's imprisonment and in April 1688 made a slave.[57] I said: "As Your Highness has observed, this incident cannot be regarded as a precedent bearing on the case under discussion. This woman should not be punished." And with these words I retired from His Highness's presence.

When I was summoned on the 7th [October 1711], I was shown a copy of Daigaku-no-Kami's opinion, which had been presented by the Rōjū. In his opinion, he had stated that: " 'Any man can become a husband; only one man can be the father.' When the daughter of Chi Chung of Chêng asked her mother: 'Which is dearer, father or husband?' her mother answered in these words.[58] It was because of this woman's complaint that the father's crime was revealed. Even in the *Analects* it is stated that it is virtuous to conceal a father's fault.[59] In the *Lü Shu*, it is laid down that those who give information about their parents' crimes should be put to death.[60] Hence this woman is guilty of a crime punishable by death for having given information about her father's crime. If her complaint was lodged in ignorance of the fact that it was her father who had killed her husband, this is a special aspect of the case. Under Japanese law, 'those who lay information about their parents' crimes are banished'; according to the commentary they were strangled."[61] (This opinion had been presented on the 5th October.) His Highess suggested we should not be guided by the words of Chi Chung's wife and further pointed out that the murder, in the case under discussion, was essentially not one that had been committed on the spur of the moment without premeditation. Also, it was not indisputable that Confucius considered it virtuous to conceal a parent's crime. His Highness therefore directed me to set out my advice in writing. When I returned home, I immediately wrote out my opinion and presented it on the 8th. It was as follows:

"I beg to present my advice concerning the incident of which I was informed on the 29th September, viz.: A certain merchant's wife, whose husband did not return from a journey, after some time heard that a man had been discovered drowned, asked the village headman to help her examine the corpse, and when she did so, found that it was indeed her husband. A thorough investigation was held, and when the full circumstances were disclosed, it was ascertained that the wife's father and brother had plotted together to kill the husband and had thrown his body into the river. The officials are in doubt as to whether the woman has committed the crime of informing on her father; the judges have expressed the opinion that she should have her property confiscated and be made a slave, while the official Confucian scholar [21] holds that she should be punished for the crime of informing on her father.[62]

"At this point, I have been ordered to give my opinion also. With all due respect, I submit that this crime is a matter which involves the three basic moral obligations and that it cannot be decided by ordinary principles. There are three points which we ought to resolve.

"In the first place, we ought to judge the case in the light of human relations. The three basic obligations concern the relation between lord and subject, the relation between father and child, and the relation between husband and wife. First of all, as regards these relations, we must recognize that lord, father, and husband are objects of equal reverence, and no priorities should be observed in serving them.

"Secondly, we ought to be guided by the mourning regulations. According to the regulations of the Sage Kings, when a woman has been promised in marriage but is living in her father's house, and when after having been married she returns to her father's house to live, upon her father's death she wears deep mourning for three years.[63] But when she is already married and living with her husband, upon her father's death, she wears mourning of the second degree for an unspecified period. Now, because far-fetched doubts seem to have crept in as regards mourning for a father in the case of a woman living in her father's house and in the case of a woman who has left her father's house and is married, these are clarified in the mourning regulations. It is stated that: 'Women's conduct is controlled by the principle of the Three Obediences, and there is no other way for them except this. Therefore, before she is married, a woman obeys her father; after marriage she obeys her husband; and on her husband's death she obeys her son. Thus, the father is the child's heaven, and the husband is the wife's heaven. The fact that a woman does not wear deep mourning twice means that there are not two heavens and that a woman cannot obey two masters at the same time.' And therefore, in accordance with the statement that a woman cannot obey two masters at the same time, we must recognize the principle that a married woman obeys her husband and does not obey her father.

"In the third place, we ought to judge the case in accordance with the circumstances. Now, any event can be either normal or abnormal, and in dealing with it, general principles or temporary expedients may be employed. Confucian scholars in ancient times spoke of employing temporary expedients to arrive at general principles.[64] According to the so-called ethical system laid down by the former Sage Kings, it was virtuous conduct for a woman living in her father's house to obey her father and for a woman who had left her father's house and married, to obey her husband.

"It is the normal morality that the lord acts like a lord, the subject like a subject, the father like a father, the son like a son, the husband like a husband, and the wife like a wife. It is an abnormal form of morality for the lord not to act like a lord, the subject not like a subject, the father not like a father, the son not like a son, the husband not like a husband, and the wife not like a wife.

"But even though the lord may not act like a lord, we do not say that the subject should not act like a subject; even though the father may not act like a father, we do not say that the son should not act like a son; even though the husband may not act like a husband, we do not say that the wife should not act like a wife. That is, even though we are faced with an abnormal form of morality, we cannot say that the normal form of morality may be disregarded.

"The case of a subject's father killing his lord is analogous to a father killing his daughter's husband. These are extreme cases of abnormal morality. If the subject is loyal to his lord, he is not filial to his father. If the wife is dutiful to her husband, she is not filial to her father. There is no greater misfortune for anyone than to be placed in a situation like this. In olden times, there were subjects who disobeyed their fathers and were loyal to their lords. Cases in point are Li Ts'ui and Shih Yen-fên of T'ang.[65] There have been cases where men's wives, disobeying their fathers and elder brothers, have been loyal to their husbands. Examples of this are the consorts of the emperors P'ing and Hsien of Han, the consort of Emperor T'ien Yüan of Northern Ch'i, and the wife of Prince of Wu.[66]

"However, there has never yet been known a case where a woman has informed the authorities that her husband has been killed by her father. There is an example where a wife knew that her husband, under orders from his lord, was going to kill her father, and she informed her father, who then killed her husband. This was Yung Chi, daughter of Chi Chung of Chêng. First of all, Yung Chi, in doubt as to which is dearer, father or husband, asked her mother and her mother replied: 'Anyone can be a woman's husband; only one man can be her father. There is no comparison between them.' (This is what Nobuatsu bases his argument upon).

"If the mother's statement and the daughter's act in informing against her husband were dutiful, it would have been unfilial, unsisterly, and immoral not to regard her father as her father and her brother as her brother, for her husband's sake.

"If there is a subject who, knowing that his father is going to kill his lord, says: 'Anyone can be one's lord; only one man can be one's father. There is no comparison between them,' and so he joins with his father in killing his lord, is this right or wrong? Chou-hsü, Prince of Wei, killed his lord. Hou, Shih Ch'üeh's son, was an accessory. Shih Ch'üeh informed the State of Ch'ên, saying: 'These two men plotted together to slay their lord.' A sage of the time said: 'Shih Ch'üeh is a loyal subject. This is a case of great duty destroying relationship.'[67]

"Confucius said: 'The father conceals the crime of the child; the child conceals the crime of the father.' (This also is quoted by Nobuatsu.) This is only normal morality. Which offense is more serious, stealing a sheep or killing one's lord?

"If we base our argument on the system of the sages of old, that a married woman considers her husband as her heaven and cannot consider her father as her heaven, if her father kills her husband, we cannot argue by the ordinary regulations about informing on fathers and mothers. Much less can we do so in this case. For this woman recognized the corpse as that of her husband after getting the village headman to turn it over, and then the officials investigated the matter and ascertained that her father and brother had murdered her husband. This is very different from knowing that her father and brother had killed her husband and informing against them.

"There is absolutely no reason to put this woman to death. If, on the day that her father's and brother's crime in murdering her husband was revealed, she had killed herself at once, she would have been dutiful to her husband, filial to her father, and sisterly to her elder brother. We would have had to say that she had shown great virtue in a case which was an extreme example of abnormal morality. However, this would be demanding perfection and would not be consonant with the tolerant attitude of the superior man toward his fellow men. Throughout the ages, there have been not a few women, who when their husbands had been killed by their fathers, although they did not go so far as to commit suicide, preserved their chastity until death. People in ancient times did not estimate their virtue lightly, simply because they did not kill themselves.

"My private opinion is that a wife who fails to preserve her chastity for her husband's sake is as blameworthy as a subject who is disloyal to his lord. If Li Ts'ui and Shih Yen-fên are accounted loyal subjects, and Chi Chung's daughter Yung Chi is accounted filial, then I cannot agree."

In the document I presented at this time I said: "According to the precedents instanced by the officials of the Hyōjōsho, this woman should be imprisoned for one year, after which her property should be confiscated and she should be made a slave. According to Daigaku-no-Kami's opinion, if this woman, knowing that her father had killed her husband, informed against him, she should be put to death. If she did not know this, she should be made a slave.

"If she is not punished, as I advise, I have a request to make. A widow who is still young is utterly bereft of protection. We cannot be sure that the color of the pine, be it ever so green, will not change as the year grows cold.[68] I am not only concerned lest she lose her chastity; I am also fearful lest the laws of the country should be broken. There are not a few people, who in accordance with the customs of Japan, have become priests or nuns to mourn the deaths of their fathers or husbands. If it is privately suggested to her that she should become a nun for the sake of her father and husband, and if we send her to a convent, have her take the tonsure, and offer the property of both her father and husband to the temple, we will be saving her from the danger of destitution and protecting both the law of the country and women's chastity."

I heard that His Highness shortly afterward gave orders in accordance with my suggestions, and Takatomo arranged it so that the woman herself petitioned to become a nun and went to a convent at Kamakura.

After the mourning period was over, the ceremony of the inauguration of the rule of the new Shōgun [25] was performed on the 7th January 1713.[69] In former generations, the heir apparent had been appointed Dainagon of the Upper Third Rank when his coming-of-age ceremony was performed, and later he had been promoted to Upper Second Rank.[70] Upon his succession, he was proclaimed Shōgun and appointed Daijin and Taishō, by Imperial Decree. But on this occasion, particularly since our lord succeeded while still a child, application first had to be made to the throne for court rank, and then an imperial decree had to be issued proclaiming him Shōgun. Accordingly, Akifusa said that I must draft the document presenting this request as under His late Highness [3]. I could not refuse this either, so I presented a draft-document.

Moreover, as regards the question of the Shōgun's name, in preceding ages it had been conferred by the lord's father, but on this occasion it was decided that he should ask the Retired Emperor [100] to write it for him, and I was told that I was to select the characters which should be submitted. So I presented both the draft of the request to the Retired Emperor and a document setting forth the characters I had selected for his name.

At this point, a letter of the 8th January [1713] was received from the throne appointing the Shōgun Dainagon of the Upper Second Rank. This must have been because he had already succeeded to the shogunate.

When the characters written by the Retired Emperor arrived in Edo with the proclamation on the 18th of the month, an auspicious day was selected, and they were formally presented on the 19th, so that the ceremony of congratulation was held on the 21st.

This day, in accordance with the custom of His late Highness, I received 30 gold *ryō* for my services and was officially commended. (Every year thereafter the same practice was observed. The rewards I received on sundry other occasions were all exactly the same as under His late Highness. Therefore I have not enumerated them.)

On the 26th January, the Shōgun's "trousering" ceremony was

held.[71] On the 17th February I received two gold *ryō*. This was because I had selected the auspicious characters for the Shōgun's seal. (This was to be used when he issued secret instructions.) This day also, Akifusa and Tadayoshi [79] informed me that three books, which His late Highness had instructed the Nagasaki magistrates to give me, had arrived in Edo and they would send them to me. (These were the *San Ts'ai T'u Hui*, the *Nung Chêng Ch'üan Shu*, and the *Ku Yin P'u*.[72]

On the 14th March [1713], I presented the program I had prepared for the Shōgun's coming-of-age ceremony. Since it was necessary to perform this ceremony with all haste, I had received orders about it previously. (I presented suggestions about all the articles employed in the coming-of-age ceremony, even the decorations for the Shiroshoin on that day.)

On the 16th April, the Shōgun proceeded to the Shiroshoin, and his coming-of-age ceremony was performed. Chūjō Naomori of Hikone performed the ceremony of placing on the headgear, and Chūjō Masakata of Aizu that of arranging the hair.[73] I witnessed the ceremony from a position behind the Shōgun's dais.

About this time, the former Sesshō, Konoe Daishōkoku [69], paid a visit to Edo, and I visited him at his lodgings many times. On the 26th April, the ceremony of the Shōgun's proclamation was held, and on this occasion also, I was seated behind the Shōgun's dais, as in the time of His late Highness.

On the 28th June, I received an increase in my house lot, in accordance with orders given by His late Highness.

On the 15th November, I composed the inscription on the memorial bell for His late Highness, Bunshō-In. This was in accordance with orders. Kao Hsüan-tai (Fukami Shin'emon) [101] did the calligraphy for the inscription.

After His Highness's death the previous year, Akifusa told me that the Densō [95, 96] had said it was the Emperor's [70] private wish that it should be left to the shogunal government to choose the characters for His late Highness's posthumous name, and showed me two or three characters which had been sent. I presented a document recommending that as the Shōgun's posthumous name is transmitted to foreign countries and to later generations, it is desirable to have completely suitable characters, and the present Shōgun should ask for one of the two characters "bun" and "shō" to be granted. The members of the Rōjū sent a reply to the Court to that effect, and an imperial decree was granted conferring both the characters "bun" and "shō." The Emperor and the Retired Emperor [100] accepted both the posthumous name for His late Highness and the name for the present Shōgun which I had selected. It was also a great honor that I was asked to compose the inscription on the memorial bell.

On the 1st December [1713] at the service for the first anniversary of His late Highness's death, in addition to those officiating, Akifusa, Tadayoshi [79], Kiyotake (Matsudaira Dewa-no-Kami) and his son Kura-no-Kami Kiyotsura, Oki-no-Kami Akiyuki [29], Awaji-no-Kami Akihira [41], Ichi-no-Kami Masanao [30], and myself, and besides us, two lords in personal attendance (Hosoi Izumi-no-Kami, Kubota Hizen-no-Kami), making ten in all, attended in full court dress.[74] (Among these, the three men Oki-no-Kami, Izumi-no-Kami, and Hizen-no-Kami were in attendance because they were the *bugyō* superintending the erection of His late Highness's mausoleum.) My attendance on this occasion was also in accordance with the rule at ceremonies in the time of His late Highness.

On the 22nd August of this year [1713], a shogunal decree was issued concerning the fishing boats on the Yamato River.[75] The facts of the case were as follows: Commodities being sent from Settsu Province to Yamato Province were loaded in river boats which brought them to Kamegase in Kawachi Province.[76] Here, since the river shallowed, they were transferred to fishing boats and distributed throughout Yamato Province. From about the Keichō era, these fishing boats had been under the control of one Yasumura, a lower official at the Tatsuta Shrine, who lived in Tachino village in Heguri District, Yamato Province.[77] With the profit from freight charges, he had repaired the Tatsuta Shrine and had presented 30 pieces of silver as transport tax to the government. (The Yasumura were hereditarily called Kiemon. As a result of Yasumura's activities, the government henceforth ceased to carry out repairs on the Tatsuta Shrine.) In 1697, the villagers of Tachino petitioned to be given control of the fishing boats, promising to pay 150 pieces of silver in tax. As Tachino was in the shogunal domains, and, moreover, the villagers had promised to pay a large tax, the then Shōgun [15] acceded to their request and terminated Yasumura's control.

In February 1708, farmers of 503 villages on both shogunal and private domains in Yamato Province presented the following petition to Miyoshi Bizen-no-Kami [68], the Nara Bugyō: "Originally, the villagers of Tachino said they anticipated that the control of the fishing boats would be carried out as heretofore, but they have increased the charges, and, in addition, even when the boats have been wrecked, they have not only failed to indemnify us for the loss of our commodities but they have also stolen whatever they wanted."

In March of the same year, dealers of dried horse-mackerel in Ōsaka also appealed, saying: "Previously, when boats loaded with dried mackerel, for sale as fertilizer for rice fields throughout Yamato Province, were wrecked, we received due compensation from the controller of fishing boats. But when the boats were wrecked in the great earthquake in October last year [1707], we demanded compensation, but the Tachino villagers ignored our demands." The Tachino villagers were summoned before the authorities and told they must pay compensation, but they did not obey. In June of the same [1708], Bizen-no-Kami informed Kyōto of this.[78] In July of the same year, when Kii-no-Kami Nobutsune [102] went to Edo, Bizen-no-Kami presented a petition and asked whether this matter should be heard in the Hyōjōsho or at Kyōto, and the Shōgun gave orders to the Kanjō Bugyōsho.

After Ogiwara Ōmi-no-Kami [51] had questioned the Nara Bugyōsho and the Daikansho about this matter, he reported that Yasumura, the original controller, had petitioned that if the control of the fishing boats were returned to him, he would pay the government 300 pieces of silver in tax, whereupon the Tachino villagers had offered to pay 320 pieces of silver in tax. "The village of Tachino," he said, "is barely 1,000 koku of land and the population is numerous. For the past 14 years, they have paid their taxes from the freight charges of these boats. It would be unjust to return the control to Yasumura. It will be best to leave the control with the people of Tachino as it is now."

A shogunal decree in accordance with the opinion of the kanjō bugyō was issued in November 1709. However, this merely dealt with the question of the control of the fishing boats, and did not resolve the dispute of the people of the 503 villages and the Ōsaka merchants with the villagers of Tachino. After His Highness had succeeded in the spring of the following year, 1710, in July Miyoshi Bizen-no-Kami [68] went to Edo to convey congratulations. On this occasion, he presented a petition through Kawachi-no-Kami Tadamine [37] asking that the dispute be decided by the Shōgun.[79] Tadamine spoke about this matter to Honda Danjō-Shōhitsu [92] and Nakayama Izumo-no-Kami [80] and the two men consulted with the members of the Hyōjō-sho. In October, the members of the Hyōjōsho jointly signed and presented a report stating: "It does not appear that formerly compensation for the cargo of wrecked boats was paid by the controller of the fishing boats. It was paid by levying, on the cargo owners, five *rin* of silver per head as sea-transit tax for each package. Moreover, the villagers of Tachino say that if the fishing boats loaded with cargo transferred at Kamegase are wrecked, compensation will be paid for that cargo, but if the river boats are wrecked between Ōsaka and Kamegase, the loss is no concern of theirs as it does not take place within the boundaries of their province. This is reasonable. If boats on which shogunal cargo is loaded are wrecked, no provision regarding compensation exists to cover that loss. The demands of the Ōsaka merchants are unjustified. The previous arrangement was a private contract; it was not a government regulation. If a decree is issued about this matter, it will become an obstruction in other cases." Masamine [37] accepted this opinion and gave orders to the members of the Hyōjōsho accordingly, and the petitioners were required to enter into a written undertaking that they would not petition again, and the same communication was conveyed to Bizen-no-Kami also through the *kanjō bugyō*.[80]

Bizen-no-Kami regarded this decision as outrageous and said to Masamine: "The judges have confined themselves to a consideration of the dispute between the Ōsaka merchants and the Tachino villagers. This case originally arose as a result of a complaint by the people of 153 villages on shogunal and private lands in Yamato Province.[81] Afterward, a complaint was also lodged by the Ōsaka merchants. Thus the complaint of the peasants on the shogunal and private domains was the primary matter under consideration, and the complaint of the Ōsaka merchants was secondary. But in discussing the secondary matter, the primary matter was lumped together with it, in the same decree, and this should not have been done."

Masamine was very annoyed and said: "A decree has already been issued in conformity with the judges' deliberations, and you will do yourself no good by reopening the question," and brushed Bizen-no-Kami's remonstrances aside.

When I went to Nara in January in the winter of the following year [1711], Bizen-no-Kami spoke to me about this matter with an expression of deep resentment. After I returned to Edo, in the spring of the same year, I took the opportunity to bring this matter up, pointing out that the decree issued on that occasion had not been a just one. Soon after, Bizen-no-Kami died, full of indignation over this matter. Thereafter, Yasumura, too, committed suicide. I did not hear directly, but perhaps as long as Bizen-no-Kami was alive, Yasumura had hoped to clear himself of the false accusation against him, but after his death, he must have thought there was no one to whom he could look for help. It was a thoroughly deplorable case.

About the era of Hōei, Ōmi-no-Kami Shigehide [51] put into operation a scheme whereby he exacted a certain amount of gold and silver as a transport tax on every article. Also Nakatsukasa-no-Shō Masatō, Masamine's father, was a very different man from his own father, and Masamine himself was a cousin, on his mother's side, of Ukyō-Daibu Terusada [38], and connected with Shōshō Yoshiyasu [31].[82] Therefore, he rose above his father and grandfather to become a member of the Rōjū. However, he was a very ill-tempered man, and one, it was said, intent on carrying out his own nefarious schemes. I suppose he had a hand in the decree of 1709. It was generally said that on this occasion, also, he first got his maternal uncle, Danjō-Shōhitsu [92], to talk matters over with the officials of the Hyōjōsho, and thus decided the matter, asserting that the Hyōjōsho had already reached this decision; and that he quashed Bizen-no-Kami's second protest on his own arbitrary authority in order to carry out his customary evil designs. In the *Ta Hsüeh* it is written: "If one man hates another because he envies his talents, or if he opposes and obstructs one who is both wise and virtuous, he is utterly unsuitable to be employed. He will not be able to ensure the safety of his descendants and the ordinary people."[83] If a man in such an office, whatever other talents he may lack, is so deficient in generosity of mind as to be unable to suffer people more gifted than himself, it will be most unfortunate for society and mankind.

So when the Shōgun succeeded, Yasumura's son, full of resentment that this affair had caused his father's death and determined to realize his father's hopes, continued to make complaint after complaint. He also carried out the repairs that Yasumura had planned on Tatsuta Shrine. But it was reported that since henceforth there would be no one to undertake this work, the shrine officials petitioned for its repair. Whatever arrangements Akifusa [24] made, the control of the fishing boats was restored to Yasumura's son, as in the past, and the taxes were remitted, while orders were given that the repair of Tatsuta Shrine should not be neglected. Akifusa showed me the copy of the decree concerning this case, saying he did so because His late Highness had spoken to me about it.

It was probably about the second week of April this year [1713] that I had remarked to Akifusa: "Recently the customs of society have gradually inclined toward luxury, and it is said that the price of commodities has increased so that the *hatamoto* find it difficult to carry out their ordinary official duties, and any commitments outside Edo involve them in the greatest hardship. Although measures framed by His late Highness dealt with this problem to some degree, it has become a deep-rooted and long-standing abuse. However keenly aware men may be in their own minds that they are exceeding what is fitting to their station in life, they seem incapable of practicing thrift in their private affairs. Although it is the same in every age, and particularly so when the ruler is a child, it is most undesirable that things should reach the stage where men cannot perform their duties because of poverty. Somehow or other, we must reform these old abuses, and I earnestly pray that the officials be consulted and decrees be issued." Akifusa, having agreed that this was most desirable, consulted with the Rōjū, and orders were given about this matter. (These orders were to the effect that I should present a proposal. Yokota Bitchū-no-Kami [76] was given instructions to notify all officials to send in their suggested remedies within four days.)

So every member of the *hatamoto* presented his solution. Akifusa showed them all to me, but they all merely said that they ought to perform their duties faithfully from early morning till late at night, and not a single one touched upon questions of administration at that time.

Akifusa told me he had said that, as His late Highness had always asked me for my opinion about such matters, they must do the same. The Rōjū had agreed this was right, so that I must give them my opinion. However, I thought that if the tone were high, few would listen and, unless I could offer proof, no one would believe, so I merely selected, from the decrees issued by previous *shōguns*, those measures appropriate to the time, and copying these out separately, presented three volumes in all.[84] But after that, even those decrees were not issued. I said that decrees ought to be issued before the Ōsaka Auxiliary Guard was changed, and it is unlikely that Akifusa also did not add his support. But after a lapse of some time, my proposals were returned to me with notes attached to them here and there to the effect: "This is difficult to do now," and "This cannot be carried out." Yet there was nothing in anything I had suggested that was not contained in decrees issued by former *shōguns*. Therefore, if these things could not be carried out now, it was not because my suggestions were impossible. What more could I do? However, it was unthinkable that decrees issued by preceding generations of *shōguns* could not be carried out now. It was just that the officials would not carry them out. It is written that: "If the people dislike the decree, they will not comply with it"[85] And certainly a *shōgun* may issue decrees, but it will be impossible to put them into effect if they do not suit the officials. However, thinking to myself, when the present Shōgun comes of age, he will ask: "At the beginning of my reign, I heard that such a thing happened, but what was done about it?" And the Shōgun will read what the officials recorded, and he will reflect that if what they said had been reasonable, I would not have offered my opinions a second time. And when he does, he will not be unlikely to conclude that they have as much as said that the regulations of former *shōguns* were useless. So I had to present proposals in reply to this. I have set down these proposals previously. When the officials' opinions had been called for and directions given that decrees should be issued, it was very reprehensible that in fact no decrees were issued. Despite my urgent representations that it did not matter whose opinion they adopted so long as they issued some decree, it finished up with no decrees being issued at all.

I obtained a copy of all my proposals on that occasion, with the notes by the members of the Rōjū, and these may be consulted. Since I selected only what was applicable to the state of affairs at that time, there was nothing in the decrees of preceding *shōguns* which was not beneficial to society and to mankind. However, it must have been because there were many matters which were not liked by the officials.

Since the 27th October last year [1712], I had anticipated that after the death of His Highness, who valued me properly, no notice would be taken of my advice. However, with respect to the gold and silver coinage only, since, although it was the cause of the greatest national distress, there was no evidence of any government official at that time suggesting any solution, I alone had put myself forward and presented a memorial in the spring of the preceding year [1712]. When I had done so for the third time, although His Highness was already critically ill, he stiffened his resolution, stopped the coinage of silver, and dismissed Ōmi-no-Kami Shigehide [51]. Whatever happened after that, the officials who have charge of the administration today well know that His Highness intended to restore the silver and gold to its former standard and continued these efforts until his death. However, now that he is dead, no one has made any representations about this matter.

Since it is written that: "A man should finish the task he has begun," from the time that I first submitted a memorial, I was firmly resolved to cure this ill. My resolution was all the stronger because His Highness had died without carrying out his plans, and people of the present day and future generations would therefore think that it was his fault. It is filial piety to carry out the plans of those who have gone before us and to complete their undertakings.[86] And since this work would heal the sufferings of future generations of Japan, I was even more resolved that I would

[212]

somehow carry out this task for the sake of His late Highness and his son, the present Shōgun. In August of this year [1713], I wrote out three volumes of proposals concerning the recoinage, and, presenting them to Akifusa, explained my ideas to him.[87] Ever since His Highness had first ordered that the standard of the gold and silver coinage should be restored to what it formerly was, many and various private proposals had been put forward by the common people.

Some said that if the new silver which had been minted since Genroku was restored to the old standard, it would be necessary to use 1,180,000 *kamme* of cupellated silver, but the amount of cupellated silver produced in one year at this time did not exceed about 4,000 *kamme*. And so it would take over 300 years to complete the work.

Some said that if the silver and copper mixed in the present new silver were separated by using the lead produced from all the silver mines throughout the country, and if the silver were minted according to the old standard, 2,762,000 *kamme* of lead would be required to carry out the refining process.[88] But the lead produced from the silver mines throughout the country at this time did not exceed 3,736 or 7 *kamme*, and so it would take more than 739 years to carry out the work. Moreover, in the process of smelting the silver from the copper, untold numbers would die of lead poisoning yearly.

Some said that the difficulties of restoring the present new silver currencies to the old standard were as described in the previous two statements. However desirable it was to return to the old standard, if the new gold currency were not restored also, the prices of gold and silver would not be properly adjusted and the prices of all commodities would necessarily be unsteady. It would therefore be best for both the gold and silver currencies if the silver were first refined sufficiently to balance the price of the new gold now circulating. (The above three opinions probably all emanated from the merchants of the Silver Mint.)

Some said that although since Genroku coins had been minted by mixing silver with gold and copper with silver, the rate of exchange between gold and silver had been so fixed that, as in former times, the price of one *ryō* of gold would be sixty *momme*. However, when the common people compared the quality of the old silver and gold coins with the new coinage, they said that the new gold fell much farther below the old standard than the new silver, and henceforth the prices of gold and silver became unsteady. After that, gold and silver were reminted in the Hōei era, and since then the silver has been reminted several times. Now there are three qualities of gold coins and six qualities of silver coins, so that even when the people exchange silver for silver, the prices vary.[89] Moreover, although the new gold in circulation is of the same quality as the old, in actual appearance it is slightly lighter and half the size of the old coin. If the silver only were restored to the old standard, the prices of gold and silver would be thrown out of balance and the silver would certainly not circulate.

Some said it was impossible both to refine new silver and regulate the prices of gold and silver by issuing decrees. But if every year 100,000 ryō of gold are issued, and the new silver is taken out of circulation, then the amount of new silver in circulation will be decreased. After that, the price of gold and silver first of all, and then the prices of all commodities will also become steady. (These two opinions probably emanated from the money changers.)

Some said the price of the new silver presently in circulation is extremely low. This is due not only to the deterioration in its quality, but also to the large quantity in circulation. If, therefore, half the quantity is called in, the price must become steady. But it is impossible to call in half the quantity without a good reason. If Great Cash is minted from good copper, and these are exchanged for the new silver presently in circulation, and all the new silver is melted up, the silver and copper separated, and pure silver held in government depositories, the copper so obtained can be used when minting Great Cash. (This was probably the opinion of the man who had previously minted Great Cash.)

Some said that to restore the gold and silver to the former standard, it is necessary first to print paper money, exchange it for new silver, and to decree that gold, paper money, and cash shall be circulated all together. Then, if new cash is minted and the deficiency in the amount in circulation is made up, a scarcity of money in the empire will be prevented and the prices of all commodities will automatically become steady. Next, if explorations for mines are undertaken throughout Japan, and gold, silver, and copper mines are developed, within about ten years, gold and silver can be issued equal to the amount circulating in the empire before Genroku. When that stage is reached, if half of the paper money can be exchanged for the reminted gold and silver, and all the paper money is burned, no one will have any objections. (This was an opinion put forward by a shrewd fellow among the high officials.)

Some said that although the quantity of the gold and silver had increased since Genroku, the quality fell short of the old standard, and the quantity was twice that of former times. As a result, during recent years the price of rice has increased yearly, yet even though it rose above famine prices in olden times, nobody died of starvation. Owing to the increase in the amount of gold and silver, no one in the empire was in want, and so the recoinage of gold and silver since Genroku cannot be said not to have brought any advantages. If the prices of gold and silver is steady, and the prices of all commodities are steady, it is better for the quantity of gold and silver to be large. But if the price of gold and silver is not steady, the prices of all commodities will increase annually because their prices are fixed by the money changers who deal in the exchange of gold and silver, by privately adjusting the relative value of the coins. If, henceforth, the coinage is restored to the old standard, we cannot forecast the harm to society from the repeated and ingenious schemes that will be devised. If those guilty of fixing exchange rates privately in defiance of public law are dealt with, and heavy sentences are imposed on several of those money changers who indulge in the practice, not only will the anxiety of the ordinary people be set at rest, but the price of gold and silver will immediately become firm, and the prices of commodities will automatically stabilize. To ordinary people, money is money and profit is profit, and it would be culpable if, owing to the machinations of such wicked merchants as these, the gold and silver minted up to now were reminted and the empire were plunged into misery again. (This was probably an opinion put forward by members of the military classes.)

As none of these opinions seemed to go to the root of the matter, I first explained in my examination of the problem why all of them were wanting in substance. Next I discussed what I thought should be done. And finally I set forth the methods. In all, I wrote three volumes.

Akifusa was also well aware of what His Highness's intentions had been, but although he was extremely anxious to carry them out by some means or other, when he heard the opinions of the general public, he thought it completely impossible and had almost given the matter up. He was therefore overjoyed to hear my views. After consulting with the members of the Rōjū, about the end of September he directed the members of the Hyōjōsho to consider measures for the restoration of the coinage to its former standard, in view of the fact that His late Highness had left instructions about the matter. (He issued this order in accordance with my draft.)

However, these officials were perpetually concerned with how to benefit themselves and their families, so it could not be expected that they would show the slightest inclination to worry about the affairs of the empire. They carelessly professed themselves completely ignorant of the matter, and as they saw no point in laying themselves open to the censure of society, not one of them bothered to reply. So, realizing no progress was being made and that no one would be anxious if no official action eventuated, I suggested that the best way would be to put a group of specially selected men in charge. Akifusa again consulted with the members of the Rōjū and on the 20th November announced the names of those selected.

Those placed in charge of the matter were: among the Rōjū, Tajima-no-Kami Takatomo [54]; among the ōmetsuke, Nakagawa Awaji-no-Kami [103]; among the kanjō bugyō, Mizuno Inaba-no-Kami [104]; among the metsuke, Ōkubo Jin'emon (the present Shimotsuke-no-Kami) [105]; and in the Kanjō Gimmi Yaku, the two men Sugioka [86] and Hagiwara [87].

About that time, a merchant of Sakai in Izumi Province, called Tani [106], set forth his suggestions about this matter and sent them to me privately through a resident of Kyōto.[90] His suggestion was not the same as I had previously advised, but it was easy to carry out at that time. I thought that at this time the opinion of a specialist in this field would be of value, so I showed

what he had written to Akifusa. He was overjoyed that, although
people in general had given the project up, nevertheless two methods of carrying it out had been brought forward. I consulted
with Akifusa and wrote to the man who had sent the letter on to
me saying that since Tani had not explained his scheme fully in
his letter, if he would come to Edo, I should like to discuss certain
details with him. Soon after, I was informed that Tani had
arrived in Edo, and I immediately sent for him and said: "It is
not a subject which a scholar like myself knows about, but it is
for the sake of the country and the people, so I beg you to explain
your plan to those in charge of this undertaking." Then he told me
that he was acquainted with a relation of Hagiwara Dono [87].
Hagiwara Dono was Suga Yoshimasa. (He was known as Genzaemon. It was entirely through the labors of this man that a start
was made on this project.) I told him I was also acquainted with
Hagiwara, and that it would be very convenient for him to explain his plan through a man with whom he had some connection.
I immediately informed Yoshimasa [87] of this development and
asked him if he would meet and question this man. Yoshimasa
replied: "Since receiving this order, I have thought about it myself and questioned others, but I have not yet arrived at any
satisfactory plan of procedure. I rejoice to hear about this."
Yoshimasa therefore met Tani, had him explain his plan, and
questioned him on points needing elucidation. He then consulted with those who had been placed in charge of this matter,
and on the 1st February 1714, he reported what he had done to
Takatomo [54].

I was first informed of this plan through a dry-goods
merchant called Washizumi Gentarō.[91] He traced his origin
to the Akai of Tamba Province. Tani Chōemon Yasutaka
[106] was a descendant of the Hotta of Owari Province.
These two men belonged to the same branches as the Hotta
and Akai who served in *hatamoto* houses, and were intimate
friends. The ancestors of these two men had, for some reason,
given up their careers as *samurai* and taken to trade. Since
they are the descendants of distinguished warriors, their
motives are not to be compared with those of ordinary merchants. They were men who combined intelligence with
nobility of mind.

[217]

Akifusa [24], of course, knew all about this from the beginning, and as those who had been placed in charge of the undertaking reported that they had not progressed beyond the stage of preliminary discussions, he gave orders that the plan was to be adopted.

Since former times, gold and copper coins had circulated in the Eastern Provinces, but silver had not been used. In the Western Provinces, silver was the chief medium of exchange, with copper coins as a subsidiary currency. As a consequence of the large issues of new silver, hardship had been particularly severe in the Western Provinces. Therefore, Tani's proposals were also chiefly concerned with the silver currency. However, it had been His Highness's order that both the gold and silver should be refined, and furthermore, it was held that, if the silver were refined but not the gold, in the end their prices would not balance. And so I consulted privately with Yoshimasa, and prevailed upon them to include the question of the gold in their discussions also.

As I said before, the people of the Eastern Provinces had never endured hardship on account of the silver coinage, and they imagined that if the gold in circulation at that time were refined, they would lose half of their wealth. Even among those charged with carrying out the undertaking were some who did not want this plan put into effect.

At this time, many people came forward maintaining that one *ryō* of refined gold should be exchanged for one *ryō* of gold in circulation at that time. It was agreed that this was a natural expectation and that it should first be inquired into, so everyone considered the matter.

The aim of the recoinage of the gold and silver first undertaken in Genroku was to double the currency circulating in Japan, so coins were minted by mixing silver with the gold and copper with the silver. Of these, although the gold coins were the same as the old standard in shape and weight, it was impossible to deceive the people, and they were aware that the newly minted coins were half silver. Therefore, commodities which hitherto could be bought for 100 *ryō*, henceforth could not be bought for less than 200 *ryō*. The same thing happened in the case of silver. And so, although it was said that the price of everything had increased, this was in fact not so. It was merely that people considered 200 *ryō* today equivalent to 100 *ryō* in former times. Thus, although the imaginary quantity of the coins had been recklessly increased, their real number was not increased. If the standard of gold and silver is hereafter restored to that of former times, people will think that 100 *ryō* of recoined gold is equivalent to 200 *ryō* of the gold that has been in circulation until now. Thus, though the imaginary number of coins is decreased, their real number will not be decreased.

Furthermore, if the prices of commodities are maintained at their present level and we set up a rule fixing the value of the gold in circulation at this time, even commodities now priced at 100 *ryō* will be able to be bought for 50 *ryō* of the new coins. So whatever is done, it will lead to the loss of half the people's money. It will be quite impossible to exchange one *ryō* of refined gold for one *ryō* of gold presently in circulation. As I mentioned above, the coins which have come into existence since the Genroku era are actually half the old standard. For example, if 100 gold *ryō* are reminted in accordance with the old standard, barely 50 *ryō* will be obtained. If 100 gold *ryō* minted in accordance with the old standard are exchanged for 100 gold *ryō* minted since Genroku, there will be a loss of 50 *ryō*. Hence, if there is no material to make coins to cover the shortage, how can the number of coins be made up? If at the time gold had been produced from the mines throughout Japan sufficient to cover the shortage, it would not have been necessary, from Genroku on, to mint coins mixed with silver to increase the gold in circulation.

The reason why this proposal was put forward was that the officials did not lack the cunning to take away with the left hand what they had given with the right. As the people have already become inured to this kind of trick since Genroku, however much the government may be relying on having their confidence in carrying this out, they will not be able to disarm their suspicions, and if the slightest deception is practiced, the situation will be much worse. Although it is an oversimplified example, since people including those in high positions had been taken in by that proposal, it was difficult to make them understand without a thorough investigation of the idea. After spending many days in long discussion on this point, in the end they decided that the principle of exchange proposed was impossible, and that the best course was to adopt Tani's advice.

A method of extracting the silver from the gold coinage of the Genroku era had been employed prior to this. In extracting the copper from the silver, as mentioned before, it was said that a great amount of lead had been used, and also that there had been many cases of poisoning. It was asked what could be done about this. However, as regards this objection, there have dwelt in Ōsaka for many years dealers who have bought and sold copper. When they saw that there was a trace of silver in the copper they had bought, they smelted it and extracted the silver. If, as was asserted, poisoning resulted through using a great deal of lead, how could these people make a living? The silver in circulation at this time is called silver, but actually there is not much more than a trace of silver in copper. Consequently, when the Ōsaka merchants attempt to extract the silver, why should they experience any difficulty? I explained this in the recoinage proposals which I had at first presented. So it was resolved that the Ōsaka merchants should be summoned and this method should be tested. It was further decided where the gold and silver would be minted and exchanged.

The officials' deliberations concerning these matters were incomprehensible to me. Yoshimasa [87] felt the same as I did. For the rest, owing to the representations of Mizuno Inaba-no-Kami [104], there was no difference of opinion concerning the new copper coins either, and the Rōjū presented their decision.

As expected, fire broke out in the factory where they smelted the silver and it spread over a wide area. Also, many cases of violation of the law occurred in the factory. The culprits were punished, and after that, it seems the law was changed.

The circulation of the new copper proved difficult, and also did not benefit the people. People of small talent who are ignorant of fundamentals, in planning what they hope will bring advantage to themselves, usually invite swift misfortune. Akifusa should remember what I said at this time.

On the 26th June, in accordance with the orders of His late Highness, the restoration of the gold and silver coinage to the old standard was announced to the people. In compliance with Akifusa's desire that I should write all the drafts in connection with this decree, I said that with respect to this one request I could not refuse, and I presented all the drafts.

Before this, on the 24th June, four officials of the Silver Mint were banished, and one was expelled.[92] Hogi [88] and Komiyama [89], two members of the Kanjōsho who had had charge of this affair, were placed under house arrest.

When the offenses committed by these men were first discussed, there were some officials who said that it was a very serious crime that officials of the Silver Mint had first of all conspired together to mint poor quality silver, and then, in defiance of the law of many generations of *shōguns*, had minted the poor quality silver in obedience to Shigehide's personal orders, and finally had brought great hardship to their country, and that they should all be beheaded.

What had happened was as follows: Though in earlier times, certificates for the minting of silver had been issued over the joint signatures of the Rōjū, since Genroku, they had been issued over the joint signatures of the *kanjō bugyō*. The recoinages of April and May 1710 and September 1711, as I have previously recorded, had, by Shigehide's arrangements been carried out by orders over the joint signatures of Hogi and Komiyama. Moreover, since the Hōei era, the minting of much poor quality silver came about because a man called Fukae [91], on orders from Shigehide, had plotted with the officials in charge of the Silver Mint, and, producing a document bearing joint signatures, had entered into agreements with them. I discussed this charge, saying their crime was indeed serious. However, when the gold and silver were recoined in the Genroku era, in violation of the laws of the Divine Ancestor [8], the certificate was not issued over the joint signatories of the Rōjū but on orders given by the *kanjō bugyō*. Therefore, the recoinages of the Hōei and Shōtoku eras were carried out on the authority of Shigehide alone. Since at that time he was chief of the *kanjō bugyō*, and in particular was acting in this undertaking under the Shōgun's orders, the officials of the Silver Mint cannot be severely condemned for obeying an order issued by Shigehide.

If punishment is inflicted on the grounds that when Shigehide alone issued the certificate, they did not object that it was a violation of the law, then it could not be denied that when the joint signatories of the *kanjō bugyō* issued the certificate at the time of the Genroku recoinage, the failure to object to this as a violation of previous *shōguns'* laws was a crime of the same magnitude. The government issues the laws, the people carry them out. When the government itself violates the law, how can we punish the people, seeing that we cannot say that they have violated the law?

When crimes are committed, there is a ringleader and accomplices and accessories, so various degrees of responsibility are involved. As Shigehide was the ringleader in this affair, he was relieved of his office and confined to his house in the time of His late Highness, but when His Highness died, a general pardon was granted to all those under official displeasure, and Shigehide later died of illness without any investigation of his crime ever having been carried out. The ringleader has thus escaped punishment. Therefore, how can we punish all those who were only his accomplices and accessories? If we put them to death, we should first exhume Shigehide's coffin and behead his corpse. Only then should we proceed to deal with his partners in crime. Even if dead men were possessed of consciousness, and even if we were to chop up that cold flesh into small pieces, what pain would a stubborn devil like Shigehide suffer? But aside from that, such a useless display of cruelty is inconsistent with the merciful government of superior men.

When I spoke about Shigehide, the officials knew that I was speaking of Shigehide's misdeeds. Furthermore, I made it clear that I had never met a single one of those who were implicated in his plot, so my reason for entering this plea was not to help them escape punishment out of any sympathy for them. It was purely for the sake of the then Shōgun that I wished them to be treated justly. I heard that as a result of my representations, they were all acquitted.

Again, later when the property of the officials of the Silver Mint was confiscated, possession was obtained of the ledger which one Fukae [91] had written with his own hand. As a result, it came to light that at the time of the minting of poor quality silver in the Hōei and Shōtoku eras, Shigehide himself took a share amounting to 260,000 *ryō*, and besides that ancient paintings and curios as presents, and his servant (Nagai Hanroku) [90] obtained 60,000 *ryō*. Some said that the servant should not escape punishment either. I also discussed this question and pointed out that as Shigehide was the ringleader in this matter, the servant, as one who, in the words of the Code, had enhanced his lord's prestige by carrying out his orders, had received the 60,000 *ryō* as his share for services rendered.[93] In line with my previous argument, I observed that Shigehide, being dead, had already escaped punishment. If his retainer's crimes were now examined, his son could not escape that punishment either. Although Shigehide's crimes had not actually been investigated, on his death, out of the 3,700 *koku* of land which he left as his estate, only 700 *koku* were granted to his son. If his father had not been guilty, why should this have been done? So the father's crime had already been visited upon the son. Now that the father's crime of accepting bribes had been revealed, to punish a second time the son who knew nothing about it would be like piling frost on snow, and this too would be inconsistent with the merciful government of superior men. If the crime of the ringleader is not subjected to investigation, it is unjust to inquire into the crimes of accomplices. To invoke severe laws in doubtful cases is even less desirable. Therefore it would be best for the government to overlook the case. As a result, this case was not proceeded with either.

In the spring of this year [1714], the officials of Nishi-no-Miya in Settsu Province made a complaint.[94] This arose because in May of the previous year, Shirakawa Haku-no-Chūjō [107] had dismissed the *kannushi* and *hafuri* from office and appointed others in their place. When this Chūjō's lower officials were summoned and interrogated, it was discovered that they had accepted bribes, trumped up seven charges against the *kannushi* and *hafuri*, confiscated their property, and either filled their positions by men without status or position, or given them their robes, and they were at a loss for an excuse to explain this conduct. The Chūjō confessed through the Densō [95, 96]: "I am responsible for all these decrees. They were not perpetrated by the lower officials," so the punishment of the lower officials was remitted and they were sentenced to expulsion, and the shrine officials who had conspired with them were either sentenced to expulsion or confined to their houses. The former *kannushi* and *hafuri* were reinstated. Control of Nishi-no-Miya was taken away from the Shirakawa Family, while orders were conveyed through the Densō that the disciplining of the Chūjō was left to the discretion of the Imperial Court. It was reported that shortly afterward he was confined to his house.

On the 17th January 1715, the Densō said through Izumi-no-Kami Tadayuki [108]: "Owing to the complaint brought by the priests of Nishi-no-Miya, in the summer of this year [1714], Shirakawa Chūjō was confined to his house. A long time has passed since then. On account of the Shintō ceremony in the Naishidokoro could he not be released?[95] The reply was that there was no difficulty about that. Akifusa asked my opinion, and I presented a draft of a decision.

The *kannushi* was Yoshii Kunai, and there were five *hafuri*; the lower official of the Shirakawa House was Usui Suketada. The man appointed as successor to the *kannushi* in May the previous year, called Hama Shōdayū, died in November of the same year. Of the priests who had slandered the *kannushi*, and merchants who had been made priests, five were expelled or had their positions taken from them in accordance with the severity of their crime.

In September of this year [1714], a decree was issued concerning a complaint by the Abbot of Sambō-In.[96] This had arisen from his complaint that he had been insulted in the street by the abbots of Hōon-In, Rishō-In, and Muryōju-In, which are branch temples of Daigoji.[97]

In March of this year, an order was dispatched from the Jisha Bugyōsho summoning the abbots of the three temples to Edo. Kii-no-Kami Nobutsune [102] thereupon sent a letter to the Rōjū pointing out that the three abbots were priests of the tutelary temple of the reigning emperor, and in particular the Abbot of Hōon-In was also the registrar of Tōji, and the Abbot of Rishō-In the vice-registrar, and that there was no example in the Shingon sect of priests currently performing the duties of that office being temporarily absent in a distant province.[98] It was asked whether there was any such example in the Tendai sect, and when Ninnaji, Daikakuji, and Yasui were questioned about their precedents, they all gave the same answer as the other three temples.[99]

When the Abbot of Sambō-In was questioned, he mentioned an instance of a visit to Edo he had made when he had been appointed the registrar of Tōji and tutelary priest of the emperor. It was recorded that the Densō [95, 96] had stated that the Emperor's private opinion was that there would be no problem so long as the abbots of all three temples did not go to Edo at the same time.

When Akifusa asked what I thought about this, I replied: "Among the precedents cited by the three temples, there is one which occurred in the Tendai sect. Among the precedents cited by the Abbot of Sambō-In, there is one which occurred in the Shingon sect. Since the abbots of the three temples are the tutelary priests of the reigning emperor, they have taken advantage of imperial favor to disregard the summons from the Bugyōsho. It is clear that the Abbot of Sambō-In has been insulted. It is undesirable for the incident to be treated lightly. A message should be sent saying one may remain in Kyōto while summoning the remainder to Edo with all speed." When a message to this effect was sent, soon afterward both the abbots of Hōon-In and Rishō-In came to Edo.

When they were questioned about the complaint of the Abbot of Sambō-In, they said that the abbots of the three temples were called *monzeki* in ancient times, and even now, together with the Abbot of Sambō-In, they had been appointed registrars of Tōji, and likewise they had been made tutelary priests of the emperor.[100] Nevertheless, the Abbot of Sambō-In had treated them as subordinates or disciple priests, for which there was no justification. The problem which arose from these assertions was discussed in all its ramifications by the *jisha bugyō*, and the questions connected with it multiplied until the incident grew into such an issue that prospects of settlement seemed remote.

When Akifusa asked me about this problem, I said to him "It is very simple to resolve arguments as trifling as this, and very regrettable indeed if the Imperial Court hears that we cannot resolve them." Perhaps Akifusa consulted with the Rōjū, for they ordered me to present my opinion. I thereupon replied: "There is no need for me to present my opinion. Ask the abbots what happened."

When they were asked: "Since Jusangō Mansai of Sambō-In, who was the seventy-third holder of the position of Chief Abbot of

Daigoji during the Ōei era, was appointed to that office, is there any example where a priest of an outside temple was appointed to the position of Chief Abbot?"[101] They replied that there was no example.

When they were asked: "By what article in the regulations issued during the Keichō era by Tōshōgū [8] is it laid down that the succession to the headship of Daigoji was entrusted to the Abbot of Sambō-In?" they replied: "We do not know."[102]

When they were asked: "Concerning the Emperor's granting the title of Daishi to the founder of the temple, when the Imperial Envoy visited the temple, the abbots of the three temples disputed concerning the seats they were assigned and did not attend the ceremony. Why was that?" they answered: "The reason the abbots of the branch temples and other temples occupy equal seats at the ceremonies of baptism and dedication of the mandala is to show respect to the Dai-Ajari at these ceremonies, and therefore these ceremonies cannot be compared to any others. But at the ceremony in question, the Abbot of Sambō-In and the abbots of the branch temples and other temples were all given equal seats, and owing to this we could not attend the ceremony." Thereupon, I presented six articles setting forth what they must answer in connection with these points:

"Generally speaking, circumstances within the country have changed with the times. Customs of olden times cannot be adhered to in affairs of the present day. With regard to the matter of the office of the Chief Abbot of Daigoji, although in ancient times the abbots of that temple were appointed by rotation, since the Ōei era, the Abbot of Sambō-In has been appointed to this office by hereditary succession. Besides that, although he was sometimes called *monzeki* and sometimes *inge*, it does not appear that in ancient times his rank was very different from what it is now.[103] In particular, when the Divine Ancestor took control of the affairs of the empire, he consulted ancient precedents, and his decisions concerning the convenience of the times became the established system for the entire line of the Tokugawa House. It is pointless to ignore the system now in force and to argue about precedents of ancient generations. Even small temples scattered through all the provinces should be aware that since the Keichō era the succession to the headship of Daigoji has been entrusted to the Abbot of

Sambō-In by shogunal decree. The abbots of the three branch temples, who had stated that their position was higher than that of the other temples in Daigoji, had replied that they did not know this. If they do not know this, they show no gratitude for the temple land which the Tokugawa House has granted them for generations. Under these circumstances, what laws could serve as the standard for this time? But even though they were unaware that for more than one hundred years the Tokugawa House has entrusted the affairs of the temple to the management of the Abbot of Sambō-In, they cannot be unaware that he has been appointed as Chief Abbot of the whole temple by imperial order.

"By virtue of the fact that in ancient times the three branch temples had the title of *monzeki*, they have asserted that they are different from the other temples. But certainly at this time the Abbot of Sambō-In holds the office of Chief Abbot of the whole temple, and the abbots of the three branch temples have shown rudeness to the Chief Abbot, who has been charged with the control of the whole temple. How can those responsible for the dispute fulfill their duty of protecting the religion of their fatherland and praying for the health of the emperor?

"Also, as regards the fact that on the day that the Imperial Envoy conferring the title of Daishi on the founder of Daigoji came to the temple, the abbots complained about the seats assigned them and would not attend the assembly, even though at that ceremony reverence for the Dai-Ajari was equivalent to reverence for Dainichi Nyorai himself. If the priests accept the meaning of the 'four blessings,' which will they consider more important, the blessing of the Buddha or the blessing of the emperor?[104] There is no reason why the Imperial Messenger cannot be treated with the same respect as the Dai-Ajari. Moreover, it is indeed a rare piece of good fortune that 800 years after the death of Abbot Shōbō, his successors could participate in the ceremony of the Emperor's conferring upon him the title of Daishi.[105] At any rate, there is nothing in their precepts to justify disregard for imperial favor or gratitude due to their founder, arising out of one small piece of selfishness.

"In questions concerning etiquette in the street, considerations such as equal rank and equal office do not enter. To take an example from court etiquette, when a minister meets the Sesshō or Kam-

[227]

paku on the road, even though the latter may be his equal in rank and office, does he therefore refuse to pay homage? In the case of the Abbot of Sambō-In, the Emperor has appointed him to the office of Chief Abbot, and the Shōgun has appointed him to the headship of the whole temple. Even though the abbots of the branch temples may have had the same rank and same office, he should be treated respectfully because of his duties."

The abbots of the branch temples, upon receiving this question-naire, could not offer a single word of explanation and presented a letter of apology in which they said: "We pray for nothing else than that the distinction between the branch temples within Daigoji be done away with, and that the whole temple may be allowed to perform its religious duties as hitherto and to offer prayers hereafter for the safety of the empire." The case was settled without further ado. (This all took place in July.)

After a shogunal decree was issued about the jurisdiction of the temple, in September [1714] the government handed down a decision which I had formulated, and the messengers of the Abbot of Sambō-In and the abbots of the branch temples took their leave and went home.[106] Soon after, a letter of thanks was sent from the Abbot of Sambō-In, and he expressed his satisfaction at the good fortune of his temple. The records of what happened at this time have almost all been lost, and now only the drafts of the ques-tionnaire and the decision sent to the abbots of the branch temples remain. (On this occasion, the Abbot of Sambō-In sent two men, Kitamura Nagato-no-Kami and Yasue Tanomo, as his messen-gers.)

On the 20th November, the ceremony of the third anniversary of His late Highness's [3] death was held, and on the 21st officials attended at the Shōgun's [25] palace and reported that the ceremony had been performed. On the following day, the 22nd, I met Akifusa [24] and told him: "I wish to discuss with you the question of my resignation. For some years, I have always spoken to you first about every matter in which I was concerned. If I were to break that custom now, you would consider that I had betrayed you, and I would be ashamed. For this reason, I now inform you of my intention to resign."

At this Akifusa was very much surprised and said: "How can you suggest such a thing? You must not forget that until his death,

His late Highness discussed with you how affairs should be handled thereafter. Only the other day they were saying even in the women's apartments: 'Is Chikugo-no-Kami [2] well? His late Highness always spoke to us about him. Now, too, we need feel no anxiety because he is here to advise.' But if you do as you say, they will think that it is my fault, and the ordinary people will think so too. I earnestly entreat you to reconsider."

I said: "You cannot have forgotten that on the 27th October of the year before last [1712] I said my service had come to an end on that day. His Highness died shortly afterward, and although I had intended resigning then, I have continued thus for two years only because I felt that in regard to the coinage, I should somehow bring the plans to fruition as His Highness had desired. Decrees were issued about this matter last June [1714].

"In the spring of the year in which he was to die [1712], His Highness said: 'I wish I could recover and go to Nagasaki to investigate the conditions there.' However, when I looked at the replies to the questions he had asked the Nagasaki Bugyō, there were many details which they still did not know about, and I replied that even if I went there myself, unless I were to stay there many days, I would be unable to uncover the information we still did not have. So, if I went there, not only the Nagasaki officials but people in general would be suspicious, and I do not think that would be to our advantage. The best time to send me would be as attaché to the officials acting as shogunal messengers when decrees are issued about Nagasaki trade. His Highness agreed that what I had said was reasonable. Since the plan was not yet put into effect, I remained in close attendance upon him until he was on the brink of death. Hereafter, when the new Shōgun comes to issue decrees about this matter in accordance with the wishes of His late Highness, unless they conform with the orders he gave me previously and with what I advised him, they will be difficult to put into effect.

"My decision to resign was made before His Highness's death, but if you now prevent me and I give up my intention to resign, how can I speak to you like this? If I say positively I cannot change my mind, you will say that my action proceeds from ill will. If it were a time of stress for the empire, if there were anything the

[229]

high officials wanted to consult with me about, as long as I live I would obey their summons as often as they wished, and advise them to the full extent of my capacities."

When I spoke in this way, he raised no further objections but merely said: "There is no way to dissuade you from something you are so determined about. However, just at this juncture, the question of the reception of the Imperial Envoy and the Envoy from the Retired Emperor [100] and of the imperial abbots is not yet concluded.[107] After this is over, you may follow the dictates of your own conscience."

Then, on the 28th [November 1714], a message came from Akifusa saying: "Something has arisen I wish to talk to you about. Please come to see me for a little while." When I arrived he said: "I have spoken to the Rōjū about what you said to me the other day. I told them that, as you were held in high esteem by His late Highness, I had sincerely tried to dissuade you, but I did not think that I had been able to do so. Should we now do as you wished, I asked, or should I try to deter you by a message from the high officials? They said they thought that since I could not stop you, they could not succeed if they tried. However, if you resign now it will be embarrassing for the present Shōgun, so I must try to stop you somehow. Whatever your feelings may be at this time, it will be a great public and private good fortune if you will nevertheless bow to the wishes of the high officials."

I said: "What you have told me is quite extraordinary. I do not know what I ought to answer. I will speak after I have considered my decision carefully," and returned home. On the following day, I presented a letter in which I said: "It is already many years since I came to this decision, yet I have continued as I have until today. It is not an idea which has arisen on the spur of the moment. When those assisting in the government have signified their wishes, it would ill become me to express my private feelings. I will accede to your request."

On the following day a letter came saying: "Thank you for informing me of your decision. Indeed it is a great private and public blessing. I have something further to say. Please come on the 2nd December at ten o'clock in the morning." I attended at that time, and when members of the Rōjū had had audience with the Shōgun and retired, Akifusa and Tadayoshi [79] invited me to accompany them to meet them. When all were seated, Akifusa said to them: "When I conveyed your wishes about this matter to him, he agreed." Masanao [62] said: "You are not yet old. Look after your health and take measures to ensure that you will be able to serve the State as long as possible." Then the others also said various things, and among them there was one who said: "Even though you may be ill in bed, pray continue to give us your advice as you have done up till now." And there was another also who said: "Put aside all concern about material matters and set your mind at ease." Kii-no-Kami Nobutsune [102] said: "It is a long time since I saw you." Yamashiro-no-Kami Tadazane [109] said: "I have not met you before, but I think what has happened today is very fortunate."

In December this year [1714], rice fields for the support of Nammyō-In were granted (50 koku). His late Highness had left instructions that this should be done on the hundredth anniversary of the death of the Divine Ancestor [8]. When I was in Kyōto, on the day that I visited Tōfukuji, I went to Nammyō-In branch temple and saw portraits of the Divine Ancestor and of the Midaidokoro [110].[108] There are portraits of the Divine Ancestor in Kyōto and Nara, and I have seen them both. There is probably no other portrait of his consort besides this one. She was the younger sister of the Taikō Hideyoshi [13], and as she was the consort of the Divine Ancestor, it is unnecessary to say that while she was alive, she enjoyed the highest respect. But as I reflected how sad it was that now her portrait should be placed within a small temple where there were no facilities for performing services in the morning and evening, as could be wished, I was involuntarily moved to tears. It is recorded in several documents that during the lifetime of Taitoku-In [46], memorial services in her honor were performed. It must have been because some pledge had been given by the Shōgun's Heir [46]. When I asked why there was no support for the care of her tomb, the priest explained that at her death rice fields in the neighborhood of Kyōto had been offered, but the resident priest had requested a gift of 1,000 ryō of gold instead, and this request had been acceded to. Thinking this strange, I later mentioned the matter to Sa Chōro of Nanzenji, and he replied that such a request had been made because during that period it was not long since the wars, and it was common for temple land to be pillaged by armed bands.[109]

On my return from the capital, in reference to this state of affairs, I said: "The Divine Ancestor had many children and their mothers also were not few, but Lady Nammyō-In [110] was his only legal wife.[110] Long ago, at the beginning of the peace between the Eastern and Western factions, Hideyoshi adopted Mikawa-no-Kami Dono [93] hoping that this would enable him to arrange a meeting with the Divine Ancestor.[111] Then he gave his younger sister as the Divine Ancestor's consort, expecting he would achieve his aim, but there was still no sign that the Divine Ancestor would visit the capital to see him. Then, in addition, the Taichō went to Edo and finally the Divine Ancestor arranged to visit the capital. At this time, the Divine Ancestor said to those whom he left behind: 'Whatever happens while I am in Kyōto, my wife will know nothing about it, and you must send her back unharmed without fail.' Records exist of what happened at that time. First, we can surmise the depth of the Divine Ancestor's concern at that time. Secondly, it was the dispensation of Providence that no harm came to the Divine Ancestor during the lifetime of the Taikō [13], but we cannot say that it was without the help of the Midaidokoro [110]. Thus her merit in her own time, and for the sake of later generations, was not small. Furthermore, she was the wife of the great ancestor of the empire, but her tomb is deserted in Kyōto and never visited by a *shōgun*. It is lamentable that the only offering she receives is a little portion of the food from the priest of a tiny temple." His late Highness, assuming correct ceremonial posture, said: "What you say is right, but if I take such a step now without some special reason, it will seem as if I am exposing the shortcomings of my predecessors. The one hundredth anniversary of the Divine Ancestor's death is near at hand; I will arrange something in expectation of that event." When he died I heard that he had given orders about the matter, and at this time this plan was carried out.

In December [1714], the envoys from Luchu arrived to convey congratulations on the Shōgun's [25] succession and to report the accession of a new king.[112] Prior to this, the style employed in the composition of the official letters sent from Luchu had been the same as in letters exchanged within Japan, but from the time of King Shōeki, they used Chinese, and also changed the style of the box in which the letter was placed.[113] However, as our administration was not like that of the Chinese court, both in the titles and in the characters employed, some unacceptable features were apparent. In particular, Luchu alone among foreign countries had employed the Japanese system of writing. I pointed out that it was desirable, from the point of view of the national polity, that the same procedures should be adhered to as in the past.

Accordingly, Akifusa asked me: "In that case, what orders should we give about it?" I replied: "There are certain forms which should be employed. In the Luchu documents, the use of the characters 'Taikun' and 'Sonfujin' to designate the *shōgun* and his consort, and also 'Daichō' for Audience, are unacceptable.[114] You should mention this informally to Satsuma-no-Kami [71], directing him to speak to the envoys in a manner appropriate to the sensibilities of that country."

Later, a letter came from Satsuma-no-Kami stating that when he had conveyed the government's wishes to the envoys, they had asked if their letters should employ the form of address used toward the emperor, and also stated that in the letters presented by Japan, it was customary to use the character for "Ue."[115] Furthermore, they wished to know how they should address Lady Ichii [60] and Lady Gekkō-In [94]. He therefore wished to know how he should reply.

A reply was sent stating: "In His late Highness's time, the use of the character 'Taikun' was discontinued. This was because 'Taikun' is a title of the emperor, and it is unbecoming to use a character which is applied to the emperor. The *shōgun's* position is below that of the emperor, but above that of the Three Lords and imperial princes.[116] Also, the titles 'Uesama' or 'Kubōsama' were used from the time of Muromachi Dono [99] on because the old styles of address to the retired emperor were adopted.[117] Similarly at that time, too, the nobles in attendance on the emperor bore the titles 'Gekkei' and 'Unkaku.'[118] In the military houses, the titles 'Nagon' and 'Sangi' were employed. The use of the character for 'Ue' derives from this. In conclusion it is suitable to use the titles 'Ten'ei-In' and 'Gekkō-In' for Lady Ichii and Lady Gekkō-In.[119] It will be satisfactory if the meth-

[233]

od of writing employed is more or less like that which we employ in addressing the King of Luchu at the present time. All their queries have arisen from their ignorance of the ancient customs of our country and the actual conditions of the present regime, so they must be instructed about the correct protocol through Satsuma-no-Kami. But whether they use only Chinese, as in the documents since the time of King Shōeki, or whether, if it is difficult to select suitable characters, in accordance with former precedents, they more or less follow the method of writing employed in Japan's ancient communications, is for Luchu to decide."

Satsuma-no-Kami reported that the ambassadors on hearing this, said: "The change in the method of writing in communications from Luchu was due to the desire of our former king, on hearing that His late Highness [3] was fond of Chinese literature, to show respect. In deference to the wishes you have now expressed, we shall henceforth follow the old way."

It is difficult to describe the present regime in Japan in Chinese. In the main, they should follow the method of writing documents employed within Korea in respect to their own affairs. This is because the *shōgun* is one degree lower than the emperor and is the lord of Japan.[120] It goes without saying that, as explained before, the title of "Taikun" should not be used for the *shōgun*. The title of "Sonfujin" in China is a form of address applied to the wives of ordinary people. Especially, in view of the fact that the consort of the Luchu king is called princess, it is very unsuitable to use a title which is inferior to that.[121] The use of the character for "dai" as a title in Japan is limited to "Daijin," but this is also applied to ordinary people in China. For instance, it is like the use of the character for the honorific "on" in our country. The reason for setting down these points is that I thought they would not like it if we forced them to use Japanese characters. Hence, if they are given these orders, they will realize that it will be difficult for them to select suitable characters, and they will probably make further inquiries of us, and when they do so, it will be in order to recommend them to follow the precedents of previous ages. As I expected, the envoys made this reply.

However, as I also wished to make some inquiries, I sent word of this, and on the 23rd January 1715, I went to Satsuma-no-Kami's house. I had an interview with Yoshitaka [71] himself. I also met the envoys from Luchu. At this time I wore a lacquered hat with a brim and court costume, but I did not use a long sword, only a short sword, and a plum-colored fan. (This fan had been given to me by the former Sesshō, Konoe Daishōkoku [69], and had butterflies and birds painted on a gold ground.)

On the 23rd December [1714], the priest of Zōjōji had presented a letter to the Shōgun [25], requesting that, as the following year was the hundredth anniversary of the Divine Ancestor's [8] death, he repair Ankokuden, which was in his temple, and perform the ceremonies there.[122] The gist of the letter was as follows: "The statue of the Divine Ancestor in Ankokuden had been sculpted under his own orders with the help of a physiognomist's magnifying glass, and as his nails and hair are preserved within it, it had been a place of particular veneration until the time of the third Shōgun [9], but since the shogunal pilgrimage was discontinued during the childhood of the fourth Shōgun [43], the sanctuary has decayed amidst the wilderness.[123] Now, this sanctuary was built 6 *ken* long and 15 *ken* wide, 66 mats were laid within the hall, and a *torii* was built before the hall. This was a tutelary fane for the whole of Japan. Also, it was called Ankokuden because for generations, ever since the time of their ancestor Taikō-In, the Tokugawa House had been adherents of the Jōdo sect, and, in particular, the Divine Ancestor inherited the secrets of this sect, and when he did, he was called Ankoku-In Tokurensha Sūyo Dōwa Daikoji.[124] Henceforth all the ceremonies from that of the forty-ninth day to the third anniversary, were performed in our temple, but after the temple at Nikkō was dedicated, these ceremonies were no longer performed in our temple.[125] But in the time of His late Highness, in continuation of the intention of the Divine Ancestor and Taitoku-In [46], our sect enjoyed a revival, and the plan of His late Highness should be continued by having the hundredth anniversary performed in our temple. Moreover, there are some recent precedents for the performances of the memorial services for Jōken-In [15] in our temple."

The officials of the Rōjū, wondering what to do about this, discussed the matter with Akifusa [24], and so he asked me what I thought. I said: "According to documents in Chōrakuji at Serata in Kōzuke Province, it does not appear that the ancestors of the Tokugawa House were hereditarily adherents of the Jōdo sect. Only in the time of Izumi-Nyūdō was his house converted to this sect.[126] According to the *Honkō Kokushi Nikki* of Konji-In, the ceremony of the forty-ninth day for the Divine Ancestor was performed at Zōjōji, but because it was a private ceremony, the Shōgun did not receive offertory money from the Retired Emperor.[127] After that, at the time of the first and third anniversaries, there was no ceremony in this temple. There is no difficulty in making decrees about this matter." So Akifusa told me to give suitable directions.

I said: "A letter must be sent to the effect that, in the first place, the temple must send the diary of the time about the performance in that temple of the ceremonies of the forty-ninth day, and of the first and third anniversaries for Tōshōgū [8]; secondly, there must certainly be some reason why the ceremonies for the seventh anniversary were not performed at that temple, and they must send the diaries of the time to elucidate this point; thirdly, may it not be that no shogunal pilgrimage has been made since the time of the fourth Shōgun [43] to Ankokuden because the Tokugawa Family has left the Jōdo sect? They must produce an explanation for this. You must first question them about these points." They replied: "The diaries of that time were destroyed in fires on various occasions and there are now no proofs. Though after the seventh anniversary there was no ceremony in our temple, we do not think that the Tokugawa Family left the Jōdo sect. However, the funeral ceremony of the first Shōgun [8] was performed at Daijuji in Mikawa Province, and he received the name Ankoku-In which has been referred to before.[128] Ever since he was granted the title of Tōshō-Daigongen in March 1617, he was generally referred to by the name he received from the Emperor.[129] Since it has gradually been forgotten that he had the title of Ankoku, if our request were granted on the occasion of the hundredth anniversary of his death, it would be the greatest good fortune for our sect."

According to the *Kokushi Nikki*, the funeral ceremony was not held in Daijuji, neither did the imperial grant of the title Tōshō take place in 1617, and so I said: "You must question them and tell them to write out what appears in the records of that temple concerning the funeral ceremony at Daijuji." Then they answered: "There is no record at Daijuji. That event is dealt with in detail in the *Mikawa Go-fudoki* written by Hiraiwa Kazue-no-Kami Chikayoshi."[130] I said: "Chikayoshi died on the 2nd February 1612, at the age of seventy in Nagoya Castle in Owari Province.[131] How could he know and record events which happened at the time of the Divine Ancestor's death? Everything they have said is lies." A letter was sent to the effect: "If all the facts are thoroughly elucidated, the Tokugawa House has been an adherent of the Jōdo sect for many generations, and Zōjōji was the traditional memorial temple of this House.[132] But such ungrounded claims as you have made are most unfitting for other temples and branch temples to hear." They immediately sent a letter of apology and there was nothing like it said again.[133]

In October this year [1714], in view of the decision to recoin silver in Kyōto also, messengers were selected from among those who had been placed in charge of the undertaking and sent there. (The three men were Mizuno Inaba-no-Kami [104], Ōkubo Jin'-emon [105], and Hagiwara Genzaemon [87], but owing to illness, Ōkubo was replaced by Marumo Gorobei [111].)[134]

They left Edo on the 24th November and returned in January the following year. In the preceding June, the silver and gold had been recoined and put into circulation, but within a short time this was obstructed, and rumors had spread that it would be most unsatisfactory for the exchange to be managed as it was. (Ever since this autumn [1714], almost all the members of the Rōjū had asked to be paid in coins formerly in circulation for the rice they sold, and if they disliked the new coins, it was natural that the ordinary people would make the same sort of criticisms).

Meanwhile, in November, the exchange rate for gold and silver was under discussion. A certain man (a merchant called Nojima Shinzaemon [112]) said: "Ever since the rate of exchange between the recently recoined gold and silver and the gold and silver previously in existence was put into effect, the prices of all commodities immediately rose. This was most unfortunate for the government and for private persons of both high and low degree. I have a good plan to alter this." High-ranking officials also spread it about that there was reason in what he said, and the common people thought: "Then the law will soon be changed," and immediately ceased to exchange gold and silver.

When I heard about this, I said: "When His Highness first gave orders about the recoinage, I expected this sort of difficulty to arise, so I stated in a document that people who in any way did anything to obstruct the circulation of the new coins for reasons of private profit should be examined and punished severely for the good of the State and future generations. It is unnecesary to stress the gravity of the offense of obstructing such a vital measure as the circulation of the new coinage. However, the reason why such rumors were spread about was because high-ranking officials had been airing the matter privately. Unless we gain the wholehearted trust of the people, it will be impossible to prevent such predicaments."

So Akifusa said: "Among the officials who were put in charge of this undertaking, those who will be best informed about the coinage are in Kyōto. Will it be feasible to give them orders about suitable measures?" I said: "If the situation is explained clearly, there will be no difficulty." He then said: "If we give them orders to take strong action now, since those best informed are in Kyōto, the populace will probably say that enforcing these measures is all Chikugo-no-Kami's [2] doing. Because I was thinking of this, I spoke as I did before." I said: "Ever since we first discussed the recoinage in the time of His late Highness, I have given no thought to my personal reputation, but only to the well-being of the State and of posterity. Do not be concerned about what the ordinary people say."

"Very well," he said, and consulted with the members of the Rōjū, and at the beginning of December they appointed officials to examine this man's proposals. (Those who received these orders were: among the *jisha bugyō*, Takebe Takumi-no-Kami; the *ōmetsuke*, Matsudaira Iwami-no-Kami [82]; the *machi bugyō*, Nakayama Izumo-no-Kami [80]; the *kanjō bugyō*, Ōkubo Ōsumi-no-Kami [81]; the *metsuke*, Suzuki Ihei [77], Nakane Hanjūrō, Semba Shichirozaemon, and Nagai Saburōemon; and Nakagawa Awaji-no-Kami [103] as before.)[135]

The gist of this fellow's ideas was that according to a statement in the *Jinkōki*, the entire population, male and female, of Japan was about 4,800,099,600, and now it must have reached several hundred times that number.[136] So if every person was taxed 12 *sen* and this was used to assist in the exchange of the old and new gold and silver and as material for minting new copper, the rate of exchange could be fixed at 70 *ryō* of new gold, or 120 *momme* of new silver, or 40 *kammon* of new copper for 100 *ryō* of gold previously in circulation.[137] Orders were given to the officials that each must present his opinion as to whether this plan was feasible, and in December they did so. They differed from one another, but they all agreed so far as to say that the scheme propounded was not without reason.

I first wrote out a document headed "Later Proposals Concerning Recoinage" and presented it to Akifusa saying: "Please show this to the members of the Rōjū.[138] Unless the officials comply with it, they will find it difficult to deal with the situation." Next I presented a document explaining fully that everything Nojima [112] had said was baseless, and I said: "Please show this document to the officials who have been placed in charge of this investigation."

Although I have made a separate record of this incident, the gist of my analysis of Nojima's plan is as follows: "Concerning the idea that we should tax everyone in Japan, although detailed records of the population for many generations appear in Chinese books, in Japanese books records exist for a few villages, but the population of Japan as a whole is not known.[139] In ancient times, in the time of Jōgū Taishi Sesshō, a census was taken and there were fewer then 5,000,000.[140] It appears that at that time the population stood at 4,969,890.[141] Also, according to one opinion, in the time of Emperor Shōmu, it was said to have been 8,631,074.[142] However, these statements do not appear in the official histories. In Chinese records, it is stated that during the Han Dynasty there were 59,594,978 people, and it has been said that never since the world began had there ever been such a large number of people as this.[143] This was the number of people in the whole of China. The previous statement concerning the population of Japan becomes even less credible.

"The statement in the *Jinkōki* is only an arithmetical example. If we compare the amount of salary rice produced in Japan at this time with the statement in the *Jinkōki*, there would be 20,000 people for every 100 *koku* of land, and there would still be 91,648 people over.[144] Even though we have had peace for 100 years, you can guess whether or not there would be more than 20,000 people in a territory of 100 *koku* by looking at your own territory.

"Then, as for imposing a 12 *sen* tax on everyone in Japan, even if there were several hundred times the number of people as there are stated to be in the *Jinkōki*, would it be as Nojima argues? Supposing there were 200 people for every 100 *koku* of land, if by putting a tax on every person we obtained material to exchange one *ryō* of old gold for one *ryō* of new, the scheme would not succeed unless we imposed a tax of 1 *kan* 300-odd *sen* on every person. The wealthy people in the empire are few and the poor are many; how ridiculous it would be to exact such a tax from those who keep father and mother, wife and child on wages of barely 50 or 100 *sen* for a full day's work.

"Not only that, but there has been a limit on the amount of copper which has been minted at various times since the middle of Kan'ei.[145] Even if we consider the amount of copper in existence before that to be equal to the amount coined since Kan'ei, we can make a rough estimate of the amount of copper which is circulating in the empire at this time.[146] It we considered putting a tax of 1 *kan* 300 or more *sen* on everyone in Japan, the number of *sen* in circulation at this time would not be one tenth of that. Where can we obtain such a large amount of coins from?

"Since ancient times in China and Japan, when taxes were imposed, the aged and the children were exempted from tax. Moreover, the difference between the upper and the lower classes was very great. Furthermore, besides itinerant priests and travelers, there are many people who ply their trade by going hither and thither, and it is difficult to determine the number of people who are born in the morning or die at night in the villages. So what means are there for recording the number of men and women in Japan without missing one, and for imposing that tax?

"If we were to compare the rich and the poor people in the empire, there would be many times more poor people than rich. Although one *ryō* of gold were to be exchanged for two *ryō* of gold and there were a loss of half, this loss would concern those above the middle class. Those in the lower classes do not make one *ryō* during the space of one year. But leaving aside the question of riches or poverty, it is a bad scheme to impose a tax without regard to position.

"Again, it is impossible to exchange gold circulating at this time for 70 *ryō* of new gold, or 120 *momme* of new silver, or 4 *kammon* of new copper. If we recoin the gold in circulation since the Genroku era according to the old standard, the number of coins will decrease by half, and so it is impossible to add 20 *ryō* of new gold in addition to the exchange rate established at this time.

"Also, if we remint the gold made since the Genroku era according to the ancient standard, we reduce it by 80 percent. But, if in exchanging the gold, we have to use 20 percent of the silver, there will only be 125,504 *kamme* or so of new silver for exchanging the silver which has been made since the Genroku era. Moreover, the method of minting the new silver is to exchange what is extracted for the silver made since the Genroku era and to make the new silver with what is exchanged.

"If we exchange the gold in accordance with the method Nojima described, and if we use new silver for this, what shall we use to exchange for the silver made since the Genroku era, and what shall we use to make the silver to exchange for that gold? If we are foolish enough to put Nojima's plan into operation, before three days have passed we will not be able to coin gold or silver. And if we cannot coin it, how can we carry out the process of exchanging gold and silver?

"Finally, when we calculate the number of copper coins we must exchange for one-tenth of the amount of gold presently in circulation, we must use 29,543,000 *kammon*. In the space of about sixteen years during the Kambun era, 1,970,000 *kan* of copper were coined.[147] Even though prices were low at that time, the government was unable to bear the expense of it and stopped coining. Recently, prices of commodities have become higher than ever before.[148] So even if 100,000 *kan* of copper were coined every year, it would be impossible to obtain, even in 290-odd years, sufficient copper to exchange for the gold now in circulation. Even if it took more than 290-odd years to recoin the gold and silver, we ought not to employ the method of taxing the people throughout the whole of Japan and using 20 percent of silver and 10 percent of copper in every 100 *ryō* of gold." I stated that I should like to hear what they all had to say about this. Since the officials were unable to say a single word in reply, I did not press the point further.

The following judgment was handed down: At this time Nojima Shinzaemon had spread this rumor and caused a stoppage in the exchange of gold and silver. He had done this in spite of the decree issued when His Highness had first given orders about the gold and silver coinages, that those who obstructed the process in any way at all should be examined and severely punished for the good of the State and of posterity. Although his crime merited punishment by death, the death sentence was remitted by one degree and he was sentenced to exile. As a result of these measures, the exchange of gold and silver was again carried on as before.

It was reported that when the man responsible for this rumor was told he had been sentenced to banishment, he immediately fell down unconscious. On hearing of this, Yamato-no-Kami Shigeyuki [61] turned to the officials and said: "How can men of this kidney perpetrate swindles of this magnitude?"An apt comment.

In the winter of this year [1714], it was decided to make a pronouncement about trade at Nagasaki in accordance with the dying wishes of His late Highness. This question had arisen at the beginning of His Highness's rule when our seaborne trade had been interrupted because our supplies of copper were not sufficient to pay for it, and the Nagasaki Bugyō reported that on this account the townspeople were approaching starvation from want of occupation.

This was because in former days, the number of Chinese ships and the yearly amount of silver for trade were not limited, but from 1685, the yearly amount of silver for trade with the Chinese ships was fixed at 6,000 *kamme* and that for the Dutch at 50,000 *ryō*.

By 1690, the yearly amount for Chinese ships was fixed at 70 cargoes.[149] But in 1695, a certain Fushimiya Shirobei was allowed 1,000 *kamme* of silver beyond this amount to trade with, and he requested to be allowed to pay in copper for the goods to the value of 1,000 *kamme* in silver, and this was permitted. This was the beginning of what was called "barter."

The next year, 1696, since he offered to pay 10,000 *ryō* in customs duty, he requested that a barter of up to 5,000 *kamme* should be permitted. This also was granted. This was the beginning of customs duty.

The next year, 1697, Takagi Hikoemon, a merchant of Nagasaki, petitioned that the fixed number of 70 ships should be increased by 10, and the amount of barter raised by 2,000 *kamme* in addition to the 6,000 *kamme* of silver, if a customs duty of 20,000 *ryō* were paid. So Fushimiya's barter was stopped and Takagi's petition was granted.

After a year had elasped, in 1699, Ogiwara Ōmi-no-Kami [51] and Hayashi Tōgorō went to Nagasaki and there issued regulations that at the Nagasaki exchange the price at which foreign cargoes could be sold to our merchants would be 70,000 *ryō* of gold paid in silver.[150] Beside this, there were the deposit money, expenses, commission, brokerage, honoraria, etc., of the Chinese and Dutchmen bringing the total to more than 110,000 *ryō*, and all outside this should be paid publicly. This was the beginning of the 70,000 *ryō* divided among the townsmen. But for the 70 shiploads with the addition of 10, and the 6,000 *kamme* of silver with the addition of 2,000, the yearly amount of copper allowed for trade was 8,902,000 *kin*.

In the beginning of foreign trade at Nagasaki, the copper that the foreigners bought for silver was sent by 16 selected copper smelters in Ōsaka. In 1697, the number of ships and amount of silver were increased, and "barter" began. Next year, 1698, an Edo merchant named Kikyōya Matahachi took over the business and was ordered to make up with silver the amount by which the yearly allowance of copper was lacking. But, as in 1699, the supply of copper was still insufficient, Kikyōya's delivery was stopped and orders were given for the Ōsaka copper smelters, and the merchants of all the other provinces as well, to send in as much as they wished. But even so, the amount collected at Nagasaki was only 7,000,000 *kin*. By 1701, orders were again given that the Silver Mint should take over the business of the Copper Mint as well and buy up all the copper the provinces produced and send it to Nagasaki. But still the yearly amount of copper required was not forthcoming and trade could not be carried on, so that the time for the foreigners to depart was exceeded and extended to the next year.

When orders were issued about this problem, although the merchants of the Silver Mint, who had received orders to send up the copper, were urged to speed this up, they said that the production of the mines in all the provinces was decreasing annually and the price was going up, so that the price must be increased or the undertaking could not be carried out.

In 1711, the officials of the Silver Mint said they would send up 4,500,000 *kin* of copper, and a certain person (a merchant named Nakagawa Rokuzaemon) applied for permission to make up the amount they could not supply and obtained it. But the price of copper rose so high that he could make no profit and was unable to carry out the transaction, and the copper needed for internal use was not available either. So even by March the following year, 1712, the officials of the Silver Mint could not supply the necessary amount, but were short 1,500,000 *kin,* so on the 22nd April, the Silver Mint's control of the work of the Copper Mint was dispensed with, and on the 24th, copper smelters of Ōsaka were ordered to take charge. However, it was said that, since the amount of copper produced by all our mines the previous year, 1711, was no more than 6,400,000 *kin*, when the 1,600,000 *kin* needed for internal use was subtracted, not more than 1,400,000 remained to be sent to Nagasaki; and the price was so high because the copper merchants would not sell it.

This being so, the townspeople of Nagasaki could not carry on their business and came near to starvation. The weaker ones got into communication with the Chinese who stayed there and traded secretly in their lodgings. The stronger ones went away and waited for the Chinese ships at sea and did business with them there. The foreigners also have not kept to their regular sea routes in recent years, but have cruised around offshore waiting to trade privately with our dishonest merchants. Then, too, they have landed and taken water and wood, and stolen the fish that our fishermen catch and the seaweed that the women and children gather. And when the people have tried to stop them, they have held them off with weapons, and when the guard-ships have approached, they have fired on them.[151] (Recently, even when Dutch ships depart, under-cover trading transactions have been carried

[244]

out. The Japanese merchants have never engaged in such practices before.)

The Nagasaki Bugyō reported these happenings and said that under these conditions the superintendence of the Nagasaki Bugyōsho could not be enforced, and that they could not handle the situation unless the shogunate issued strict decrees.

The reason why the Chinese and others behave like this is probably because of the lenient way foreigners were treated in the Jōkyō and Genroku eras. Our people were enjoined not to be hostile to foreigners, and when the lower officials of the Bugyōsho were threatened by the Chinese, and drew their swords and wounded them slightly, they were dismissed on the spot. In consequence, foreigners developed a bad habit of doing what they liked.

When I heard this, I said that our country has from ancient days been famous as one that surpassed all others in its martial qualities, and it is quite intolerable that it should be thus insulted by these foreign merchants. Written orders must be given by the *bugyō* to the Chinese and also to the *daimyō* of the Western Provinces and the Chūgoku Region as to how they are to act. These orders were put into effect in June 1714.[152]

In preparing the decree admonishing the Chinese, orders were given directing Fukami Shin'emon [101], Miyake Kyū-jūrō, and Muro Shinsuke [98] to present drafts, and that presented by Fukami was employed with various alterations. I wrote the draft of the orders given to all the *daimyō*. Orders were given that when any of these foreigners appeared from time to time in home waters, and disembarked, the people must burn their boats and kill those who came in them; and when Japanese ships approached foreign ships, they must arrest them.

Before this, in March during the spring of this year [1714], because copper was lacking as currency for foreign trade, the Nagasaki Bugyō (Komakine Higo-no-Kami and Hisamatsu Bingo-no-Kami) and the lower officials (the Nagasaki *machi doshiyori*, chief of whom was Takagi Sakuemon) were asked their opinions about this.[153] But the various opinions presented did not seem to be of much use, and so, as it was my duty to write the drafts enforcing, a second time, the decisions made in the time of His late

Highness, I wrote out 211 major and minor items (consisting of eight volumes) and presented them. It is difficult to explain what was involved here because it is like seeking for a thread in a tangled web with many loose ends. If you wish to know about it all in detail, you must consult the documents "Regulations for Trading Ships" and "New Precedents for Trading Ships" which I wrote on two occasions.[154]

There is no need to discuss what happened prior to the establishment of the Tokugawa shogunate, but from 1601, there was no particular fixed place for foreign ships to come and trade. That was about the time of the Wan-li era of the Ming Dynasty and there was a strict prohibition on ships going abroad so that Chinese ships did not come as they do now.[155] At Nagasaki, only European vessels came to stay. By the beginning of Kan'ei, orders were issued that foreign vessels might come to Nagasaki and trade, but the Dutch ships were going to Hirado in Hizen, and it was not until the latter part of the era that they changed to Nagasaki.[156] Both *daimyō* and merchants went out to trade with foreign lands under the *shōgun's* official seal, but in 1634 this was stopped.[157]

In those days, the number of foreign ships and the amount of silver for trade were not fixed, but in 1685, for the first time, a fixed amount was allotted for trade, 6,000 *kamme* of silver for Chinese ships, and 50,000 *ryō* of gold for the Dutchmen, and in 1690, the total number of Chinese ships was fixed at 70.[158] This was the K'ang-hsi era of the Ch'ing Dynasty, and the Chinese emperor relaxed the prohibition against trade so that as many as 200 Chinese ships arrived.[159] From 1695, besides the fixed amount of silver, copper began to be used, and a barter system was set up, and in 1698 the number of Chinese ships was increased by 10 to 80, while an extra 2,000 *kamme* of silver was allowed. (I have dealt roughly with these changes in a previous note.)

As the number of Chinese ships was fixed, if any beyond that number came, they were sent back loaded and not allowed to trade. Even if the ship was one of the permitted number, the amount of silver was fixed for each, and each ship was only allowed to trade in goods up to the value of 160 *kamme* of silver. The rest was called surplus freight. But since it was not their purpose to go back empty-handed after braving the wind and the sea for long distances, or to bring a lot of goods and make little profit on them, they tried to sell what they brought somehow or other. Our people also had to pay duties when they bought things within the permitted amount, so that they had large expenses and small profits, and thus they tried to buy these surplus goods that were to be returned, and every year this illicit trade increased. (It was known by various names, such as "outside buying," "agents' buying," "smuggled goods," and "sly buying.")[160]

In the time of His late Highness, the Nagasaki Bugyōsho was asked to inform him of the amount of gold, silver, and copper spent at Nagasaki for foreign trade. From 1601 to 1647, 46 years in all, they had no information, but for the period of about 60 years from 1648 to 1708, the amount of gold that went abroad was 2,397,600 *ryō* and of silver, 374,229 *kamme*. As to copper, before 1662, for a period of 61 years, they knew nothing, but from 1663 to 1707, that is, for 44 years, the amount exceeded 1,114,498,700 *kin*.[161] This was the only total that the *bugyō* could give from the year 1648 onward.

Trade prior to that was not confined to Nagasaki alone. As I mentioned before, foreign ships called at various Japanese ports to trade, while Japanese ships also called at various foreign ports. Besides this, it was impossible to ascertain in full the numbers of those who went to Korea from Tsushima and those who went to Luchu from Satsuma Province.

Therefore, if we calculate the sum of gold and silver that has gone to foreign countries for the 107 years since the Keichō era on the basis of the information given by the Nagasaki Bugyōsho and compare it with the amount of gold and silver produced in our country within the same period, we can see that we must have lost a quarter of the gold and three-quarters of the silver.[162] Therefore, in another century we shall have lost half our gold, and all the silver will have gone before that period is out. As for copper, not only is what we have now not enough for foreign trade, but insufficient for internal needs as well.

We ought not to lower the dignity of our country for the sake of gain as we do in thus throwing away the time-honored treasures of our produce in exchange for the ephemeral novelties that come from abroad. If this must be done to obtain such things as drugs and books, we should estimate the amount we now need for use here and the amount that all the provinces produce annually, and then establish what is to be sent abroad from Nagasaki, Tsushima, Satsuma, and other places. I do not understand why the authorities did not take all these measures but only fixed the amount of gold, silver, and copper for Nagasaki.

But even if these amounts are fixed from now on, if, as previously, the number of ships to come each year and the freight carried in each one are not fixed, we shall still have the same illicit trading as we have at present. Thus, we must first consider the total yearly production of gold, silver, and copper that can be exported abroad, and then decide on the yearly sum that is to be used for foreign trade at Nagasaki. Next, the amount that is to be carried as freight on each foreign ship is to be reckoned, and both the number of ships and the amount of freight are to be fixed. In this way, the cargo they bring can be bought up, and we shall not lose our treasure through illicit trade, nor will the foreigners treat the laws of our country with contempt as has happened hitherto. Our national prestige will be widely honored, and our wealth will last forever.

The ordinary people of Nagasaki were ruined and reduced to starvation, and this was indeed a problem of the poor people and not the rich. If the cause is studied, it is clear with whom the blame lies, so it is unnecessary to discuss the matter in detail. *Bugyō* were appointed, the regulations for public trading were laid down, and as in Kyōto and Ōsaka, *metsuke* were dispatched and authorized to exercise supervision. This concerned not only trade at Nagasaki, but was also appropriate to the Western Provinces and the Chūgoku Region. Since the document I presented at this time was the gist of what had been decided in the time of His late Highness, it merely set forth those precedents and regulations.

Writing out regulations and setting forth precedents is like trying to destroy the snake in Mount Ch'ang, whose tail defends its head, and vice versa, or whose head and tail mutually assist each other.[163] It is not permissible to insert or leave out a single case of the many. However, this supervision was in the event not put into effect in the time of His late Highness because no one gave any thought to the interests of the State and of posterity, but talked a lot of nonsense about matters of which they were completely ignorant. The people of Nagasaki hoped there would be many foreign ships and many foreign commodities; the officials of the Bugyōsho hoped that without reducing the amount of transport tax paid, the people under their control would be able to make a living (the way the officials schemed to increase the wealth of their own families was a separate issue); the merchants throughout the country hoped that many foreign goods would come so they could buy cheaply and sell at a large profit; when textiles and drugs were imported in large quantities, the general populace, on rushing to buy them, thought only of the cheap price. Henceforth, people who do not think about the future and are misled by theories of every description will also inevitably be in trouble if they try to change the law without proper consideration, exactly as has happened in the past.

In the spring of the following year, 1715, in the middle of February, messengers left Edo for Nagasaki to communicate the "New Regulations for Sea-borne Trade" to the Nagasaki Bugyō. (These were the ōmetsuke, Sengoku Tamba-no-Kami [113], and the otsukaiban, Ishikawa San'emon, accompanied by several officials of the Kanjōsho.[164] They arrived about the end of March, and at the beginning of April the orders were given out to the townspeople and then to the Chinese and others. (The document that was read out by them was one that I had composed.) To those who said they would abide by our laws, a certificate was given and they were allowed to come again to trade. Those who would not submit to these laws were not allowed to trade and were expelled on the spot. In June of the same year, the *daimyō* of the Western Provinces and the Chūgoku Region also received commands about these new regulations.

It was probably about the spring of 1715 that a lampoon was written on the gate of a member of the Rōjū. The message stated that people of the three provinces of Settsu, Kawachi, and Izumi were distressed and made a complaint about Hōjō Awa-no-Kami Ujihide [114]. Akifusa asked me privately what I thought about this incident. I said: "If what is written is the truth, the complaint should have been presented to the government. It was not necessary for the fellow to conceal his name. He must certainly be a small-minded wicked man, and he has done it in order to satisfy a private spite. If you give this lampoon to Awa-no-Kami, he will probably know who has written it. It is most unfitting for the government to take action against the *bugyō* because of such things. Even if the *bugyō* have made mistakes, if you show that you have faith in them, they will mend their ways and it will be very fortunate for the future." Akifusa consulted with the Rōjū, and when he sent the lampoon to Awa-no-Kami's house by the hand of Matsumae Izu-no-Kami (since Matsumae was a relative of Hōjō), it was found to be a completely groundless statement.[165] Soon after, there was a lampoon complaining about the *bugyō* written by the people of Sado Province. As before, this was also given to the *bugyō*. (It was given to Kōno Kan'emon.)

It happened at this time that the Rōjū consulted together and said that certain high-ranking office-holders, including *bugyō*, must be deprived of their office. Sagami-no-Kami Masanao [62] said: "I have never ever heard things about these people." Yamashiro-no-Kami Tadazane [109] did not say anything. At that time, Akifusa said sadly: "These happenings are unfortunate," and I replied: "I feel the same as you. We must stop them." After the ceremonies for the one hundredth anniversary of the Divine Ancestor's death were concluded, this question was again referred to, but it was said: "It would be bad policy to issue decrees punishing these people, in view of the fact that at this time an amnesty for criminals has been granted. If it is impossible to stop this matter, it would be best just to change their positions without giving any special reason," and the affair died down without people arguing about it any further.

Among the many whose dismissal from office was discussed at this time, including *orusu*, *ōmetsuke*, *machi bugyō*, *kanjō bugyō*, was one who had a very fine reputation.[166] But this discussion was not without reason. However, it is probably out of place to write this down. Two of them were soon unfortunately deprived of office. The rest are still fulfilling their duties without any interference.

At the beginning of the summer of this year [1715], the Shōgun [25] fell ill, and when medicine proved of no avail, physicians were summoned. When I left the palace at about two o'clock on the afternoon of the 11th August, I met Yamashiro-no-Kami Tadazane hurrying in. My attendants told me that Yamato-no-Kami Shigeyuki [61], with only a few attendants, had also entered in great haste. I thought it strange, and when I went out the east gate, I found that a lot of people had congregated, and they said that they had seen one of Tadazane's palanquin bearers collapse out of breath. I was even more perplexed when an order was issued summoning everyone to attend on the following day. This was because at this time Kii-no-Kami Nobutsune [102] was on duty and he may have misunderstood the report, but under the impression that the Shōgun was very ill, he notified the members of the Rōjū. That evening, these officials went so far as to discuss what they would do if the Shōgun died, and Akifusa, for the first time, revealed to them the instructions left by His late Highness [3]. However, shortly afterward the Shōgun responded to treatment, and after only a month had passed, on the 10th October, Nobutsune had a stroke.[167] Things which happen in life are unexpected.

Soon after the Shōgun was born, he had been very ill. But because the medicine prescribed by a doctor called Yamada Sōen Hōgen proved so efficacious, he had been regularly kept on this Hōgen's medicines only, and no other doctors had been consulted.[168] Owing to his illness this year, it seems that his usual nourishment was reduced, and since the medicine was changed, it might have seemed a matter for concern. People came to my house and discussed the Shōgun's illness, and because Nobutsune and Tadayoshi [79] believed the rumors, a commotion arose, and the incident of the 11th August occurred.

Now, among those who heard the instructions left by His late Highness that evening, it seems that there were as many as three or four who devised schemes for private advancement for the time when the Shōgun would be dead. It is said that they were all hereditary retainers, and they were all people who had received great favors during the rule of both His late Highness and the present Shōgun. Among them, one or two are still in office. It seems one cannot trust people.

When His late Highness was still an ordinary feudal lord, a certain member of the Wakadoshiyori presented him with a map of the Western Palace.[169] On the following day, His Highness was installed in the Western Palace as the adopted son of the then Shōgun [15]. His Highness was not pleased at this man's action and showed him no favor after his succession. The fellow died soon afterward. I consider His Highness's behavior highly laudable.

In the winter of this year [1715], the marriage of the daughter (Yaso-no-Miya) of the Retired Emperor [100] to the Shōgun was announced, and in the spring of the following year it was reported that Bungo-no-Kami Masataka [97] was to be appointed envoy in this matter.[170] This was the first such example since the military had got control of the country. Although it all seems like a fleeting dream now, it was a very fortunate thing.

The dispute between the villages of Ukawa and Uchishita and the village of Kita-Komatsu in the Shiga District of Ōmi Province, which I mentioned earlier, arose, as I said before, from the disclosure of the cunning swindle practiced many years ago by the Kita-Komatsu villagers. When Akifusa showed me the draft of the judgment prepared by the members of the Hyōjōsho, saying that the case had already been decided since Ukawa village had clear documentary evidence dating from the Ōei era, I found it contained certain incomprehensible points. When he therefore produced a map of the district and showed it to me, the decision was, as I had thought, incomprehensible. So I said: "It will be very improper if the decision goes this way." Akifusa thereupon told me that the members of the Hyōjōsho had changed their minds halfway through the case, and since it had been impossible to reach a decision without an on-the-spot survey of the actual ground, it had been resolved that first of all, the fiefs of the *jitō* up to that time would be transferred elsewhere, and then an order would be given for this survey to be carried out, and that in this winter, official inspectors had been appointed.

There was no room for doubt in this case, as the boundaries were clearly defined in the documents of the Ōei era. It was even more evident that the documents produced by the Kita-Komatsu villagers were forgeries. Despite this, the case had dragged on without a decision from the time of His late Highness until now. Rumor had it that although the case should have been decided, subsequent to Kii-no-Kami Nobutsune's [102] appointment as a member of the Rōjū, the resolution arrived at by the Hyōjōsho had been reversed;

this was because when Nobutsune had first made a pronouncement in Kyōto, he had twice said that the claims of of Kita-Komatsu were reasonable. In view of this, there was some reluctance at that time to give a decision reversing that one. But while things stood thus, Nobutsune had had a stroke, so the members of the Hyōjōsho had changed their minds again.

It may have been about the summer of this year that a retainer of Kurokawa Samon, called Watanabe Shōemon, came to my house and met a servant of mine and told him there was something he wanted to tell me about this case. When my servant told him I knew nothing about it, the fellow said: "I will conceal nothing. I have come because one Otowa Shōbei, a retainer of Kawachi-no-Kami [37], told me to explain to your master what has actually happened in this case." My servant replied that he had been warned never to meddle in such matters, and it was quite impossible, and drove the fellow away. This Kurokawa had been the *jitō* of Kita-Komatsu. After that, Masamine [37] again told the members of the Hyōjōsho that the documents of the Ōei era constituted a stumbling block in the case, and some officials found this hard to comprehend. The difficulty in deciding the case had arisen since the time of His late Highness. It cannot be thought that it was because Nobutsune had been appointed to the Rōjū. There must have been some explanation for it. So even now, though a land survey has been carried out, I wonder how it will be decided. These matters are difficult to comprehend.

It also happened in the winter of this year that the Bugyōsho reported that a certain man had slain his uncle. They sent a report setting forth a precedent where Nobutsune had given a judgment about a man who had slain his uncle in the summer of this year. Akifusa, thinking the case complicated, had inquired into the details of the story at that time. Whereupon they replied that when Nobutsune had heard that at the beginning of the rule of His late Highness, there was a precedent in which a man who had slain his uncle had been sentenced to death by decapitation, he had consequently told them to follow that precedent.[171] I was asked what was the best thing to do about this.

[253]

I replied: "Ordinary law requires that a man who has committed murder be put to death. Even in the Code, there are examples of punishment for those who have murdered their parents or uncles or aunts.[172] It is a cause of some anxiety that in the time of His late Highness, a man who had killed an uncle was sentenced to beheading like an ordinary murderer, and that that should be accepted as a precedent for the future. Why has such a decree been issued?"

According to what I heard later, in the time of His late Highness, a man who was a retainer of Inaba Tango-no-Kami Masatomo [115] had killed his uncle. Inaba had said that as this man was guilty of rebellion, he could not punish him privately, and asked for directions from the government, whereupon a judgment was given in accordance with what was written in the Code. Remembering that, Akifusa asked the members of the Rōjū about the case at that time, and they replied that the report of Tango-no-Kami and the directions given to him were in existence, and they had given judgment in accordance with that precedent.

Among recent precedents, a man who slays his lord or parents is sentenced to death by decapitation with the saw, and his wife and children are also put to death.[173] The man who had slain his uncle was sentenced to death by the saw, but the punishment against his wife and children was remitted.

The precedent, of which Nobutsune had been informed by the Bugyōsho, does not seem to have occurred during the time of His late Highness.

At the beginning of the following year [1716], about midnight on the 24th January, fire broke out in the house of Tadayoshi [79] and spread to a large number of houses.[174] (Tadayoshi's house lay to the north of a street called the Daimyōkōji, and many of the *daimyōs*' houses burned down.)[175] The fire was not extinguished until nearly twelve o'clock on the morning of the 25th, the day of the lunar New Year. It was a strange sight to behold those in fireman's gear and those in ceremonial costume rushing hither and yon.

On the 4th February, fire again broke out and spread to many buildings. Among them, the gaol caught fire and a large number of prisoners escaped. There were many among them who had been in prison for 16 or 17 years, and now it was not known why they had been imprisoned, their relatives had died, and their identities could not be established. An inquiry came from the Bugyōsho to Akifusa asking how they should deal with the escapees they apprehended, and Akifusa asked me about what should be done.

I replied: "Since those who were imprisoned had committed crimes of varying degrees, if they had not escaped they would of course have been punished in accordance with the seriousness of their original crimes. But now that this calamity has occurred, many have broken the law and escaped. This is no light offense. However, it is the natural feeling of the lower orders to think that if they escape at such a time, they might be free of danger once and for all. And what a dreadful thing that large numbers of people have been confined in prison without having their crimes investigated for such a long time. Why is it that they were excluded from the benefit of special and regular amnesties during all that time? It would be a pitiful thing if we punished all of them severely now. There would be no limit to such happenings in the future. I think that henceforth, a law should be framed whereby those who do not escape from prison at such times should have the punishments for their original crimes reduced by one degree, and those who do should have their punishments increased by one degree. But first, those in prison whose crimes have not been investigated should be pardoned and released, and then the remainder who did not escape should all have their punishments relaxed by one degree. Then after that, those who escaped and whose whereabouts are not known should not be sought out. All these events have occurred because none of the *bugyō* have either shame or pity. It is a thoroughly regrettable affair." (The draft of this document is still in existence, but probably they did not accept my suggestions. I saw no sign that any edict was issued in accordance with what I had said.)

Similarly, there was a report that the pickled corpse of a man who had killed his lord seven or eight years before would be punished in accordance with the law as a warning to those who were in prison. The withered corpse was bound with a rope and crucified. (He was a fellow who had killed Asai Uemonbei, a

[255]

samurai of Hotta Izu-no-Kami Masatora.)[176] Official acts of this kind can only be called thoroughly unseemly.

At this time, judgment was pronounced concerning a kidnapping which had been much talked about since the spring of the previous year [1715]. The case was as follows: An apothecary (called Seibei) of Suidō-chō had had in his employ two young brothers born in Ise Province (of whom the elder brother was called Tarobei and the younger brother Tōbei), but the younger boy had suddenly disappeared.[177] In the spring of the previous year, the elder boy discovered that his brother was living in a beggar's house and told his master. The master went at once to the beggar's house and took the child away. A *rōnin* called Yamada (given name, Masaemon) came to the apothecary's house and claimed that the child in the beggar's house was the son of a man called Dōsan (given name, Shichisuke) who lived in Kai Province. "Six years ago, his father put him in my keeping," Yamada said, "and I apprenticed him to a certain doctor, but he proved a dullard and so I gave him to the beggar. What right have you to take him away?" From this an argument had arisen and the dispute had been taken to court.

Both Dōsan of Kai and the father of the children from Ise were summoned to the Hyōjōsho and interrogated, but the judges could not decide whose child it was, and meanwhile both Dōsan and the young child who had been given to the beggar died. In view of this, it was asked whether Yamada should be released. (This was in the report of the *machi bugyō*, Nakayama Izumo-no-Kami [80].)

I had heard about this matter from the beginning, so I spoke to Akifusa and he investigated the case again. The following report was made: "The father of the child from Ise lived on the fief of Tōdō [116] and when he was sent for, some retainers of Izumi-no-Kami [116] brought him. When all were assembled at the Hyōjōsho, first Dōsan was called, and the young child was asked: 'Is this your father?' He replied: 'I have never seen him before.' Whereupon Dōsan beat the child over the head, crying: 'Don't you know your own father?' and the child ran away. Next, the man from Ise was called, and when the child saw him, he wept aloud and ran to the man, saying: 'This is my father.' The child also knew the men who had come with his father and thanked

[256]

them for bringing him. However, since neither Dōsan nor Yamada would give in, it was impossible to pronounce judgment."

I presented a recommendation to the effect that now that Dōsan was dead, Yamada would probably give in and that they should interrogate him. This advice was adopted and he was summoned and interrogated, but he replied that it was difficult to say if the child was really Dōsan's, since it had all happened a long time ago. I said: "If he maintains this attitude, the case will never be settled. However, even if he will not give in, there can be no doubt that the father and brothers were one family and that they and Tōdō's retainers were all known to each other. But what a terrible thing it was that while the case dragged on, the child died and Dōsan also died far from his home, and quite unnecessarily. (He was over seventy years of age.) How can the officials be so cruel? Anyway, what could Dōsan have done with his own child? But if this question is now investigated, the case will never be decided. In short, the best thing to do is to remit the death sentence on Yamada by one degree and banish him." In the end, sentence was pronounced in accordance with my advice.

This was a typical example of the lack of pity in criminal cases displayed by all the *bugyō* belonging to the Hyōjōsho. Someone suggested that the story that the child belonged to the man from Kai may have arisen because Yamada, by some trick, had kidnapped a child belonging to a man from Ise, had given him to the beggar, and then had said it was Dōsan's child. If the case were to be thoroughly investigated, clear evidence that this was so would probably be found. But I thought it would do no good to tell officials who sent in reports like the above that the evidence was plain, so I advised as I have explained.

There was another case which was talked about in the summer of the year before last [1714]. The *bugyō* reported that the daughters of a man (called Shinsuke) of Funatsu village in Muro District, Kii Province, had been kidnapped.[178] The story was that five years ago, in the winter of 1711, a man called Ogiya (given name, Dōju), who was an innkeeper at the post-station of Shinagawa in Musashi Province, had given his servant (a clerk called Kihei) 20 gold *ryō* and told him to go and buy some servant girls.[179] The servant went around from one place to another and finally came to Funatsu village in Muro District, Kii Province, and there he met a poor man and his wife who had two daughters. He told them that if they would hire these two girls out as servants to his master, they would do well out of it.

About November, he brought back the two daughters with their parents, but as they could not pass the barrier at Imakire, in Tōtōmi Province, he at once conspired with a man (called Tarozaemon) at the post-station of Mitsuke who said he could arrange matters.[180] Tarozaemon got some people (called Okachi and Kahei) from Naka-Osakabe village to help him, and by traveling along the road through the mountains they arrived at the post-station of Mitsuke. Here, Kihei proposed to sell the two girls for 25 *ryō*, but the father would not consent to this. (When Kihei explained that he intended to sell them as maid-servants to an inn, the father said that he did not wish to force his children into such a life.)

In December, they arrived at Shinagawa. Kihei's master, Dōju, on seeing the two sisters, said: "Why ever did you go and buy such young girls?" and drove them and his servant out of the house. As Kihei had to support not only himself but the father and mother and two daughters as well, he went to his master and complained bitterly, and his master said: "Well then, you will have to sell the girls as prostitutes." As the father and mother now had no friends to help them, they could do nothing but agree to that plan. The master immediately consulted with a go-between (called Ichizaemon, a resident of Asakusa and a procurer by trade) and sold the girls for 105 *ryō* to a house in the Shin-Yoshi-wara (to a man called Tomoeya Gen'emon, a brothel keeper), telling him the two girls came from Suruga Province.[181] (The elder girl was called Yuki and the younger Shime). Of the 105 *ryō*, he gave 34 *ryō* 2 *bu* to the go-between, 7 *ryō* each to his servant Kihei and the girls' father, and took all the rest for himself.

Later, the father and mother, having no one to help them, went to the go-between and complained about their daughters. He arranged to send the parents to the house of their daughters' master, but meanwhile, in April in the spring of 1712, the mother died. Those who heard this story were sorry that both father and children had come to this pass, but over and above this, those who were implicated were alarmed that if the fact of the family's by-passing the Imakire Barrier were to be known, they would be held guilty of a grave offense. So when they heard that the father was going to complain about what had happened, they cajoled him in all sorts of ways. He consequently hesitated for some time but after two years, in May in the summer of 1714, he complained to Kii Dono [26], who reported the affair to the *bugyō* and sent the father along to them.

In due course, those implicated were summoned to the Hyō-jōsho for questioning, and while the usual long inquiry dragged on, the father died in prison in May in the summer of last year, 1715. But at this point, the officials wrote out a record of their deliberations as follows: "Although the father had at first not understood about by-passing the barrier, once he had become aware of what he had done, he should have reported it immediately; his delay cannot be viewed lightly. Therefore, should they behead his corpse and send it to Kii Dono to expose at his native place, and give his two daughters to their present master, or should they make them slaves? Should they crucify or behead those who had been implicated in the by-passing of the barrier, and should they expel or banish the Shinagawa innkeeper?"

I said: "Since the father had not known about passing the barrier for many years, he cannot be blamed for not reporting the matter. When he did learn about it, although he did not report it for one year, we cannot blame him seriously for the time he let elapse, because the old man, foolish enough to have been kidnapped with his wife and daughters, had been hoodwinked by people. It is clear in the regulation of January 1620 that the victims of kidnapping must be restored to their original lord, so how can these girls be given to their present master? It is not necessary to discuss the crime of those who participated in the illegal passing of the barrier. The innkeeper of Shinagawa cannot escape the death penalty. Furthermore, in the regulations of generations of *shōguns*, laws have been promulgated about the buying and selling of people. They are for such cases as this. The innkeeper, whose servant kidnapped these people and illegally passed the barrier, sold them for 105 *ryō*, of which he gave away 48 *ryō* 2 *bu*, taking all the remainder for himself. He has committed a very serious crime. Moreover, if Kihei's master had not sent him to buy maid-servants, this dreadful crime would never have

[259]

happened. So he is the chief malefactor." This was my advice and finally everything was decided as I said, and the two daughters were sent back to Kii Dono.

The document containing my recommendations concerning this incident is still extant.[182] In recent times, in cases of this kind, everything had been decided in accordance with what was said by those who recorded the depositions on the day and who were called clerks of the Hyōjōsho.[183] In this case, the Shinagawa innkeeper, the Shin-Yoshiwara brothel keeper, and his confederates had bribed the officials and prevailed upon them to declare them innocent, and the officials of the Hyōjōsho, as usual, had given in to what the clerks said and submitted the preposterous proposal I outlined. It is a terrible thing that these officials interpret the criminal code of Japan as they wish.

On the 5th April [1716], a letter was received from Izumi-no-Kami Tadayuki [108] stating: "On the 4th just past, the Densō [95, 96] had brought a communication from the Retired Emperor [100] to the effect that Kōsei Shōnin, in charge of soliciting subscriptions for Tōdaiji, had made the following claim: "Tōdaiji is a national tutelary fane, founded by Emperor Shōmu. Therefore, after it burned down in the fire of the Jishō era, by a request of Retired Emperor Go-Shirakawa a decree of the Retired Emperor was sent all over Japan, and it was rebuilt.[184] Later again, following the fire of the Eiroku era, a special decree of Retired Emperor Ōgimachi was circulated throughout the country, but it did not succeed because the times were unpropitious.[185] In the time of the former Abbot Kōkei, a message was sent to the Shōgun, and contributions were called for throughout Japan, and the Daibutsuden was built. I, Kōsei, have succeeded him. Although I have built the two-storied middle gate, the cloister and other places have not yet been constructed. I humbly request that in accordance with the precedents of the Kenkyū and Eiroku eras, you will permit a decree to be circulated by the Retired Emperor. As the precedents for the Retired Emperor's decree are clear, the Shōgun will surely not refuse. Is there any obstruction to granting the order as requested? A brief statement of the Retired Emperor's direction for me to advise him confidentially, and copies of the Retired Emperors' decrees during the Kenkyū, Eishō, Eiroku, and Genki eras are attached."[186]

When Akifusa consulted me about this request, I presented a draft of what he should reply. The gist of it was: "With regard to subscriptions for Tōdaiji, there is nothing to prevent the Retired Emperor from issuing a decree in accordance with the request by the Shōnin. But with regard to the precedent of the Kenkyū era, an imperial decree was first sent to Kamakura, and then the Shōgun issued a directive to the whole of Japan. However, Kōkei Shōnin did not request the Retired Emperor to issue a decree. Instead, he made his request through the Shōgun, and a tax was imposed on all the provinces. So this case was quite different from what happened in the Kenkyū era. Although at that time a tax was imposed on all the provinces, in recent times the finances of the empire have been exhausted and it seems there are many provinces which would now be unable to obey such an order. However, the construction of the Daibutsuden and the two-storied middle gate has already been completed. Now, if an imperial decree is issued for the construction of the cloister and the other parts, certain provinces may not obey this second request, and it will be unfortunate if the impression is given that it is sometimes impossible to carry out an imperial decree. If Kōsei Shōnin, desiring to carry out his predecessor's plans, fails in his request, the extensions would not be difficult to carry out. However, matters of this kind must be discussed in secrecy. It is a foregone conclusion that if the Retired Emperor were to issue a decree, the Shōgun should immediately send a directive to the whole country." When the shogunal government sent this reply, the Retired Emperor said: "I never expected it would be possible to carry this out. But it was difficult to ignore the Shōnin's request, so I said what I did. What you say is reasonable. I shall not issue a decree."

On the 18th April [1716], the members of the Rōjū held a consultation. This was in connection with a report from the Nagasaki Bugyō (Ōoka Bizen-no-Kami Kiyohira) to the following effect: In the spring of the previous year, the "New Regulations for Sea-borne Trade" had been fixed.[187] Among the Chinese who had received trading licenses from the interpreters, the merchants who came from Fukien and Canton brought their licenses at the appointed time and engaged in business, but no ships came from Nanking and Ningpo.

While they were wondering about this, in the spring of this year a man called Li T'ao-shih from Fukien came and said: "Last year when the merchants of Nanking and Ningpo received licenses from Japan and returned to their home country, a lampoon appeared suggesting that these merchants had come to China under secret instructions from Japan. (This, it was said, was because the era name of Japan appeared in the license.) Soon after, two men called Chuang Yün-ch'ing and Hsieh Hsieh-yün reported this lampoon to the authorities. The reason was that they had originally been unable to obtain licenses. They conspired with those who had received licenses, including men called Hu Yün-k'ê and Tung I-jih, and when they made that false charge, all the licenses were confiscated by the government, and no one was permitted to come to Japan. As I also reside in Ningpo, I too had my license confiscated along with them. Having no other means, I went to Canton and came here from there." According to this fellow's story, it seemed as if the Chinese Viceroy, Provincial Governor, and Superintendant of Customs at Canton have consulted together, and considering that it will be difficult to put the new regulations of Japan into effect, plan to send a large number of ships to trade here as before.[188] However, his story could not be accepted without reserve, and they must get hold of those who come here from now on and talk with them again. They would detain Li T'ao-shih.

When Akifusa asked me what I thought about this, I stated emphatically: "Even within Japan, it is still difficult to put the laws into effect. The refining of the coinage is a case in point. And it is much more difficult to do so outside Japan. It was for this reason that when the new regulations were first put into effect, I said that difficulties would not be resolved until three to five years had passed. When the Korean Embassy came in the time of His late Highness, the variety of opinions which were put forward by all and sundry, including the high officials, was astounding, but since His Highness made a decision, everything was carried out in accordance with his order. At this time, when there is a child *shōgun*, even if I were to give my opinion, no one would act upon it. Therefore I have no advice I wish to offer positively."

It seems that a consultation with the Rōjū then took place,

and word came that they wished to speak to me. When I accordingly went on the 18th, Tadayoshi [79] came to greet me, and led me to where the officials of the Rōjū usually assembled. They told me that since this matter had first been brought up by Kawachi-no-Kami Masamine [37], everyone, including Masamine, had had much to say. The gist of what they said was that, in the spring of the previous year [1715], in fulfillment of His late Highness's plans, the regulations for trade at Nagasaki were put into effect. But the report which had been sent at this time from the Bugyōsho was as had been explained. If the situation was as has been described, not only was it impossible to carry out the present government's orders at this time, but they felt that the plans of His late Highness would come to nought. As His late Highness had consulted me about this matter, they would give orders in accordance with whatever I advised. All those present were in agreement on this.

I replied: "As I told Akifusa, the report sent by the Nagasaki Bugyō at this time was what I expected from the day discussions were begun about this in the time of His late Highness, and I do not think that things will change now. But I am already old and infirm, and I do not think I will live to see the matter settled. After all, whatever happens, if no changes whatsoever are made in the regulations issued in the spring of last year, they must eventually function properly. I have no other advice to give."

Akifusa then said: "His Highness also stated it would be a long time before difficulties were resolved." And the others admitted that at all events they had no other recourse but to abide by my counsel in issuing decrees. I replied: "In view of this, I can no longer refuse. I will present my suggestions without fail," and returned home. (Various observations were voiced, but I have only set down the common tenor of their remarks.)

I immediately presented a draft of directions to be sent down to the Bugyōsho. My advice was: "Li T'ao-shih has confessed that the Chinese officials will not permit Chinese merchant ships to come to our country. T'ao-shih came here secretly, in defiance of the laws of his own country. A crime is a crime anywhere. We do not permit those who do not obey the laws of our country to come. How can we permit those who break their own laws to come? He must be sent back at once."

Soon after, another report came from the Nagasaki Bugyōsho, that a man of Ningpo called Chu Wu-chên had been permitted to come to Nagasaki, and a copy of his passport from Chênhai County was presented with that report. When I saw this passport, I said that this man had not obtained permission to come to Japan. Prior to this, copies of passports brought by merchants who came every year had been produced. (All the passports issued to merchants who came to Japan were endorsed for travel to Nagasaki. The endorsement on Wu-chên's passport referred to the East only.)

I presented a draft which was to be sent to the Bugyōsho. The gist of it was, as in the case of Li T'ao-shih, the passport that Chu Wu-Chên had brought was not a permit to come to Japan.

On the morning of the 25th April [1716], in the region of the Sagami River (i.e., the Banyū River) a young *samurai* who had killed a robber had been detained by the men of Nakajima in that neighborhood and had been brought to the Daikansho.[189] When the incident was looked into, it was ascertained that the *samurai* was called Sakai. (His personal name was Jōhachi and he was about twenty years old.) On his way to Suruga Province, between Totsuka and Fujisawa, a big man began following him, and when he got near the river, the fellow had put his hand into the *samurai's* bosom and stolen his purse, so the *samurai* drew his sword and cut him down with one stroke.[190] When the local people were interrogated about the man who had been killed, they replied that they did not know anything about him but that he might be a robber plying up and down the highway. It was also said that this young *samurai* was a retainer in the house of Honda Tōtōmi-no-Kami Masatake and that he had recently run away from his lord's house.[191] Although his slaying of the robber was a fine deed, since he had run away from his lord's house, he had, for the time being, been put in prison on the grounds that his offense could not be overlooked.

I told Akifusa that if this man were punished, the rest of the robber-band would spread a false report, and that if the story got about that he had been punished for killing a robber, in the future people traveling along the highway would suffer beyond endurance at the hands of robbers. However, I said there was a way to deal with the matter and he should delay his decision for a while.

I sent a message to Asakura Yoichi Kagetake telling him there was something I wanted to see him about.[192] He came at once, and I asked him if someone had recently run away from his master's house. He replied: "That is so. A man called Sakai has run away and killed a robber near the Sagami River." I told him that it was because of that man that I had asked him to see me and said: "It will be very cruel if, despite the fact that the young fellow has killed a robber, he is punished because he has run away from his lord's house. What should we do?" "I see," he said, and came the next day and told me he had spoken to his lord who had agreed not to inflict any punishment on the man. I told him that that was wise, and reported what had happened to Akifusa. On the grounds that since the *samurai* had killed a robber, no judgment would be passed on him, he was pardoned.

The following is another incident which occurred about this time. Yamato-no-Kami Shigeyuki [61] happened to meet Okino-Kami Akiyuki [29], Akifusa's younger brother, and said: "I cannot do anything about the merchant you asked me about." Akiyuki said: "What are you talking about?" Trouble arose as a result, an inquiry was held, and it was discovered that the servant of a certain man (called Suzuka Sonoemon, a retainer of a chamberlain like Akiyuki, who was called Magaribuchi Shimotsuke-no-Kami [28]), had brought Shigeyuki a letter, purported to be from Akiyuki, saying that he had received orders that a merchant called so-and-so was to be placed in charge of the Silver Mint. This was because Shigeyuki was in charge of the gold and silver coinage and Akiyuki's wife was connected with him in some way. Those implicated in this conspiracy were immediately arrested and all were punished. (No fewer than eight persons were involved.)

I said that such incidents as these have arisen because recently bribery has been practiced openly, and there have been many cases of officials accepting bribes by taking advantage of such family connections. Unless we put a stop to merchants asking to be put in charge of this or that undertaking, we cannot expect this sort of incident to cease. In particular, it is essential to take measures to prevent bribery. So Akifusa consulted with the officials of the Rōjū, and they issued regulations.

A similar incident had happened to me in the previous

year [1715]. A priest of a certain temple came to my house as messenger for someone who asked if I could get him placed in charge of the trade at Nagasaki, and said if he got the office, he would give me 500 *ryō* of gold as a reward to begin with (called at the time a "gift in anticipation"), and after he was appointed, he would send each of my sons 300 *ryō* a year in gratitude for my assistance. This is something I have first-hand knowledge of. Such proposals were made even to people like me. You can imagine what happened in the case of people who had great influence.

On the 11th June [1716], a decision was given by the government in a case which had aroused wild speculation among the common people, and which concerned a notorious robber who had been arrested in Echigo Province in the winter of the previous year. The facts were as follows: Some men had informed Funakoshi Saemon [117], who was in charge of the apprehension of robbers, that a notorious robber was living in the wilds between Yasushiro and Toguchi in Kambara District, Echigo Province.[193] Hearing that he had a large band of followers, at the end of October the previous year, 1715, Funakoshi had sent two retainers there with those who had brought the information as guides. (The names of the men who had reported the matter were Kaemon of Tatsuishi village in Kōzuke Province, and Shichiroemon of Menuma village in Musashi Province.[194] Funakoshi's retainers were Matsuno Ichibei, aged fifty-one, and Tazawa Kandayū, aged sixty. These were *dōshin* in the *osakite*.) They had arrived there on the 4th November and had captured the chief and four of his followers. (The robber's name was Gozaemon. He was fifty-two at the time.)

When they had first tried to place them in the custody of the people of Yasushiro (which was in the fief of Obama Magosaburō), these people had argued that the robbers had always lived between the territory of Yasushiro and Toguchi, so they ought not to be placed in Yasushiro's custody only. The police officers questioned the people of Toguchi (which was in the fief of Mizoguchi Hōki-no-Kami Shigemoto [85]), but they said the robbers had never lived in their territory, so the officers did not know what to do. They then tried to place them in the custody of the people of Chibara, since this was the Shōgun's domain.[195] (The *daikan* was Nose Gombei.) But they said: "Despite the fact that the robbers' domicile is not under the control of either Yasushiro or Toguchi, that is no reason why you should place them in the custody of our district."

When the officers inquired about Shibata Castle, which was held by Mizoguchi, the feudatory of Toguchi, they were told it was 8 or 9 *ri* away, and from there back to Edo by the Shinano road was over 100 *ri*.[196] When they next inquired about the shogunal fief of Izumozaki, they were told that it was 6 or 7 *ri* away, and from there to Edo was over 80 *ri*.[197] So, thinking that if they went to Izumozaki, put their prisoners in charge of the Daikansho there, and then returned to Edo, the road from there to Edo would be more convenient, they left Chibara on the 7th of the same month [November], with their prisoners and with bearers to carry their bows, spears, and swords, making a party of 14 or 15 persons, and arrived at Izumozaki toward dusk on the 8th (since there was a Daikansho there under Kameda Saburōbei). But when they said that they wanted to place the arrested men in the custody of this office, those in charge during the *daikan*'s absence said: "It is the rule, when robbers are arrested, to place them in the custody of the authorities of the place where the arrest is effected. We cannot understand why you have brought them here to commit them." Here, too, they were unable to find anyone willing to accept custody of them. Their traveling funds had run out, having had to convey such a large party from one place to another, and furthermore, since they would not be allowed through the barrier at Hatsuzaki with their prisoners (for they had no passports for them), they took them back to Kashiwazaki and after consulting together, untied their prisoners, released them, and returned to Edo and reported the matter.[198]

Saemon reported this matter on the 26th November and dispatched his officers again. A shogunal order was also sent to Mizoguchi. On the 22nd December, the robber, his son, and three of his men were arrested, and a report was received on the 3rd January, 1716, that they had been committed to the custody of the authorities at Toguchi. (The prisoners included Gozaemon, his son, and three of his men.) Within a few days, the remainder of his band were all apprehended and Mizoguchi's retainers escorted them to Toguchi. After that, orders were sent to the *ōmetsuke* and the *kanjō bugyō*, and an inquiry was held.

At this time, the order to Funakoshi to apprehend the

robbers was withdrawn. Also, the officers who had arrested them were placed under house arrest. This was because the Rōjū had consulted together and decided that when Funakoshi had first dispatched his officers, he ought to have given firm orders. But there was no precedent for giving firm orders beforehand in such cases. The impasse occurred on this occasion because of the objections raised by the authorities at Yasushiro and Toguchi. So why was Funakoshi dismissed from superintendence of the case? Three men, Yokota Bitchū-no-Kami [76], Ise Ise-no-Kami [118], and Sugioka Yatarō [86] were now placed in charge of the case.

These officials first of all sent for the robbers and the men from Yasushiro, Toguchi, and Chibara, interrogated them and took down their depositions, and advised that first of all messengers should be sent to ascertain whether the place where the robbers lived belonged to Yasushiro or Toguchi. When Akifusa asked me about this, I said: "Where they live has no bearing on the case. According to the robbers' present statement, in the beginning they applied to the authorities at Yasushiro and Toguchi for permission to live on their borders. They say this was because they did not wish to belong to either place. Their statements agree with the depositions of the men from Yasushiro. Also, if we look at a map, we see that the place they live in is less than three *tan* in extent, and on the side contiguous with Toguchi village there is a small cedar plantation. This is where the Toguchi people say their boundary extends to. So when they first gave that area to the robbers to live in, it is clear that they had already abandoned all claim to that ground and had arranged matters so that they would not be involved in any future trouble. So whoever owns the land at the present time, the officers sent to arrest the robbers would probably have been unable to commit them to anyone's custody. It is a waste of time to argue about such irrelevancies. What you should first find out is whether the men alleged to be robbers are indeed so." Accordingly, the order to send men to survey the ground was cancelled. (What stupidity to send so many officers to survey a plot of land in a case of this nature!)

After that, when I read the record of the interrogation of the men alleged to be robbers, I found that the father had originally been a farmer in Chibara village. (His name was Heisaburō.)

He had lost his father at the age of seven and had been adopted by his uncle on his mother's side, but his uncle, too, had died when he was nine. (His uncle's name was Nizaemon.) After that, he begged for a living and when he was thirteen came to live in the house of a villager of Chibara. From the age of fifteen, he had been employed by people of Nagamine, Kitakata, and Tsukioka, and after about ten years he lived for four years or more (in Mitsuke Niigata) in the house of an aunt on his mother's side, and then married the daughter of a farmer (called Kyūzaemon) of Mitsuke Shimmachi and had one son.[199] This son is the prisoner now called Chōzō (who is twenty-three at the present time). But Heisaburō's wife was an intractable woman, and he had no desire to remain in her parents' house. So at the end of four years, he abandoned his wife and child and worldly goods and, applying for help to a priest of Kan'onji at Yotsuya, he rented some land. After he had cultivated a farm and ricelands, he took away the son born of the wife he had abandoned earlier, brought him to Kan'onji, and married a woman of Gosenchō village.[200] At this time, hearing that because of some money the villagers of Gosenchō had lent him, they were going to kill him, he fled from Yotsuya with his wife, and after appealing for protection in various places, obtained land from the people of Yasushiro and Toguchi, built a house, cleared riceland, and had lived there for twelve years.

Then the people in the neighboring district consulted together and every year presented him with rice and beans (one *to* two *shō* of rice, and soybeans per household) and requested him to protect them against robbers. This was because for two years after he first left Yotsuya, he had associated with robbers and had friends among them, so he was able to make an agreement with the robbers not to enter the villages of the neighborhood in which he lived. The weapons he had in his house were to use against robbers. His followers were all men he had cared for when, like himself formerly, they had no one to help them. By day, he set them to work in the fields, and by night he had them make the rounds of the villages. He was helped by the village people, obtained a settled occupation, and his wealth increased. Why, he asked, should he commit robbery when there was nothing he lacked?

At this point, the villagers were summoned and questioned,

and they all said the same as he. They produced documents to show that on the 18th September, 1707, the men of 15 villages (besides Yasushiro and Toguchi, 13 villages in the fief of Shibata) had entered into a signed agreement with this man, stipulating that he would protect them against robbers. Also, ten years ago when robbers had entered a temple called Tōzanji at nighttime, he had, on being ordered to do so, immediately sought out the robbers, got back all the stolen articles, and handed them over to the temple.

Also, when his followers were sent for and questioned, they said that though he treated his men kindly, he ruled his house strictly and would not let them bring a single article into the house they could not account for. Then, when he was asked why in the beginning he had said at Funakoshi's house, that he had carried out robberies at various places and killed many men, he replied he could not endure the terrible torture, and since escape seemed impossible, he hoped for a quick release by death, and that if they sent for the people of those places and questioned them, they would soon know whether or not he was telling the truth. (He made the statement on the 1st May [1716].)

When men from Kitakata, Tsukioka, Todai, and Kurosaka were sent for and asked whether he had ever committed robbery or murder in those villages, they all presented written testimonies that such allegations were totally untrue.[201] Among them, the *ōjōya* of Mizoguchi's [85] fief (called Sukezaemon, *ōjōya* of the fief of Shibata) stated that if he had committed murders in these villages, he would certainly have been informed of it, but no such report had ever reached him. In particular, it had been asserted that 15 years before, Gozaemon had entered the house of one Jirosaku in Tsukioka village, stabbed him to death, and also stabbed a servant, but actually the Jirosaku in question had died three years ago of illness and had not been stabbed by anyone.

When I read this report, I said that this man's control of robbers was surely aimed at doing away with robbery, and so it was necessary to reach a decision about what the man had done until this time. Robbers existed, even in olden times in the age of the Sage Kings, and laws were framed to control them. However, in those ages the government was virtuous, the people were well disposed, and as a natural result there was no strong urge to com-

[270]

mit robbery. The vulgar proverb says: "Lice on the body, rats in the house, and robbers in the state," and even though robbers are arrested and executed daily until their corpses pile up into mountains and their blood flows until rivers run, I do not think that in this degenerate age robbery will ever cease.[202] Not only did this man turn over a new leaf, but for 12 years people have forgotten what robbery is in the 15 villages in his neighborhood. However much you probe into his past offenses, it is out of the question to condemn him to death.

From ancient times until the present day, Echigo, Shinano, and Kōzuke provinces have been noted for their high number of robberies. Men from the 15 villages therefore conferred together and arranged for this man to maintain a watch. If he is punished now because his former offenses have been brought to light, henceforth the people in these villages will not be able to rest quietly at night. Furthermore, besides this man, there are many others in these provinces who formerly committed robberies but have now become law-abiding citizens. And if they come to the conclusion that in the long run, the law will catch up with them, why should they suffer hardship while passively awaiting death? If they have only one day to live, they will devise some way to lift themselves out of poverty. So your efforts to control robberies will have the contrary effect of increasing them.

In the *Ta Hsüeh*, it is written: "Renew the spirits of the people"; in the *Analects*: "Do not punish people for old offenses"; and in the *Chou I*, it says: "The superior man changes completely; the man of small mind reforms outwardly only. A severe upheaval invites misfortune. If you hold fast to righteousness, you will enjoy prosperity."[203] What I hope you will do is release this man, let him move his residence to Mizoguchi's fief, place him and his men under Mizoguchi's jurisdiction, and let them maintain their protection of the neighboring villages against robbery as they have done until now. Also, if my advice is taken, in passing judgment on this man, no sentence will be passed on the people of Yasushiro, Toguchi, or Chibara. Furthermore, what could Funakoshi's officers do when, having arrested the men, they could find no one to accept custody of them, and their traveling funds were exhausted? However, having let them go, when they went to arrest them again, since they were men of ripe years experienced in this work, they apprehended them all without letting one escape. They should therefore be rewarded rather than punished. They are certainly not guilty of the slightest crime. The advice I gave was as above. (The draft of the proposal must still be in existence.) And the case was eventually decided in accordance with my suggestions.

Another incident also occurred about this time. When those under sentence of banishment were sent to their places of exile, the *bugyō* sent in a report about the banishment of the inhabitants of a village called Koremasa, about ten *ri* distant from Edo. According to this report, in August of last year [1715], the men of that village had assembled, numbering 1,400 or 1,500, had forced their way into the village of Shimo-Koganei, and had cut down bamboos, trees, and crops. Because of this, the three ringleaders had been sentenced to banishment and confined in prison. But in the spring of this year, when the prison burned down, some of them escaped. The others were to be sent to their place of banishment now.

I said: "Why has no report been made about this incident until now? The case must be inquired into strictly." When the details of the case were investigated again, it appeared that it originally arose from a quarrel between the villagers of Koremasa and Shimo-Koganei concerning the fields from which they gathered horse-fodder.[204] On the 4th August the year before [1715], the men of Koremasa had called together the neighboring villagers and armed with bows, spears, and other weapons had burst into Shimo-Koganei, sounding the conch and raising a war cry. When they attacked, the people of that village took flight, whereupon the assailants destroyed all the furniture and possessions in one farmer's house, and cut down trees and trampled crops.

When this was reported to the Daikansho, the *daikan* (whose name was Amamiya Kambei) sent for them, but they did not obey his summons. And they attacked again on the following day, cutting down trees and trampling crops as before. On these two days, more than 57,700 trees and an incalculable number of bamboo were cut down. Even if every man cut down two or three trees each, the number of men involved would exceed 20,000.

I said: "The Shimabara Revolt in former days did not involve more than 30,000 men.[205] I cannot understand what the *bugyō*

[272]

were thinking of in not sending in a report until now, in spite of the fact that such an outbreak has occurred in a place not ten *ri* from Edo. Seeing that *shōgun* after *shōgun* has issued strict orders prohibiting the assembly of groups, the *bugyō* cannot be unaware of this." Therefore, they were questioned a second time as to why they had not reported the incident at the time. They replied: "Since this incident occurred on shogunal lands, we reported it to Ise Ise-no-Kami [118] (because he was on duty that month as *kanjō bugyō*). He was summoned by the Hyōjōsho on the 1st September 1715 and consulted with the members of that body, and they decided that they could not punish them all because they were too numerous, and that the best thing to do was to sentence the ringleaders to exile. The ringleaders were exiled on the 29th November. When the clerks of the Hyōjōsho were consulted about the precedents in such a case, they replied that it was usual to report such matters when those sentenced to banishment were dispatched to their places of banishment, and therefore we did not report the matter at the time. When we now, on the receipt of the present order, summoned the clerks and questioned them, their replies were all different, but when all is said and done, Ise-no-Kami is to blame."

When Akifusa asked me what he should do about this case, I said: "As the officials of the Hyōjōsho have already passed judgment, sentencing the three ringleaders to banishment, it would be unwise to issue another shogunal decree upsetting their judgment. However, it is very unfortunate that such a serious matter has been handled in this way. The best thing to do, therefore, is to order the rest of the offenders to apprehend the escaped men at once, and if they do not apprehend and hand them over within a reasonable time, after two or three warnings, arrest the chief offenders among the others, and sentence them to banishment, and from the remainder, collect fines and give part to the people of Shimo-Koganei."

I wonder what decision the Rōjū came to. I heard that at any rate Ise-no-Kami was dismissed. (Touching this matter, I do not understand why, when the ringleaders had been sentenced to banishment by the unanimous decision of the officials of the Hyōjōsho, it was considered to be the fault of one man, Ise-no-Kami.)

As I have noted before, in recent times, the officials of the Hyōjōsho have entrusted their responsibilities to petty officials, called clerks of the Hyōjōsho, with the result that cases remain undecided and men are left to languish in gaol, even after a lapse of many years. I therefore explained in detail the sufferings this caused the ordinary man. Consequently, since the officials of the Hyōjōsho decided that they would henceforth hear cases themselves, the Rōjū first dismissed the clerks and gave orders to the *bugyō* that if cases were not decided within 100 days, the fact should be reported.

Shortly afterward when the Shōgun [25] died, as had happened on the death of His late Highness [3], all those who had been dismissed from office were pardoned, and Ise-no-Kami also returned to duty. I wonder what happened about the incident at Koremasa village? Also with regard to the orders given to the *bugyō*, I heard that Kawachi-no-Kami Masamine [37] told the *bugyō* that recent orders that cases which had not been decided within 100 days must be reported, were now canceled, and everyone rejoiced. The *bugyō* must have been relieved, but how the people must have suffered!

At the end of the spring of this year [1716], the Shōgun again fell ill, and medicine being of no avail, he died on the 19th June about four o'clock in the afternoon. Toward evening, in accordance with the dying injunctions of His late Highness, Kii Dono [26] was installed in the Ni-no-Maru, and on the following day, the 20th June, it was announced that the Shōgun had died the previous evening.[206] On the 26th June, he was interred at Zōjōji.

The 26th June was the date of the fall of Ōsaka Castle.[207] Under the Chou Dynasty, the date Chia-tzŭ was not used.[208] Of all the days and months in the year, why should the Shōgun's death have happened on this particular day?[209] I attended the funeral ceremony, as I had done on the previous occasion. Henceforth, there was a new Shōgun [26], and I did not serve him.

On the 1st July, I vacated my room in the Naka-no-Kuchi. About this time, all the personal attendants of the late Shōgun, including Akifusa, Tadayoshi [79], and others, were dismissed.

As the official duties that Akifusa, Tadayoshi, and others had been entrusted with until this time will become difficult to understand as time goes by, I shall deal with them here. From the time of the Divine Ancestor until that of the second Shōgun, the officials called "Joint Signatories" did not rise above Daibu of the Fifth Rank, and their salaries were also low.[210] In the time of the third Shōgun [9], from about the period of his visit to Nijō Palace, they were given Fourth Rank and were made chamberlains.[211] About that time, Hotta Kaga-no-Kami Masamori [119], who had at first been appointed a "Joint Signatory," was shortly afterward relieved of this position and became a personal attendant to the Shōgun, and through him were conveyed the Shōgun's orders to the Rōjū and the Rōjū's reports to the Shōgun. It was in this age that the Tairō and Wakadoshiyori were established. In the time of the fourth Shōgun [43], since a boy had succeeded, the members of the Rōjū acted as advisers to the administration, and hereafter Masamori occupied a unique position. In the time of the fifth Shōgun [15], Makino Bingo-no-Kami Narisada, who had been in the Shōgun's service from the time when he was an ordinary feudal lord, served as intermediary between the Shōgun and the Rōjū, as Masamori had done in an earlier reign.[212] Later, Yanagisawa Dewa-no-Kami Yasuakira [31] was permitted to use the Shōgun's [15] family name, granted a syllable of the Shōgun's personal name, was appointed Shōshō of the Fourth Rank, and rose to be feudatory of Kai Province.[213] After this, all the members of the Rōjū were drawn from among his protégés, and all affairs of government great and small were decided as this man wished. The Rōjū simply became his mouthpiece and did not meet the Shōgun more than five or so times a month.

Then, when His late Highness [3] succeeded, although he had daily sessions with the Rōjū, its members were all proverbial "*daimyōs*' sons," and none had studied classical ethics nor had any knowledge of present-day affairs.[214] For many years, they merely transmitted the orders they received, and were, as I have said before, completely ignorant of the financial condition of the empire, and naturally even more so of the importance of administrative matters. Therefore, fearful of His Highness's perspicacity, they were often perplexed for an answer, and normally His Highness privately conveyed his opinion through Akifusa, then waited for the officials to reach agreement among themselves, after which he summoned them to his presence and gave his orders.

In matters difficult to comprehend, discussion went back and forth many times with Akifusa as intermediary. His Highness simplified into easily comprehensible terms matters difficult to grasp, and only when they had understood did he give orders. He never imposed his orders arbitrarily, however trifling the question was. So anything the members of the Rōjū wished to say, they said through Akifusa.

Akifusa, from his childhood, had always served at His Highness's side, and His Highness knew him thoroughly, and hence entrusted these duties to him, but perhaps he still had some reservations about him, for later, he appointed Tadayoshi [79] to the same position and gave orders that Tadayoshi was to take his seat with the Rōjū in the order of precedence, according to rank and office. Thus until recently, Akifusa took a higher seat than Bungo-no-Kami Masataka [97], and Tadayoshi was given a seat lower than Masataka. All these years, from the time when His Highness had been an ordinary feudal lord long ago, Akifusa had devoted himself to public affairs from early morning till late at night and did not return home more than three or so times a year. His duties became even heavier after His Highness's death, for since the Shōgun [25] was a child, the members of the Rōjū took it in turns to remain on duty in the palace at night, so for the space of five years, Akifusa did not return home at all. At his death, His Highness had left instructions that everything was to be carried on as when he was alive. So thereafter, Akifusa as before discussed with the Rōjū what orders the shogunate should give, and these were issued after the members had reached agreement. Petitions from below were also discussed by the members of the Rōjū with Akifusa and decisions were made by the agreement of the members. Officials like myself were also consulted because, in accordance with the directions left by His Highness, Akifusa followed the same arrangements as in his time.

From his childhood, Akifusa had never had leisure to study, but he had a very fine character, and in most respects he was not inferior to the sages of old. Hence affairs after the death of His late Highness were entrusted to him, and he served as the young Shōgun's adviser at this time. His management of affairs of state, both great and small, won the admiration of the people, and he never made a mistake. It is rare indeed to find such a man in a degenerate age. But it seems that now people are uttering detractions against him. It stands to reason that if Akifusa had not been fit to hold such an office, he could have been dismissed by the Rōjū, even in the time of His late Highness. It would have been even easier to dismiss him during the time of the young Shōgun.

It seems that it was said that everything was carried out as he wished, and, worse, that the country was administered as people like myself wished. But when Akifusa's opinions differed from those of the Rōjū, he could take no action. And this was much more the case with people like myself who only answered when the Rōjū asked us questions and who lacked the power to put a single suggestion into effect. There were many occasions when I gave my honest opinion, but the Rōjū did not agree with it, so it was not put into effect.

But there is no point in talking about these things.

In a time of normalcy the hereditary retainers of the Tokugawa House have until now been very anxious because the Shōgun has been a child. But now they congratulate themselves that the House will henceforth be stable and criticize the rule of the late Shōgun [25], putting the blame on Akifusa, but in one hundred years' time when public opinion has become settled, their abuse will be discredited.[215]

I, Chikugo-no-Kami Minamoto Kimmi of the Lower Fifth Rank Second Grade, close this account at about the middle of July 1716.[216]

NOTES

PREFACE

[1] My parents: father, Arai Masanari (1601–82); mother, surname Sakai (Fujiwara Sept) (1617–78).

[2] grandfather: Arai Kageyu, d. 1609.

[3] Hakuseki retired when Yoshimune succeeded the 7th Shōgun.

[4] At this time, Hakuseki held court rank (conferred 1709) but no official position (retired 1 July 1716); the date (text Hinoe-saru 10m 4d) was the 4th anniversary of the 6th Shōgun Ienobu's death, not necessarily the actual date of the preface.

The signature and date are followed by a seal which reads "Gen Kan no In" and means "Seal of Minamoto Kageyu." "Gen" is Minamoto, Hakuseki's sept, and "Kan" the first syllable of "Kageyu," his familiar name, or *zokumyō*.

BOOK I

[1] grandmother: d. 31 May 1604, aged 49. See n. 6, bk I. Shimozuma-no-Shō, in S. W. Makabe dist., Hitachi prov. (region N. E. pres. Shimozuma, Ibaraki pref.).

[2] Arai: name of village in Nitta dist., Kōzuke prov. (Gumma pref.), formerly written 荒居 as now.

[3] old nurse: in the feudal period, children of middle and upper classes were brought up by carefully selected nurses of a high caliber who not only nursed but also educated them, and who hence enjoyed a closer relationship with them than their own mothers did.

[4] Perhaps Tagaya Hiratsune, descended from a retainer of the Arai House.

[5] In about 1634.

[6] Hakuseki's date for his grandmother's death, Keichō 9y 3m 3d is incorrect; see n. 1, bk. I.

[7] Kōtokuji: then in Asakusa, Edo (now in Nakano, Tōkyō).

[8] The Sengoku period which lasted until 1600.

[9] Kohō: Chinese equivalent for Mimbu-no-Shō (see Appx. 1), properly Kohōrō; also read Kobu.

[10] Censor, an inspector, or police officer who secretly reported any misdemeanor or deviation from duty to his lord.

[11] The S. is the direction of honor, hence it would be disrespectful for a retainer to enter his lord's mansion from the S.

[279]

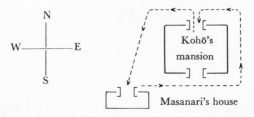

¹² Under the *sankin kōtai* (alternate attendance) system, the *hannen kōtai* (half yearly attendance) rule applied to the *fudai* (hereditary) *daimyō*. The Kohō's fief is pres. Kururi, Kimitsu dist. (Chiba pref.), 21,000 *koku*.

¹³ Hakuseki's father, as a *metsuke*, remained in the Edo mansion.

¹⁴ The Kohō became Honorary Commandant (an auxiliary guard changed every 6 mths.) at the Tokugawa stronghold at Sumpu (text: Surugafujō), capital of Suruga prov. (Shizuoka pref.). Masanari went to Kururi Castle, the Kohō's own seat.

¹⁵ 1649: text Shōhō 6y, a mistake for Keian 2y; text Nikkōzan, in Shimotsuke prov. (Tochigi pref.), founded 1617 (completed 1636) to enshrine Ieyasu's remains; all *daimyō* were required to serve for a term on fire duty within the precincts.

¹⁶ Ōsaka Castle was built by Toyotomi Hideyoshi in 1583; in Tokugawa times the *Ōsaka jōdai* was stationed there to guard the Kinki region (the district around Kyōto); this consisted of 4 *daimyō*, entrusted with the duty of guarding the 4 gates of Ōsaka Castle, who replaced each other every 8 mths.

¹⁷ Mishima post-station: one of the 53 post-stations of the Tōkaidō in Izu prov. (Shizuoka pref.).

¹⁸ Sanuki: a coastal town, Kimitsu dist., Kazusa prov. (Chiba pref.), now merged with Ōnuki to form Ōsawa-machi.

samurai-taishō: a *samurai* commanding one division of 4000 or 12,500 men, according to different sources, under the command of a general; the term came to be used as synonym for an "elder," who in times of peace assisted in the administration.

Satomi: the Satomi Family were in possession of Iiyama Castle in Awa prov. (Chiba pref.), 120,000 *koku*; Satomi Tadayoshi was dispossessed in 1614.

¹⁹ monkey-leader: itinerant entertainer who exhibited monkeys trained to dance and took up a collection from spectators.

²⁰ Takeda of Kai: descended from Seiwa Genji, established in Takeda, Kita-Koma dist., Kai prov. (Yamanashi pref.). When Takeda Katsuyori (1546–82) was defeated in 1582 by the armies of Oda and Tokugawa and committed suicide at Temmokuzan (Kai prov.), the House of Takeda was destroyed.

²¹ Sōma: lord of Nakamura Castle in Sōma dist., Iwaki prov. (part of Fukushima pref.), 60,000 *koku*. In the Battle of Sekigahara, the Sōma sided against Ieyasu, and their fief was confiscated, but later they were reinstated. When the line failed, Tsuchiya Tadanao's 2nd s., Katsutane (afterward Tadatane), was adopted and married to a dtr.

²² Tsuchiya Tadanao was a hereditary retainer of the Takeda House, s. of Masatsune, who married Okabe Tamba-no-Kami's dtr. and died with Takeda Katsuyori.

²³ adopted son: Gunji Masanobu who served in the House of Sōma.

²⁴ Shisawa: in Hyōgo pref., at that time it was the fief of the Ikeda Family.

²⁵ Hayashida: in Ibo dist., Harima prov. (Hyōgo pref.), territory (100,000 *koku*) of Takebe Masunaga (1603–72).

²⁶ Takataki according to *Dai Chimei Jiten*; Matsumura reads Kōtaki; in Ichihara dist. (Chiba pref.),

²⁷ The annexation of Awa prov. (Hyōgo pref.) by the Satomi Family is said to have taken place in 1496; the family was dispossessed in 1614 and became extinct in 1622; the lord of Shisawa, whom Takataki served, may have been Ikeda Teruzumi.

²⁸ Mutsu: Rikuoku, N. part of the ancient prov. of Mutsu (orig. comprising the

N.E. of the main Japanese island) including 8 dist. in Aomori pref. and 1 in Iwate pref.

San'yōdō: one of the 8 territorial divisions of Japan, in the S.W. of the main island.

Kashinokinosaka: a very steep slope in the Hakone mountains, Sagami prov. (Kanagawa pref.), now Hatajuku.

[29] Higai: 1.97 km from Kashinokinosaka.

[30] The name of the Daijō Family was derived from the office of Taira Kunika (ca. A.D. 930), a magnate of Hitachi prov. (Ibaraki pref.); the descendant of his nephew succeeded to the office and adopted the surname.

[31] Kohō's second son: Tsuchiya Shikibu Katsutane became the adopted s. of Sōma Daizen-no-Suke Yoshitane and changed his title to Nagato-no-Kami Tadatane.

Mutsu branch: held 60,000 koku at Nakamura, Iwaki prov. (Fukushima pref.).

[32] From 郡司 to 軍治.

[33] Takeda Katsuyori opposed Tokugawa Ieyasu and Oda Nobutada, but fell, transfixed by the arrows of 6 of the enemy, at Temmokuzan, Higashi-Yamanashi dist., Kai prov. (Yamanashi pref.) in 1582, aged 27.

[34] Seikenji: a temple in Kōzumachi, Ihara dist., Suruga prov. (Shizuoka pref.).

[35] coming of age: gembuku, a ceremony for boys between 12 and 15 or 16 when they changed their style of dressing to signify they were adults, having the top of the head shaved, and gave up their childhood names to adopt their jitsumyō, or given names.

[36] Matsushita Iwami-no-Kami Nagatsuna was enfeoffed with 30,000 koku at Miharu in Tamura dist., Iwaki prov. (Fukushima pref.) in 1628, but on his death in 1644 his House became extinct.

[37] Tenneiji: a temple of the Sōdō sect, E. of Ōme (pres. Nishi-Tama dist., Tōkyō).

[38] elder councilor: i.e. became a member of the Rōjū (in 1665).

[39] Shinchō Ki: a 15 vol. life of Oda Nobunaga, from 1568 to 1582, by his private secretary Ota Gyūichi.

[40] Prob. during Toyotomi Hideyoshi's campaign, 1592–98.

[41] daughter: Niwa's dtr. married Asano Takumi-no-Kami Naganao (1610–72).

Niwa Saishō: Niwa Nagashige (1571–1637); Saishō is the Chinese equivalent of Sangi (councilor), a position he attained in 1632.

[42] Nihommatsu: Niwa Nagashige's widowed younger sister retired to his fief, which at the time of her husband's death was 50,000 koku at Tanakura Castle, Higashi-Shirakawa dist., Iwashiro prov. (Fukushima pref.). It was Nagashige's son, Mitsushige, who was transferred (100,000 koku) to Nihommatsu Castle, Adachi dist., Iwashiro prov. (Fukushima pref.) in 1643.

[43] Furuta Daizen-Daibu: Furuta Shigeharu (1578–1625) resided at Hamada Castle, Naka dist., Iwami prov. (Shimane pref.).

[44] Bansan: nickname composed of the first characters of his surname, Sakai, and familiar name, which may have been Saburō.

[45] He refused to serve the Kohō's heir, who was unworthy of his position.

[46] the 27th: elsewhere in text given as 28th.

[47] He was dispossessed in 1679; his s. received 3,000 koku.

[48] Tatsunao: some texts give Michinao; Sadanao is given in the pedigree in Hakuseki's Hankampu.

[49] The Great Meireki Fire on 2–3 March 1657. On two successive days, fire raged through Edo, killing tens of thousands of people and destroying buildings over 400 city blocks.

[50] Now, the streets from Mansei Bridge in Kanda (in Chiyoda-ku) to Asakusa Bridge along the Kanda River.

[51] Nambu Toshinao: a mistake for Nambu Shigenao, who held 130,000 koku at Morioka (in Rikuchū). Nambu Toshinao had died in 1632. He had 2 s., Shigenao and Shigenobu. Shigenao died in 1664 when Hakuseki was 8, while his heir had died in 1651. His adopted s. Katsunao (the 3rd s. of Hotta Masamori) had also died in 1659. In 1662 when Hakuseki was 6, he therefore had no heir. In accordance with his will, the shogunate permitted his younger brother Shigenobu to succeed him.

[52] unicornis: narwhal's tusk.

[53] Ceremony: for boys from 5 to 9, and for girls from 7 to 11; a lucky day of the month is chosen and the cord is discarded and the sash (*obi*) is put on for the first time; text lit. "undoing cord or belt."

hakama: long wide trousers resembling a divided skirt, in ancient times mostly worn for the first time at the age of 3, in later times at 5 or 7; the custom was observed in the case of girls also.

[54] Illustrated story book written in *kana*, 2 vols., not extant.

[55] A temple in Ueno in Edo (now Ueno Park, Taitō-ku, Tōkyō). Erected by Shōgun Iemitsu in 1625, the principal temple took its name from the Kan'ei era (1624-44). Six *shōguns* were buried there, but the temple burned down in 1868.

[56] Written in the form of correspondence and covering practices of daily life, they first arose at the end of the Heian period (ca. 1192) and flourished until Tokugawa times. *Meikō Ōrai*, ascribed to Fujiwara Meikō, but probably by a priest of early Muromachi, and *Teikin Ōrai* (see n. 60, bk. I) are representative examples.

[57] commentary: the *Taiheiki Hyōban Shiyō Rijin Mukyokushō* in 50 vols. by the lay-priest Eikō, Wada Shimotsuke-no-Kami Sukenori, a critical study of the military operations in the *Taiheiki*. According to one opinion, although the preface is dated 1476, it is actually a work of the Tokugawa period and has some connection with Nichiō, a priest of the Hokke sect. *Taiheiki* is a historical work of 41 vols. attributed to the priest Kojima (d. 1374) of Hieizan, but author actually unknown.

[58] Imagawa: a *daimyō* family descended from the Seiwa Genji; Norikuni (1294-1384) was a relative of Ashikaga Takauji who rewarded him for his military support with large domains in Tōtōmi and Suruga (Shizuoka pref.), which were inherited by his 1st s., Noriuji, and his descendants.

verse-capping: see n. 69, bk. II.

[59] The first poem refers to an old tale which appears in the *Chan-Kuo-Ts'ê* (Chin and Han dynasties), in which P'ang-ts'ung explains to the King of Wei the origin of rumors; if one man makes an assertion, he is not believed; if two men make an assertion, one half-believes and half-doubts; if three men make an assertion, one believes completely.

Zōsu: a priestly title indicating rank, below a head priest, but here probably used merely with the meaning of "priest."

Enoshima: a small island off the coast of Sagami prov. (today the coast of Katase at Fujisawa in Kanagawa pref.).

[60] *Teikin Ōrai*: a primer in the form of letters and answers; it teaches a letter-writing style to primary-school children by presenting models suitable for all 12 mths. of the year. The style is quasi-Kambun. The author is said to have been Gen'e (1269-1350), a monk who expounded the Confucian doctrines of the Han and T'ang dynasties (207-907) and agitated against Hōjō rule.

[61] Composed by Nakae Tōju (1608-48), in 5 vols., pub. in 1649. It discusses literature, the military arts, Buddhism, etc., in the form of questions and answers between a disciple called Teijū and a master called Tenkun.

[62] Way of the Sages: Confucian philosophy.

[63] Or *Little Learning*, in 2 vols. 6 chs. supposedly written by the Sung Confucianist Chu Hsi but actually compiled by his disciple Liu Tzŭ-ch'êng. A book containing lessons in social intercourse, hygiene, official etiquette, speech, and ethics for primary school and culled from ancient and later books.

[64] *Ssŭ Chên*: the *Four Precepts* or prohibitions against impropriety of speech, movement, seeing, and hearing, taught by Confucius to his disciple Yen Hui, stated in the *Analects*, bk. 12.

Ch'êng Tzŭ: the great Confucianist Ch'êng I-ch'uan (1033-1107) of Northern Sung (960-1126). A disciple of Chou Tun-i whose teachings he transmitted, and known as Ch'êng the Enlightener (who originated the theory of *T'ai Chi*, later developed into Chu Hsi philosophy).

[65] *Four Books*: the *Ta Hsüeh* (*Great Learning*), the *Lun Yü* (*Confucian Analects*), the

Chung Yung (Doctrine of the Mean), *Mêng Tzŭ (Mencius)*, established in the Sung period (960–1280) as the sacred scriptures of Neo-Confucianism.

Five Classics: the *I Ching (Book of Changes)*, the *Shu Ching (Book of History)*, the *Shih Ching (Odes)*, the *Li Chi (Book of Rites)*, and the *Ch'un Ch'iu (Spring and Autumn Annals)*.

⁶⁶ *Yün Hui*: the *Ku Chin Yün Hui Hsüeh Yao*, a phonetic dictionary in 30 vols.; there is also a *Yün Hui Hsiao Pu* (or appendix) in 3 vols.

Tzŭ Hui: composed by Mei Ying-tsu, a dictionary in 12 vols. with an introduction and epilogue, published during the Ming Dynasty (1368–1644).

⁶⁷ He took service with Hotta Masatoshi.

⁶⁸ Yamagata: chief town of Yamagata dist. (later Mogami), in Dewa (later Uzen) prov. (Yamagata pref.), where his lord Hotta Masanaka had been transferred.

⁶⁹ Literally, presents given as a courtesy; usually bundles of dried meat.

⁷⁰ clan mansion: castle in Kōfu (fief 330,000 *koku*), in Nishi Yamanashi dist., Kai prov. (Yamanashi pref.), at which time Bunshō-byō (Ienobu, the 6th Tokugawa Shō-gun), was called Tsunatoyo, before he was recognized as the Shōgun's Heir.

⁷¹ Based on a sentence in the *Chung Yung (Doctrine of the Mean)*: "What others do once I do a hundred times; and what others do ten times, I do a thousand times."

⁷² Uematsu: Uematsu Chūbei, descendant of a retainer of Imagawa in Suruga prov. (Shizuoka pref.) who had taught Hakuseki Chinese poetry when he was a child.

⁷³ Satomi Yoshitaka: built Kururi Castle in 1522 and spent his last years there, having taken the tonsure and adopted the name Taisō.

⁷⁴ younger sister: O-Made, married Yamamoto Shinsuke Yasuchika, d. 7 June 1677.

⁷⁵ Oda Naifu Jōshin: Oda Nobuo (1558–1630), Nobunaga's 2nd s. Attained rank of Naidaijin (of which Naifu is the Chinese form) in 1585, but after quarreling with Toyo-tomi Hideyoshi in 1590 he became a lay-priest with the name Jōshin.

⁷⁶ At this time intermarriage between *samurai* and merchant families was not yet wide-spread.

⁷⁷ A quotation from Mencius, *Kung Sun Ch'ou*, vol. 1.

⁷⁸ merchant: Kawamura Zuiken (1617–99). Rose from courier to entrepreneur. His fortunes were founded on timber speculations after the Meireki Fire; he also under-took flood-control work and canal communications; became a *hatamoto* with 150 *hyō*.

⁷⁹ Ling Shan: Ryōzen, one of the 36 peaks of Higashiyama in Otagi dist. in Yama-shiro prov. (pres. Higashiyama-ku, Kyōto), and Ryōzanji, a branch temple of Seihōji (Tendai sect), founded 1004, have been suggested, but the fable suggests a Chinese source and this is a common geographical name in China.

⁸⁰ Kurokawa Dōyū, d. 1691, Confucian scholar and physician from Aki prov. (Hiroshima pref.), author of *Yōsufushi*, etc.

⁸¹ Hotta incident: text "Chikushū no koto"; Masatoshi was killed in a barracks in Edo Castle by a relative by marriage, Inaba Masayoshi, a member of the Wakadoshi-yori, who was cut down on the spot.

⁸² wife and family: Hakuseki makes very few references to his wife and children in this work; mention of his wife is confined to this instance, the presents given her by Shōgun Ienobu, and the latter's concern for her safety at the time of the earthquake. Hakuseki probably married when he obtained a position (at age 26) in the Hotta House (1682), where his wife's family was also connected as retainers; his wife was dtr. of Asakura Nagaharu of the Kusakabe Sept; d. age 71, 22 Aug. 1739. He had by this time begun raising a family, but his 1st dtr., Shizu, was short-lived, prob. dying at birth (1687) when Hakuseki was 31. His 2nd dtr., Kiyo, was born 1689. When he submitted his resignation (at the beginning of 1691), his wife was pregnant with his 1st s., Akinori. See Appx. 4. for information on Hakuseki family.

⁸³ His lord was concerned that Hakuseki's wife was pregnant.

⁸⁴ Kōtokuji: within Hōonji in Asakusa in Edo.

⁸⁵ younger brother: Hotta Masatoshi's 3rd s. (1666–1728), by a concubine, received 10,000 *koku* of his father's inheritance and afterward held a fief at Katata, in Ōmi prov. (Shiga pref.), 1698; he later changed his name to Masataka; he founded a junior branch of the family.

[86] east of the castle: E. of Edo Castle, now within Kōtō-ku; in 1691 Hakuseki moved to Honjo (a farm on the Sumida River).

[87] Tani: identity not certain, but perhaps Tani Jinzan (1663–1718), a pupil of Yamazaki Ansai and Shibukawa Shunkai, a Confucianist in the Tosa clan, skilled in the calendrical arts and the Suika sect of Shintō; author of *Shindai Kan'endo Den* and other books.

a lord: Hotta Masanaka, son of Hotta Masatoshi, whose assassination bore the marks of being in accord with Shōgun Tsunayoshi's will.

[88] a master: Kinoshita Jun'an, overshadowed by Hayashi Nobuatsu.

[89] Tani was urging him to join the official school of Hayashi Nobuatsu, in high favor with Shōgun Tsunayoshi.

[90] Ancient states in what is now Honan; after leaving Lu, having despaired of the Duke's behavior, Confucius, accompanied by several disciples, wandered from state to state, and was in Ch'ên in 495–94 B.C. and 491 B.C., and in Ts'ai in 490–89 B.C. Between Ch'ên and Ts'ai, their provisions became exhausted and they suffered great distress for 7 days.

[91] Lord of Kaga: family descended from Maeda Toshiie (1538–99), who had been the chief of the 5-member council of state appointed by Toyotomi Hideyoshi to guard the interests of his s. Hideyori; at this time his great-great-grands., Maeda Tsunanori, held 1,027,000 *koku* at Kanazawa in Kaga prov. (Ishikawa pref.).

Okajima: 1666–1709 Okajima Tatsu (nickname Chūtsū), nom-de-plume Sekiryō.

[92] Kōfu was the capital of Kai prov. (Yamanashi pref.). The lord of Kai, Tsunatoyo (later Ienobu) was nephew of the then Shōgun, Tsunayoshi, and stood next in succession.

[93] One day's ration for 1 man was 5 *gō*; 30 men's rations for one year were therefore about 54 *koku*.

[94] reasons of his own: being in favor with Tsunayoshi, it would have been impolite to form a connection with the Kōfu house, next in line to the shogunate, at a time when Tsunayoshi still hoped to beget a son of his own to succeed him.

[95] Itō Jinsai (1627–1705), Confucianist of Kyōto, founder of the Kogakuha, a school which rejected the Sung commentaries and followed the Confucian texts themselves; also studied ancient Japanese literature.

[96] Tsuda: Tsuda Echizen-no-Kami Masatsune, at that time Geki.

[97] *Ta Hsüeh: The Great Learning*, one of the *Four Books*; a work used by the Sung philosophers in the 13th century A.D. as the source of later Confucian political philosophy; orig. contained in the *Li Chi*.

[98] *Chin Ssŭ Lu*: a book written by Chu Hsi and Lü Tsu-ch'ien of Sung (in 14 vols.) containing 622 important everyday phrases, divided into 14 classes, taken from the speech of 4 learned men.

[99] *Shih Ching*: the *Odes* or the *Book of Poetry* is one of the *Five Classics*. A collection of very ancient poems, hymns, and songs from various Chinese states, said by Han scholars to have been compiled by Confucius himself; contains valuable evidence regarding ancient customs and beliefs.

Li Chi: the *Book of Rites,* a work in 17 vols. dealing with ceremonies and regulations concerning coming of age, marriage, funerals, ancestor worship, attendance at court, visits of courtesy, bearing gifts; one of the 3 books on rites; said to have been composed by the Duke of Chou.

[100] following year: text, this year 11m 20d.

[101] painting teacher: Inō Jakusui (1655–1715), given name Terunobu, studied Confucianism under Itō Jinsai; appointed to Maeda Clan of Kaga in 1693.

[102] In the *Shikyōshōshiki* (8 vols.).

[103] *Shu Ching*: the *Book of History* is one of the *Five Classics*, a collection of very old documents, speeches, orations, and harangues which are the earliest literary source for Chinese history.

[104] Three Dynasties: Hsia (2205–1766 B.C.), Shang (1766–1122 B.C.), and Chou (1122–249 B.C.).

[105] Ssŭ-ma Kuang: conservative statesman and famous historian (1018–86) in the time of Shên Tsung (1068–85), 6th emp. of the Sung Dynasty. A native of Shensi prov., he attained the highest degree (Hanlin) in literature under the old system. He criticized unavailingly the "New Laws," or revolutionary economic policy of Wang An-shih, and, in his disappointment, poured all his energy into the composition of the *Tzŭ Chih T'ung Chien.*

Tzŭ Chih T'ung Chien: in 294 vols., composed on the order of Ying Tsung in 1066 and completed in 1084 under Shên Tsung. It is a chronological account of the reigns of 113 emps. for 1362 years, from 403 B.C., during the Chou Dynasty, to A.D. 959, in the Late Chou Dynasty. The title means "A revelation of successive administrations to serve as a guide in government."

Chu Hsi: a Sung Confucianist (1130–1200) who was the founder, or perfector, and organizer of Neo-Confucianism which had a tremendous influence during the Tokugawa period; author of *Shih Chi Chuan, Ssŭ Shu Chi Chu, Chin Ssŭ Lu,* and (reputedly) *Hsiao Hsüeh.* See n. 63, bk. I.

T'ung Chien Kang Mu: a short title for *Tzŭ Chih T'ung Chien Kang Mu,* a new introduction to the *Tzŭ Chih T'ung Chien,* divided into *Kang,* an outline of history, by Chu Hsi and others, and *Mu,* or critical commentary, composed by his disciple, Chao Shih-yüan.

[106] same year: text has "the following year, Kinoto-i (i.e., Genroku 8y) 1m. 24d."

[107] following: text has simply 12m 21d.

[108] *Ch'un Ch'iu: Spring and Autumn Annals,* the first accurate chronological history written in China, is a chronicle of the feudal state of Lu, from 722–481 B.C., of which Confucius was a native. Chinese orthodox tradition assigns the *Ch'un Ch'iu* to Confucius himself, but this attribution cannot be substantiated and is not accepted by foreign scholars.

Chou I: another name for the *I Ching,* the *Book of Changes,* a work of great antiquity, used as a book of divination. Consists in its present form of two separate texts, one part comprising rhymed interpretations of ordinary country omens, and the other a divination manual containing formulas, such as have been deciphered on oracle bones and tortoise shells; much space is given to the interpretation of the 8 trigrams or Pa Kua.

[109] *Tso Chuan*: one of the "Three Commentaries" on the *Ch'un Ch'iu,* a work of 30 chs. attributed to a certain Tso Ch'iu-ming (ca. 300 B.C.?) of whom nothing definitely is known; it throws light on the obscure events laconically listed in the *Ch'un Ch'iu* and explains its formal language.

Kung Yang: one of the "Three Commentaries" on the *Ch'un Ch'iu*; a work of 11 chs., said to have been based on traditions related by Kung-yang Kao, and later recorded by his great-grands. Kung-yang Shou and Hu-mu Tzŭ (Kung-yang Shou's disciple).

Ku Liang: one of the "Three Commentaries" on the *Ch'un Ch'iu,* a work of 11 chs. compiled by Ku-liang Ch'ih of Lu.

Hu Chuan: abbreviation for *Ch'un Ch'iu Hu Chuan,* a commentary of 30 chs. on the *Ch'un Ch'iu,* compiled by Hu An-kuo of Sung.

[110] 1702: Hakuseki has mistaken Kanoto-hitsuji (1691) for Kanoto-mi (1701); the amended date 12m 19d of 1701 is given.

[111] *Hsü Pien*: abbreviation for *T'ung Chien Kang Mu Hsü Pien,* supplement to the *T'ung Chien Kang Mu,* in 24 vols., composed by Ch'en Ching of Ming.

[112] same year: text has next year, Kanoto-mi 1m 11d.

[113] Record of the feudal lords; a *hankan* is a guardian of the royal house, hence, a feudal lord.

[114] *Hsiao Ching*: another name for the *Hsiao Hsüeh.* See n. 63, bk. I.

Chou Li: a book in 6 vol. on the rituals of the Chou Dynasty, attributed to the Duke of Chou, with a supplement by a later hand; deals with etiquette.

I Li: another book in 17 vols. as above; deals with ceremonies.

[115] *Ta Hsüeh Yen I*: a work (1235) written by Chên Tê-hsiu of S. Sung on the significance of the *Ta Hsüeh* (a philosophical treatise on good government, in 43

vols.) and based on references from the classics and histories. Ch'iu Chün of Ming considered Chên Tê-hsiu's work incomplete and therefore wrote a supplement, *Ta Hsüeh Yen I Pu*, in 160 vols.

[116] 1695: a mistake for 1694, the date indicated by an entry in *Hakuseki Nikki*.

[117] An entry in *Hakuseki Nikki* indicates this event is correctly assigned to 1695 (12m 21d), 1696 in Western reckoning.

[118] *Six Classics*: the *I Ching, Shu Ching, Shih Ching, Ch'un Ch'iu* and *Li Chi* (as in the *Five Classics*) with the addition of either the *Yüeh Chi* (*Book of Music*) or the *Chou Li*, a book on ritual.

[119] Chikuko: the library of Mao Chin of the Ming Dynasty (1368–1643), with a collection of more than 80,000 vols., besides many books reprinted under his personal supervision.

[120] Sakakibara Gensuke: Sakakibara Kōshū (1656–1706), a native of Izumi prov. (Ōsaka pref.) sprung from the Shimoyama of Iga prov. (Mie pref.), but adopted by his maternal grandfather; official Confucianist of the Kii or Kishū House and the author of many works.

Kii House: text has Nanki, or Southern Ki, the Kishū clan, descended from Ieyasu's 8th s., Yorinobu, held 550,000 *koku* at Wakayama, Nagusa dist., Kii prov. (Wakayama pref.); one of the "Three Houses" from whom the *shōgun* could be selected. Yoshimune, the 8th Shōgun, was then lord.

[121] Two groups of odes in the *Shih Chi*, or *Book of Poetry*.

[122] In the Tokugawa House, the 1st, 15th, and 28th days of each month were called the "Three Days" and were ceremonial days.

seasonal celebrations: the so-called *gosekku*:
7th day, 1st month (*Jinjitsu*, day for eating the 7 greens)
3rd day, 3rd month (*Jōmi*, or Dolls' Festival)
5th day, 5th month (*Tango*, or Boys' Festival)
7th day, 7th month (*Tanabata*, or Festival of the Weaver Star)
9th day, 9th month (*Chōyō*, or Chrysanthemum Festival)

[123] Hakuseki moved to Yushima Tenjin Shita on the 22 March 1694.

[124] Kanda Myōjin: shrine in Kanda in Edo (in pres. Soto Kanda, Chiyoda-ku, Tōkyō).

[125] Asakura Yosan: younger brother of Hakuseki's wife.

[126] Fujieda Masanori (1658–1726), a retainer of the Kōfu clan, afterward attached to the *yoriai*.

[127] Tatsu-no-Kuchi: the area before the Wadakura Gate beneath the Western Palace in Edo Castle, the outlet for the water from the castle moat.

[128] A gate in the wall of Edo Castle, E. of the Sakurada Gate, no longer in existence.

[129] clan mansion: the mansion of the Kōfu or Kai clan was in Sakurada, and was near the Hibiya Gate; the "great gate" was a two-storied gate at the entrance.

[130] The entrance near the storeroom for clothes and supplies.

[131] As Hakuseki came to pay a ceremonial visit to inquire about his lord Tsunatoyo's safety, so Tsunatoyo goes to visit Shōgun Tsunayoshi.

[132] Yanaka: a region overlooking a valley to the W. of Ueno.

[133] Western Palace: a mansion in the Seijō or Nishi-no-Maru, in the W. part of Edo Castle, residence of the *shōgun's* heir.

[134] A reception room behind the entrance porch in the front of the accounts office gate, which is the center on the S. side, or front, of a military man's house.

[135] A room in Edo Castle where a priest was on duty to announce the time.

[136] The Hon-maru, i.e. the central and most important part of Edo Castle, containing the *shōgun's* apartments.

[137] New Year's Day according to the lunar calendar (Hōei 2y 1m 1d).

[138] Yagiū Munefuyu (1613–75), became Tsunayoshi's instructor in swordsmanship in 1661.

[139] Suwabe: Suwabe (Bungorō) Sadakata.

Hōki-no-Kami Masatake: Honda Masatake, a mistake for Masanaga. Masatake, 2nd s. of Sakakibara Hisamasa, was adopted (1693) by Honda Masanaga, had the title Tōtōmi-no-Kami, and d. 1721. Masanaga (1645–1711) this year (1705) became a member of the Rōjū in the Western Palace, and had the title Hōki-no-Kami.

[140] Text has Hinoto-inu; Hakuseki's mistake for Hinoe-inu (1706).

[141] Hama: in Shiba.

[142] *sarugaku*: here means Nō.

[143] Ienobu's 1st s., d. in infancy; mother Ukon no Kata (dtr. of Ōta), later known as Hōshin-In.

[144] Ōta Naiki: Ōta Masasuke, younger br. of Iechiyo's mother.

[145] Inscribed "Hōei Tsūhō" (currency of the Hōei era) on the obverse, and on the reverse, Eikyū Senjō; weight 2 *momme* 5 *bu*. The issue of this coin was the idea of Inagaki Tsushima-no-Kami Shigetomi, member of the Rōjū.

[146] About this time many "disturbances" were noted, but no explanation of this particular phenomenon is available. Confucianists regarded natural phenomena as manifestations of Heaven's disapproval of the manner of government.

[147] A palace for Tsunayoshi to retire to, inside the Tayasu and Shimizu Gates of Edo Castle; the houses in Iidamachi and Bammachi were cleared away as a precaution against fire.

[148] Part of Tsunayoshi's Kindness to Animals Statutes. His Buddhist policy of placating spirits of warriors slain in battle by the Tokugawa Family was showing kindness to creatures. It was also forbidden to use horses for express delivery of news.

[149] On 11 Nov. 1708, the *metsuke* issued an order that the "Ten Mon Pieces" were to be circulated and accepted in payment of tax in shogunal and private domains.

[150] On 3 Dec. 1708, it was decreed that: (1) animals were to be kindly treated; (2) if horses being ridden got tired on the road, they were to be stabled and looked after at any mansion in the vicinity; (3) horses hired out by post-stations were not to be overtaxed and strict attention to caring for them both in shogunal and public domains was to be observed.

[151] Tsunayoshi died of smallpox, aged 64.

BOOK II

[1] (1) the abolition of the Great Cash; (2) the stoppage of the removal of houses from the N. of the castle; (3) the abolition of the Kindness to Animals Statutes.

[2] Copper coins inscribed "Hōei Tsūhō" coined in 1708.

[3] The relocation, since about July 1708, of houses in Hakuseki's neighborhood to make a firebreak for the construction of a palace for Tsunayoshi to live in with a favorite concubine.

[4] Genna Regulations: the *Buke Shohatto*, circulated in 1615. See n. 73, bk. II.

"In Explanation of the Laws of the Divine Ancestor": commentary on the "Regulations of the Genna Era," no longer extant. See n. 74, bk. II.

[5] Buzen-no-Kami Naoshige: Kuroda Naoshige, afterward Naokuni, at this time a page.

"when I am dead": text lit. "even for a hundred years hereafter."

[6] "corpses . . . pickled in brine": When prisoners died before judgment was passed on them, their corpses were preserved in order that sentences might be executed on these.

[7] In a palliated form of *junshi* or "suicide to follow one's lord"; at this time 11 of Tsunayoshi's close attendants took the tonsure.

[8] A prohibition had been issued on 28 June 1663.

[9] Jugō: contraction of Junsangō, a title which guaranteed its possessor a revenue

equal to that bestowed on any of the three empresses (the reigning empress, the dowager empress, and the arch-dowager empress), given to princes and ministers; later became merely honorific.

[10] four [sons]: Matsudaira Hideyasu, and Tokugawa Yoshinao, Yorinobu, and Yorifusa, the 2nd, 7th, 8th, and 9th s. of Tokugawa Ieyasu, and founders of the Houses of Echizen, Owari, Kii, and Mito.

[11] Aizu Dono: Hoshina Masayuki (1611–72), 3rd s. of Shōgun Hidetada by a concubine, was adopted by Hoshina Masamitsu, the daimyō of Takatō, Shinano prov. (Nagano pref.), 30,000 koku; after he succeeded to his fief (1631) he was in 1636 given Yamagata, Dewa (Yamagata pref.), 200,000 koku; in 1644 he was transferred to Wakamatsu, Mutsu prov. (Fukushima pref.), 230,000 koku. Iemitsu entrusted the guardianship of his s. Ietsuna to him. He was granted the name Matsudaira and was celebrated as an administrator and scholar. Aizu is the dist. in Mutsu (Iwashiro) where Wakamatsu is situated.

[12] two sons: Iemitsu had 3 s., Ietsuna, Tsunashige, and Tsunayoshi; Ietsuna became Shōgun. Tsunashige (1644–78) received the fief of Fuchū, Kai prov. (Yamanashi pref.), 250,000 koku in 1661. Tsunayoshi (1646–1709) received the fief of Tatebayashi, Kōzuke prov. (Gumma pref.), 350,000 koku.

[13] Ietsuna (held office 1651–80) succeeded his father at the age of 11 and d. without issue, aged 40; Tsunayoshi was a younger br.

[14] a son: Tsunayoshi had a s., Tokumatsu, who d. aged 5, in 1683; his mother was a concubine.

no children after that: Tsunayoshi's lack of issue was the cause of his publishing his Kindness to Animals Statutes. See n. 150, bk. I.

[15] Genkō, Kemmu: era names during the reign of Emp. Go-Daigo; Genkyō (1321–24) (also read Genkō) is prob. a mistake for Genkō (1331–34), which is written with a different 2nd character; Kemmu was 1334–35, the period referred to is prob. 1331–35.

[16] The founder of the Tokugawa shogunate, Ieyasu, provided financial support and built palaces for the emp. and retired emp. and instituted the practice of reconstructing the Ise shrines. Iemitsu reestablished the custom of dispatching an envoy to Ise bearing offerings (1646). Tsunayoshi revived the Daijōe, the first ceremony performed by an emp. in honor of his ancestors after his coronation (1687) and repaired the tombs of successive generations of emps. (1697), etc.

[17] custom: that of the imp. offspring taking Buddhist vows.

[18] estates: the imp. court held various estates, e.g. presented by Oda Nobunaga and Toyotomi Hideyoshi, and confirmed and augmented by the Tokugawa shōguns.

[19] Divine Ancestress: Amaterasu-ō-mikami.

[20] Takakura-no-Miya: Prince Mochihito (1150–80), 2nd s. of Emp. Go-Shirakawa (1156–58).

Hei Shōkoku Nyūdō: lay-priest Dajōdaijin Taira Kiyomori (1118–81), who on taking the tonsure in 1168, adopted the name Jōkai and was nicknamed Dajō-Nyūdō. Shōkoku is the Chinese title equivalent to Dajōdaijin; nyūdō means lay-priest.

[21] Abbot of Nashimoto: Prince Morinaga (1308–35), s. of Emp. Go-Daigo, who wished to place him on the throne but was opposed by Hōjō Takatoki. Morinaga became a bonze, but when Takatoki attempted to depose Go-Daigo, raised an army against him. At first defeated, he again rallied his supporters, and after Takatoki's destruction, was named Sei-i-taishōgun.

[22] Hide-no-Miya: Prince Naohito (1703–52), founded imp. house of Kan'in.

Retired Emperor: Emp. Higashi-yama (1687–1709), reigned during shogunate of 5th Shōgun Tsunayoshi.

princess: see n. 170, bk. III.

previous Shōgun: Hakuseki, writing when Yoshimune had become Shōgun, so referred to Ietsugu, but at the time of his memo the latter was a baby.

[23] The imp. line, established as a result of Hakuseki's memorial, continued the succession when the reigning emp. d. without issue in 1779; the present emp. of Japan is a descendant in the 7th generation from Naohito.

[24] some highly born person: Ichijō Kaneteru, of a leading branch of the Fujiwara Family.

[25] The shogunal estates yielded 8 million *koku* but half was under the control of *fudai daimyō* and *hatamoto*, leaving 4 million in charge of stewards dispatched by the central government.

[26] customs: instituted 1696; dues imposed on merchants and craftsmen.

transport tax: instituted in 1697.

[27] biannual salaries: pensions paid to *hatamoto* who had no personal domains.

[28] The imp. palace was destroyed by fire in April/May 1708 and reconstruction completed Nov. 1709.

[29] mausoleum: in Kan'eiji.

[30] after the eruption of Mt. Fuji on 26 Dec. 1707.

[31] for Tsunayoshi's widow.

[32] A policy of debasing the coinage to balance the budget had been initiated by Ogiwara Shigehide. Coinage was carried out by mints, known as *za*, which were a special kind of monopolist guild, under direct shogunal control. The copper mint was a government monopoly, the operation of which was carried out through a chartered company.

[33] money: in Ōsaka Castle, to ensure the stability of Bakufu currency.

[34] In Ieyasu's time, 36 ingots were cast, the gold ingots weighing more than 40 *kamme* and the silver more than 30; in 1659, 24 gold ingots and 260 silver ingots were cast.

[35] *Chou I*: (see n. 108, bk. I) Hsi Tz'ŭ Chuan Hsia (Postscript Pt. II).

[36] the *Analects*: the discourses of Confucius to his disciples, but prob. compiled by their disciples at the end of 5th, early 4th c. B.C. Ref. here is to Bk. I, ch. 5.

[37] *Ta Hsüeh*: (see n. 97, bk. I) commentary of Ts'êng, ch. 10, para. 19.

[38] Ōhiroma: where the *daimyō* above a certain rank assembled.

Goshoin: two halls, one in white wood, and one in black lacquer.

[39] Fêng-I: once relieved the starvation of Kuang-wu's army N. of the Yellow River.

[40] Shogunal amnesty under which crimes including the 8 forms of insubordination (e.g., desecration of an imp. tomb, betrayal of one's lord, unfiliality, etc.), premeditated murder, wilful murder, illicit coinage, robbery with violence, and theft were pardoned.

[41] *bugyō*: here in charge of the administration of justice.

[42] ordinary amnesty: an amnesty under which crimes not involving the death penalty were pardoned.

[43] Kuan Chung: (?–644 B.C.) minister of Kung-tsŭ Chiu, later became prime minister of Duke Huan of Ch'i during "Spring and Autumn" period; author of *Kuan Tsŭ*.

[44] K'ung-ming: (181–234) general, and later prime minister, to King Liu Pei during Three Kingdoms period; author of *Chu-ko Wu Hou Wên Chi*.

[45] Hsün Yüeh: (178–213) philosopher of Later Han dynasty, attached to the imp. court during reign of Emp. Hsien; author of *Shên Chien* (5 vols.) and *Han Chi* (30 vols.).

[46] Quotation from the commentary of Hsiang attached to the divination of Chieh in the *I Ching* (see n. 108, bk. I): "the thunder shower fell because heaven and earth relaxed, whereupon all the plants and trees spread their foliage," referring to the gratitude of the released prisoners.

[47] fire-hook coolies: fire-fighting was largely demolition; hooks were used to pull down roofs.

[48] Goban-iri: ceremony of entry into the *gobanshū*; the first step in promotion in the shogunate, restricted to the s. of certain officials.

[49] 27th April: text has "18th day of the same," mistake for 4 m 18d, which was 27 May.

[50] *hoi* costume: a court robe with a round stand-up collar but no crest, worn by lower ranks.

[51] sandal-bearer: his duty was to carry and present the *shōgun's* footwear when he alighted from his palanquin.

[52] this year: text has "the following year."

[53] banners: used to indicate the location of the commander in a battle.

[54] The Korean Embassy visited Japan in 1711.

[55] Tōshōgū at Nikkō: text Nikkōzan, the mausoleum of Tokugawa Ieyasu.

[56] *Atake-Maru*: a warship constructed by the 3rd Shōgun Iemitsu in 1633, demolished in 1682 because of financial difficulties.

[57] Nagasaki Bugyō: in charge of foreign trade and coast defenses.

[58] *onando*: shogunal supplies storehouse.

fox-bewitching: possession of a human being by a fox's spirit leading to abnormal behavior.

[59] The Serata were ancestors of the Tokugawa.

[60] Kōzuke Province: pres. Gumma pref.

[61] Family descended from Minamoto Yoshishige, grands. of Yoshiie. Yoshishige's s., Yoshisue, was the founder of the Tokugawa branch.

[62] Yagiū: also read Noushi, but given reading has the authority of the *Dai Nihon Chimei Jisho* (Fusambō); in Saitama pref.

Otsuhata: Matsumura reads Koshihata, but readings in Miyazaki and *Dai Nihon Chimei Jisho* suggest as given; this estate lies athwart pres. Tōkyō, Kanagawa, and Saitama prefs.

[63] Naka-no-Kuchi: entrance between the porch and the kitchen.

Hasuike Gate: within the Sakashita Gate.

[64] the Roman: Giovanni Battista Sidotti (1668–1714), the last Christian missionary to enter Japan during the seclusion.

[65] notably in *Seiyō Kibun*.

[66] concerning foreign trade and the livelihood of Nagasaki citizens.

[67] notably *Nagasaki Goyō Shomotsu*.

[68] The armor worn by Tokugawa Ieyasu at the Battle of Nagakute (1584) in support of Oda Nobuo (also read Nobukatsu) against Toyotomi Hideyoshi.

[69] Verse-Capping Party: a ceremonial poetry contest borrowed from the imp. court in the Muromachi period as part of the shogunate's New Year celebrations. Participants composed successive stanzas of a series of 100 traditional 31-syllable poems; each pair of stanzas had to make a complete poetic statement.

[70] supplementary proposals: *Heijikōgi*, but nothing with this title extant; *Hakuseki Nikki* records under this date that *Chōsen Heirei Jigi Zoku* was presented.

[71] two volumes of proposals: *Ōsetsujigi*, perhaps incorporated in the *Chōsen Ōsetsu Ki*.

[72] the New Regulations: the *Hōei Buke Shohatto* or "Laws for the Regulation of the Warrior Houses."

[73] The *Genna Rei*, the *Buke Shohatto* or "Regulations of the Warrior Houses" issued in 1615.

[74] Commentary on the New Regulations: the *Shinrei Kuge*.

[75] Jōei Shikimoku: a code of the *samurai*, published in 1232 by Miyoshi Yoshitsura for Hōjō Yasutoki, containing laws enacted since the time of Minamoto Yoritomo.

Kemmu Shikimoku: a code of the *samurai* published in 1336, compiled for Ashikaga Takauji by officials of the shogunate and noted bonzes.

[76] government on literary principles: the keynote of Ienobu's reign, under Hakuseki's guidance, was government in accordance with Confucian principles.

succeedings ages: the reigns of the 3rd, 4th, and 5th *shōguns*, but the particular reference is to the *Buke Shohatto* of 1681.

kana: actually, the 1681 regulations were written in Chinese, but Chinese of a distinctly Japanese cast, i.e. having *kana* intermixed.

[77] 'Jōsai': here a term for a decree issued under the *shōgun's* seal.

[78] codes and regulations: text has *ritsuryō kyakushiki*, criminal and civil codes, ordinances, and operation rules, beginning in 701; by contrast to the systematization and detail of this body of law, the regulations in question were merely practical rules for the control of the *buke*.

[79] see n. 60 bk. I.

⁸⁰ 'Uesama': "the one on high."

⁸¹ Rokuon-In: Ashikaga Yoshimitsu (1358–1408); 'Kubō' was an honorific title orig. reserved for the emp.

⁸² 'Jōchō,' 'Jōbun': orig. meant "reaching the emp.'s ears, coming to the emp.'s knowledge."

⁸³ biannual salaries: *kirimai*, see n. 27, bk. II.

⁸⁴ Rice Bulletin: a bulletin posted in Edo Castle, fixing the standard price of rice, and hence the conversion rate for salaries paid in cash.

⁸⁵ "Tenka": "empire."

⁸⁶ "Tenka Taihei": "the empire at peace."

⁸⁷ supernatural beings: text has *shinsen*=wizard, or Taoist hermit with supernatural powers.

⁸⁸ Possession of human beings by foxes was a widely held belief.

⁸⁹ laid out in 1710 behind the Nishi-No-Maru in Edo Castle.

⁹⁰ *T'ung Chien Kang Mu*: see n. 105, bk. I.

⁹¹ Chuang Tsung: (923–25) he was fond of theatrical entertainments, even taking part in them himself, and eventually lost his throne.

⁹² *Yüan Ch'ü Hsüan*: a collection of representative Yüan-period operas published 1616 by Tsang Chin-shu.

⁹³ record . . . written by Daigaku-no-Kami Nobuatsu: the *Butokutaiseiki* (1686), 30 vols., covered the history of the Tokugawa House from Ieyasu's antecedents to the Ōsaka campaigns.

⁹⁴ *Ch'un Ch'iu*: see n. 108, bk. I.

⁹⁵ A warning to Ienobu that his actions will be criticized by future historians.

⁹⁶ The Taikō (Toyotomi Hideyoshi) tried for a long time to inveigle the Divine Ancestor (Tokugawa Ieyasu) into submission.

⁹⁷ Lao Lai: a philosopher of Ch'u (740–330 B.C.) who, at the age of 72, donned a dancing costume and performed before his parents in order to cheer them, giving no indication that he himself was an old man.

⁹⁸ Nobuatsu's history: see n. 93, bk. II.
father: Tokugawa Hirotada (1526–49).
biography of Uemura: (Dewa-no-Kami Iemasa) vol. 4, pt. II.
Hankampu: see n. 113, bk. I.

⁹⁹ Hayashi Nobuatsu, though a staunch Confucianist, had never been a *samurai*.

¹⁰⁰ Ichijō-In: a branch temple of Kōfukuji belonging to the Hossō sect.

¹⁰¹ mansion at Fushimi: the castle at Fushimi in Yamashiro prov. (Kyōto pref.) built by Toyotomi Hideyoshi in 1594, was destroyed in the Battle of Sekigahara (1600). Ieyasu built a new mansion there (1604), where he lived until he retired to Sumpu in Suruga prov. (Shizuoka pref.) in 1607; he demolished Fushimi in 1623.

¹⁰² Daijō-In: another branch temple of Kōfukuji, also of the Hossō sect.
Yuima Service: at Kōfukuji, on the 10th–16th days of the 10th month of the lunar calendar, at which the Yuima (Vimalakirti) sutra is expounded.

¹⁰³ Midaidokoro: the then Midaidokoro, consort of the 5th Shōgun, Tsunayoshi.

¹⁰⁴ Bugyōsho: the Jisha Bugyōsho.

¹⁰⁵ visited Kyōto: to meet Hideyoshi in 1586 in ratification of a peace after the battles of Komaki and Nagakate in 1584.

¹⁰⁶ *Kugyō Bunin*: a record of the dates of appointment of court nobles to high rank.

¹⁰⁷ the Takeda of Kai: Takeda Shingen and his son Katsuyori; Ieyasu defeated Shingen at Mikata-ga-Hara in Tōtōmi prov. (Shizuoka pref.) in 1572.

¹⁰⁸ own province: Ieyasu had received Tōtōmi as his reward in 1568 when he allied with Takeda Shingen against Imagawa Ujizane and built a castle at Hamamatsu (1570).

¹⁰⁹ Hieizan and Miidera: since 987, a violent quarrel had existed between Enryakuji, seat of the Tendai sect, on Mt. Hiei (see n. 112, bk. II) and Onjōji or Miidera (a temple N. W. of Ōtsu in Ōmi prov. [Shiga pref.]), seat of the Jimon branch of the Tendai sect. The quarrel was over rights of control of priestly punishments and frequently flared up into armed combat.

[110] Ietsuna's consort was a Takatsukasa, and Ienobu's a Konoe, *kuge* families descended from the Fujiwara.

[111] The villagers' livelihood was cutting timber.

[112] national tutelary fane: Enryakuji had been built in 8th c. to protect the imp. palace from noxious influences from the N. E.

polluted: ground dedicated to the protection of the imp. house must be ritually clean.

[113] Five Controllers: (*Go-Shi*) since Nara period (710–84), were officials chosen from the temples and shrines.

[114] yellow robes: *kōe*, usually forbidden to ordinary priests.

[115] Matsui Hyōbu: in the service of the prince abbot.

[116] Shōgo-In, Emman-In, and Jissō-In were 3 imp. temples of the junior branch of the Tendai sect (in Sakyō-ku, Kyōto) attached to Miidera; the heads of these temples served as administrators of Miidera for 3 years at a time.

[117] Jōshin-In: also read Jōjin-In.

[118] Taiseiden: the Yushima Seidō, a hall for the worship of Confucius in the Yushima Kōbunkan, the academy presided over by Hayashi Nobuatsu.

[119] ceremony of worshiping Confucius: biannual ceremony consisting of offering fruit and vegetables.

[120] ancient kings: the so-called Sage Kings of China.

[121] *chêntungpai*: an obeisance with handclapping.

"nine obeisances": 9 modes of bowing detailed in the *Chou Li*, ch. *Ta Chu*, varying according to the position of the head, use of the hands, the genuflections involved, etc.

Chêng Ta-fu: Chêng Hsüan (127–200), a Later Han commentator on the etiquette of the Chou dynasty and on the Confucian classics.

[122] Luchu: the Ryūkyū islands, over which China claimed suzerainty at this time.

[123] An extraordinary privilege even for members of the Rōjū.

[124] disciplining: no historical evidence remains to throw light on the offense.

Zenkōji: of the Tendai Jōdo sect, a branch temple of Kan'eiji, probably founded during the reign of Empress Suiko (593–628); enjoyed protection of the Tokugawa; situated in Nagano.

[125] Seiyō-In Den: Ienobu's father, Tsunashige (1644–78), 3rd s. of Iemitsu, lord of Fuchū Castle in Kai prov. (Yamanashi pref.) with 350,000 *koku*.

[126] Kan'eiji at Ueno: text has Tōeizan ("the Hieizan of the East").

[127] Shiroshoin: hall in *shōgun's* palace used for transaction of matters of internal concern.

[128] When traveling on government business, a seal or certificate entitled an official to requisition a stated number of bearers and horses.

[129] Capital of Ōmi prov. (Shiga pref.).

[130] coming-of-age ceremony: the *gembuku*, see n. 35, bk. I. Nakamikado succeeded to the throne at the age of 10, and at this time he was 11; thus the ceremony was performed early; text has "next year."

[131] Uji: town in Kuze dist. Yamashiro prov. (Kyōto pref.) on Uji River.

[132] on New Year's Day according to the lunar calendar.

[133] Gates forbidden to all below rank of the Rōjū, except those with special permission.

[134] As part of the preparations for the Korean Embassy, in order to demonstrate the prosperous state of Japan's defenses, the warships *Takeda Maru, Asuka Maru, Kokirin Maru,* and *Tenchi Maru* were repaired.

[135] Those entitled to be received in audience were allowed to wear *hoi* costumes; this marks Hakuseki's formal promotion to the rank of *hatamoto*.

[136] I.e., raised to lower 5th rank lower grade and given a title.

[137] lodgings: at Higashi Honganji.

[138] set out from Edo for Ōsaka.

[139] separate documents: *Heiji Kōgi, Ōsetsu Jigi, Shugō Jiryaku, Kokushofukugō Kiji,* etc.

[140] ten years: actually about 8 years; the order withdrawing troops from Korea was issued in 1598, and the first Korean Embassy visited Japan in 1607.

[141] *Sōgyōki:* history of Ieyasu's life from 1542 to 1615 by Matsudaira Shimōsa-no-Kami Tadaaki.

[142] Korean embassies visited Japan in 1624 and 1636 (Kan'ei) and 1682 (Tenna).

[143] Refers to story about the founding of the state of Lu; Hakuseki recounts it in the *Buke Kan'i Shōzokukō.*

[144] inquiries: from Hayashi Nobuatsu.

[145] King (or hegemon) of Japan, a change of title from "Nippon Koku-Shu (master of Japan) Minamoto Iemitsu" to "Nippon Koku-Ō" (king of Japan), had been surreptitiously effected at the desire of the Korean Envoys in 1624; owing to disturbances in the Tsushima clan, it was discovered in 1636, and the shogunal official involved was punished.

[146] In 1631 a quarrel had broken out between Sō Yoshishige, *daimyō* of Tsushima, and his retainer, Yanagawa Suketsugu; because Yanagawa's retainer, Matsuo Tomoyasu, plotted to make Yanagawa a direct retainer of the shogunate, which was hostile to Yoshishige.

[147] subject: i.e., the 1st s. of a prince, indicating "of the upper 1st rank."

[148] Chinese books: first in the *Chou I* (see n. 108, bk. I).

[149] rustic scholars: Amenomori Hōshū (1668–1755) and Matsuura Kashō, pupils of Kinoshita Jun'an, who opposed Hakuseki in this argument.

[150] According to other documents, since the alteration had been made after the envoys had left Seoul, there was considerable resentment at the Korean court.

[151] Tokumatsu, the heir of the 5th Shōgun Tsunayoshi, was at that time (1682) 4 years old.

[152] Tandai: an office under the Kamakura and Ashikaga shogunates in charge of military affairs, policing, and justice in Kyūshū and the 2 islands of Iki and Tsushima.

Korea probably no longer wished that custom: the discontinuance of this custom actually aroused great indignation in Korea, but contrary to their real feelings, they submitted out of fear of Japanese military might.

[153] Togunegi-Fūsu: Tongnae-Pusa, pref. governor of Tongnae, dist. in S. Kōchang pref. 9 km. N. of Pusan. The transcription is given by Hakuseki.

[154] According to the custom of using odd numbers in matters concerning auspicious occasions.

[155] four places: Kyōto, Ōsaka, Sumpu, Edo.

[156] administrators: members of the Rōjū.

[157] councilors: high officials.

[158] *changchangkwan:* Korean officials.

[159] during audience with the *shōgun.*

the Three Houses: the Owari (Nagoya), Kii (Wakayama), and Mito (Hitachi) branches of the Tokugawa House, founded by the 7th, 8th, and 9th s. of Ieyasu, from whom the *shōgun* could be chosen in the event of the failure of the main line.

[160] taboo: the letter from the *shōgun* contained a character in the posthumous name of Chungjong (1506–44), the 11th ruler of the Yi dynasty, an ancestor of the then king of Korea, Sukchong (1675–1720), separated by 7 generations.

[161] The Korean letters contained a character used in Iemitsu's name.

[162] not to return to Korea alive: i.e., to commit suicide in protest.

[163] When Confucius was a minister in the state of Lu, at a meeting with ministers from Ch'in, he obtained the return of Lu territory through his diplomatic prowess.

[164] Ts'ao Mo: a brave general.

Mao Sui: a diplomat.

[165] A quotation from the *I Ching* (see n. 108, bk. I); *Hsi Tz'ŭ Chuan Hsia* (Postscript pt. II).

[166] Among the disciples of Hayashi Nobuatsu.

[167] "two bodies but one mind": in order to teach and succor mankind Buddha manifests himself in various aspects.

[168] San'yō Chōrō: chief abbot of Enkōji, founded in 1601, through Ieyasu's endowment, at Fushimi in Yamashiro prov. (Kyōto pref.) for the education of lay or clergy.

[169] moved: after the destruction of the Hōjō in 1590 moved to Edo Castle.

school: perhaps founded by Ashikaga Yoshikane (?–1199) in Ashikaga dist. later Shimotsuke prov. (Tochigi pref.). It had been very active for about 2 c. before the Keichō era (1596–1615) as an important center of Chinese studies and Confucianism.

[170] Sōroku: in Zen and Shingon sects, an administrator in control of monks.

[171] his family: the first Hayashi, namely Dōshun (1583–1657), served 4 generations of shōguns.

[172] Yamamoto Dōki: A lay-priest, given name Kansuke, a native of Mikawa, expert in military strategy in the employ of Takeda Shingen, killed in the battle of Kawanakajima.

[173] Takeda: given name Harunobu (1521–73); was a great general during the Sengoku period; held Kai prov. (Yamanashi pref.); fought with Uesugi Kenshin for 20 years.

Uesugi: Uesugi Kenshin (1530–78), given name Terutora, held Echigo prov. (Niigata pref.).

[174] natural philosophy: "kakubutsu" appears in the Ta Hsüeh, meaning "the true nature of things."

[175] Teikin Ōrai: see n. 60, bk. I.

[176] Kamakura Shōgun: text has Kamakura Dono, Minamoto Yoritomo (1147–99) and his descendants.

[177] Kamakura Kanryō: text has Kamakura Dono, governor of the E. provs., the first permanent kanryō or kubō being Ashikaga Takauji's s., Motouji; the office became hereditary in his family, and then passed to the Uesugi.

[178] "Congratulatory Banquet": banquet held when the Ashikaga shōgun was appointed daijin or minister.

[179] "Kaimon": gate in the mansion of a daijin; kai or huai became a synonym for daijin in Chou times in China as 3 huai trees were planted in the Chinese imp. palace; huai is a kind of locust tree from the flowers of which a yellow dye was extracted. A kaimon would be appropriate for the Konoe Family.

[180] Taiheiki: see n. 57, bk. I; the reference to yari ("long spear") appears in the ch. on the battle at Miidera, and this is said to be the first appearance of the word in literature.

"long-spear room": appears on the map, claimed to be that of the Kamakura palace, transmitted from ancient times and also on a map said to be of the shōgun's palace at Kyōto; it was probably an armory.

[181] Nijō Palace: constructed by Ieyasu in 1602 in Kyōto as a residence for shogunal visits.

[182] hip-roofed gate: a front gate with a roof-ridge (mune), built only in residences of a shōgun, a retired emp., or a prime minister.

Chinese gabled gate: a Chinese-style gate, having round pillars surmounted by a curved gable, and with ornate doors.

[183] Nanzenji: founded 1291 in Kyōto by Emp. Kameyama; Konji-In, a branch temple, founded end of 16th c., and moved to Fukuchi Machi, Sakyō-ku, Kyōto, in 1619.

Juraku-Dai: famous mansion constructed by Toyotomi Hideyoshi in Kyōto in 1586, largely demolished after his nephew Hidetsugu's death in 1595.

[184] Diary of Ishin Sūden [63] whose posthumous name was Honkō Kokushi. In 46 vols., covers the years 1620–33 and gives details of the shogunates of Hidetada and Iemitsu.

[185] Ōgaki: in Ampachi dist. (Gifu pref.).

[186] Kazuo: a mistake for Kazunobu (1658–1730); was transferred to Tanaka in 1705.

[187] Tanaka Castle: ancient castle E. of the post-station of Fujieda, in Shida dist. (Shizuoka pref.).

[188] Murakami: Iwafuna dist. (Niigata pref.); Matsudaira Terusada moved there in 1710.

[189] Kurokawa: a village in N. Kambara dist. (Niigata pref.).

[190] Ikkō sect: also called Jōdo Shinshū or true Jōdo sect; founded in 1224; especially turbulent against *daimyō* in the 16th c.

[191] father and mother of the people: quotation from the *Ta Hsüeh* (see n. 97, bk. I); commentary of Tsêng, ch. 10.

[192] Tadamoto: s. of Naomoto (5th s. of Yūki Hideyasu, who was the 2nd s. of Ieyasu, ancestor of Matsudaira of Echizen); moved to Murakami in 1649.

[193] three great rivers: Shinano, Akano, Ara rivers in Echigo prov. (Niigata pref.).

[194] eight divisions: each division was under the control of an *ōjōya* attached to the fief of Murakami; in following paragraph text has ten *ōjōya*.

[195] Sakaimura: in Echigo prov. (Niigata pref.).

[196] 29th January: a mistake for 18 Jan. 1712.

Shinobazu Pond: now in S. W. of Ueno Park, Tōkyō.

[197] No longer extant.

[198] Shirogane-chō: present Nihonbashi Muromachi and Nihonbashi Hon-chō, Chūō-ku, Tōkyō.

[199] Dutchmen: merchants from the trading post at Deshima in Kyūshū paid a ceremonial visit to Edo in the spring of each year. In 1712 these were Cornelis Lardijn, Paulus Simons, Willem Wagemans, and Joan Heusler.

countries of the southwest: Europe and S. E. Asia; for his works on world geography, see n. 201, bk. II.

[200] Actually met them on 2 and 10 April 1712 only.

[201] In *Seiyō Kibun*, *Sairan Igen*, *Oranda Kō* and *Oranda Kiji*.

[202] Gate and fire guard at Edo castle, guard at Ōsaka and Sumpu castles, handling of communications with the court and temples, building and engineering works, and disbursement of expenses for the entertainment of foreign envoys.

[203] military service: a system of requisitioning soldiers and horses in numbers proportionate to the income of a fief.

[204] service was first fixed: in 1616, military service was fixed for those below 10,000 *koku*.

[205] revised: in 1633, military service was fixed for those above 10,000 *koku*.

thereafter: another revision was carried out in 1649.

[206] "First . . . them": a quotation from the *Analects* (see n. 36, bk. II), *Tzŭ Lu* 13, Confucius replying to Jan Yu.

"When . . . understand": transmitted as the words of Kuan Chung (of the "Spring and Autumn" period), when assisting Duke Huan of Ch'i, in vol. on *Mumin* (Shepherd the People).

[207] returned from Kyōto: after attending coronation and coming-of-age ceremony of Emp. Nakamikado in 1710–11.

Tōkaidō: road along the coast.

[208] highways: set up in 1659, consisting of *ōmetsuke* and *kanjō bugyō*, and having charge of maintenance of the 5 highways: the Tōkaidō, Nakasendō, Kōshūkaidō, Nikkōkaidō, and Ōshūkaidō.

[209] auxiliaries: additional bearers were requisitioned from villages adjacent to post-stations.

[210] Arai Ferry: a short ferry journey from Maisaka to Arai on Lake Hamana (Hamanako) in Tōtōmi prov. (Shizuoka pref.); as this was close to the Hakone Barrier, there was strict surveillance.

Nakasendō: road over the mountains joining the Tōkaidō at Kusatsu.

[211] inn inspectors: supervised provision of bearers and horses at the post-stations.

[212] along the N. shore of Lake Hamana.

[213] tax: imposed in 1705.

Daibutsuden: hall, rebuilt by Tsunayoshi, housing the Daibutsu, a large statue of Buddha, nearly 16 m. high, cast in 746.

Tōdaiji: erected in Nara 728 as headquarters of the Kegon sect. eruption: 1704.

[214] No longer extant.

[215] ceremonies: an annual festival on 4m 17d at Nikkōzan, dedicated to Ieyasu.

[216] Equivalent to "too many cooks spoil the broth"; conflicting advice proffered by passers-by will hamper proceedings.

[217] another document: not extant.

[218] prohibited: by a decree of 29 July 1709.

[219] Shōgun's mother: text has Ichi no Onkata, Keishō-In of the Honjō Family.

[220] consort: Jōkō-In, of the Takatsukasa Family.

[221] children's mothers: his concubines.

[222] Amenomori Tōgorō Toshiyoshi: see n. 149, bk. II.

[223] Hsüan Tsung: reigned as Ming Huang (712–56); nephew of the empress Wu. *fêngliuchên*: the emp. at the head of his nobles, and his consort at the head of 100-odd palace ladies, engaged in a playful contest with flowering branches, the vanquished being forced to drink as a fine.

[224] Yao and Shun: two ancient rulers during the golden age of China, said to have reigned 2357–255 B.C. and 2255–205 B.C. respectively.

[225] A reference to a passage in the *Shih Chi*, Biography of Chou Yang, which says that even though 2 men may have been friends from their youth, if they do not understand each other's hearts, they are nothing more than new acquaintances. The *Shih Chi* (Historical Memoirs) is a history of China from legendary times to early Han by Ssŭ-ma Ch'ien (145–87 B.C.).

[226] Hōin Yōboku: Kano Tsunenobu (1636–1713), painter.

[227] Memorial service on the 33rd anniversary of Ietsuna's death.

[228] Torii Tadahide: became member of Wakadoshiyori in 1711.

[229] Norisato: also read Norimura.

[230] whatever his hereditary retainers said: Hakuseki shows sympathy for a *rōnin*, because he himself had had experience as one.

[231] Matsudaira Iki-no-Kami: Matsudaira Yoshinori became *goshoimbangashira* in 1710.

[232] Ta Yü: founder of the Hsia dynasty (2205–1765 B.C.), was famous for control of the waters of the Yellow River.

Pê I: a minister of Emp. Shun.

[233] Ta-szŭ-k'ung: chief of the bureau in charge of civil affairs.

[234] board of audit: Kanjō Gimmi Yaku.

[235] 6th August: a mistake for 5 Oct.

[236] Shigehide: became *kanjō bugyō* in 1696.

[237] sandalwood: more properly aloeswood or "lign aloes."

[238] a sandalwood pavilion: the Ch'ên-hsiang T'ing in the time of Ching Tsung (825–27).

rebellion: of An Lu-shan in 755 during the reign of Hsüan Tsung.

[239] old standard: Keichō standard, 862 parts of gold to 132 parts of silver; the gold coin was the *koban* weighing 4 *momme* 8 *fun*.

increase in the quantity of silver: subsequent to 1695, the standard fell to 564 parts of gold to 432 parts of silver, the weight remaining the same.

[240] Reminting had been carried out in the Genroku era: in "Genrokugin" (1695–1706) the proportion had become 646 parts of silver to 352.6 parts of copper with 1.4 parts of gold; in "Hōeigin" (1706–10) the silver fell to 507 parts, other 491.8 (incl. 1.2 of gold).

[241] Nagasaki Hanzaemon: Nagasaki Motonaka.

[242] reminted the silver: coins known as "Futatsuhōjigin" or "Eijigin" minted in 1710, silver 416 parts, other 595.2 (incl. 0.8 of gold).

[243] "Kenjikin": 1710 and 1714, gold 834 parts, silver 165.5 parts.

[244] debased silver: coins known as "Mitsuhōjigin," minted in 1710 and 1711, silver 326.5 parts, other 672.7 parts (incl. 0.8 of gold).

[245] national emergency: Hakuseki writing of 1710, concerned at rumors of the first

minting of "Mitsuhōjigin," referring to the alarming report of the state of the treasury.
²⁴⁶ new rewards: an increase of 500 *koku* in 1710.
²⁴⁷ palace: see n. 31, bk. II.
²⁴⁸ Silver Mint: established 1598 in Fushimi, moved to Edo 1612.
²⁴⁹ minted in 1711; 204 parts of silver to 795.8 parts of other metals (incl. 0.2 of gold).
²⁵⁰ 30-odd years: actually 22 years, 1688–1710 since Hakuseki is writing of 1710.
²⁵¹ in ancient times . . . every three years: a quotation from the *Shu Ching*; see n. 103, bk. I, *Shun Tien* (Book of Shun).
²⁵² Shiga pref.
²⁵³ Funatsu: perhaps pres. Funatsu in Kita-Muro dist., Mie pref.
Shinohara: in Hamana dist. in Shizuoka pref.
²⁵⁴ Nihommatsu: pres. Nihommatsu city in Fukushima pref.
Niwa Tadashige: afterward Hidenobu, warden of Nihommatsu Castle.
²⁵⁵ silver recoined: the "Yotsuhōjigin," 1711; see n. 249, bk. II.
²⁵⁶ what Shun did: ref. to *Ch'un Ch'iu Tso Chuan* Bk. 6 Duke Wên, 18th year, winter: when he became emp., Shun utilized the services of 16 good ministers and got rid of 4 bad ones; Hakuseki had got rid of one bad minister.
²⁵⁷ *Twenty-one Histories*: a collection of histories from ancient times to the Yüan dynasty.
²⁵⁸ "That which . . . no end": a quotation from the *Yōshihōgen*.
²⁵⁹ the Three Houses: of Owari, Kii, and Hitotsubashi from which the heir could be chosen.
²⁶⁰ Owari Dono: Tokugawa Yoshimichi, at that time 24.
²⁶¹ my several sons: Iechiyo, Daigorō, Nabematsu (later Ietsugu), Torakichi; only Nabematsu survived at this time.
²⁶² Refers to Tadanaga's death; ill feeling arose between Tadanaga and Iemitsu, who obliged him to commit suicide.
²⁶³ The Ōnin war (1467–77) arose because of a quarrel between Shōgun Ashikaga Yoshimasa and his younger brother Imadegawa Yoshimi.
²⁶⁴ what was done: Ieyasu succeeded his father Hirotada at the age of 8.
²⁶⁵ what was to be done after his death: that Yoshimune (Kii Dono) was to succeed if his own son died.
²⁶⁶ Ietsugu d. 1716.
²⁶⁷ discussed: actually to wait for public opinion to become clear, since only if the people acquiesced in the restoration of the coinage to its former standard could the undertaking be successful.
²⁶⁸ Aoyama Akiyuki: later Yasunari (1658–1732), since 1705 a member of the *gosobashū*.
²⁶⁹ Mizuno: Mizuno Shinhachi in the *okonando*.
²⁷⁰ quotation from the *Analects* (see n. 36, bk. II), Li Jên, Bk. 4. ch. 7.
²⁷¹ pamphlets: chiefly *Honchō Hōka Tsūyō Jiryaku*.
²⁷² gold . . . silver: of old gold 20,000 *ryō*, old silver 400,000 *kamme*.
²⁷³ official statements: i.e., on the licensed trade, and therefore not including the illicit trade.
²⁷⁴ Five Cereals: rice, wheat, millet (*awa*), millet (*kibi*), beans.
²⁷⁵ Five Metals: gold, silver, copper, iron, tin.
²⁷⁶ quotation from the *Shih Ching*, see n. 99, bk. I.
²⁷⁷ countries of the south and west, Korea, and the Luchus: Holland, Siam; Korean trade was with Tsushima; Luchuan trade was with the Satsuma clan.
²⁷⁸ Cotton was introduced in the late Nara or early Heian period and became a substantial crop in the Tokugawa period; tobacco was introduced from Portugal in the late Sengoku period, and spread so rapidly that its production was severely restricted under the Tokugawa shogunate.
²⁷⁹ search: Emp. Suinin dispatched Tajima Mori to China in A.D. 61 to seek "the fruit of perpetual scent," but when he returned after 10 years, Suinin was already dead.
²⁸⁰ Ichijō-In-no-Miya: Emp. Reigen's s., Sonshō Hōshinnō.

scarlet robes: granted only by imp. decree.
281 head: Shinkan Daisōjō.
282 his will: in 4 parts: (1) to *daimyō*; (2) to Bakufu officials; (3) to the Rōjū; (4) concerning the reminting of the currency.
283 Zōjōji: in accordance with Ienobu's will; temple in Shiba, Tōkyō, established 1393, of the Jōdo sect, chosen by Ieyasu to contain the funeral tablets of his family.
284 mourning period: 49 days.
285 populace grieving: in the *Shu Ching* (see n. 103, bk. I), Canon of Shun, ch. 4., para. 13.
286 critical scribblings: lampoons.
287 had happened: in 1673–80 when Shōgun Ietsuna was young.
288 recorded in *Hakuseki Nikki* as 3 Oct. 1708.

BOOK III

1 earlier: when Ienobu discussed with him the question of the succession.
2 far-reaching plans: the restoration of the currency and the regulation of trade at Nagasaki.
3 history of the Divine Ancestor: the *Sosō(go)jitsuroku* was planned because of dissatisfaction with Hayashi Nobuatsu's history of the Tokugawa family, the *Butokutaiseiki*, but never written.
4 Imp. messengers to Tōshōgū at Nikkō and Ise Jingū, ceremonies held annually in the 4th and 3rd months, respectively.
5 *I Li*: one of the 3 classics on rites (see n. 114, bk. I) in ch. on mourning. A distinction is made in the degree of mourning for children who die between the ages of 16 and 19, 12 and 15, 8 and 11, under 7, and under 3 months; for children under 7 it is stated that no mourning is observed.
6 *Bukukiryō*: other readings are *Fukkirei*, *Bukkiryō*; compiled on Tsunayoshi's order, under the direction of Hotta Masanaka, by Hayashi Nobuatsu and others, completed 1684, revised and enlarged 1686, 1688, 1691, promulgated 1693.
7 sages of old: the Duke of Chou and Confucius who wished to stabilize the 5 human relationships, i.e. between lord and retainer, father and son, husband and wife, elder and younger brothers, and between friends.
8 regulations of Japan: the Yōrō Codes, i.e. the Taihō Ritsuryō of 701 revised and enlarged in 718, supplemented by three great collections of ordinances (*Kyakushiki*) in 811, 868, and 907.
9 The Genroku Regulations (1693) state: for children under 7 years mourning is not worn; the parents keep the house for 3 days; neither is mourning worn by children under 7 years.
10 regulations of Japan: in the *Sōsōryō*: "Mourning is observed for lord, parents, husband, master, for one year."
11 many children: four sons and one daughter.
12 'heart mourning': in the *I Li*: "Confucius died . . . and all his disciples put on mourning for 3 years; within those 3 years they finished their heart mourning and left . . . but only one disciple built a house by the grave."
13 Ying Tsung, Shih Tsung: 5th emp. of Sung (1064–67) and 11th emp. of Ming (1522–66).
14 One of the basic ideas of Neo-Confucianism; the word "divine" refers to the principle of reason in the universe.
15 *I Li*: it is doubtful whether the Duke of Chou composed *I Li* (see n. 114, bk. I); he assisted Emp. Wu's successor, Ch'êng (1115 B.C.), to establish ceremonial; *I Li* sets out the forms for coming of age, marriage, funerals, festivals, audience at court, visits of courtesy, etc.

Chia Li: the short title of *Wên Kung Chia Li* ("Household Rites of Duke Wên") in 12 vols. by Chu Tzŭ (Chu Hsi).

regulations of the Ming Court: see n. 17, bk. III.

[16] *Shintō Bukukiryō*:appears as ch. 11 in *Shintō Shoseki Mokuroku* by Yoshida Kanehiro, included in his *Jingi Teiyō*, and sets forth the length of mourning for relatives, etc.

Yoshida-Ke Bukukiryō: sets forth the mourning rites in the Yoshida House.

Kinri Bukukiryō: sets forth the mourning rites in the Imp. Court.

[17] *Hui Tien*: a complete description of the Ming court composed by Imp. Decree, in 3 parts, *Chêng Tê Hui Tien* (180 vols.) pub. 1511, *Chia Ching Hsü Hsiu Hui Tien* (53 vols.) not pub., and *Wan Li Chung Hsiu Hui Tien* (228 vols.) pub. 1587.

Chi Li: short for *Ta Ming Chi Li* (53 chs.) consisting of a collection of regulations of etiquette compiled by decree of Emp. T'ai Tsu by Hsü K'uei in 1370 plus additions and corrections in 1530.

[18] *Sōsōryō*: 17 articles dealing with matters ranging from imp. tombs and robes to regulations relating to mourning.

[19] *Kachōyojō*: in 30 vols. by Ichijō Kanera, 1472; in one passage occurs the following: "Touching mourning for parents by children of 7 and under, nothing appears anywhere in the *Ritsuryō Kyakushiki* (see n. 8, bk. III) about their wearing mourning. The result is that at the present time, it has been decided that children under 7 years do not have to wear mourning or keep within doors at all."

[20] documents: still extant; one is entitled *Kokusō Jigon*.

Kokusō Seigi: written 1713, by Muro Kyūsō in reply to Hayashi Nobuatsu's assertions regarding mourning.

[21] *Shu Tu Tsa Ch'ao*: compiled by Lu Shên of the Ming dynasty.

Pi Chi: short for *Pao Yen T'ang Pi Chi*, in 450 chs. revised and pub. by Ch'ên Chi-ju, an unexampled bibliophile of the Ming dynasty.

Ch'ien Pai Nien Yen: in 12 vols. compiled by Chang Sui of Ming about 1620, a study of matters concerning the classics and history; Nobuatsu referred to a passage in vol. 12 of this work in particular.

[22] Ch'i-wang Fang: placed on the throne in 239; in 240 the era name was changed to Chêng-Shih (Shōji); Ch'i was deposed in 254.

Kao-kuei-hsiang-kung: placed on the throne after Ch'i Wang-fang with the new era name of Chêng-yüan (Shōgen) in 254, this being changed again in 256.

Wei: a state which existed 220–65.

Wu Ling: successful contender for the throne; the era name was changed to T'ien-chêng (Tenshō) in 551, but, his reign lasting only one year, the era name was again changed in 552.

Liang: a state set up in 502.

Yang: 9th emp. of Chin, ascended the throne in 1224, the era name being changed to Chêng-ta (Shōdai); overthrown in 1234.

Chin: a state established early 12th c.

Shun: of Yüan, overthrown in 1368, the 28th year of Chih-chêng (Shishō).

Yüan: a dynasty established by Kublai (1260–95).

[23] Chêng-t'ung: Ying Tsung ascended the Ming throne in 1436, era name Chêng-t'ung (Shōtō), at the age of 8, affairs being in the hands of the eunuch Wang Chên. The Mongols were very active at this time, and Wang Chên was defeated in 1449 at Tu-mu-pao and the Emp. held captive for a year.

Chêng-tê: (Shōtoku) in 1506 Wu Tsung came to the throne at the age of 15 completely under the domination of eunuchs; his misrule led to many palace intrigues and popular uprisings; d. in 1521 without an heir.

[24] King Hui of Liang neglected administration and Mencius condemned him, holding him responsible for the year's harvest being poor.

[25] The 8 decades of a man's life from 1–10 years to 70–80 years.

[26] Quotation from the *Li Chi* (see n. 99, bk. I); the names referred to are the *yōmyō* (childhood name) and at *gembuku* (see n. 35, bk. I) his *jitsumyō* (real name); in China at 50 a man was addressed by names indicating his order of seniority among his brothers.

²⁷ *Ch'un Ch'iu:* see n. 108, bk. I.

the 'Four Beginnings': New Year's Day—the beginning of the year, the month, the day, and the hour; explained in the *Shih Chi (The Historical Records)*, one of the dynastic histories of China.

²⁸ Quotations from the *Chung Yung (Doctrine of the Mean)* ch. 29, and from the *Analects*, (see n. 36, bk. II), Sayings of Yao (no. 20). The *Doctrine of the Mean* is a work in 49 chs. attributed to K'ung Chi, grands. of Confucius; it contains a mystical development of the Sage's dicta.

²⁹ Sagami-no-Kami Tokimasa: Hōjō Tokimasa (1138–1215), first *shikken*, father-in-law of Minamoto Yoritomo.

³⁰ The 15th and last Ashikaga Shōgun (1568–73), set up by Oda Nobunaga; relations became strained, and Nobunaga deposed his protégé who sought asylum with Mōri Terumoto (1553–1625) in Aki (Hiroshima pref.).

³¹ Tōji-In Den: Ashikaga Takauji (1305–58), overthrew the Hōjō, seized power 1338.

³² the Italian: Hakuseki interrogated the Sicilian priest Sidotti in 1709 and left a detailed account in *Seiyō Kibun.*

the Dutch: merchants from Deshima who made annual courtesy visits to Edo.

³³ turmoil: the War of the Spanish Succession.

³⁴ Chang Yü-hsien: orig. an official in Po Lo county; in 942 established himself on the throne but was slain in 943.

Chung-t'ien-ta-kuo-wang: Great King of the Kingdom of Middle Heaven.

³⁵ Fang La: according to Sung chronology, usurped the throne from 1120–21 but was soon taken prisoner.

³⁶ T'ai Tsung: the 3rd Ming emp. Ch'êng Tsu, gained the throne by force of arms and reigned 1402–24, actually 23 years; he changed the era name in 1403.

³⁷ Kuang-Wu: Liu Hsiu, ruled 25–57 as Emp. Kuang-Wu; struggled against the usurper Wang Mang who had seized the throne in A.D. 9, and established the Later (or Eastern) Han dynasty.

³⁸ Go-Daigo: (1318–38) used Gen'ō (1319–20) at his inauguration; resolving to rid himself of the Hōjō Shikken, he raised armies from the court nobility and militant Buddhist monks but was defeated and exiled.

³⁹ Murakami: rulcd 947–67, assuming the government instead of appointing a *kampaku* thus diminishing the power of the Fujiwara; Tenryaku lasted from 947 to 956.

Wên Tsung: of the Yüan dynasty, ascended the throne in 1329; the era name was changed in 1330. Wên Tsung d. in 1332.

⁴⁰ This theory of era name change is connected with the sexagenary cycle in which the years are distinguished by attaching to each a combination of 2 signs selected in consecutive order, one from the *Jikkan*, or 10 Calendar Signs, and one from the *Jūnishi*, or 12 Zodiac Signs. According to the *Iwei* (expounding a prophetic view of history), which appeared at the end of the Former Han, the first year of an epoch (21 cycles of 60 years = 1260 years) bearing the signs Kanoto-tori is a year when "revolutions" are likely; while in the first year of every 60-year cycle, Kinoe-ne, there are liable to be "reformations"; "multiple disaster years" are, according to the Yin-Yang theory, marked by a conjunction of 3 of the 8 guardian gods. The 8 guardian gods were supposed by ancient astrologers to inhabit and control certain points of the compass, and hence to be in charge of the orientation of good and bad luck.

⁴¹ Era name actually changed 22 May 1199.

⁴² 23rd February 1218: actually Sanetomo was assassinated 13 Feb. 1219.

Sanetomo: (1192–1219), 2nd s. of Minamoto Yoritomo, 3rd Kamakura Shōgun.

10th May (1218): era name actually changed 27 May 1219.

⁴³ Yoshikatsu: Hōkyō-In was Yoshiakira (1330–67), the 2nd Ashikaga Shōgun; Yoshikatsu, 7th Ashikaga Shōgun, was Jishō-In (1433–43).

16th March: era name was actually changed 7 March 1368.

⁴⁴ Yoshihisa: 9th Ashikaga Shōgun (1465–89) d. of illness in the camp.

15th September: era name actually changed 16 Sept. 1489.

⁴⁵ 27th January: actually Yoshimochi d. 3 Feb. 1428.

Yoshimochi: 4th Ashikaga Shōgun (1394–1423).

[46] 20th February: actually era name changed 10 June 1428.

[47] Shōkō: actually Emp. Go-Hanazono, who ascended the throne 7 Sept. 1428; Shōkō ascended the throne 5 Oct. 1412 and d. 30 Aug. 1428.

[48] 3rd February: actually Yoshimitsu d. 31 May 1408.

7th March: actually Yoshikazu, 5th Ashikaga Shōgun, d. 17 March 1425.

[49] "revolution" year: actually a "reformation" year, since it was the year Kinoe-ne according to the sexagenary cycle.

[50] Yoshinori: 6th Ashikaga Shōgun (1394–1441), slain at a feast.

[51] father: Hayashi Shunsai (also called Shunkatsu, and Gahō) (1618–80); Nobuatsu was Shunsai's 2nd s. and Shunsai was Razan's 3rd s.

[52] in ancient times: in the *Analects* (see n. 36, bk. II) Yang Huo, Bk. 17 ch. 21: Tsai Wo asked Confucius if 3 years' mourning for parents were not too long: Confucius replied that if 3 years' mourning by eminent people resulted in the neglect of public affairs, one year was sufficient, but he later explained why 3 years' mourning had been decreed.

[53] a man: called Ihei, 39 years old; his wife was Mune, his brother-in-law Shirobei, his father-in-law Jingobei.

Matsushiro-no-Shō: a part of pres. Matsushiromachi in Hanishina dist. (Nagano pref.)

[54] Kawagoe-no-Shō: a part of pres. Kawagoe city in central Saitama pref.

[55] three days passed: text 13 Sept. (the 1st day of the new month).

[56] *I Li*: see n. 114, bk. I.

[57] Convicted criminals were assigned from prison to private owners.

[58] in the *Tso Chuan* (see n. 109, bk. I), Duke Huan 15th year, para. 4.

Chêng: a feudal state (in pres. Honan) of the 7th c. B.C.

the daughter asked: she secretly informed her father of her husband's plot to kill him on orders from the lord of Chêng, hence the father killed his daughter's husband.

[59] *Analects*: (see n. 36, bk. II) in *Tzŭ Lu*, Bk. 13. ch. 18 para. 2.

[60] *Lü Shu*: codes of the Sui and T'ang dynasties.

[61] Japanese law: the Yōrō *Ritsuryō*. See n. 8, bk. III.

commentary: a note to the *Tōjōritsu*, a law of the Tokugawa period.

[62] judges: the magistrates of the Hyōjōsho..

[63] regulations: of the ancient Chinese rulers as codified in the *I Li*, (see n. 114, bk. I).

deep mourning: orig. a garment made of coarse linen of which the bottom edge was left unhemmed.

[64] As stated in the *Analects*; the words used are *kei* (general principles or unchangeable norms), and *ken* (temporary expedients or emergency measures).

[65] Li Ts'ui, son of Li Huai-kuang; learning of Huai-kuang's intention to revolt against his lord, Tê Tsung (779–805), Ts'ui informed Tê Tsung, who put Huai-kuang to death, whereupon Ts'ui committed suicide; Shih Yen-fên, a barbarian from beyond China's western borders, became the adopted s. of Li Huai-kuang; Yen-fên sent a guest, Kao Ch'êng-i, to warn Tê Tsung, whereupon Yen-fên was put to death by Huai-kuang.

[66] Three women who refused to obey their fathers when ordered to betray their husbands: dtr. of Wang Mang, the usurper who placed Emp. P'ing of Han on the throne at the age of 8 in A.D. 1; dtr. of Ts'ao Ts'ao, founder of the Wei dynasty (220–65), consort of the last emp. of the Later Han; perhaps consort of Emp. Hsüan (578–80) of N. Chou dynasty (557–89), for which N. Ch'i is a mistake; the fourth example unidentified.

[67] recorded in the *Tso Chuan*, under date of the 4th year of Duke Yin (see n. 109, bk. I).

[68] from the *Analects* (see n. 36, bk. II) Tzŭ Han, Bk. 9, ch. 27, meaning the widow may lose her chastity under difficult conditions.

[69] mourning period: of 49 days, expired 2 Jan. 1713.

⁷⁰ coming-of-age ceremony: see n. 35, bk. I.

⁷¹ See n. 53, bk. I.

⁷² *San Ts'ai T'u Hui*: composed by Wang Ch'i of Ming in 106 vols. dealing with astronomy, geography, plants, mechanisms, etc.

Nung Chêng Ch'üan Shu: composed by Hsü Kuang-ch'i (1562–1633) of Ming in 60 vols. on agriculture.

Ku Yin P'u: a catalogue of ancient books and other seals.

⁷³ Chūjō Naomori: Ii Naomori, at this time Sachūjō, of Hikone, on the E. shore of Lake Biwa (Shiga pref.).

Chūjō Masakata: Matsudaira (Hoshina) Masakata, at this time Gonchūjō, of Aizu (part of pres. Fukushima pref.).

arranging the hair: the hair was bound in a queue.

⁷⁴ Matsudaira Kiyotake (Ienobu's younger br.), Matsudaira Kiyotsura (Kiyotake's s.), and Hosoi Yasuaki, and Kubota Tadahide (in the Konando).

⁷⁵ a river running through pres. N. Nara and central Ōsaka prefs.

⁷⁶ Settsu Province: occupied parts of Hyōgo and Ōsaka prefs.

Yamato Province: Nara pref.

Kawachi Province: part of Ōsaka pref.

⁷⁷ Tatsuta Shrine: In Tachino, pres. Misato village, Ikoma dist., Nara pref.

Tachino: also read Tatsuno, but the *Dai Nihon Chimei Jisho* (Fusambō) supports given reading. There is a Heguri village in Ikoma.

⁷⁸ Kyōto: the Kyōto Shoshidai.

⁷⁹ Kawachi-no-Kami Tadamine: mistake for Inoue Kawachi-no-Kami Masamine.

⁸⁰ Masamine: name given correctly here; see previous note.

⁸¹ 153: a mistake for 503.

⁸² Masatō: Inoue Masatō.

his own father: Masatoshi.

⁸³ *Ta Hsüeh*: (see n. 97, bk. I.) ch. 10, para. 14, Declaration of Duke of Ch'in.

⁸⁴ *Hakuseki Kengi*, nos. 1, 2, 3.

⁸⁵ Appears in *Ta Hsüeh* (see n. 97, bk. I) ch. 9, para. 4 of the Commentary of Tsêng.

⁸⁶ Quotation from *Chung Yung* (see n. 28, bk. III), ch. 19, para 2.

⁸⁷ proposals: the *Hakuseki Kengi* nos. 4, 5, and 8.

⁸⁸ old standard: pre-Genroku. See n. 239, bk. II.

⁸⁹ three qualities of gold coins: "Keichōkin," "Genrokukin," "Kenjikin." (see ns. 239, 243, bk. II).

six qualities of silver coins: "Keichōgin," "Genrokugin," "Hōeigin," "Futatsuhōjigin," "Mitsuhōjigin," "Yotsuhōjigin." See ns. 239, 240, 242, 244, 255, bk. II.

⁹⁰ Sakai: S. of Ōsaka, pres. Ōsaka pref., port for Chinese trade in the Muromachi period.

⁹¹ trading under the name Kameya, descended from Minamoto Yorisue, from Akai village, Hikami dist., Tamba prov. (Hyōgo pref.).

⁹² I.e., expelled from his residence and not permitted to return; banishment, a more serious punishment than expulsion, involved sending the convicted to designated islands.

⁹³ the Code: the Yōrō *Ritsuryō*. See n. 8, bk. III.

⁹⁴ Nishi-no-Miya: (near pres. Nishinomiya city) in Muko dist., Settsu prov. (Hyōgo pref.).

⁹⁵ Naishidokoro: Imp. Sanctuary, the repository of the sacred mirror in the imp. palace, called the Ummyōden (pres. Kashidokoro).

⁹⁶ Daisōjō Kōken, appointed 1707; tutelary temple of the reigning emp. charged with offering prayers for the emp.'s well-being.

⁹⁷ temple of the Shingon sect in Uji dist., Yamashiro prov. (Kyōto pref.). With Kongō-In, Rishō-In, Hōon-In, and Muryōju-In became known as the Five Monzeki, temples administered by an imp. prince; their abbots took turns administering Daigoji, but Sambō-In eventually acquired the greatest prestige.

⁹⁸ Tōji: main temple of the Tōji branch of the Kōgi denomination of the Shingon sect, founded by Kōbō Daishi.

⁹⁹ Tendai sect: introduced from China by Dengyō Daishi.

¹⁰⁰ *monzeki*: title by extension given to prince-administrators.

¹⁰¹ Mansai: s. of Imakōji Morofuyu of the Nijō; adopted s. of Ashikaga Yoshimitsu.

¹⁰² regulations issued during the Keichō era: the *Daigoji Shohatto* 16 Sept. 1609 and the regulations sent to Sambō-In on 8 July 1613.

¹⁰³ *inge*: the retreat of an abbot (*monshu*), hence an abbot.

¹⁰⁴ Dainichi Nyorai: one of the deities in the Buddhist trinity.

the 'four blessings': a Buddhist expression, conferred on all creatures; that of heaven and earth (or the Three Treasures), of the Monarch, of one's parents, and of the people at large; the Three Treasures are the Buddha, the Law, the Priesthood.

¹⁰⁵ Shōbō: (832–909) famous priest of the Shingon sect, posthumous title Rigen Daishi.

¹⁰⁶ September: text has 8m; according to the *Tokugawa Jikki* actually the end of 7m (early part of Sept.).

¹⁰⁷ These had come for the 3rd (actually 2nd) anniversary of Ienobu's death.

¹⁰⁸ Tōfukuji: the headquarters of a subdivision of the Rinzai denomination of the Zen sect.

¹⁰⁹ Nanzenji: chief temple of a subdivision of the Rinzai denomination of the Zen sect founded by Retired Emp. Kameyama in the Zenrinji Den, a detached palace, in 1291.

¹¹⁰ many children: Ieyasu had 11 sons and 4 daughters.

only legal wife: this is not true. In 1558 Ieyasu married the daughter of Sekiguchi Chikanaga, vassal of the Imagawa with whom he was a hostage. She bore his eldest son Nobuyasu (1559) who with his mother was accused (in 1579) of treason against Ieyasu's overlord Nobunaga. Nobuyasu was sentenced to commit suicide. His mother was put to death by one of Ieyasu's retainers.

¹¹¹ Eastern and Western factions: i.e., Tokugawa Ieyasu, who at this time was lord of the 5 provinces of Mikawa, Tōtōmi, Suruga, Kai, and Shinano (in the Kantō or E. region) and Toyotomi Hideyoshi, whose headquarters were in Ōsaka (in the Kansai or W. region).

¹¹² 26th generation of the Luchu dynasty, Shōkei.

¹¹³ King Shōeki: 25th generation of the Luchu dynasty, the former king.

¹¹⁴ 'Taikun': great lord.

'Sonfujin': respected consort.

'Daichō': meaning "the *shōgun* hears."

¹¹⁵ "Ue": meaning "on high."

¹¹⁶ Three Lords: the Dajōdaijin, the Sadaijin, and the Udaijin.

imperial princes: Shinnō.

¹¹⁷ 'Uesama': formerly a title of respect for the emp. but in the Muromachi and Edo periods used of the *shōgun*.

'Kubōsama': orig. a term of respect for the Imp. Court, but in the Kamakura and Muromachi periods applied to the Bakufu. From the time of the 3rd Shōgun Ashikaga Yoshimitsu, applied to the *shōgun*.

¹¹⁸ 'Gekkei': moon lords, officials of the 3rd rank and above. The Imp. Court was equated to heaven, the emp. to the sun, and hence the nobles to the moon.

'Unkaku': cloud dwellers, nobles of the 5th and 6th rank. The palace was compared to regions above the clouds.

¹¹⁹ Ten'ei-In, Gekkō-In: Buddhist names upon taking the tonsure at Ienobu's death.

¹²⁰ The Confucian view of the state current in the Tokugawa period respectfully placed the emp. above the *shōgun*, but by regarding the *shōgun* as the "hegemon," provided the theoretical basis for his power.

¹²¹ princess: text has "kisaki"; in ancient times the 2nd consort of the Japanese emp.; after the Taihō Code, a wife of lower rank.

¹²² Ankokuden: small temple sacred to the spirit of Ieyasu behind the Zōjōji, temple of Jōdo sect in Shiba (pres. Tōkyō).

¹²³ statue: according to the *Go Bettō Anryūin Gyoki*, the origin of the statue of Ieyasu

in the Ankokuden was as follows: After the New Year's ceremonies in 1601 were concluded, Ieyasu said: "This is the same year (in the sexagenary cycle) as the year of my birth, and therefore I should observe certain taboos but it is very difficult for an old man to observe taboos," and therefore he ordered a wooden image of himself to be sculpted as a substitute. Depicted as wearing court costume, he had the color of his skin, the wrinkles in his face, the folds of his costume, and his exact body measurements minutely copied, and himself plucked out hairs to be inserted in the image's temples. He kept it by his side for 2 or 3 years and had clippings from his hair and nails placed in its hollow inside.

[124] Taikō-In: Nitta Yoshishige, grands. of Yoshiie, and ancestor of the Nitta House.
-In, Daikoji: posthumous titles conferred on people of high rank.

[125] Because the divine spirit was transported to another location; Ieyasu's remains were removed from Kunōzan to Nikkō in 1617.
temple at Nikkō: text has Nikkōzan.

[126] Izumi Nyūdō: Tokugawa Nobumitsu (1390–1465), ancestor of Ieyasu in the 6th generation.

[127] Honkō Kokushi Nikki: in 46 vols.; diary of the priest Sūden of Konji-In; Honkō Kokushi, title of respect granted to Sūden.
offertory money: for the purchase of incense to offer to the spirit of the departed.
Retired Emp. Go-Yōzei, 107th emp. (1587–1611).

[128] Daijuji: a temple of the Chinzei branch of the Jōdo sect in Nukada dist., Aichi pref.; founded by Matsudaira Izumi-no-Kami Nobumitsu, though according to one opinion by his s., Chikatada, in 1475.

[129] Tōshō-Daigongen: "Eastern-luminary-great-puissant-manifestation"; this title suggests a combined Shintō and Buddhist deity.

[130] Mikawa Go-fudoki: in 45 vols. attributed to Hiraiwa Chikayoshi but actually the work of Hosoi Ujinori. Treats of the ancestry of the Tokugawa House, and the times of Ieyasu and his retainers, up to the Sekigahara campaign.
Hiraiwa Kazue-no-Kami Chikayoshi, a native of Mikawa, s. of Hiraiwa Chikashige, a retainer of Ieyasu; became the tutor of Tokugawa Yoshinao when he received Kai prov. in fief in 1603; when Yoshinao was transferred to Owari, he became lord of Inuyama Castle, with an income of 100,000 koku.

[131] 2nd February 1612: this date and age do not agree with Hakuseki's version in the Hankampu, according to which he d. on 1 Feb. 1611, aged 71. Ieyasu d. 1616.

[132] memorial temple: where funerals, masses for the dead are performed.

[133] Yoshimune, disregarding Hakuseki's contrary arguments, restored the Ankokuden immediately upon his succession and endowed it with 500 koku. It was Hakuseki's recommendations at this time that constituted one of the chief reasons for coolness between the two.

[134] Marumo: Matsumura reads Maruke but the Dai Nihon Jimmei Jisho gives only Marumo.

[135] Takebe Takumi-no-Kami: Takebe Masataka (1637–1715), appointed jisha bugyō in 1714; also read Tatebe.

[136] Jinkōki: in 3 vols., by Yoshida Mitsuyoshi, pub. 1627, the 1st Japanese textbook on arithmetic.
4,800,099,600: This figure can be read in two ways: in the Jinkōki it is read as 48,099,600, while Hakuseki took it as 4,800,099,600. The population at this time was about 25,000,000.

[137] new gold: the Musashi koban and the ichibuban, coined during 1714, containing 856.9 parts of gold to 142.5 parts of silver.
new silver: "chōgin" and "mame-ita-gin," coined 1714–36, e.g., the "mitsuhō" and the "yotsuhō," whose compositions were respectively: gold, 0.8; copper, 672.7; silver, 326.5; and gold, 0.2; copper, 795.8; silver, 204.0.

[138] "Later Proposals Concerning Recoinage": Hakuseki Kengi no. 7.

[139] tax: this would have been a miscellaneous tax to be collected by the Bakufu in cash in proportion to income, as distinct from military service and labor.
Japan: text has "the 66 provs." = the whole of Japan.

[140] Jogū Taishi Sesshō: another name for Shōtoku Taishi (572–621).

[141] 4,969,890: it is not known whence Hakuseki derived this figure, but according to the *Shōtoku Taishi Denki*, compiled by Fujiwara Kanesuke, the figure is given as 4,988,842.

[142] Emperor Shōmu: (724–48).

8,631,074: it is not certain what the source is, but according to the *Hyakushō Bukuro* by Nishikawa Joken, in the time of Shōmu the population was more than 8,631,000.

[143] Chinese records: in the *Ti-li-chih* (or *Topographical Annals*) in the *Han Shu* (History of the Former or Western Han dynasty) (206 B.C–A.D. 23) in 120 vols.

[144] amount of salary rice: i.e., in both shogunal and private domains, which about the middle of the Tokugawa period was about 24,000,000 *koku*.

100 *koku* of land: land producing 100 *koku*.

20,000 people . . . 91,648 people over: if the population stood at 4,800,099,600 and the total rice production at 24,000,000 *koku*, there would be 20,000 people for every 100 *koku* of land and 99,600 people over. There is a discrepancy between the population figure Hakuseki has in mind here and the figure previously quoted for the population figure given in the *Jinkōki*.

[145] Copper was minted in 1626, 1629, 1636. The currency coined at these times was called "Old Kan'ei Currency"; after 1636 also much "New Kan'ei Currency" was coined (Kan'ei era, 1624–44).

[146] before that: in the Kamakura and Muromachi periods, Sung and Ming copper *sen* were imported from China and in the Sengoku period large quantities of Yung-lo currency (i.e., Ming currency of the period 1403–25); in the Momoyama period currency issues were made in the Tenshō and Bunroku eras (1573–95) and in the Tokugawa period in the Keichō and Genna eras (1596–1624).

[147] The Kambun era was 1661–73; in 1663, the Kyōto Daibutsu was melted down and it yielded 40,000,000 *kammon* according to the secret records of the Gold and Silver Mints; the discrepancy with Hakuseki's statement is unexplained.

[148] There was a sharp rise in prices in 1714 owing to the currency confusion.

[149] 1690: Hakuseki's mistake for 1688.

[150] exchange: cargo allotment center, established in 1603, but in 1672 altered to the Kamotsukaisho (or cargo exchange); the former was orig. an organization for private trade. Owing to the trade restrictions during the seclusion period, foreign trade was brought under the control of the shogunate and it became a government exchange.

[151] guard-ships: to guard Nagasaki harbor, muskets, sailors, look-outs, police for the control of Chinese merchants, guardships, and messengers were maintained.

[152] Appears in *Tokugawa Jikki*, vol. 8.

Chūgoku: S. W. Hondō; comprising 16 provs.

[153] Komakine Masakata and Hisamatsu Sadamochi became Nagasaki Bugyō in 1m 1710.

[154] No longer extant.

[155] Wan-li: 1573–1619.

Chinese ships: at first entered any port but from 1636 they were restricted to Nagasaki.

[156] foreign vessels: Portuguese ships.

Hirado: N. E. coast of Hirado Island in Nagasaki pref.

[157] To China and the South Seas; the actual prohibition was dated 5m 1635.

[158] 1690: text has Genroku 3 but actually 1688.

[159] K'ang-hsi: 1662–1722.

[160] Respectively, going out to meet the foreign ships to trade; agents acting as intermediaries between the cargo owners and *tonya* or wholesale merchants; purchasing goods and arranging profit margins; clandestine exports and imports.

[161] 1,114,498,700: here the *ichioku ichiman* of the text is to be read as *jūichi oku*.

[162] 107 years: 1596–1703.

[163] appears in the *Chiu Ti P'ien* of Sun Tzŭ.

[164] Ishikawa San'emon: Ishikawa Masasato.

[165] Matsumae Izu-no-Kami: Matsumae Yoshihiro.

[166] *orusu*: a mistake for *orusui*.

[167] 10th October: so the text; actually 9 Oct. according to the *Tokugawa Jikki*.

[168] Yamada Sōen Hōgen: Yamada Masakata (1661–1741), a pediatrician attached to the women's apartments in the *shōgun's* palace (1709); Hōgen was a rank given to physicians, granted Yamada in 1712; salary 300 *hyō*.

[169] a certain member: Katō Etchū-no-Kami Akiyoshi, d. 8 Feb. 1712.

[170] Yaso-no-Miya: dtr. of Retired Emp. Reigen, b. 1714; mother, dtr. of Matsumuro Bitchū-no-Kami Shigeatsu.

[171] Text has "there was a precedent where . . . the law for *geshunin* had been put into effect." Orig. *geshunin* meant a man who had killed someone with his own hand. In the Tokugawa period it meant the punishment of townsmen by decapitation. It was considered the punishment applicable to those who committed murder in the course of quarrels or arguments, or in other unpremeditated ways.

[172] Code: the Yōrō Ritsuryō, see n. 8, bk. III.

[173] saw: a method of inflicting death in which an incision was made in both shoulders of the criminal, and he was exposed for two days, passers-by being permitted to saw at his neck at will, and after he was dead, his body was crucified.

[174] beginning of the following year: text has at the end of this year; Shōtoku 5y. 12m 31d = 24 Jan. 1716.

[175] Daimyōkōji: a narrow street (close to pres. Tōkyō station) between 2 canals.

[176] Hotta Masatora: the 2nd s. of Hotta Masatoshi, see n. 67, bk. I.

[177] Suidō-chō: Koishikawa (pres. Bunkyō-ku, Tōkyō).

[178] Funatsu: pres. Kita-Muro dist., Mie pref.

[179] five years ago: from the beginning of 1716 to the winter (= end) of 1711 would, according to our reckoning, be 4 years.

Shinagawa: a post-station on the Tōkaidō, Ebata dist., Tōkyō pref.

[180] Imakire: (Matsumura reads Imagiri) Shizuoka pref. The inspection barrier at the Arai Ferry (see n. 210, bk. II) where special scrutiny was given to the going and coming of women.

Mitsuke: post-station on the Tōkaidō, a town on the S. plateau in Iwata dist. in Tōtōmi prov. (Shizuoka pref.).

[181] Shin-Yoshiwara: the pleasure quarters in the N. part of Asakusa (pres. Taitō-ku) in Tōkyō.

[182] No longer extant.

[183] clerks: text has *hyōjōsho tomeyakunin*, low-ranking officials responsible to the *kanjō bugyō* of the judiciary department, chiefly in charge of the investigation of criminal cases.

[184] fire: the Daibutsu was destroyed by Taira Shigehira in 1180.

Go-Shirakawa: 77th emp. (1156–58); after his abdication he continued to govern during the reigns of his three successors until his death in 1192.

decree: Go-Shirakawa issued a decree in 1181; the Daibutsu was recast in 1185 and the hall was reconstructed in 1190.

[185] fire: in 1567 during the struggles between Matsudaira Hisahide and the Miyoshi: the temple was not restored till 1708.

Ōgimachi: text Ōgimachi-In; 106th emp. (1558–86).

unpropitious: the emp's own coronation ceremony was postponed for 3 years for lack of funds. His reign was disturbed by civil wars, for during these years took place the contest between Takeda Shingen and Uesugi Kenshin, the end of the Ashikaga shogunate, the rise and death of Nobunaga, and the rise of Hideyoshi. Emp. Ōgimachi issued decrees for the restoration of Tōdaiji in 1568 and also in 1570.

[186] Kenkyū: restoration by imp. decree of Retired Emp. Shirakawa, in 1190.

Eishō: the decree during Eishō is not known.

Eiroku, Genki: 1568, 1570.

[187] Ōoka Bizen-no-Kami Kiyohira: a mistake for Kiyosuke (1679–1717) who became Nagasaki Bugyō in 1711.

[188] Viceroy: Governor-general, highest local official during Ming (1368–1644) and Ch'ing (1644–1912) dynasties, chiefly in charge of military affairs.

Provincial Governor: during Ming and Ch'ing dynasties, chief of local civil administration.

[189] Sagami: runs through central Kanagawa pref.; the Banyū is its lower reaches.

[190] Totsuka: pres. Totsuka-ku, Yokohama city.; then a post-station on the Tōkaidō.

Fujisawa: pres. Fujisawa city, Kanagawa pref., then a post-station on the Tōkaidō.

[191] Honda Tōtōmi-no-Kami Masatake: lord of Numata Castle in Kōzuke prov. (Gumma pref.) adopted s. of Honda Masanaga, succeeded to Masanaga's estates in 1711.

[192] Asakura Yoichi Kagetake: father-in-law of Hakuseki's eldest s. Akinori, retainer of Honda Masatake.

[193] Yasushiro and Toguchi: (Miyazaki and Matsumura read Ajiro) in pres. Ōmo village, Minami-Kambara dist., Niigata pref.

[194] Tatsuishi: (Matsumura reads Tateishi) in pres. Ono village, Tano dist., Gumma pref. (neighboring Niigata pref.).

Menuma: in pres. Menuma, Ōsato dist., Saitama pref. (neighboring Gumma pref.).

[195] Chibara: (Matsumura reads Kayahara) in pres. Ōmo village (see n. 193, above).

[196] Shibata: pres. Shibata City, Niigata pref. The distance given is incorrect; it was about 15 *ri* as the crow flies.

[197] Izumozaki: harbor in Santō dist., central Niigata pref.

[198] Hatsuzaki: perhaps in pres. Kakizaki city, Naka-Kubiki dist., Niigata pref.

Kashiwazaki: pres. Kashiwazaki city, Niigata pref., then a post-station in the Hokurikukaidō.

[199] Nagamine . . . and Tsukioka: in pres. Higashi-Honjōji, Sanjō city, Minami-Kambara dist., Niigata pref.

Kitakata: 2nd character may be wrong; prob. Kitagata, in pres. Ōmo village (see n. 193, above).

Mitsuke Niigata: (Matsumura reads Shinkata) perhaps pres. Niigata village, near Mitsuke, Minami-Kambara dist, Niigata pref.

Mitsuke Shimmachi: in pres. Niigata village (as above).

[200] Yotsuya: near Kariyata River (tributary of the Shin-Shinano) prob. within its Minami-Kambara stretch.

Gosenchō: perhaps in pres. Gosen city, Naka-Kambara dist., Niigata pref.

N. B. Commentators do not identify remaining two place names in this incident:

[201] Todai: 2nd character may be wrong; perhaps in pres. Mitsuke, Minami-Kambara dist., Niigata pref.

Kurosaka: there is a Kurosaka in pres. Kirishima village, Santō dist., Niigata pref., about 12 km from Ōmo village (see n. 193, above).

[202] "Lice . . . state": 97th stanza of the *Tsurezure Gusa*: "Touching these matters there are numerous things which destroy them. Lice on the body; rats in the house; robbers in the state. The ignoble have wealth; the cultivated humanity, and the priest the law."

[203] *Ta Hsüeh*: (see n. 97, bk. I) 2nd of the 3 principles initially enunciated.

Analects: (see n. 36, bk. II) Bk. 5 Kung-Ye Ch'ang, ch. 22.

Chou I: (see n. 108, bk. I) Hexagram 49 Kê Kua (Revolution).

[204] Koremasa: pres. Koremasa, Tōkyō pref.

Shimo-Koganei: pres. Koganei City, Tōkyō pref.

[205] Shimabara Revolt: in 1637 at Shimabara Castle in Minami-Takagi dist. in Hizen prov. (Nagasaki pref.).

[206] Ni-no-Maru: a part of Edo Castle.

[207] At the Ōsaka Summer campaign, on 26 June 1615 Ieyasu overthrew the heir, Hideyori, of his former lord Toyotomi Hideyoshi.

[208] Chia-tzŭ: in Japanese Kasshi, the day of the month distinguished by the cyclical characters, Kinoe-ne, regarded as a day when prosperity is overthrown; 26 June 1716 had these cyclical characters.

²⁰⁹ this particular day: it seemed like retribution that Ietsugu's funeral took place on the anniversary of the day the line of Toyotomi Hideyoshi came to an end.

²¹⁰ "Joint Signatories": text has *Hōshorembanshū*, i.e., members of the Rōjū.

²¹¹ visit to Nijō Palace: visit in the autumn of 1632 to the Nijō Palace of Empress Myōshō. In his *Buke Kan'i Shōzokukō*, Hakuseki notes the conferring of lower 4th rank 2nd grade and the appointment as chamberlains of 2 members of the Rōjū as occurring for the first time on this occasion.

Fourth Rank: text reads *shihon* (4th princely rank), but *shii* (4th court rank) is meant.

²¹² Makino Narisada: (or Shigesada) rose from an income of 2,000 *koku* to 20,000, beginning in the entourage of Tokumatsu, Tsunayoshi's son, and becoming *sobayōnin* in 1681.

²¹³ family name: Matsudaira.

syllable: *yoshi*.

²¹⁴ "*daimyōs*' sons" : i.e., dull and ignorant.

²¹⁵ late Shōgun: text has *Zendai* which context suggests refers to Ietsugu though commentators say Ienobu.

²¹⁶ close this account: refers to the point at which Hakuseki concludes the narrative, not the actual date he finished the composition.

The signature and date are followed by three seals. The first is the same as at the end of the Preface. The second, below and to the left, reads "Gen Kimmi (no) In," meaning "Seal of Minamoto Kimmi." The third, immediately beneath that, reads "Kyūji Shōroku," meaning "Written by my own hand."

BIOGRAPHICAL NOTES

1. Ema Ekian; Gemboku; a native of Kyōto, physician.
2. Arai Hakuseki (1657–1725) (Minamoto); Kimmi, Kageyu; Chikugo-no-Kami (1711); Chu Hsi Confucianist, studied under Kinoshita Jun'an; from 1693 lecturer to Tokugawa Tsunatoyo, lord of Kai, afterward 6th Shōgun Ienobu; instituted "literary government"; author of *Hankampu* (1702), *Tokushi Yoron* (1712), *Seiyō Kibun* (1715), etc.
3. Tokugawa Ienobu (1662–1712) (Minamoto); Tsunatoyo, lord of Kai, Bunshō-In, Bunshōbyō, His Highness, His late Highness (text *Ue*, *Zendai*); 6th Shōgun (1709–12).
4. Ryōya; (Shin, Ōtani); (former) *Jūji* of Kōtokuji (in Hōonji, Asakusa, Edo).
5. Tsuchiya Toshinao (1607–75) (Minamoto); the Kohō; Mimbu-no-Shō (1621); took part in the Ōsaka summer campaign at age 8; selected as a *fudai daimyō*, but suffered many illnesses and lived much retired; fief 20,000 *koku* at Kururi, Kazusa (1612).
6. Seki; old Seki; friend of Hakuseki's father, Masanari; served in Tsuchiya clan.
7. Gunji Masanobu (1636–1703); Ichiya, Yaichiemon, Chihō; adopted s. of Hakuseki's father.
8. Tokugawa Ieyasu (1542–1616) (Minamoto); Ōgosho (1605–16), Divine Ancestor, Tōshōgū, Tōshō Daigongen, Ankoku-in Tokurensha Suwa Dōwa Daikoji; 1st Tokugawa Shōgun (1603–5).
9. Tokugawa Iemitsu (1603–51) (Minamoto); Takechiyo, Taiyū-In; 3rd Shōgun (1622–51); 2nd s. of Hidetada.
10. Tsuchiya Yorinao; Yoshū; Iyo-no-Kami (1675); s. of Toshi-

nao; fief 20,000 *koku*, Tsuchiura, Hitachi (1675); confiscated 1679; s. received 3,000 *koku* at Tanaka, Suruga (1681).

11. Hotta Masatoshi (1634–84) (Ki); Ki-Masatoshi, Shōshō Masatoshi; Chikuzen-no-Kami; Tairō (1681–84), fief 115,000 *koku* at Koga, Shimōsa (1681).

12. Kinoshita Jun'an (Kinri) (1621–98); Heinojō, Naomiki, Kyōsei, Kyōsei Boku Sensei, Boku Sensei; Chu Hsi Confucianist, b. Kyōto, studied under Matsunaga Sekigo, served in House of Maeda of Kaga, lecturer to Tsunayoshi (1682); established school Bokumon; disciples Arai Hakuseki, Muro Kyūsō, Amenomori Hōshū, Gion Nankai, Sakakibara Kōshū; author of *Kinri Bunshū*, etc.

13. Toyotomi Hideyoshi (1536–98); Taikō (1592–98); general who served Oda Nobunaga and after his assassination seized supreme military power from 1585 until his own death.

14. Nishiyama (Abiru) Juntai (Yoshiyasu) (1660–88); Kempo; b. Tsushima, studied under Kinoshita Jun'an.

15. Tokugawa Tsunayoshi (1646–1709); Jōken-In; former Shōgun; 5th Shōgun (1680–1709); fief 150,000 *koku* at Tatebayashi, Kōzuke (1661–80); patron of arts and letters, promulgated Kindness to Animals Statutes, whence called Inu-Kubō; 4th s. of Iemitsu.

16. One of Seki's sons; Seki.

17. Hotta Masanaka (1662–94) (Ki); Sōshū; Shimōsa-no-Kami; fief 100,000 *koku* at Yamagata, Dewa (1685); Fukushima, Mutsu (1686); with Abe Masatake edited *Butokutaiseiki* (1683); s. of Masatoshi.

18. Arai Akinori (1691–1741) (Minamoto); Hakuseki's eldest s.

19. Kōriki Tadahiro; Yoshū; Iyo-no-Kami; employed in Kai clan (1683); salary 3,000 *hyō*; in 1693 *koshōkumibangashira*.

20. Toda Tadatoshi; Chōshū; Nagato-no-Kami; elder Kai clan, became Nishimaru *osobashū*.

21. Hayashi Nobuatsu (1644–1732) (Fujiwara); Hōkō; Daigakuno-Kami (1691), grands. of Razan (Dōshun) [74], 2nd s. of Shunsai; became head of House 1680, served 5 *shōguns* from Ietsuna to Yoshimune.

22. Yoshida Tōhachirō (Funabashi Mareyoshi, Han'emon), employed in Kai clan (1693); salary 40 men's rations; later transferred to *nando*.

23. Koide Ariyuki; Tosa-no-Kami; became Nishimaru *osobashū*.
24. Manabe Akifusa (1667–1720) (Fujiwara); Kunai; Ukyō; Echizen-no-Kami; served Ienobu from his youth, and became *sobayōnin*; became *daimyō* (1707); fief 50,000 *koku* at Takasaki, Kōzuke (1710); Murakami, Echigo (1717); s. of Nishida Kiyosada.
25. Tokugawa Ietsugu (1709–16) (Minamoto); Nabematsu, Yūshō-In; pres. Shōgun; previous Shōgun; 7th Shōgun (1715–16); 4th s. of Ienobu.
26. Tokugawa Yoshimune (1684–1751); Yūtoku-In, Kii Dono; pres. Shōgun; 8th Shōgun (1716–45); fief 555,000 *koku* at Wakayama, Kii (1705); 3rd s. of Mitsusada of Kii.
27. Inoue Masakata; Tōtōmi-no-Kami; became Nishimaru *osobashū*; younger br. of Masamine.
28. Magaribuchi (Magabuchi) Kagehira; Shimotsuke-no-Kami; *fushin bugyō* (Inspector of Works).
29. Manabe Akiyuki (1674–1730) (Fujiwara); Shuzen; Oki-no-Kami; at first *koshō*; *yoriai* (1716); salary 2,150 *koku*; younger br. of Akifusa.
30. Murakami Masanao; (Fujiwara) Ichi-no-Kami; *koshōkumi*.
31. Yanagisawa Yoshiyasu (formerly Fusayasu, Yasuakira) (1658–1714) (Matsudaira by grant); Yatarō, Hozan, Shōshō Yoshiyasu; Dewa-no-Kami, Mino-no-Kami; Rōjū (1706–9); became Tsunayoshi's *sobayōnin* (1688); fief 150,000 *koku* at Kōfū, Kai (1704); s. of a *samurai*.
32. Shibazaki Jūroemon (1633–1705); Masakatsu; served in Kai clan as a riding master; *kobushin* (1705); salary 250 *hyō*.
33. Murata Jūroemon (1647–1724); Hisanobu; served in Kai clan as master in swordsmanship; Nishi-no-Maru *konando* (1705); *yoriai* (1716); salary 300 *hyō*.
34. Hattori Tōkurō (1667–1721); Yasutsune, Kansei; Confucianist in Kai clan, studied under Kinoshita Jun'an; author of *Dan'en, Sōkan Shōshūshū, Kansei Nikki*. (All editions of *Oritaku Shiba no Ki* and the Tōdai Shiryō Hensanjo edition of *Hakuseki Nikki* [Iwanami Shoten] read Tōkurō; the *Dai Jimmei Jiten* [Kōdansha] gives Tōgorō; in my opinion, the *Jippitsu Bon* also reads Tōgorō.)
35. Hattori Seisuke (?–1729); Yasutaka (Masayuki), Gakei; calligrapher; s. of Kansei.

36. Doi Genshirō (1693–1757); Motonari, Confucianist in Kai clan.

37. Inoue Masamine (earlier Masamichi); Kawachi-no-Kami; Rōjū (1705–22). Hakuseki sometimes gives Tadamine by mistake.

38. Matsudaira Terusada; Ukyō-Daibu; at this time *sobayōnin;* castellan of Murakami (maternal cousin of Inoue Masukata).

39. Nagai Naohiro (text Naohira) (earlier Noritake, Norishige); Izu-no-Kami; Wakadoshiyori (1704). (Some, including *Dai Niho-Jimmei Jisho,* read Iga-no-Kami, but the Tōdai Shiryō Hensanjo's *Hakuseki Nikki,* Miyazaki, and Matsumura read Izu; the *Jippitsu Bon,* in my opinion, reads Izu.)

40. Ōkubo Norishige (at other times Noritake, Norihiro); Nagato-no-Kami; Wakadoshiyori (1706).

41. Manabe Akihira (1671–1725); Iga-no-Kami, Awaji-no-Kami; in 1708 *koshō;* Nakatsukasa-no-Shō (1705); fief 500 *koku* (1710), 1,500 *koku* (1715); younger br. of Akifusa.

42. Matsudaira Tadayoshi (Tadachika); Iga-no-Kami; Wakadoshiyori (1685); *sobayōnin* (1705).

43. Tokugawa Ietsuna (1639–80); Gen'yū-In (Kubō); 4th Shōgun (1651–80); eldest s. of Iemitsu.

44. Ogasawara Nagashige; Sado-no-Kami; Rōjū (1697–1705, 1709–10).

45. Kuben Hōshinnō, Abbot of Rinnōji, Nikkō Jugō (1690–1715); 6th s. of Emp. Go-Sai.

46. Tokugawa Hidetada (1579–1632) (Minamoto); Taitoku-In, Tokubyō; 2nd Shōgun (1605–23); 3rd s. of Ieyasu; had 3 s. Iemitsu, Tadanaga, Hoshina Masayuki.

47. Tokugawa Tadanaga (1606–33); Suruga-Dainagon, Suruga Dono, Dainagon (1624); fief 550,000 *koku,* Suruga, Kai, Shinano, Tōtōmi; younger br. of Iemitsu.

48. Hōjō Takatoki (1303–33) (Taira); 14th Kamakura Shikken (1310–33), weak and dissolute ruler; threatened by imp. forces, committed suicide.

49. Nobuko, dtr. of Takatsukasa Fusasuke; Midaidokoro; Ōmi-daidokoro; consort of Tsunayoshi.

50. Ōkubo Tadatomo (Norihiro); Kaga-no-Kami; Rōjū (1677–98). See 53.

51. Ogiwara Shigehide (1658–1713); Ōmi-no-Kami (1695);

kanjōkumigashira, 1683, Kanjō Gimmi Yaku (1687); *kanjō bugyō* (1696); dismissed 1712; fief 3,700 *koku*.

52. Inagaki Shigetomi (Shigenaga) (1673–1710); Tsushima-no-Kami (1693); Wakadoshiyori (1699).

53. Ōkubo Tadamasu (1656–1713); Kaga-no-Kami (1705); Rōjū (1705–13); s. of Tadatomo. Hakuseki sometimes gives his father's name (see 50) by mistake.

54. Akimoto Takatomo; Tajima-no-Kami (1659); Rōjū (1699–1707).

55. Murakami Masakuni; Inaba-no-Kami, Noto-no-Kami; in 1710, *koshō*.

56. Kōkai; Sōjō, Abbot of Chōrakuji.

57. Konoe Motohiro (1648–1722); (the present) Taikō, Konoe Daishōkoku, Konoe Shōkoku, Shōkoku, the former Sesshō; Kampaku (1690); Dajōdaijin (1709); court noble, antiquarian; nephew of Emp. Go-Mizu-no-O; Ienobu's father-in-law.

58. Konoe Sakihisa (Harutsugu, Sakitsugu) (1536–1612); Ryōzan, Tōgu-In; Kampaku (1582); Dajōdaijin (1582); calligrapher, antiquarian, historian; sided with Ieyasu against Toyotomi after Nobunaga's assassination.

59. Konoe Nobutada (earlier Nobumoto, Nobusuke) (1565–1614); Sambō-In, Jirō Gimi, Sammyaku-In Den, former Kampaku; (1605); Jusangō (1605); distinguished man of letters and calligrapher (founded Konoe-ryū); author of *Sambō-In Nikki*; s. of Sakihisa.

60. Hiroko, dtr. of Konoe Motohiro; Midaidokoro, Ōmidaidokoro, Ten'ei-In, Lady Ichii; consort of Ienobu.

61. Kuze Shigeyuki; Yamato-no-Kami; Wakadoshiyori; Rōjū (1713–20).

62. Tsuchiya Masanao; Sagami-no-Kami; Rōjū (1687–1718).

63. Ishin Sūden (1569–1633) (Isshiki); Zen; Den Chōrō, Enshō Honkō Kokushi; Chōrō of Nanzenji; Jūshoku of Konji-In; served Ieyasu, Hidetada, Iemitsu; wrote *Honkō Kokushi Nikki* (abbr. to *Kokushi Nikki* in text), which was discovered by Hakuseki in 1712.

64. Ichijō-In Den (1699–1746); Morokata, Taki-no-Miya, Kōshō-gen-In; Hossō; (Sonshō) Hōshinnō (1709); Bettō of Kōfukuji (1719); 37th Monshu of Ichijō-In; 13th s. of Emp. Reigen.

65. Daijō-In Den; Shinkan Daisōjō; Hossō; Bettō of Kōfukuji (1699).

66. Konoe Takataka; Tarō Gimi; Daiō-In; Sōjō, Monshu of Ichijō-In; s. of Sakihisa.

67. Shingyō (?–1709); Mibota-In Den (Sabodai-In); Hōshinnō; Monshu of Ichijō-In; 10th s. of Emp. Go-Mizu-no-O.

68. Miyoshi Nagahiro (?–1711); Bizen-no-Kami; Nara Bugyō (1707).

69. Konoe Iehiro (1667–1736); former Sesshō, Konoe Daishōkoku; Sesshō (1709–12); Kampaku (1707); Dajōdaijin (1710); Jugō (1725); poet, painter, calligrapher; continued Konoe-ryū school; s. of Motohiro.

70. Nakamikado (1702–38); 114th emp. (1710–35).

71. Shimazu Yoshitaka (Minamoto); Satsuma-no-Kami; fief at Kagoshima, Satsuma.

72. Sō Yoshikata (Taira); Tsushima-no-Kami; fief at Fuchū, Tsushima.

73. Hirata Naokata, Naoemon (Taira); elder in House of Sō.

74. Hayashi Dōshun (Razan) (1583–1657); studied Chu Hsi philosophy under Fujiwara Seika; 1st official Confucianist to the Tokugawa shogunate, served 4 *shōguns*.

75. Minamoto Yoritomo (1147–99); Kamakura Udaishō, Kamakura Dono; 1st Shōgun (1192–99).

76. Yokota Yoshimatsu; Bitchū-no-Kami; *ōmetsuke*.

77. Suzuki Toshio; Hida-no-Kami; *metsuke*.

78. Hotta Gen'emon; Michiaki; *metsuke*.

79. Honda Tadayoshi (1690–1751); Nakatsukasa-Tayū; Rōjū (1734–35); Jijū; a 5th-generation descendant of Honda Tadakatsu, Ieyasu's companion in arms; succeeded to Murakami in 1709; fief at Koga, Shimōsa (1712).

80. Nakayama Tokiharu; Izumo-no-Kami; *kanjō bugyō* (1702–14); rewarded for flood control in Sagami and Suruga (1710), and for judicial services (1711).

81. Ōkubo Tadayoshi; Ōsumi-no-Kami; *kanjō bugyō* (1708–16) in charge of inspection of highways for the reception of the Korean Envoys in 1711.

82. Matsudaira Norikuni; Iwami-no-Kami; in charge of inspection of highways for the reception of the Korean Envoys in 1711.

83. Matsudaira Norisato (mura); Izumi-no-Kami; fief at Kama-yama, Ise (1710); suspended 1712, but reinstated after 2 months.

84. Matsudaira Norikane; Samon; *yoriai*; actually, as a result of the incident related, his salary was reduced from 5000 to 3000 *koku*.

85. Mizoguchi Shigemoto; Hōki-no-Kami (1694), succeeded to fief in 1706.

86. Sugioka Yatarō; Yoshitsura; Kanjō Gimmi Yaku.

87. Hagiwara (Suga) Genzaemon, Yoshimasa; Hagiwara Dono; Hōki-no-Kami (1736); *kanjōkumigashira* (1701); Kanjō Gimmi Yaku (1712); Ni-no-Maru Rusui (1716); salary 500 *hyō* (1712).

88. Hogi Yaemon; Kintō; a head of the Kanjōsho.

89. Komiyama Tomoemon; Masayuki; a head of the Kanjōsho.

90. Nagai Hanroku; retainer of Ogiwara Shigehide.

91. Fukae Shōzaemon; ledger-keeper.

92. Honda Tadaharu; Danjō-Shōhitsu; *jisha bugyō* (1702); reward-ed for judicial services in 1711; resigned in 1713.

93. Hashiba Hideyasu (1574–1607); Mikawa-no-Kami Dono, Yūki Dono, Mikawa-no-Kami; fief 67,000 *koku* at Echizen; 2nd s. of Ieyasu, adopted by Yūki Harutomo (1590).

94. Okiya-no-Kata, Teruko, dtr. of Shōda (Gentetsu) Akinori; Sakyō-no-Tsubone; Gekkō-In; Ietsugu's mother.

95. Tokudaiji Kin'akira (Fujiwara): Dainagon; Densō; Kuge.

96. Niwata Shige'eda (Uda-Genji); Dainagon; Densō; Kuge.

97. Abe Masataka; Bungo-no-Kami; Rōjū (1711–17).

98. Muro Kyūsō (1658–1734) Shinsuke; Bakufu Confucianist, pupil of Kinoshita Jun'an, adherent of Chu Hsi philosophy, served Yoshimune; author of *Suruga-Dai Zatsuwa*.

99. Ashikaga Yoshimitsu (1358–1408); Rokuon-In; Muromachi Dono; 3rd Shōgun (1367–95).

100. Reigen (1654–1732); Retired Emperor; 112th emp. (1663–86).

101. Kao Hsüan-tai (Fukami Shin'emon); b. Nagasaki; grand-father Chinese; studied medicine; in temporary employ of Satsuma-no-Kami; became Bakufu Confucianist (1710) at Hakuseki's recommendation; salary 200 *hyō*.

102. Matsudaira Nobutsune (Katahara); Kii-no-Kami; Kyōto Shoshidai (1697).

103. Nakagawa Nariyoshi; Awaji-no-Kami; *ōmetsuke* (1712).

104. Mizuno Tadakuni; Tsushima-no-Kami, Inaba-no-Kami; *kanjō bugyō* (1712).

105. Ōkubo Jin'emon; Tadataka; Shimotsuke-no-Kami; *metsuke* (1710); *fushin bugyō* (1714).

106. Tani Chōemon; Yasutaka; a merchant; descended from the Kii branch of the Tokugawa, from Hotta village, Nakajima dist. (Owari prov.).

107. Shirakawa Masafuyu; Haku-no-Chūjō; Sukenobu; grands. of Emp. Kazan (985–86), became Jingi-Haku, and was granted the surname Shirakawa; thereafter his descendants were appointed hereditarily.

108. Mizuno Tadayuki; Izumi-no-Kami; castellan of Okazaki; Wakadoshiyori (1711).

109. Toda Tadazane; Yamashiro-no-Kami; Rōjū (1714–29); fief at Utsunomiya, Shimotsuke.

110. Asahi-no-Kata (1543–90); Nammyō-In; Midaidokoro; uterine sister of Hideyoshi, wife of Ieyasu (1586), dtr. of Chikuami.

111. Marumo Gorobei; Toshio.

112. Nojima Shinzaemon; merchant.

113. Sengoku Hisanao; Tamba-no-Kami; appointed 1695.

114. Hōjō Ujihide; Awa-no-Kami; Ōsaka Machi Bugyō (1709), administrator of Settsu, Kawachi, Izumi, Harima provs.; fief 3,400 *koku*.

115. Inaba Masatomo; Tango-no-Kami; Rōjū (1701–7).

116. Tōdō Takatoshi; Izumi-no-Kami; fief at Ise.

117. Funakoshi Saemon; *osakite teppō kumigashira.*

118. Ise Sadatoki; Ise-no-Kami (1712); *fushin bugyō* (1712); *kanjō bugyō* (1714–21).

119. Hotta Masamori (1608–51); Kaga-no-Kami; Rōjū (1633–51); Hyōjōsho; promoted to chamberlain in 1640; on Iemitsu's death, committed *junshi.*

Appendix 1
Glossary of Titles, Offices, and Names

Titles of feudal *daimyō* were courtesy honors only and usually had no relation to the functions, emoluments, or places of residence of the bearers. These titles derived originally from those granted to nobles of the Imperial Court; in Tokugawa times, they were granted to *daimyō* and *hatamoto* in effect at the will of the *shōgun* and tended to become hereditary in certain families.

The most numerous were titles meaning originally governor of a province: as Hida-no-Kami, literally governor of Hida province. The titles Satsuma-no-Kami and Tsushima-no-Kami were exceptional in that their holders were actually the *daimyō* of Satsuma and Tsushima respectively. In sobriquets formed of a province name plus "Dono," the person referred to held the province in question in fief.

Other titles derive from the names of the ministries and bureaux, guard companies, and provincial administrations of the Imperial administration as organized at the time of the Taika Reform (649). Great variety exists in the reading of titles, some authorities inserting, and some omitting the particle *no* (of) between the name of the ministry or bureau and the grade. For uniformity's sake, I have followed Matsumura's readings, though Kindaichi Kyōsuke has some entries in his *Kogo Jiten* which disagree. Entries in the following list include the councils (*kan*), ministries (*shō*), bureaux (*shiki*), etc., from which titles appearing in the text were derived and the various grades of titles held. Officials of the Tokugawa bureaucracy, the contemporary Imperial Court, and Buddhist and Shintō institutions, of which mention are made, as well as names, nicknames, and sobriquets are also listed.

Court rank was granted to both men and women. Under the Taihō Code (702), a concordance of offices and court ranks was drawn up. *San-I* (Honorary Rank) meant holding court rank without office. Fifth rank second grade was the lowest rank admitted to the Imperial Court, and it was rare for members of the military classes to receive higher than third rank.

b. = Buddhist
o.i.c. = Old Imperial Court
t.b. = Tokugawa bureaucracy
s. = Shintō

Ban	*t.b.* guards.
Bugyō	*t.b.* magistrate(s).
Bugyōsho	*t.b.* magistrates' office.
Bugyōshū	*t.b.* magistrates.
Bunshōbyō	*b.* Chinese equivalent of *Bunshō-In*, q.v.
Bunshō-In	*b.* posthumous name for Tokugawa Ienobu.
Chikara	a common name, originally a nickname derived from *Chikara-ryō*, one of the bureaux in the *Mimbu-shō*, q.v.
Chōrō	*b.* a superior in a temple.
Chōshū	*o.i.c.* Sino-Japanese form of Nagato-no-Kami, used as a nickname.
Chūjō	*o.i.c.* upper division, second grade in *Sakone-fu*, *Ukone-fu*, q.v.
Dai-Ajari (or *Azari*)	*b.* chief expounder of the doctrine of a sect.
Daibu	*o.i.c.* first grade in *Daizen-shiki*, *Ukone-fu*, *Ukyō-shiki*, q.v.
Daigaku-ryō	*o.i.c.* a bureau in the *Shikibu-Shō*, ministry in charge of ceremonies, rewards, and the university.
Daijin	*o.i.c.* *Naidaijin*, q.v.
Daikan	*t.b.* local stewards on shogunal lands, having control of tax collection, etc.
Daikansho	*t.b.* stewards' office.
Daimyō	*t.b.* holders of fiefs above 10,000 *koku*.
Dainagon	*o.i.c.* privy councilor.
Daishi	*b.* a priest who has had the honor of instructing the emperor in his doctrine.

Daishōkoku	Chinese form of *Dajōdaijin*, q.v.
Daizen-shiki	*o.i.c.* a bureau in the *Kunai-shō*, ministry in charge of the collection and employment of taxes in kind for use in the palace.
Dajōdaijin	*o.i.c.* chief of the *Dajōkan*, q.v.
Dajōkan	*o.i.c.* the council of state.
Danjō-tai	*o.i.c.* the high court of justice.
Den	1. *b.* alternate pronunciation of Dono, attached to abbots. 2. as above, attached to ladies of high degree.
Densō	*t.b.* two court nobles in charge of communications between the shogunate and imperial court.
Dono	used in nicknames: 1. added to a province name to indicate a prominent personage who resided there, e.g., Suruga Dono; 2. added to a surname to indicate a prominent personage, e.g., Yūki Dono; 3. added to the name of a residence to indicate a prominent personage, e.g., Muromachi Dono; 4. merely a courtesy title.
Dōshin	*t.b.* minor officials under a magistrate, inferior to *Yoriki*, q.v.
Geki	*o.i.c.* secretary in *Dajōkan*, q.v.
Gen'yu-In	*b.* posthumous name of Tokugawa Ietsuna.
Gobanshū	*t.b.* members of the guards, included the *Koshōkumi, Shoimban, Ōban, Kojūninkumi.*
Gonchūjō	*o.i.c.* acting *Chūjō*, q.v.
Hafuri	*s.* priest, under control of *kannushi*, q.v.
Haku	*s. Jingi-haku* (also read *kami*), first grade in *Jingikan*, q.v.
Hatamoto	*t.b.* bannermen, holders of fiefs below 10,000 *koku*, direct retainers of the *shōgun*, many of whom were employed in the bureaucracy.
Hōgen	*b.* "eye-of-the-law," also granted to physicians, etc.

Hōin	*b*. "seal-of-the-law," also granted to artists, etc.
Hōshi	*b*. posthumous title granted to priests.
Hōshinnō	*b*. title given to imperial princes who entered a monastery.
Hyōjōsho	*t.b*. supreme court.
Hyōjōshū	*t.b*. judges.
Ichii	first rank, specific title for Tokugawa Tsunayoshi's mother.
Ichi-no-tsukasa	*o.i.c.* under a bureau in charge of Kyōto administration.
Jingikan	*s*. department in charge of ceremonies, superintendence of priests, etc.
Jisha Bugyō	*t.b*. superintendent of temples and shrines.
Jitō	*t.b*. stewards of shogunal lands with tax rights.
Jō (or *Shin*)	*o.i.c.* third grade in *Sakyō-shiki*, q.v.
Jō	*o.i.c.* third grade in *Saemon-fu, Uemon-fu*, q.v.
Jōken-In	*b*. posthumous name of Tokugawa Tsunayoshi.
Jusangō (or *jugō*)	honorific title originally giving the bearer the right to an income equivalent to that received by the three empresses: the reigning, dowager, and arch-dowager.
Kachizamurai	low ranking *samurai*, took van of procession as part of the guard when *shōgun* traveled.
Kamakura Kanryō (*Kamakura Dono*)	governor of the Kantō or eastern provinces.
Kami	*o.i.c.* first grade in *Daigaku-ryō, Ichi-ryō, Kazue-ryō*, q.v., provincial administration.
Kanjō Bugyō	*t.b*. superintendent of finance.
Kanjō Gimmi Yaku	*t.b*. board of audit.
Kanjō Kumi Gashira	*t.b*. chief financial clerks.
Kanjōsho	*t.b*. finance department.
Kanjōshū	*t.b*. clerks in *Kanjōsho*, q.v.

Kannushi	*s.* superior of a shrine, whose chief function was to present the morning and evening offerings to the *kami* (gods).
Kazue-ryō	*o.i.c.* bureau in the *Mimbu-sho* in charge of receipt and verification of imposts and taxes sent from provinces.
Kobushin Bugyō	*t.b.* superintendent in charge of maintenance and repairs.
Kohō	*o.i.c.* Sino-Japanese form of *Mimbu-shō*, specifically Tsuchiya Toshinao.
Kojōya	See *Shōya.*
Kokushi	*b.* a priest of the Zen sect who has had the honor of instructing the emperor in his doctrine.
Konando	*t.b.* personal attendants of the *shōgun.*
Kubō	an honorific title at first reserved for the emperor; applied to the *shōgun* from the time of the third Ashikaga Shōgun, later applied to the *Kamakura Kanryō*, q.v.
Kura-ryō	*o.i.c.* bureau in the *Nakatsukasa-shō*, entrusted with imperial seal, robes, treasures.
Kyōto Shoshidai	*t.b. shōgun's* representative in Kyōto.
Machi Bugyō	*t.b.* city magistrate in Edo, Kyōto, Nagasaki.
Machi Doshiyori	*t.b.* assistants to *Machi Bugyō*, q.v.
Metsuke	*t.b.* surveillance officer.
Midaidokoro	*shōgun's* consort.
Mimbu-shō	*o.i.c.* ministry of home affairs, in charge of census, taxes, communications, agriculture, etc.
Miya	*o.i.c.* title of a prince or princess
Monzeki	*b.* 1. a temple whose abbot is an imperial prince; 2. imperial prince who is abbot of a temple.
Naidaijin	*o.i.c.* Minister of the Interior in the *Dajōkan*, q.v.
Naifu	*o.i.c.* alternate form of *Naidaijin*, q.v.
Naiki	*o.i.c.* secretary in *Nakatsukasa-shō*, q.v.

Nakatsukasa-shō	*o.i.c.* ministry in charge of transmission of orders, formulation of ordinances, the keeping of records, etc.
Nara Bugyō	*t.b.* Nara city magistrate.
Nyūdō	*b.* lay-priest, lay-nun ("bonze" or "ama"), a man or woman who entered a religious order on retirement.
Ōban	*t.b.* wardens of Edo, Kyōto, and Ōsaka castles.
Ōgosho	specific title for Tokugawa Ieyasu, signifying Retired Shōgun.
Ōjōya	See *Shōya.*
Okachishū	*t.b.* foot soldiers.
Okonandoshū	personal servants of the *shōgun* in charge of small duties like hairdressing.
Ōmandokoro	mother of a Kampaku (Regent) specific title for Toyotomi Hideyoshi's mother.
Ōmetsuke	*t.b.* chief surveillance officer.
Ōmidaidokoro	*shōgun*'s relict.
Ōrusui	*t.b.* had charge of the security of the women's apartments in Edo Castle.
Osakite	*t.b.* had charge of the security of the main keep of Edo Castle, and acted as bodyguard when the *shōgun* went outside the castle precincts; also assisted in fire prevention and arrest of robbers within Edo.
Osobashū	personal attendants on the *shōgun* or the *shōgun*'s heir, serving in rotation.
Otsukaiban	*t.b.* couriers
Rōjū	*t.b.* senior council which controlled certain sections of the bureaucracy.
Rōnin	a lordless *samurai.*
Sachūjō	*o.i.c.* here abbreviation of *Sakone-no-Chūjō.* See *Sakone-fu, Chūjō.*
Saemon-fu	*o.i.c.* one of the six departments of household troops.

Saishō	See *Sangi*.
Sakone-fu	*o.i.c.* one of the six departments of household troops.
Sakyō-shiki	*o.i.c.* bureau in charge of the eastern section of Kyōto.
Samurai	*t.b.* man-at-arms.
Sangi	*o.i.c.* honorary privy councilor.
Sesshō	*o.i.c.* Regent, title held by Konoe Iehiro.
Shinnō	sons and brothers of the emperor.
Shō	*o.i.c.* lower division, second grade in the *Nakatsukasa-shō*, *Mimbu-shō*, q.v.
Shōgun	*t.b.* abbreviation of *Sei-i-taishōgun* (originally dispatched by Imperial Court against native tribes), later military ruler of Japan.
Shōhitsu	*o.i.c.* lower division, second grade in *Danjō-tai*, q.v.
Shōnin	*b.* a title of respect for priests of great sanctity.
Shōshō	*o.i.c.* lower division, second grade in *Sakone-fu*, *Ukone-fu*.
Shōya	*t.b.* headmen of villages, towns, or districts; there were grades: *Ōjōya*, *Kojōya*.
Sobashū	*t.b.* chamberlains.
Sobayōnin	*t.b.* grand chamberlain, intermediary between *shōgun* and *Rōjū*, q.v.
Sōjō	*b.* highest rank of priests, corresponding to privy councilor.
Sōshū	*o.i.c.* Sino-Japanese form of Shimōsa-no-Kami, used as a nickname.
Sosō	literally Divine Ancestor, specifically Tokugawa Ieyasu.
Taichō	See *Ōmandokoro*.
Taikō	*o.i.c.* 1. Retired Regent, specific title for Toyotomi Hideyoshi (formerly Kampaku); 2. also refers here to Konoe Motohiro, who held the title at the Imperial Court.
Taikun	title for *shōgun* used in correspondence with Korea during early Tokugawa period, and

	also in dealings with Europeans, 1854–67.
Tairō	*t.b.* prime minister
Taishō	*o.i.c.* 1. first grade in *Ukone-fu*, q.v. 2. here used as an abbreviation of *Ukone-no-Taishō*.
Taitoku-In	*b.* posthumous name of Tokugawa Hidetada.
Taiyū-In	*b.* posthumous name of Tokugawa Iemitsu.
Tandai	provincial governor under early shogunates.
Tayū	*o.i.c.* upper division, second grade in *Naka-tsukasa-shō*, *Mimbu-shō*, q.v.
Tennō	emperor
Tōshōgū	*b.* posthumous name of Tokugawa Ieyasu.
Udaijin	*o.i.c.* Minister of the Right in the *Dajōkan*, q.v.
Udaishō	*o.i.c.* abbreviation of Ukone-no-Taishō. See *Ukone-fu*, *Taishō*
Uemon-fu	*o.i.c.* one of the six departments of household troops.
Ukone-fu	*o.i.c.* one of the six departments of household troops.
Ukyō-shiki	*o.i.c.* bureau in charge of western section of Kyōto.
Wakadoshiyori	*t.b.* junior council, in charge of certain sections of the bureaucracy.
Yoriai (*Yoriaishū*)	*t.b.* unemployed *hatamoto*, q.v., with an income over 3,000 *koku*.
Yoriki	*t.b.* minor officials under a magistrate, divided into two companies.
Yoshū	*o.i.c.* Sino-Japanese form of Iyo-no-Kami, used as nickname.
Yūshō-In	*b.* posthumous name of Tokugawa Ietsugu.
Zōsu	*b.* next below a head priest of a temple.

Appendix 2
The Sexagenary System

The Japanese divided time into cycles of 60 years, each year being identified by a combination of 1 of 10 calendrical, with 1 of 12 zodiacal signs. They also used era names which were changed to mark important events for auspicious reasons.

The 10 calendrical signs consist of five pairs representing the elements: *ki* (wood), *hi* (fire), *tsuchi* (earth) *ka(ne)* (metal), and *mizu* (water); each pair consisted of an "elder" and a "younger" member *e* ("elder brother") and *to* ("younger brother"). The 12 zodiacal signs are: *ne* (rat), *ushi* (ox), *tora* (tiger), *u* (hare), *tatsu* (dragon), *mi* (serpent), *uma* (horse), *hitsuji* (ram), *saru* (monkey), *tori* (cock), *inu* (dog), *i* (boar).

The first year of the cycle is therefore *kinoe-ne*. The years 1624, 1684, 1744 were *kinoe-ne*. The year 1600 was *kanoe-ne*. Years are often referred to by the zodiacal signs only, as Year of the Ox, etc. Various superstitions exist about children born in certain years.

Era Names

Era names appearing in the text and their dates, listed in alphabetical order.

N = Northern Dynasty

Bun'an	1444–1449		Kan'ei	1624–1644
Chōkyō	1487–1489		Keichō	1596–1615
Eiroku	1558–1570		Kempō	1213–1219
Empō	1673–1681		Kenkyū	1190–1199
Entoku	1489–1492		Kōhō	1716–1736
Genkō	1331–1334		Meireki	1655–1658
Genkyō	1321–1324		Ōan	1368–1375 (N)
Genkyū	1204–1206		Ōei	1394–1428
Genna	1615–1624		Ōnin	1467–1469
Genroku	1688–1704		Shōchō	1428–1429
Hōei	1704–1711		Shōji	1199–1201
Jōji	1362–1368 (N)		Shōō	1288–1293
Jōkyū	1219–1222		Shōtoku	1711–1716
Kakitsu	1441–1444		Teikyō	1684–1688
Kambun	1661–1673		Tenna	1681–1684

Appendix 3
Measures

Capacity

		1 *gō*	=	.18	liters	=	.318 pts.
10 *gō* =		1 *shō*	=	1.8	liters	=	3.18 pts.
10 *shō* =		1 *to*	=	18	liters	=	3.97 gals.
4 *to* =		1 *hyō*	=	72	liters	=	1.99 bushels
10 *to* =		1 *koku*	=	180	liters	=	4.96 bushels

Weight

160 *momme*	=	1 *kin*	=	600	gm.	=	1.32 lbs.
1000 *momme*	=	1 *kan* (*kamme*)	=	3.75	kg.	=	8.27 lbs.

Length

		1 *bu*	=	3.03	mm.	=	.12 in.
10 *bu*	=	1 *sun*	=	3.03	cm.	=	1.2 in.
10 *sun*	=	1 *shaku*	=	30.3	cm.	=	.994 ft.
6 *shaku*	=	1 *ken*	=	1.82	m.	=	1.99 yd.
10 *shaku*	=	1 *jō*	=	3.03	m.	=	3.31 yd.
60 *ken*	=	1 *ri*	=	3.93	km.	=	2.44 miles

Area

1 sq. *ken*	= 1 *tsubo*	=	3.31 sq. m.	=	3.95 sq. yds.
1 *chō*	= 60 *ken* × 50 *ken*	=	.992 ha.	=	2.45 acres

Cloth Measure

		1 *bu*	=	3.79	mm.	=	.15 in.
10 *bu*	=	1 *sun*	=	3.79	cm.	=	1.5 in.
10 *sun*	=	1 *shaku*	=	37.9	cm.	=	1.243 ft.
10 *shaku*	=	1 *jō*	=	3.79	m.	=	4.14 yds.

Appendix 4
Pedigrees

Arai Pedigree

Kageyu ----- Masanari ----
d. 1609
(m. Someya
d. 1604)

Masanari ----
1601–82
(m. Sakai
d. 1678)

- Masanobu
  1636–1703
  (adopted, s. of
  Gunji)
- Matsu
  1651–53
- Yone
  1652–54
- Tatsu (Tei)
  1653–71
- Hakuseki ----
  1657–1725
  (m. Asakura)
- Made
  1660–78
  (m. Yama-
  moto)

Hakuseki ----
1657–1725
(m. Asakura)

- Shizu
  b./d. 1687
- Kiyo
  1689–94
- Akinori
  1691–1741
  (m. Asakura 1721)
- Masu (Den)
  ?1693–?
  (m. Ichikoka
  1718)
- Kichi
  1694–96
- Saburojirō
  b./d. 1696
- Yoshinori
  ?1699–1723
- Yasu
  1703–5
- Mura (Chō)
  (1705–6)
- Ben
  1706–?
  (m. Ishigaya 1723)

Tsuchiya Pedigree
(from *Hankampu*)

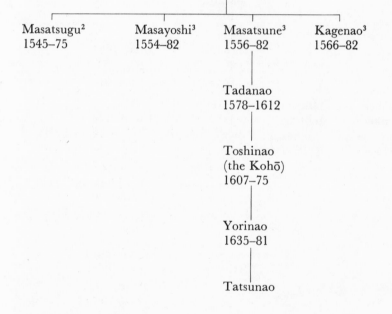

Kanamaru Fujitsugu[1]

Toratsugu

Torayoshi

Masatsugu[2]
1545–75

Masayoshi[3]
1554–82

Masatsune[3]
1556–82

Kagenao[3]
1566–82

Tadanao
1578–1612

Toshinao
(the Kohō)
1607–75

Yorinao
1635–81

Tatsunao

[1]served Takeda of Kai
[2]killed at Battle of Nagashino. Takeda Katsuyori was defeated at this battle by Oda Nobunaga and Tokugawa Ieyasu.
[3]killed at battle of Temmokuzan. Katsuyori perished with all his family at this battle.

Tokugawa Shōguns

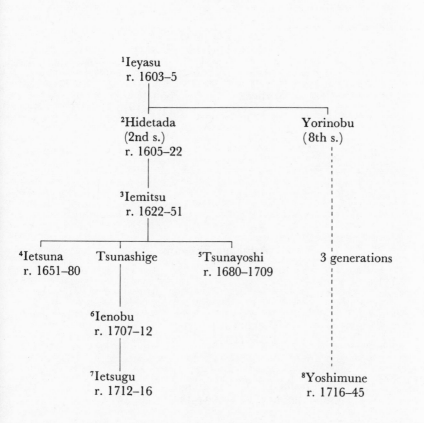

Minamoto Shōguns

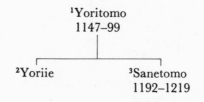

[1]Yoritomo
1147–99

[2]Yoriie   [3]Sanetomo
                    1192–1219

Ashikaga Shōguns

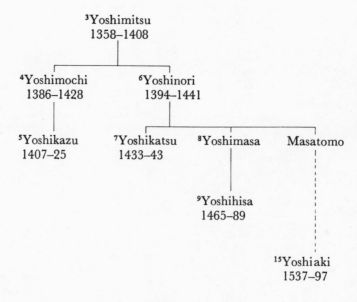

[3]Yoshimitsu
1358–1408

[4]Yoshimochi   [6]Yoshinori
1386–1428   1394–1441

[5]Yoshikazu   [7]Yoshikatsu   [8]Yoshimasa   Masatomo
1407–25   1433–43

                                   [9]Yoshihisa
                                   1465–89

                                                    [15]Yoshiaki
                                                    1537–97

Appendix 5
Selected Chronology

Year	Hakuseki's Age	Event
1601		Hakuseki's father, Masanari, born
1604		Hakuseki's grandmother dies
1609		Hakuseki's grandfather dies
1613		Hakuseki's father runs away to Edo
1631		Hakuseki's father takes service with Tsuchiya Clan
1657	1	great Edo fire; Hayashi Razan dies; *Dai Nihon Shi* begun; Hakuseki born
1659	3	copies ideographs from *Ueno Monogatari*
1660	4	attends lectures on *Taiheiki*
1662	6	Uematsu teaches him a Chinese poem; Nambu Toshinao wishes to adopt him; Wakadoshiyori established
1663	7	attack of smallpox; *junshi* (suicide on the death of one's lord) prohibited
1664	8	practices calligraphy; Hayashi Shunzai begins editing *Honchō Tsūgan*
1665	9	"trousering" ceremony; helps with his father's correspondence
1666	10	Kohō's mother died; Yamaga Sokō banished
1667	11	copies out and learns *Teikin Ōrai*; practices *kendō*
1669	13	looks after Tsuchiya Toshinao's correspondence
1670	14	*Honchō Tsūgan* completed
1671	15	elder siter Tatsu dies
1673	17	reads *Okina Mondō*; composes a Chinese poem

1674	18	goes to Kazusa with Tsuchiya Toshinao; dissensions in the clan; Hakuseki under house arrest
1675	19	Tsuchiya Toshinao dies; Yorinao succeeds; father Masanari retires
1677	21	Hakuseki expelled from clan; composes *haikai*; meets Nishiyama Juntai (Abiru)
1678	22	mother and younger sister Made die; Kawamura Zuiken's offer of marriage alliance
1679	23	Tsuchiya fief reduced; Hakuseki reinstated as *samurai*; Hotta Masatoshi becomes a member of Rōjū.
1680	24	Shōgun Ietsuna dies; Tsunayoshi succeeds
1681	25	Hotta Masatoshi becomes Tairō
1682	26	Hakuseki engaged by Hotta Masatoshi; father dies; Korean envoy writes preface to Hakuseki's Chinese poems; Kinoshita Jun'an becomes Bakufu Confucianist
?	?	marries daughter of Asakura Nagaharu, Hotta retainer
1684	28	Hotta Masatoshi assassinated
1686	30	accompanies Hotta Masanaka to Yamagata; enters Kinoshita Jun'an's school; writes *Yamagata Kikō*
1687	31	Kindness to Animals Statutes issued; Emperor Higashiyama ascends throne; eldest daughter Shizu born but soon dies
1688	32	Abiru dies; Yanagisawa Yoshiyasu becomes *sobayōnin* (grand chamberlain)
1689	33	daughter Kiyo born
1691	35	eldest son Akinori born; leaves Hotta Clan and goes to Edo; becomes a teacher; Hayashi Nobuatsu becomes Daigaku-no-Kami
1692	36	gives up offer of employment in Maeda Clan to Okajima Sekiryō
1693	37	?(?3rd) daughter Masu (Den) born; discussions on engagement as lecturer by Kōfu Clan; begins *Nikki*
1694	38	beings lectures; daughter Kiyo dies; Akinori

		seriously ill; (?4th) daughter Kichi born; Matsuō Bashō dies
1696	40	Ogiwara Shigehide becomes *kanjō bugyō*; daughter Kichi dies; 2nd son Saburojirō born but soon dies
1697	41	long illness; great Edo fire
1698	42	great Edo fire; house burned down; buys suit of armour with money received to repair house
1699	43	Kinoshita Jun'an dies; Kawamura Zuikan dies; ? 3rd son Yoshinori born
1700	44	Mito Mitsukuni dies
1701	45	writes *Hankampu*
1702	46	presents *Hankampu*; incident of the 47 Rōnin
1703	47	5th daughter Yasu born; Doi Motonari enters household; adoptive brother Gunji Masanobu dies; great Kantō earthquake; Edo fire; house at Yushima burned
1704	48	Akinori's coming-of-age ceremony; Ienobu proclaimed Heir; Hakuseki becomes *yoriai* in Western Palace
1705	49	daughter Yasu dies; Hakuseki writes *Dōbun Tsūkō*; 6th daughter Mura (Chō) born 7th
1706	50	daughter Ben born; daughter Mura (Chō) dies
1707	51	receives house lot near Kiji Bridge and builds house there; severe earthquakes and eruption of Mt. Fuji
1708	52	Sidotti lands on Yakushima and is brought to Edo
1709	53	Tsunayoshi dies; Ienobu becomes Shōgun; presents three urgent proposals; repeal of Kindness to Animals Statues; proposal for the establishment of princely house of Kan'-in; great amnesty; consulted about finance; eldest daughter ill with smallpox; proposals for the regulation of Nagasaki trade; proposal for renovation of armaments; Yanagisawa Yoshiyasu retires; Emperor Higashiyama

		dies; Ietsugu born; given a fief of 500 *koku*; proposals for the reception of the Korean Embassy; assigned a room in Naka-no-Kuchi in Main Palace; interrogation of Sidotti; *Honchō Gunkikō, Honchō Hōka Tsūyō Jiryaku*
1710	54	Further proposals concerning the Korean Embassy; new draft of *Buke Shohatto*; meets Konoe Motohiro; report on the complaint by the Yase villagers; establishment of princely House of Kan'in; visits Kyōto to witness coronation of Nakamikado
1711	55	witnesses Nakamikado's coming-of-age ceremony; meets Luchu princes; visits Ōsaka and Nara; leaves Kyōto and returns to Edo; recommends Muro Kyūsō for employment by Bakufu; proposals for the reception, banquet, and farewell for the Korean Envoys; complaint of Echigo villagers; report on the trial of the widow at Kawagoe for "informing" on her father; *Hakuseki Shisō*; given court rank and title Chikugo-no-Kami; meets Korean Envoys; offers resignation over problems concerned with their reception; fief increased to 1,000 *koku*; great Edo fire; proposals for fire-fighting regulations
1712	56	meets Dutch merchants; has son Yoshinori examined by Dutch physician; illness; proposals concerning post-stations; dispute between villages of Ukawa-Uchishita and Kita-Komatsu; illness; residence transferred to Ogawa-chō; report on Buddhist robes of Ichijō-In-no-Miya; dispute in Matsudaira House; lectures on *Tokushi Yoron* begun; proposal for the revival of the Kanjō Gimmi Yaku (Board of Audit); proposals concerning judiciary; impeachment of Ogiwara Shigehide; advice to Ienobu on the succession; Ienobu dies; Ietsugu succeeds; proposals for the recoinage announced; dispute

about Ietsugu's mourning; dispute about the era name

1713 57 Ietsugu's coming-of-age ceremony; proposals concerning financial straits of *samurai; Sairan Igen*; meets Konoe Iehiro; house lot increased; long illness; proposals concerning the recoinage; report on the Yamato River fishing boats

1714 58 porposals for regulation of Nagasaki trade; meets Dutch merchants; complaints of the officials of the Nishi-no-Miya and the Abbot of Sambō-In; offers resignation; application of the Abbot of Zōjōji in connection with 100th anniversary of Ieyasu's death; later proposals concerning coinage; Sidotti dies in prison; Yanagisawa Yoshiyasu dies

1715 59 meets Luchu Envoys; new regulations for Nagasaki trade; *Seiyō Kibun*; *Honchō Gunkikō*; Ietsugu betrothed to imperial princess

1716 60 escape of prisoners during a fire; meets Dutchmen; revises *Koshitsū* and *Koshitsū Wakumon*; Ietsugu dies; Yoshimune succeeds; Hakuseki offers resignation; gives up room in Naka-no-Kuchi; income reduced; *Oritaku Shiba no Ki* begun

1717 61 great Edo fire; gives up house lot; moves to rented rooms at Isshiki-chō, Fukagawa; *Buke Shohatto* of Tsunayoshi's time revived; former ceremonies for reception of Korean Embassy revived; buys a house and lot at Yanagi-chō, Koishikawa

1718 62 name of Kan'in bestowed on princely house; daughter Masu (Den) marries Ichioka Masanori

1719 63 *Tōga, Tōinfu, Nantōshi*

1720 64 begins corresponding with Sakuma Tōgan; *Ezoshi*; great Edo fire; *Dai Nihon Shi* presented to Bakufu; ban on foreign books other than those dealing with Christianity relaxed

1721	65	great Edo fire; house burned down; moves to new house on substitute grant of land at Rokken-chō, Naitō Shuku; eldest son Akinori marries daughter of Asakura; national census; (?) Hakuseki begins corresponding with Asaka Tampaku, *Keihō Tenrei*
1722	66	grandson dies; *Sombu Heihō Taku,* begins writing *Shigi;* Konoe Motohiro dies
1723	67	Ose Fukuan dies; son Yoshinori dies; grandson Kunitak aborn; daughter Ben marries Ishigaya Kiyotora; *Arai Kakai*
1724	68	Hayashi Nobuatsu retires; completes *Shigi*; revises *Tokushi Yoron*; revises *Seiyō Kibun*
1725	69	revises *Sairan Igen*; falls ill and dies
1739		at Bakufu request Akinori presents *Honchō Gunkikō, Tōga;* Hakuseki's wife dies, aged 71
1789		Hakuseki's great-grandson Shigeyoshi at Bakufu request presents *Hankampu*
1793		at Bakufu request Shigeyoshi presents *Seiyō Kibun*
1795		Shigeyoshi's son Kaneyoshi at Bakufu request presents a number of Hakuseki's works
1880		wife of Takichi (descendant in 8th generation) presents Hakuseki's collected works to Imperial Court
1907		Hakuseki posthumously granted Upper Fourth Rank

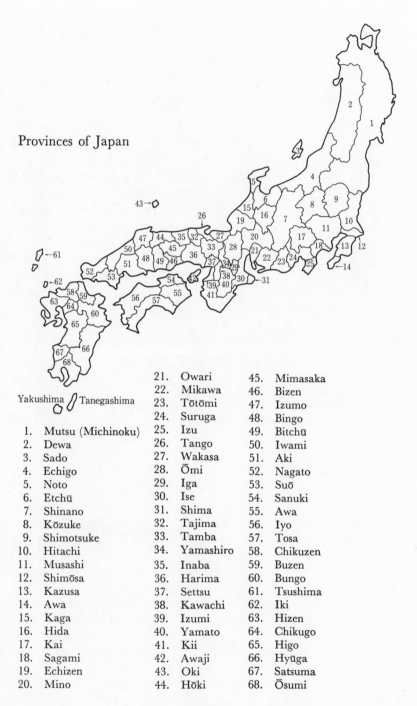

Provinces of Japan

Yakushima   Tanegashima

1. Mutsu (Michinoku)	21. Owari	45. Mimasaka
2. Dewa	22. Mikawa	46. Bizen
3. Sado	23. Tōtōmi	47. Izumo
4. Echigo	24. Suruga	48. Bingo
5. Noto	25. Izu	49. Bitchū
6. Etchū	26. Tango	50. Iwami
7. Shinano	27. Wakasa	51. Aki
8. Kōzuke	28. Ōmi	52. Nagato
9. Shimotsuke	29. Iga	53. Suō
10. Hitachi	30. Ise	54. Sanuki
11. Musashi	31. Shima	55. Awa
12. Shimōsa	32. Tajima	56. Iyo
13. Kazusa	33. Tamba	57. Tosa
14. Awa	34. Yamashiro	58. Chikuzen
15. Kaga	35. Inaba	59. Buzen
16. Hida	36. Harima	60. Bungo
17. Kai	37. Settsu	61. Tsushima
18. Sagami	38. Kawachi	62. Iki
19. Echizen	39. Izumi	63. Hizen
20. Mino	40. Yamato	64. Chikugo
	41. Kii	65. Higo
	42. Awaji	66. Hyūga
	43. Oki	67. Satsuma
	44. Hōki	68. Ōsumi

[337]

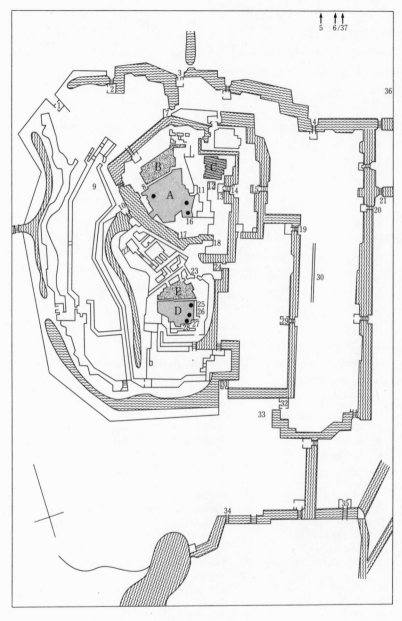

Edo Castle

A Main Palace
B Women's Apartments in Main Palace
C Ni-no-Maru
D Western Palace
E Women's Apartments in Western Palace

1. Tayasu Gate
2. Shimizu Gate
3. Kiji Bridge
4. Kanda Bridge
5. Kanda Myōjin (near Yushima)
6. Shōhei Bridge
7. Takehashi Gate
8. Shiroshoin
9. Fukiage Garden
10. Momijiyamashita Gate
11. Naka-no-Kuchi
12. Ōtesan (Hyakuningumi) Gate
13. Naka Gate
14. Uchisakurada Gate
15. Ōte Gate
16. Gogenkan Gate
17. Hasuike (= pond)
18. Hasuike Gate
19. Wadakura Gate (Tatsu-noKuchi)
20. Gofuku Bashi
21. Nihon Bashi
22. Momijiyama
23. Ura Gate
24. Sakashita Gate
25. kitchens
26. Naka-no-Kuchi
27. Great Gate
28. Tokei-no-Ma
29. Babasaki Mon
30. Daimyōkōji
31. Sotosakurada Gate
32. Hibiya Gate
33. Sakurada (Kai Clan) Mansion
34. Tora-no-Mon
35. Shibaguchi Gate (Nishikuruwa Gate)
36. Shirogane-Chō
37. Shinobazu Pond

The Arai Ferry

INDEX

Abe Masataka, 182, 252, 276
Abiru. *See* Nishiyama Juntai
administration, 4, 28, 96, 114, 115,
145, 164, 175–76, 180–82, 183,
197–98, 247–48
Akimoto Takatomo, 197, 203, 216,
217
Amenomori Hōshū, 30, 132, 160
amnesty, 105–6, 107–8
Analects, 103, 199, 271
Ankokuden petition, 235–36
Arai Akinori, 16, 70, 108–9
Arai Hakuseki: advice, drafts, memorials, reports of, for *shōgun*, Rōjū,
93, 94, 96–99, 99–104, 107, 108,
110, 113, 117–18, 122, 123, 127,
147, 152, 154, 162–63, 174, 204,
210–12, 213–16, 221, 231–32, 255,
260; appointment in Western palace, 85, 89; at ceremonies, 55,
109, 128, 129, 144, 205, 206; character of, 30–31; children of, 16,
30, 70, 87, 107, 108–9, 128; civil
and criminal cases, etc., opinions
on, 119–26, 161–62, 182–83, 197–
204, 206–10, 228, 237, 257, 259–
60, 261, 262–65, 270–73; and
Confucian studies, 61–62; early
education of, 58–63; emoluments
of, 72–73, 76, 77, 87, 89, 127, 129,
130, 175, 204–5; estates of, 112,
130–31; forebears of, 37; government, views on, 2–3, 4–7, grandmother of, 37; Hayashi Nobuatsu,
opinion of, 28, 30, relations with,
96, 119, 138–39, 186–91, 196–97;
on history, 9, 10, 14; Hotta Clan,
service in, 69–71; house arrest of,
63–66; house lots of, 89, 161, 205;
Ienobu, lectures to, 75–78, opinion
of, 28, relations with, 21, 26, 30,
78, 84, 87, 94, 136–37, 185, 212,
229, service to, 21, 26, 30, 77, 140;
illnesses, 30, 58, 159; inscriptions
written by, 205–6; Kaga Clan,
recommendation to, 71; Kai

(Kōfu) Clan, negotiations with, 63,
72–73; and Kinoshita Jun'an, 62–
63; on Korean Envoys, 62, 130–
46; literary composition of, 62;
on Luchu Envoys, 129, 232–34;
Manabe Akifusa, opinion of, 28,
30; marriage proposals to, 67, 68–
69; mother of, 30, 35; Ogiwara
Shigehide, opinion of, 28, 104–5,
164–72, 174; and poetry, 9, 15,
59–60, 62; promotions of, 109,
130; on religion, 9, 11; resignation
offer by, 228–31; as *rōnin*, 66–69,
70–72; as scholar, 9–11; self-portrait of, 29–31; on *shōgun's* title,
114–15, 233–35; sisters of, 30, 54,
56, 57, 67; as *samurai* 3–4, 11–13,
27, 77; and swordsmanship, 61;
on treasury, 99–104; as teacher,
71; and Tsuchiya Clan dissension,
64–65; wife of, 23, 30, 70, 79,
82, 87, 128; Yoshimune, relations
with, 7–9. *See also* Confucianism;
Nippon Koku-Ō; Nippon Koku
Taikun; *rangaku*
Arai Kageyu, 4, 14, 16, 37, 38
Arai Masanari, 4, 14, 16, 29, 30,
37–57, 60
armaments, 110
Asahina, 45
Asahi-no-Kata, 231–32
Asaka Tampaku, 14, 15
Asakura Kagehira, 79
Asakura Kagetake, 264–65
Ashikaga-no-Shō school, 137
Ashikaga: Takauji, 6; Yoshiaki, 193,
Yoshihisa, 195; Yoshikatsu, 196;
Yoshikazu, 196; Yoshimitsu, 196,
233; Yoshimochi, 195; Yoshinori,
196
Ashizawa, 42–43
Atake-Maru, 110
autobiography, 1, 17–23, 24, 28

Bakufu, 2, 3, 5, 6, 28, 31
Board of Audit, 5, 162–64, 172

INDEX

Buddhism, 18, 40, 55
Bukukiryō, 186, 189

cases, civil and criminal: Echigo robber band, 266–72; Funatsu ship
pillage, 173, 182–83; inter-village
dispute, 272–73; kidnapping case,
256–57; Murakami farmers' protest, 146–51; murder of an uncle,
253–54; Matsushiro-no-Shō murder of son-in-law, 197–204; sale of
daughters, 257–60; *samurai* kills
robber, 264–65; Shiga District
boundary dispute, 172–73, 252–
53; Yamato River fishing boat dis-
pute, 206–10; Yase trespassing
dispute, 122–23
Cellini, Benvenuto, 17, 18, 21–22
Ch'ên Ch'ing Piao, 18
Chêng Pan-ch'iao, 18
Ch'êng Tzŭ, 61
chia-chuan, 19, 20
Chia Li, 189, 190
Chi Chung, 199, 202
Ch'ien Pai Nien Yen, 191
China, trade with, 179, 242–46, 249
Chin Ssŭ Lu, 73
Chōshū. *See* Toda Tadatoshi
Chou, Duke of, 189, 190
Chou I, 74, 76, 102, 271
Chou Li, 75
Christianity, 11, 13, 31
Chu Hsi, 22, 74, 189
Ch'un Ch'iu, 74, 118, 192
Chu Tzŭ. *See* Chu Hsi
coinage, 4–5, 8, 26, 90, 101–4, 166–
70, 173–74, 178, 182, 212–21, 237–
42
Confucianism, 1, 2, 5–6, 7, 8, 11,
13–14, 22, 24, 26–27, 71, 103, 118,
136, 186–90, 192, 196, 198–203,
234, 254, 270–72
Copper Mint, 243–44
corruption, 5, 119, 139–40, 170, 171,
219, 222, 251, 253, 265–66

Daigaku-no-Kami. *See* Hayashi Nobuatsu
Daijō-In Den, 119, 120, 126
daimyō, 2, 7, 10, 105, 107, 145, 146,
153, 158, 246, 275
Dōbun Tsūkō, 11
Doi Motonari, 14, 85, 89
Dutch, 13, 152, 194; trade, 242–43,
246. See also *rangaku*

Echizen Kurobei, 50–52
economy, 2–3, 4, 164–66, 210, 215.
See also coinage
Edo Benkei, 9
Edo fires, 76, 151–52, 254–55
Ema Ekian, 35, 61
emperor, 115, 132, 233
era name, dispute over, 191–97
Ezoshi, 11, 14

Five Classics, 61
Forty-Seven Rōnin, Incident of, 7
Four Books, 61, 73, 74, 75
Fuji eruption, 90
Fujieda Masanori, 79, 80, 81
Fujiwara House, 6, 37
Fujiwara Kanezane, 20
Fukae Shōzaemon, 170, 174, 222
Fukami Shin'emon, 205, 245
Fukuō Jiden, 17
Fukuzawa Yukichi, 17, 23
Funakoshi Saemon, 266–68
Furukawa Tesshi, 1, 6, 25
Furuta Daizen-Daibu, 54–55
Fushimiya Shirobei, 242–43

Genji Monogatari, 190, 191
Genna Regulations, 94, 113, 114
Genroku Regulations, 187–88
giri vs *ninjō*, 12
Goban-iri, 108
Go-Toba, Ret. Emp., 15
Great Cash, 90, 93, 101, 214
Gukanshō, 10
Gunji: Ichirobei, 52: Masanobu, 52,
66; Yaichiemon, 52
Gyokuyō, 20

Hagiwara Yoshimasa, 163, 216, 217,
218, 220, 237
Haisho Zampitsu, 17
Hakuseki Kengi, 26
Hakuseki Nikki, 9, 23, 24, 25, 26
Hama Shōdayū, 224
Hanazono Tennō Shinki, 20
Hani Gorō, 16, 22, 29
Hankampu, 9, 10, 19, 75, 118
Hashiba Hideyasu, 176, 232
hatamoto, 105, 108, 153, 210
Hattori Seisuke, 85, 89
Hattori Tōkurō, 85, 89
Hayashi Dōshun (Razan), 138, 196
Hayashi Nobuatsu, 8, 24, 28–29, 30,
73, 86, 96, 113, 118–19, 127, 138,
143, 186–91, 196–97, 199, 202, 203

INDEX

Hide-no-Miya, 99
Hirata Naokata, 132, 139
Hogi Yaemon, 169, 221
Hōjō: Takatoki, 193; Tokimasa, 193; Yoshiaki, 193; Ujihide, 249–50
Honchō Hōka Tsūyō Jiryaku, 26
Honda: Masanaga (text Masatake), 87, 264; Tadaharu, 173, 209; Tadayoshi, 148, 206, 231, 251, 254, 263, 274
Honkō Kokushi Nikki, 143, 236
Hoshina Masayuki, 97
Hosoi Yasuaki, 206
Hotta: Clan, 9; Gen'emon, 148, 150; Masamori, 275; Masanaka, 69, 70; Masatora, 256; Masatoshi, 5, 8, 21, 56, 69; Owari branch, 217; Toshihiro, 71
Hsiao Ching. See *Hsiao Hsüeh*
Hsiao Hsüeh, 61, 73, 75
Hsün Yüeh, 106
Hu Shih, 17, 18
Hsiao Ya, 77
Hu Chuan, 75

Ichijō-In Den, 119, 126
Ichijō-In-Miya, scarlet robe of, 180–81
Iidamachi relocation, 90
Ikenishi Gonsui, 9
I Li, 75, 186, 189, 190, 198
Imakōji (Ashikaga) Mansai, 224–28
Imperial Court, 5, 6, 97–99; Northern and Southern, 97
Inaba Masatomo, 254
Inagaki Shigetomi, 100
Inoue: Masakata, 81, 85, 87, 88; Masamine (text sometimes Tadamine), 87, 149, 182, 208, 209, 253, 274; Masatō, 209, Masatoshi, 209
Ise Sadatoki, 268, 273–74
Ishikawa: Gensaku, 58; Masasato, 249
Ishin Sūden, 114, 138
Itō Jinsai, 73

Jien, 10
jih-chi, 19, 20
Jijū-Den, 126
Jinkōki, 238–40
Jinnō Shōtōki, 10
jitsuroku nikki, 20, 23
judiciary, 5, 30, 253–54, 255, 256–57, 266–72, 274
Juraku-Dai, 142

Kachōyojō, 190, 191
Kai (Kōfu) Clan (House), 14, 24, 73, 77
kambun nikki, 20
Kambe: 53, 54; Jūbei, 53, 54; Saburōemon, 53
Kao Hsüan-tai. *See* Fukami Shin'e-mon
Katō, 43–44
Katō Ukon, 185
Kawamura Zuiken, 69
Keihō Tenrei, 14
kikō-nikki-zuihitsu-haibun genre, 18
Kikyōya Matahachi, 243
Kindness to Animals Statutes, 91, 94–95
Kinoshita Jun'an, 14, 58, 62, 63, 71, 72, 73, 77
Kishin Ron, 11
Kitabatake Chikafusa, 10
Kōfukuji dispute, 119–26
Kohō. *See* Tsuchiya Toshinao
Koide Ariyuki, 73, 81, 85, 87, 88
Kojikiden, 11
Kōkai, 111, 112
Kokusho Sōmokuroku, 16
Kokusō Jigen, 25
Kokusō Seigi, 25
kokutai, 11, 139, 141
Komiyama Tomoemon, 169, 221
Konoe: Hiroko, 112, 159, 160, 188; Iehiro, 126, 129, 169, 205, 235; Motohiro, 111, 115, 119, 121, 122, 126, 143, 159, 160; Nobutada, 111, 120, 121; Sakihisa, 111, 119; Takataka, 120, 121, 124
Korea, 2, 131, 132, 134, 135, 136–37, 179
Korean Envoys, 8, 25, 30, 62, 110, 113, 130–41, 143–46, 171
Kōriki Tadahiro, 72
Koshitsū, 9, 10, 14
Koshitsū Wakumon, 9, 10, 14
Kōsei Shōnin, 260, 261
Kōyō Gunkan, 9
Kuben Hōshinnō, 96
Kubota Tadahide, 206
Kugyō Bunin, 121
Ku Liang, 75
Kumazawa Banzan, 3
K'ung-ming, 106
Kung Yang, 75
Kuroda Naoshige, 94
Kurokawa Dōyū, 69
Ku Yin P'u, 205

Kuze Shigeyuki, 112, 137, 141, 185, 250–51, 265

lampoons, 182, 249–50
Li Chi, 74, 189
lieh-chuan, 19, 20,
Li Mi, 18
Li T'ao-shih, 262–64
Lü Shu, 199
Li Ts'ŭ-ming, 20
Luchus, 11, 129, 232–34; trade with, 179

Magaribuchi Kagehira, 82, 265
Maeda Sadaemon, 162
Makino: Narisada, 275; Rokurozaemon, 58
Manabe Akifusa, 12, 81, 84; at ceremonies, 206; character of, 28, 30, 276–77; dismissal of, 274; duties of, 274, 276; as go-between with shōgun, 76, 86, 89, 93, 99, 102, 103, 108, 109, 130, 136, 137, 159, 161, 167, 277, with Rōjū, etc., 185, 196, 210, 211, 225, 228–29, 235, 238, 249, 250, 252, 254, 255, 256, 261, 262, 263, 264, 276–77; as possessor of documents, 174, 175; as recipient of secret information, 177, 178, 216, 217, 218, 251
Manabe: Akihira, 93, 128, 159, 206; Akiyuki, 82, 206, 265
Man'yōshū, 15
Marumo Toshio, 237
Matsudaira: dispute, 161–62; Kiyotake, 206; Kiyotsura, 206; Nobutsune, 207, 231, 251, 252–54; Norikane, 161–62; Norikuni, 162, 238; Norisato, 161; Sadanobu, 17, 21–22, 23; Tadamoto, 148; Tadayoshi, 94; Terusada, 88, 94, 95, 108, 146, 149, 209; Yoshinori, 162
Matsumae Yoshihiro, 250
Meiji, 7, 11,
Meireki earthquake and fire, 78–83, 110
Mencius, 192
Midaidokoro. See Asahi-no-Kata; Konoe Hiroko; Takatsukasa Nobuko
Mikawa Go-fudoki, 237
military arts, 15, 61
Minamoto: Sanetomo, 195; Sept, 36, 37, 98; Yoritomo, 6, 142, 195
Miyazaki Michio, 9
Miyoshi Nagahiro, 126, 207–9
Mizoguchi Shigemoto, 162, 266

Mizuno: Shinhachi, 178; Tadakuni, 216, 220, 237, Tadayuki, 224, 260
Motoori Norinaga, 11
mourning dispute, 185–91
Murakami: Masakuni, 109; Masanao, 87, 116–17; 159, 165, 206
Murata Jūroemon, 84, 85, 86, 87
Muro Kyūsō, 14, 25, 30, 198

Nagai:Hanroku, 170, 223; Naohiro (text Naohira,) 89; Saburōemon. 167, 238
Nagasaki, 8, 112
Nagasaki Motonaka, 167
Naitō: Kazunobu (text Kazuo), 146; Masachika, 57
Nakagawa Nariyoshi, 216, 238
Naka-no-Kuchi, 85, 115, 274
Nakamikado, Emp., 196
Nakane Hanjūrō, 238
Nakayama Tokiharu, 149, 238
Nambu Toshinao, 58
Nantōshi, 11, 14
Nammyō-In proposal, 231–32
Neo-Confucianism, 11, 18
"New Precedents for Trading Ships," 26, 246
New Regulations, 113–15
nien-p'u, 19
Nihonshoki, 10
Nijō Palace, 142, 275
Nikkō Jugō. See Kōkai
Nippon Koku-Ō, 2, 26, 132, 138, 140
Nippon Koku Taikun, 132, 138, 139, 233
Nishi-no-Miya complaint, 223–24
Nishiyama Juntai, 62, 63
Nitta House, 111
Niwa: Tadashige, 173; Saishō, 54
Niwata Shige'eda, 181, 205, 225, 260
Nojima Shinzaemon, 237–42
Nung Chêng Ch'üan Shu, 205

Oda Nobuo, 67
Ogiwara Shigehide: accounting by, 115–16; character of, 28; civil case on, 207; and coinage, 164–77, 221; crimes of, 222–23; daimyō duties, 146; dismissed, 24, 30, 164; Hakuseki's relations with 24, 30; on trade, 243; and transport tax, 209; on treasury, 100–104
Ōgosho. See Tokugawa Ieyasu
Ogyū Sorai, 6, 9, 31
Okabe Motome, 44–45
Okajima Sekiryō, 71, 72

Okina Mondō, 61
Okiya-no-Kata, 188, 233
Ōkubo: Jin'emon, 216, 237; Norishige, 89; Sakyō, 89; Tadamasu (text, sometimes Tadatomo), 101, 137; Tadatomo, 100; Tadayoshi, 149
Ōmidaidokoro. *See* Takatsukasa Nobuko
Ōoka Kiyosuke (text, Kiyohira), 261
Oritaku Shiba no Ki, 1, 15–17, 20–26
Ose Fukuan, 14, 15
Ōta Masasuke, 89
Owari Dono. *See* Tokugawa Yoshimichi

pi-chi, 18
Pi Chi, 191
portents, miracles, 90, 111, 116–17, 181
post-station system, 154–58
prison break, 254–55

rangaku, 11, 12–13
Reigen, Ret. Emp., 204, 252, 260
"Regulations for Trading Ships," 26, 246
Rōjū, 8, 22, 25, 30, 88, 100, 128, 137, 172, 177, 182, 209, 210, 216, 225, 235, 237, 238, 250, 251, 262, 273, 276
rōnin, 4, 9, 14
Rousseau, 17, 18, 21–22
Ryōya, 39, 48

Sairan Igen, 11, 15, 31
Sakai Tadazane, 81
Sakakibara Kōshū, 77
Sakuma Tōgan, 8, 14
Sambō-In's complaint, 224–28
samurai, 3, 4, 12, 13, 27, 41, 52, 56, 67, 68, 69, 70, 86, 98, 146, 173, 217, 264–65
sankin kōtai, 3, 4
San Ts'ai T'u Hui, 205
San'yō Chōrō, 137
sarugaku, 89, 117–18
Satomi: House, 43, 50; Yoshitaka, 65
Seclusion, 4
Seiyō Kibun, 11, 13, 17
Seki: 13, 45, 58, 61, 64, 65, 66; son of, 12, 13, 64, 65
Sekigahara, 124
Semba Shichirozaemon, 238
Sengoku Hisanao, 249

Sesshō (former Sesshō). *See* Konoe Iehiro; Konoe Motohiro
Shibazaki Jūroemon, 84, 85, 87
Shigi, 9, 10, 11, 15
Shih Chi, 18
shih-chi, 19
Shih Ching, 74, 75
Shihaku Gi, 26
Shihaku Shinrei, 26
Shikimoku, 114
Shimazu Yoshitaka, 129, 233, 234, 235
Shimizu House, 53
Shimozuma-no-Shō, 37
Shinchō Ki, 54
Shingyō, 120, 124, 125, 126
Shinkokinshū, 15
Shirakawa Masafuyu, 223–24
shishōsetsu, 19
shōgun, 2, 3, 5, 6, 7, 8, 114–15, 132, 147. *See also* Nippon Koku-Ō, Nippon Koku Taikun
Shōgun's mother. *See* Okiya-no-Kata
Shōkō-In Den, 125
Shu Ching, 74, 75
Shu Tu Tsa Ch'ao, 191
Sidotti, Giovanni Battista, 13, 31, 112, 194
Silver Mint, 221, 243–44, 265
Six Classics, 76
smallpox, 106–7
Sōgyōki, 131
Sombu Heihō Taku, 15
Sōshū. *See* Hotta Masanaka
Sōsōryō, 190
Sō Yoshikata, 132, 133, 134, 138, 139, 140, 144
Ssŭ Chên, 61
Ssŭ-ma-Ch'ien, 18, 19
Ssŭ Shih Tzŭ Shu, 17, 18
Sugioka Yatarō, 163, 216, 268
Suminokura Ryōnin, 67
Sung Wen, 18
Sung Tung Yang Ma Shêng Hsü, 18
Sun Yat-sen, 18
Suruga Dono. *See* Tokugawa Tadanaga
Suwabe Sadakata, 87
Suzuki Toshio, 148, 150, 238

Ta Hsüeh, 73, 103, 209, 271
Ta Hsüeh Yen I, 76
Taiheiki, 59, 142
Taikō. *See* Konoe Iehiro; Konoe Motohiro; Toyotomo Hideyoshi
Taiseiden, 127

INDEX

Takagi: Hachibei, 162; Hikoemon, 243
Takataki Kichibei, 49
Takatsukasa Nobuko, 100, 106, 107, 120
Takebe Masataka, 238
Takeda: House, 44, 53, 121, 140; Tamba-no-Kami, 112
Takenaka Kunika, 16
Tani Yasutaka, 216–18
Taoism, 18
Tashiro Shōi, 9
Ta Ya, 77
Teikin Ōrai, 61, 114, 141–42
Ten Mon Pieces. *See* Great Cash
Toda: Tadatoshi, 72, 73, 81, 85, 86, 87, 88; Tadazane, 231, 250
Tōdō Takatoshi, 256–57
Tōga, 11, 14
Tōinfu, 14
Tokudaiji Kin'akira, 181, 205, 225, 260
Tokugawa: Hidetada, 97, 117, 143, 176, 231, 235; Hirotada, 118–19; House, 97, 111, 235–36, 237; Iechiyo, 89; Iemitsu, 53, 97, 235; Ietsuna, 95, 96, 97, 120, 124, 235, 236; Ieyasu, 3, 6, 53, 94, 96, 97, 102, 110, 117, 119, 120–21, 124, 125, 131, 137, 164, 175, 176, 185, 231, 235, 236, 237; Nobumitsu, 236; shogunate, 6; Tadanaga, 97, 176; Tsunayoshi, 8, 25, 81, 86, 91, 93, 94, 95, 96, 97, 99, 100, 103, 109, 110, 113, 119, 122, 127, 153, 155, 156, 164, 166, 235; Yoshimichi 175, 176; Yoshimune, 2, 5, 7, 8–9, 21, 24, 160, 259, 260, 274
Tokugawa Ienobu: 2, 7, 8, 14, 21, 24, 25, 30, 76–77, 82, 83, 85, 86, 87, 90, 91, 96, 97, 103, 107, 109, 110, 111, 112, 120–21, 129, 130, 135, 141, 142, 143, 146, 155, 170, 172, 187, 196, 210; administration of, 96, 114, 115, 145, 164, 175–76, 180–83, 197–98, 247–48; character of, 26, 28; and coinage, 99–102, 166, 167, 173–74; *daimyō*, opinion of, 88, 108; death of, 177–78, 181; death anniversaries of, 17, 206, 228; filial piety, 118–19, 185; Hakuseki's lectures to, 1, 16, 73–75, 78, 86; illness of, 175; interment of, 181–82; and Kindness to Animals Statutes, 94–95; and *kokutai*, 136; and learning, 74–76, 234;

memorial bell for, 205–6; as Nippon Koku-Ō, 132; and portents, 116–17; posthumous name of, 205–6; and procedures, 113, 127; relations with Hakuseki, 84, 136–37, 159, 185; and *sarugaku*, 117, 160; and trade, 179
Tokugawa Ietsugu: 7, 14, 16, 17, 21, 22, 24, 25, 27, 30, 210, 232; and coming-of-age ceremony, 205; death of, 274; illnesses of, 250–51, 274; inauguration of, 204; mourning for Ienobu by, 25, 185–91; as Serata, 111; "trousering" ceremony of, 204
Tokugawa Jikki, 28
Tokugawa Kinrei Ki, 26
Tokushi Yoron, 6, 9, 10, 15, 24
Tokutomi Sohō, 2, 28
Tomita Kakushin, 59
Torii Tadahide, 161
Tōshōgū, 42, 110, 158
Toyotomi Hideyoshi, 59, 118, 131, 231–32
trade, 3, 4, 8, 179, 242–49, 261–64
treasury, 99–104, 174. *See also* coinage
Tsêng Kuo-fan, 20
Tsêng Wên Chêng Kung Jih Chi, 19–20
Tso Chuan, 74
Tsuchiya: Clan, 12, 14, 30, 52, 53; Kazunao, 53, 54; Masanao, 113–14, 130, 138, 182, 231, 250; Masatsugu, 53; Masatsune, 53; Tadanao, 44, 45; Tatsunao, 56, 66; Toshinao, 13, 39, 40, 41, 42, 43, 44, 45, 48, 50, 52, 53, 54, 55, 58, 59, 60, 61, 63, 64, 65, 66, 67; Yorinao, 55, 62, 66
Tsuda Masatsune, 73
T'ung Chien Kang Mu, 74, 75, 117
Twenty-one Histories, 175
Tzŭ Chih T'ung Chien, 74
Tzŭ Hui, 62

Uematsu Chūbei, 9, 59, 60
Ueno Monogatari, 59
Uesugi House, 140
Uge no Hitogoto, 17
Usui Suketada, 224

Washizumi Gentarō, 217
Wêng T'ung-ho, 20
Wêng Wên Kung Kung Jih Chi, 20
Western learning. *See rangaku*

Yagiū House, 86

[346]

Yamada Masataka, 251
Yamaga Sokō, 17, 21–22, 23
Yamamoto: Den'a, 85; Dōki, 140;
  Genchō, 58, 85
Yanagisawa Yoshiyasu, 84, 88, 90,
  94, 95–96, 100, 108, 209, 275
Yao and Shun, 7, 26
Yaso-no-Miya, 252
Yasumura Kiemon, 206–9
Yōboku, 161
Yokota Yoshimatsu, 148, 150, 167,
  268

Yoshida Tōhachirō, 85, 86
Yoshii Kunai, 224
Yoshū. *See* Tsuchiya Yorinao
Yüan Ch'ü Hsüan, 117
Yuasa Jōzan, 3
Yüeh Man T'ang Jih Chi Ch'ao, 20
Yūki Dono. *See* Hashiba Hideyasu
Yung Chi, 202
Yün Hui, 62

Zōjōji, 181, 236, 237

THE LIBRARY
ST. MARY'S COLLEGE OF MARYLAND
ST. MARY'S CITY, MARYLAND 20686